Mystery, Violence, and Popular Culture

A RAY AND PAT BROWNE BOOK

Series Editors
Ray B. Browne and Pat Browne

Mystery, Violence, and Popular Culture

Essays by

John G. Cawelti

THE UNIVERSITY OF WISCONSIN PRESS
POPULAR PRESS

The University of Wisconsin Press
1930 Monroe Street
Madison, Wisconsin 53711

www.wisc.edu/wisconsinpress/

3 Henrietta Street
London WC2E 8LU, England

1   3   5   4   2

Printed in the United States of America

Library of Congress Cataloging-in-Publication Data
Cawelti, John G.
Mystery, violence, and popular culture / by John G. Cawelti.
p.   cm.
"A Ray and Pat Browne book."
ISBN 0-299-19630-5 (cloth: alk. paper)
ISBN 0-299-19634-8 (pbk.: alk. paper)
1. Popular culture.   2. Popular culture—United States.
3. Violence in popular culture.   4. Mystery in literature.
I. Title.
HM621.C39   2004
306—dc222   003020569

Table of Contents

Acknowledgments

Earlier versions of the previously published essays in this volume appeared in the following publications:

"Beatles, Batman, and the New Aesthetic," *Midway 9* (Autumn 1968): 49–70.

"The Concept of Formula in the Study of Popular Culture," *Journal of Popular Culture* 3.3 (Winter 1969): 381–90.

"God's Country, Las Vegas, and the Gunfighter: Differing Visions of the West," *The American West* 9.4 (1972): 273–83.

"Notes toward an Aesthetic of Popular Culture," *Journal of Popular Culture* 5.2 (Autumn 1972): 255–68.

"Myths of Violence in American Popular Culture," *Critical Inquiry* 1.3 (March 1975): 521–41.

"The Gunfighter and the Hard-Boiled Dick: Some Ruminations on the American Fantasies of Heroism," *American Studies* 16.2 (Winter 1975): 49–64.The Writer as a Celebrity: Some Aspects of American Literature as Popular Culture," *Studies in American Fiction* 5.1 (Spring 1977): 161–74.

"Chinatown and Generic Transformation in Recent American Films," *Film Theory and Criticism,* ed. Gerald Mast and Marshall Cohen, 2nd ed. (New York: Oxford UP, 1979), 503–20.

"With the Benefit of Hindsight: Popular Culture Criticism," *Critical Studies in Mass Communication* 2.4 (December 1985): 365–79.

"Symbols of Ethnicity and Popular Culture," *Dominant Symbols in Popular Culture,* ed. Ray B. Browne, Marshall W. Fishwick, and Kevin

O. Browne (Bowling Green, OH: Bowling Green State U Popular P, 1990), 83–95.

"Literature, Race, and Ethnicity in America," in W. M. Verhoeven, ed. *Rewriting the Dream: Reflections on the Changing American Literary Canon.* Costerus New Series 33 (Amsterdam: Rodopi, 1992), 3–21.

"Faulkner and the Detective Story's Double Plot," *Clues* 12.2 (Fall/Winter 1991): 1–15.

Masculine Myths and Feminist Revisions: Some Thoughts on the Future of Popular Genres," *Eye on the Future: Popular Culture Scholarship into the Twenty-First Century in Honor of Ray B. Browne,* ed. Marilyn F. Motz, Jack Nachbar, Michael T. Marsden, and Ronald J. Ambrosetti (Bowling Green, OH: Bowling Green State U Popular P, 1994), 121–32.

"Popular Culture/Multiculturalism," *Journal of Popular Culture* 30.1 (Summer 1996): 3–20.

"Canonization, Modern Literature and the Detective Story," *Theory and Practice of Classic Detective Fiction,* ed. Jerome H. Delamater and Ruth Prigozy (Westport, CT: Greenwood, 1997), 5–15.

"The Question of Popular Genres Revisited," *In the Eye of the Beholder,* ed. Gary Edgerton (Bowling Green, OH: Bowling Green State U Popular P, 1997), 67–84.

"Detecting the Detective: Critical Approaches to Detective Fiction,"*ANQ* 12.3 (June 1999): 44–55. This essay has been revised here to include an extension of reviews of D. J. H Jones's *Murder at the MLA* (U of Georgia P, 1993) and Jon Thompson's *Fiction, Crime, and Empire: Clues to Modernity and Postmodernism* (U of Illinois P, 1993), which appeared in *ANQ* in. 8:1 (Winter 1995), and of Gordon Kelly's *Mystery Fiction and Modern Life* (Jackson: UP of Mississippi, 1998), which appeared in the *Journal of American History* in March 1999.

"The Literature of Mystery: Some Reconsiderations," *Storytelling: A Critical Journal of Popular Narrative* 1.1 (Spring 2001): 4–35.

The following were originally presented as conference papers and are published here in revised essay form for the first time:

"Classics and Commercials, Cowboys and Canons," PCA-ACA Conference, Las Vegas, NV, March 1996."The Internationalization of Popular Genres," international conference sponsored by the Centre de recherche en littérature québécoise and the Quebec City International Book Fair in the Humanities and Social Science, Quebec, Montreal, September 1997. "Take That, You Commie Rat! The Hot Underside of the Cold War and the Myth of Espionage," " Cold War Culture: Film,

Fact, and Fiction," Indiana University, Bloomington, IN, 19 February 1999.

"Mystiquing the Western, or, How I Started Doing Popular Culture," *Film and History* conference, "The American West(s) in Film, TV, and History", Kansas City, MO, November 2002.

General Introduction

When Pat and Ray Browne of the Popular Press originally suggested I compile a collection of my essays, I didn't have enough time to make the revisions I realized would be necessary in some works that went back as far as the 1960s. However, when I retired in 2000, I thought it might be an interesting challenge to look back at the various things I had written and researched to see if there were any threads of continuity. I wasn't too surprised to discover that the majority of my essays had concentrated on three themes: the theory of popular genres, the role of violence in American culture, and the literature (and film/TV) of mystery. This collection consists of what I thought were the most useful and coherent of the essays I had written over some forty years on these themes.

My enjoyment of westerns and detective stories was the driving force behind my early literary and cultural scholarship and turned me toward the study of popular culture. When I began to think about popular culture in the late 1950s, mass culture criticism, with its largely negative view of it, was the predominant approach. A few critics, like Leslie Fiedler, were beginning to say more complex things about popular culture and I soon discovered that there were other scholars like Ray Browne and Russell Nye who were working along the same lines. I realized that if I was going to explore the reasons for my own delight in popular genres rather than merely confessing my depravity, I would have to develop a new way of conceptualizing, or, in today's jargon, of "theorizing," works of popular culture. My initial attempt at this was to use the concept of formula to suggest that works of popular culture were not simply degraded specimens of traditional literature but had formal patterns and thus a unique aesthetic.

This approach, which I developed in early essays like "The Concept of Formula" and "Notes Toward an Aesthetic of Popular Culture," now seems oversimplified to me and I no longer think there is such a clear difference between popular generic works and more "canonic" literature. However, at the time, this approach was useful in that it enabled us to think of popular works in much more positive terms and to explore their artistry. The study of formula coincided with several other contemporaneous "aesthetic" approaches to popular culture as the French auteur theory of film.

My own work seems to have proceeded in two main directions from that early attempt to articulate a distinctive concept of popular culture. One was toward finding a way to manage the formal analysis of popular culture so as to go beyond the oversimplification of the invention vs. convention or original vs. formulaic distinction without losing sight of the positive artistic qualities of popular art forms. The other was toward discovering how to use this richer and more complex idea of the forms of popular culture for the purposes of cultural or historical analysis.

The mass culture critics essentially believed that works of popular culture either reflected the interests of capitalist power or expressed the ideologies of dominant classes. My own work increasingly attempted to transcend what I felt was the great oversimplification of this equation of ideology with the forms of the western and the detective story. While I did not doubt that these genres were popular because they reflected important individual and cultural interests, I was unconvinced that class interest or ideology, at least as defined by the then existing Marxist tradition, were complex enough concepts to define the relationship between popular genres and culture.

Evidently I was not alone in my concern, for, since the 1950s, cultural and historical scholarship and criticism has been particularly rich in new ways of conceptualizing the relationship between literary work, popular and canonical, and culture. In addition to an enriched vocabulary of ideological analysis produced by the critical movement known generally as "cultural studies" and by the followers of individual cultural analysts like Walter Benjamin and Louis Althusser, other approaches like myth-symbol analysis, French structuralism and poststructuralism, and Gramscian hegemonic analysis have all contributed new methods of cultural analysis. In fact, it's been difficult to keep up with all the new theories. Clearly one important task of the next generation of cultural historians will be the evaluation and synthesis of the complex legacy of critical theory produced during the latter part of the twentieth century. Some of my later essays have attempted to come to terms with at least some of the new theories though I would hesitate to say with what degree of success.

I've found that I tend to test my own ideas about theory, or my attempts to synthesize aspects of critical theory, by applying them to three main areas or problems. One is the tragic predominance of violence in American life, an issue that must be of great concern to any thinking American. To what extent do such popular genres as the western or crime and detective stories, with their emphasis on violence, affect the climate of it in America? Do violent films and television programs produce mass murderers or lead to massacres in schools and workplaces? Or are these genres more symptomatic than causal? Empirical researchers continue to try to answer this question, but on the whole, it seems to me that their analyses are made less persuasive by the overly simple way they define violence in popular genres. The essays on the subject in this volume reflect my attempt to develop a more complex analysis of the issue of violence in American culture.

Another issue that has become increasingly important in American studies is that of multiculturalism. Up until the 1950s, American cultural history was usually conceptualized through grand myths like the idea of the frontier, or of the progressive movement toward democratization, or of the increasing Americanization of immigrants as formative factors of American history. However, in the second half of the twentieth century, American scholars and historians increasingly abandoned these mesamyths frontier theory and began exploring the role of cultural conflict as a defining factor in the development of America. More recently, sexism and racism in America have become increasingly central to our understanding of its development. Like many other scholars, I have tried to use gender and race theory to explore the evolution of literature and popular culture in America and a number of my essays have worked on these issues.

Finally, ever since being hooked on Sherlock Holmes in my early teens, I have loved reading mystery stories. Since this is a taste shared by a remarkable number of other people not only America, but increasingly throughout the world, I've come to see the literature of mystery as reflecting a central aspect of modernity. In my earlier work (*Adventure, Mystery and Romance*, for example) I deal primarily with the formal aspects of mystery stories, but I've become increasingly fascinated by the seemingly paradoxical relationship between mystery and modernity. The last section of essays in this collection traces the evolution of that interest.

I suspect that this introduction has imposed a kind of logical coherence on the development of my popular culture scholarship that it certainly did not possess as it happened. In reality I moved from one topic to another more by accident than by design. Above all, my work has been shaped from beginning to end by the responses of my students to it at the various places I have taught, especially the Universities of Chicago and Kentucky, and by my colleagues and fellow scholars who have generously supported and encouraged my scholarly struggles. As a symbolic expression of gratitude to all of these companions in the pursuit of literary and cultural insight,. I would have dedicated this book to Ray and Pat Browne, had I not already dedicated *The Six-Gun Mystique Sequel* to them. In place of the Brownes, then, I dedicate this collection to my students, past, present, and, I hope, future.

In the course of nearly half a century researching and writing about popular culture, I have incurred innumerable debts in help, support and inspiration. That scholarship is a collaborative enterprise has been proved to me over and over. I've tried to list at least some of the most important names in my previous volume. As this may be my last chance at this kind of acknowledgment, I'd like to concentrate on a few here. My parents, Donald G. and Florence M. Cawelti, helped me get a wonderful education and encouraged me to think I could make a difference in some area of scholarship. My good friend Arthur Wrobel of the University of Kentucky gave much support and counsel over the years and used his sharp editorial eye to rescue me from many howlers. And finally Mary Catherine Flannery, Jon Anthony Fasanelli-Cawelti, Andrea N. Cawelti, and Jonathan P. Flannery, wife, and children, made it all worthwhile.

Section 1

Evolving Views of Popular Culture

1

The Concept of Formula in the Study of Popular Literature

This essay, published in the *Journal of Popular Culture* in winter 1969, aroused a great deal of interest and seemed to have quite an influence on the early development of popular culture studies. I now find it oversimplified in many ways, particularly in the gross distinction it makes between convention and invention and between formulaic and non-formulaic works. The distinction between form and formula now seems much more complicated as well. However, I have left the essay pretty much as it was as an example of early popular culture theory. I think the reason it was influential is that it seemed to acknowledge the aesthetic significance of even the most generic works of popular culture, which had been dismissed by the mass culture theorists of the 1950s as trash or worse.

≋

The growing interest among humanistic scholars and teachers in popular culture is one of the more exciting academic trends of the present day. This field of study represents a great expansion in the range of human expression and activity subjected to the scrutiny of historians and scholars of the arts. Consequently, one of the central problems in giving some shape to our inquiries into popular culture has been the need for analytical concepts that might enable us to find our way through the huge amount of material, which is the potential subject matter of studies in popular culture. Moreover, we badly need some way of relating the various perspectives, historical, psychological, sociological, and aesthetic, that are being used in the investigation of such phenomena as the western, the spy story, pop music, the comic strip, film, and TV.

To some extent, students of popular culture have simply applied to a wider range of materials the historical and critical methods of traditional humanistic scholarship. This practice has led to more complex analyses of such popular forms as the detective story and richer, more carefully researched accounts of the development of various popular traditions. Approaching the materials of popular culture with the traditional arsenal of humanistic disciplines is certainly a necessary first step. Nonetheless, the analysis of popular culture is somewhat different from that of the fine arts. When we are studying the fine arts, we are essentially interested in the unique achievement of the individual artist, while, in the case of popular culture, we are dealing with a product that is in some sense collective. Of course it is possible to study the fine arts as collective products just as it is possible to examine individual works of popular culture as unique artistic creations. In the former case, the present discussion should apply with some qualifications to the fine arts, while in the latter, the traditional methods of humanistic scholarship are obviously the most appropriate, with some allowance for the special aesthetic problems of the popular arts.

Students of popular culture have defined the field in terms of several different concepts. When scholars were first interesting themselves in dime novels, detective stories, etc., they thought of them as subliterature. This concept reflected the traditional qualitative distinction between high culture and mass culture. Unfortunately, it was really too vague to be of much analytical use. Even if one could determine where literature left off and subliterature began, a distinction that usually depended on the individual tastes of the inquirer, the term suggested only that the object of study was a debased form of something better. Like many concepts that have been applied to the study of popular culture, the idea of subliterature inextricably confused normative and descriptive problems.

Four additional concepts have come into fairly wide use in recent work: a) the analysis of cultural themes; b) the concept of medium; c) the idea of myth; and d) the concept of formula. I would like to deal briefly with the first three, mainly by way of getting to a fuller discussion of what I consider the most promising concept of all.

The analysis of cultural, social, or psychological themes is certainly a tried and true method of dealing with popular culture. In essence, what the analyst does is to determine what themes appear most often or most prominently in the works under analysis and to group different works according to the presence or absence of the themes he is interested in. Unfortunately, there is a certain vagueness about the concept of theme. Such various things as the ideal of progress, the Oedipal conflict, racism, and innocence have all been treated as themes. In effect, a theme turns out to be any prominent element or characteristic of a group of works that seems to have some relevance to a social or cultural problem. Though the vagueness of the concept can be cleared up when the investigator defines the particular theme or set of themes he is interested in, the concept of theme still seems inadequate because it depends on the isolation of particular elements from a total structure. This not only tends to oversimplify the works under investigation, but to lead to the kind of falsifying reduction that translates one kind of experience into another. Thus, a story of a certain kind becomes a piece of social rhetoric or the revelation of an unconscious urge. No doubt a story is or can be these things and many others, but to treat it as if it were only one or another social or psychological function is too great a reduction. What we need is a concept that will enable us to deal with the total structure of themes and its relationship to the story elements in the complete work.

The concept of medium has become notorious through the fascinating theories of Marshall McLuhan, Walter Ong and others who insist that medium rather than content or form as we have traditionally understood them ought to be the focus of our cultural analyses. This concept seems to have a particular application to studies in popular culture because many of the works we are concerned with are transmitted through the new electric media, which McLuhan sees as so different from the Gutenberg galaxy, the media associated with print. The concept of medium is an important one and McLuhan is doubtless correct that it has been insufficiently explored in the past, but I am not persuaded that more sophisticated studies of the nature of media will do away with the need for generalizations about content. I am sure that we will need to revise many of our notions about where medium leaves off and content begins as the new studies in media progress, but for the present, I would like to forget about the idea of medium altogether with the explanation that I'm concerned with a different kind of problem, the exploration of the content of the popular media.

One more distinction along these lines is necessary. In this paper I will be concerned primarily with stories and with understanding the various cultural significances of these stories. While a large proportion of popular culture can be defined as stories of different kinds, this is certainly not an exhaustive way of defining popular culture. Just as there are other arts than fiction, so there are works of popular culture that do not tell stories. With additional qualifications the concepts I am seeking to define are applicable to the analysis of other expressions of popular culture than those embodied in stories, but to keep my task as simple as possible, I have chosen to limit myself to the discussion of stories.

The most important generalizing concept applied to cultural studies in recent years is that of myth. Indeed, it could be argued that the concept of formula developed in the course of this paper is simply another variation on the idea of myth. But if this is the case, I would argue that distinctions among meanings of the concept of myth are worth making and naming, for many different meanings can be ascribed to the term. In fact, the way in which some people use the term myth hardly separates it from the concept of theme, as when we talk about the myth of progress or the myth of success. There is also another common meaning of the term, which further obfuscates its use, namely myth as a common belief that is demonstrably false, as in the common opposition between myth and reality. Thus, when a critic uses the term "myth" one must first get clear whether he means to say that the object he is describing is a false belief, or simply a belief, or something still more complicated like an archetypal pattern. Moreover, because of the special connection of the term "myth" with a group of stories that have survived from ancient cultures, particularly the Greco-Roman, the scholar who uses the concept in the analysis of contemporary popular culture sometimes finds himself drawn into another kind of reductionism, which for example, explains James Bond's popularity in terms of classical myths. But if the retelling of myth is what makes something popular, why on earth didn't Mr. Fleming simply retell the ancient myths?

Because of this great confusion about the term "myth," I propose to develop another concept that I think I can define more clearly and then to differentiate this concept from that of myth, thereby giving us two more clearly defined generalizing concepts to work with. Let me begin with a kind of axiom or assumption that I hope I can persuade you to accept without elaborate argumentation: all cultural products contain a mixture of two kinds of elements, conventions and inventions. Conventions are elements that are known to both the creator and his audience beforehand — they consist of things like favorite plots, stereotyped characters, accepted ideas, commonly known metaphors, and other linguistic devices, etc. Inventions, on the other hand, are elements that are uniquely imagined by the creator, such as new kinds of characters, ideas, or linguistic forms. Of course it is difficult to distinguish in every case between conventions and inventions because many elements lie somewhere along a continuum between the two poles. Nonetheless, familiarity with a group of literary works will usually soon reveal what the major conventions are and therefore, what, in the case of an individual work, is unique to that creator.

Convention and invention have quite different cultural functions. Conventions represent familiar shared images and meanings and they assert an ongoing continuity of values; inventions confront us with a new perception or meaning that we have not realized before. Both these functions are important to culture. Conventions help maintain a culture's stability while inventions help it respond to changing circumstances and provide new information about the world. The same thing is true on the individual level. If the individual does not encounter a large number of conventionalized experiences and situations, the strain on his sense of continuity and identity will lead to great tensions and even to neurotic breakdowns. On the other hand, without new information about his world, the individual will be increasingly unable to cope with it and will withdraw behind a barrier of conventions as some people withdraw from life into compulsive reading of detective stories.

Most works of art contain a mixture of convention and invention. Both Homer and Shakespeare show a large proportion of conventional elements mixed with inventions of great genius. Hamlet, for example, depends on a long tradition of stories of revenge, but only Shakespeare could have invented a character that embodies so many complex perceptions of life that every generation is able to find new ways of viewing him. So long as cultures were relatively stable over long periods of time and homogeneous in their structure, the relation between convention and invention in works of literature posed relatively few problems. Since the Renaissance, however, modern cultures have become increasingly heterogeneous and pluralistic in their structure and discontinuous in time. In consequence, while public communications have become increasingly conventional in order to be understood by an extremely broad and diverse audience, the intellectual elites have placed ever higher valuation on invention out of a sense that rapid cultural changes require continually new perceptions of the world. Thus we have arrived at a situation in which the model great work of literature is Joyce's *Finnegans Wake*, a creation that is almost as far as possible along the continuum toward total invention as it is possible to go without leaving the possibility of shared meanings behind. At the same time, there has developed a vast amount of literature characterized by the highest degree of conventionalization.

This brings us to an initial definition of formula. A formula is a conventional system for structuring cultural products. It can be distinguished from form, which is an invented system of organization. Like the distinction between convention and invention, the distinction between formula and form can be best envisaged as a continuum between two poles; one pole is that of a completely conventional structure of conventions—an episode of the Lone Ranger or one of the Tarzan books comes close to this pole; the other end of the continuum is a completely original structure that orders inventions—*Finnegans Wake* is perhaps the best example, though one might also mention Resbais's film *Last Year at Marienbad,* Eliot's *The Waste Land,* or Beckett's *Waiting for Godot.* All of these works not only manifest a high degree of invention in their elements but unique organizing principles. *The Waste Land* makes the distinction even sharper for that poem contains a substantial number of conventional elements—even to the point of using quotations from past literary works—but these elements are structured in such a fashion that a new perception of familiar elements is forced upon the reader.

I would like to emphasize that the distinction between form and formula as I am using it here is a descriptive rather than a qualitative one. Though it is likely for a number of reasons that a work possessing more form than formula will be a greater work, we should avoid this easy judgment in our study of popular culture. In distinguishing form from formula we are trying to deal with the relationship between the work and its culture, and not with its artistic quality. Whether or not a different set of aesthetic criteria are necessary in the judgment of formal as opposed to formulaic works is an important and interesting question, but necessarily the subject of another series of reflections.

We can further differentiate the conception of formula by comparing it to genre and myth. Genre, in the sense of tragedy, comedy, romance, etc., seems to be based on a difference among basic attitudes or feelings about life. I find Northrop Frye's suggestion that the genres embody fundamental archetypal patterns reflecting stages of the human life cycle a very fruitful idea here. In Frye's sense of the term genre and myth are universal patterns of action that manifest themselves in all human cultures. Following Frye, let me briefly suggest a formulation of this kind—genre can be defined as a structural pattern that embodies a universal life pattern or myth in the materials of language. Formula, on the other hand is cultural; it represents the way in which a culture has embodied both mythical archetypes and its own preoccupations in narrative form.

An example will help clarify this distinction. The western and the spy story can both be seen as embodiments of the archetypal pattern of the hero's quest, which Frye discusses under the general heading of the mythos of romance. Or if we prefer psychoanalytic archetypes these formulas embody the Oedipal myth in fairly explicit fashion, since they deal with the hero's conquest of a dangerous and powerful figure. However, though we can doubtless characterize both western and spy stories in terms of these universal archetypes, they do not account for the basic and important differences in setting, characters, and action between them. These differences are clearly cultural and they reflect the particular preoccupations and needs of the time in which they were created and the group that created them: the western shows its nineteenth-century American origin while the spy story reflects the fact that it is largely a twentieth-century British creation. Of course, a formula articulated by one culture can be taken over by another. However, we will often find important differences in the formula as it moves from one culture or from one period to another. For example, the gunfighter western of the 1950s is importantly different from the cowboy romances of Owen Wister and Zane Grey, just as the American spy stories of Donald Hamilton differ from the British secret agent adventures of Eric Ambler and Graham Greene.

The cultural nature of formulas suggests two further points about them. First, while myths, because of their basic and universal nature, turn up in many different manifestations, formulas, because of their close connection to a particular culture and period of time, tend to have a much more limited repertory of plots, characters, and settings. For example, the pattern of action known generally as the Oedipus myth can be discerned in an enormous range of stories from Oedipus Rex to the latest western. Indeed, the very difficulty with this—myth as an analytical tool—is that it is so universal that it hardly serves to differentiate one story from another. Formulas, however, are much more specific: westerns must have a certain kind of setting, a particular cast of characters, and follow a limited number of lines of action. A western that does not take place in the West, near the frontiers, at a point in history when social order and anarchy are in tension, and that does not involve some form of pursuit is simply not a western. A detective story that does not involve the solution of a mysterious crime is not a detective story. This greater specificity of plot, character, and setting reflects a more limited framework of interest, values, and tensions that relate to culture rather than to the generic nature of man.

The second point is a hypothesis about why formulas come into existence and enjoy such wide popular uses. Why of all the infinite possible subjects for fictions do a few like the adventures of the detective, the secret agent, and the cowboy so dominate the field? I suggest that formulas are important because they represent syntheses of several important cultural functions, which, in modern cultures, have been taken over by the popular arts. Let me suggest just one or two examples of what I mean. In earlier more homogeneous cultures religious ritual performed the important function of articulating and reaffirming the primary cultural values. Today, with cultures composed of a multiplicity of differing religious groups, the synthesis of values and their reaffirmation has become an increasingly important function of the mass media and the popular arts. Thus, one important dimension of formula is social or cultural ritual. Homogeneous cultures also possessed a large repertory of games and songs, which all members of the culture understood and could participate in both for a sense of group solidarity and for personal enjoyment and recreation. Today, the great spectator sports provide one way in which a mass audience can participate in games together. Artistic formulas also fulfill this function in that they constitute entertainments with rules known to everyone. Thus, a very wide audience can follow a western, appreciate its fine points, and vicariously participate in its pattern of suspense and resolution. Indeed one of the more interesting ways of defining a western is as a game: a western is a three-sided game played on a field where the middle line is the frontier and the two main areas of play are the settled town and the savage wilderness. The three sides are the good group of townspeople who stand for law and order but are handicapped by lack of force, the villains who reject law and order and have force, and the hero who has ties with both sides. The object of the game is to get the hero to lend his force to the good group and to destroy the villain. Various rules determine how this can be done; for example, the hero cannot use force against the villain unless strongly provoked. Also, like games, the formula always gets to its goal. Someone must win, and the story must be resolved. This game dimension of formulas has two aspects. First, there is the patterned experience of excitement, suspense, and release, which we associate with the functions of entertainment and recreation. Second, there is the aspect of play as ego enhancement through the temporary resolution of inescapable frustrations and tensions through fantasy. As Piaget sums up this aspect of play:

> Conflicts are foreign to play, or, if they do occur, it is so that the ego may be freed from them by compensation or liquidation, whereas serious activity has to grapple with conflicts, which are inescapable. The conflict between obedience and individual liberty is, for example, the affliction of childhood [and we might note a key theme of the western] and in real life the only solutions to this conflict are submission, revolt, or cooperation, which involves some measure of compromise. In play, however, the conflicts are transposed in such a way that the ego is revenged, either by suppression of the problem or by giving it an acceptable solution. . . . [I]t is because the ego dominates the whole universe in play that it is freed from conflict. (71)

Thus, the game dimension of formula is a culture's way of simultaneously entertaining itself and of creating an acceptable pattern of temporary escape from the serious restrictions and limitations of human life. In formula stories, the detective always solves the crime, the hero always determines and carries out true justice, and the agent accomplishes his mission or at least preserves himself from the omnipresent threats of the enemy.

Finally, formula stories seem to be one way in which the individuals in a culture act out certain unconscious or repressed needs or express in an overt and symbolic fashion certain latent motives that they must give expression to but cannot face openly. This is the most difficult aspect of formula to pin down. Many would argue that one cannot meaningfully discuss latent contents or unconscious motives beyond the individual level or outside of the clinical context. Certainly it is easy to generate a great deal of pseudopsychoanalytic theories about literary formulas and to make deep symbolic interpretations, which it is clearly impossible to substantiate convincingly. However, though it may be difficult to develop a reliable method of analysis of this aspect of formulas, I am convinced that the Freudian insight that recurrent myths and stories embody a kind of collective dreaming process is essentially correct and has an important application on the cultural as well as the universal level; that is, that the idea of a collective dream applies to formula as well as to myth. But there is no doubt that we need to put much more thought into our approach to these additional dimensions of formula and about their relation to the basic dimension of a narrative construction.

My argument, then, is that formula stories like the detective story, the western, the seduction novel, the biblical epic, and many others are structures of narrative conventions that carry out a variety of cultural functions in a unified way. We can best define these formulas as principles for the selection of certain plots, characters, and settings, which possess in addition to their basic narrative structure the dimensions of collective ritual, game, and dream. To analyze these formulas we must first define them as narrative structures of a certain kind and then investigate how the additional dimensions of ritual, game, and dream have been synthesized into the particular patterns of plot, character, and setting that have become associated with the formula. Once we have understood the way in which particular formulas are structured, we will be able to compare them, and also to relate them to the cultures that use them. By these methods I feel that we will arrive at a new understanding of the phenomena of popular literature and new insights into the patterns of culture.

2

Notes toward an Aesthetic of Popular Culture

This is another period piece and like "The Concept of Formula" shows definite signs of its age. It hardly seems necessary, now, to explain the *auteur theory* at such length. In fact it has been superseded in film criticism by all sorts of new concepts. However, at the time this was published (in the *Journal of Popular Culture* of autumn 1972), it was still news to a lot of us. In fact, I really learned about it from my hyper-film-conscious students at the University of Chicago — Charles Flynn, Marvin Meisel, Terry Fox, Barbara Bernstein, and many others — to whom I will always be grateful. I've reprinted it here and resisted the temptation to annotate or revise some of the more dubious assertions because I think the essay illustrates something of the dialectic between traditional humanists and those of us who were trying to create a new approach to popular culture. The mildly patronizing treatment of Hitchcock seems especially egregious. Audiences and critics alike art have long recognized that portly genius as a great master of the art of film.

Whenever criticism feels the impact of an expanded sensibility, it becomes shot through with ideological dispute. In quieter, more stable artistic times, the critic, unburdened by the clash of methods and criteria, can focus his attention on his real task, the exploration and interpretation of individual works of art. But before he can do so with any hope of being understood and accepted by others, he must share with them at least a basic core of assumptions about the nature and value of artistic work. For almost three decades now, the criticism of literature, despite a variety of tangential currents, has flowed fairly smoothly from certain key assumptions of the "new criticism": the integrity and unity of the individual work, the intricate analysis of structure as the key to meaning and value, and the central value of complexity of expression as manifested in artistic devices like tension, irony, ambiguity, etc.

But the impact of the new media, the growth of a new pop culture, and the widening range of artistic interests and tasks have opened again the Pandora's box of aesthetic controversy. The resultant confusion is most apparent in film criticism — at present the most highly developed though most pungently polemical area of criticism involving modern popular forms. Compared to film, other modes of popular art such as pop music, comedy, and formula literature like detective stories have remained critically inarticulate, except for the work of reviewers. To a considerable extent these modes of popular art still bear the lingering stigma of cultural inferiority that long prevented film criticism from coming into its own. Indeed, the problem of the relationship between popular art and so-called high or serious art has always been the crux of any attempt to create a popular aesthetic. In this paper, I would like to explore this difficulty and to suggest how some of the recent concepts of film criticism have made possible a better approach to the analysis and criticism of the popular arts.

The traditional way of treating the popular arts has been in effect to deny that they are arts at all, or at least not arts in the same sense as the high arts. This practice has age-old authority since it was first and most compellingly set forth by no less a critic than Plato. In the *Gorgias,* Socrates arrived at a fundamental distinction between "arts," which are rational methods for using true knowledge to good ends, and nonarts, or "knacks" as Socrates calls them, which are capable of moving the mind through pleasure. However, these "knacks" are irrational because they concern not truth, but what pleases. Thus they are practiced by a combination of instinct and trial and error and cannot, like arts, be taught or meaningfully discussed. As examples of knacks as opposed to arts, Socrates distinguishes cookery from medicine and make-up from gymnastics. Cookery and medicine both concern themselves with diet. However, where medicine prescribes not what pleases, but what the doctor's knowledge tells him is best for the body to eat, the cook seeks primarily to please, irrespective of the consequences for health. Similarly, the gymnast prescribes exercises aimed at the creation of a healthy body, while the make-up man has the knack of creating a beautiful appearance without concern for the actual state of the body. In the same way, rhetoric, Socrates argues, is not an art based on true ends, but a knack for creating the appearance of conviction: its true and rational counterpart is legislation, the art of prescribing what is right for the health of the state.

Many modern critics have used the Platonic distinction between art and knack to distinguish "high" or "serious" art from the popular or mass arts; in contemporary parlance the Platonic notion of knack has been replaced by such terms as entertainment or "kitsch." But the basic idea remains the same; arts dedicated to higher purposes are opposed to arts that have simple pleasure or an appeal to the baser emotions as their primary goal.

Today, though many critics have consciously abandoned the negative, pejorative approach that long dominated the discussion of popular culture, the traditional Platonic distinction between art and nonart has a way of lingering on in more positive forms. Much current critical treatment of such film directors as Alfred Hitchcock reflects this tendency. O. B. Hardison, for instance, completely retains the traditional Platonic distinction, but he believes that the rhetorical knacks, which Plato condemns, are significant arts, which have their own meaningful purposes and are highly valuable in their own way. Thus, for him, Hitchcock is not an artist in the true sense, but a high quality professional creator of entertaining melodrama:

> Nobody would seriously compare Hitchcock to a dozen directors and producers who have used the film medium as an art form. Eisenstein, Chaplin, Ford, Bergman, Olivier, Fellini—the list could be expanded—have qualities undreamed of in the world of cops and robbers and pseudo-Freudian melodrama, which is the world where Hitchcock reigns supreme. (137-38)

While explaining and defining his distinction between "professional" and "artist" Hardison goes on to create a superb contemporary formulation of Plato's *Gorgias* distinction:

> Consider the professional a rhetorician. The purpose of art, says Aristotle, is to give pleasure. Not any kind of pleasure, but the sort that comes from learning. The experience of art is an insight, an illumination of the action being imitated. Rhetoric, on the other hand, is

oriented toward the market place. Its purpose is not illumination but persuasion, and its governing concept is that the work produced must be adjusted to the mind of the audience. Rhetorical art succeeds by saying what the audience has secretly known (or wanted to know) all along. Its language is disguised flattery, its norm fantasy, and its symbols surrogates for unconscious cravings. Given the passionate desire that everyone has to suspend disbelief, almost anything works, as witness the comic book and the exploits of Mike Hammer and James Bond; but some kinds of rhetoric work better than others. [and here Hardison departs sharply from Plato] just as there is good and bad art, there is good and bad rhetoric. (138)

Hardison's essay is somewhat ambiguous on the relative value of art and rhetoric. At times he seems to be saying, like Socrates, that rhetoric is an Inferior mode of creation: ("Nobody would seriously compare Hitchcock to a dozen directors and producers who have used the film medium as an art form"). But, on the other hand he seems to suggest that rhetoric, though different from art, is equally valid: "If [Hitchcock's thrillers] are rhetoric and shaped by the needs of the audience, they are just as significant as art and just as necessary" (152). This uncertainty about the aesthetic value of Hitchcock's work leads Hardison to a particular mode of analysis of his films. Instead of treating them as independent works, Hardison examines Hitchcock's thrillers as embodiments of the middle-class mind of the twentieth century. "Because Hitchcock has continued to produce successful thrillers for over thirty years, his films are a kind of contour map of the middle-class mind during this period" (150).

This approach implies that the work of "rhetorical" or popular artists like Hitchcock is successful because it embodies or expresses the values of the popular mind in a particularly effective or direct fashion. This assumption, shared by many scholars and critics of the popular arts, has made social and psychological analysis the dominant mode of interpretation and analysis in dealing with this kind of material. Thus, the distinction between high art and popular art has led to two quite different modes of discussion: high art is commonly treated as aesthetic structure or individual vision; the popular arts are studied as social and psychological data.

There is certainly some validity to this practice if we assume that what is popular embodies cultural attitudes to a greater extent than that which is not. However, such an approach does have some problems. First of all, what is popular at any given time is not all "rhetorical" art.

Indeed, as Frank Luther Mott's study of bestsellers has shown, many novels which we would call high art have, over a longer period of years, sold as well as many ephemeral bestsellers. This is perhaps not as clear in the case of the newer media of film and TV. Nonetheless, films that belong unquestionably to the category of high art—e.g., the works of Bergman, Fellini, Antonioni and Godard—have been quite popular. Correspondingly, many films clearly designed solely for rhetorical purposes have not been successful. Thus, there is no necessary connection between popularity and those qualities of a work, which Hardison designates as rhetorical. The fact that a work is designed to please the audience clearly does not mean that it will become popular. Otherwise most Hollywood films and pulp novels would achieve the popularity of Hitchcock at his best, and works created primarily with a view to an artistic expression of the creator's vision would inevitably fail. A second difficult question is what psychological process or mechanism makes the expression of commonly held values popular with the public. Is it simply that we find comfort in repetitions of received opinions? But if this is the case, why go to all the trouble of constructing a fiction? If this theory of popularity is correct we should all be satisfied with Fourth of July Speeches and sermons from the church of our choice. Moreover, if we look at some of the most successful popular works, they seem as much to contradict popular views as to affirm them. One of the strongest middle-class values is a respect for law and order and a high valuation of stability and respectable enterprise. Yet in Hitchcock's thrillers, respectable citizens become involved in situations of peril and intrigue where the established machinery of law and order is helpless. Perhaps this is vicarious adventure, which springs from the impulse to escape an overly stable and restrictive life. Then Hitchcock is successful because he reflects basic conflicts in the middle-class mind. This is essentially the way Hardison views Hitchcock: his films embody the subconscious need to engage in adventures without destroying the framework of reason and stability: "No matter how we may plot our situation on the charts of reason, the subconscious needs to view life as an epic quest through alien territories and the domains of strange gods, underwritten by providence and with the payoff guaranteed. Hitchcock's thrillers present this fantasy in palatable modern guise" (152).

But if this means that Hitchcock's thrillers constitute an exploration and resolution of the complex conflicts between the conscious mind and the devious subconscious, how do we differentiate this from art? Why is the insight into human life produced by such a work of art any less than that of say, Dostoyevsky's *Crime and Punishment?* Hardison would reply, I think, that Hitchcock's exploration and resolution is more formulaic, more stereotyped than Dostoyevsky's. But, if this is the case, are we not just saying that Hitchcock is an inferior artist? In these terms is not the distinction between high art and popular art simply a means of evading the obvious conclusion that most popular artists are inferior artists, no matter how much pleasure they may give?

Several other difficulties attend the definition of the popular arts along the Platonic lines of truth vs. rhetoric. Are we then to say that high art is not rhetorical, does not depend for much of its effectiveness on a skillful manipulation of audience attitudes and feelings? If all art depends on emotional effect to some extent just where do we draw the line between rhetoric and art? To some extent this depends on the audience and not on the innate character of the work. To a person without much education or sophistication, a soap opera may well be an important source of truths about life. Is it then entirely rhetorical for such a person? Moreover, it is a notorious fact that the popular art of one century often becomes the high art of another. Shakespeare and Dickens certainly thought of themselves as popular artists writing for a heterogeneous public and the media in which they worked were the mass media of their day. Today their status as classics is unchallenged. Does this mean that some mysterious process has transmuted Hamlet and Bleak House from rhetoric into art? From audience flattery into illumination?

I find it impossible to answer these questions very satisfactorily and I invariably run into such mare's nests whenever I try to separate the high arts and the popular arts in this fashion. I recommend that we turn our attention to the work of a different school of film critics, who have managed to surmount this problem. This group is known as the auteur critics after a term first given wide currency in an essay by the French critic and director François Truffaut.[1] To understand the particular emphases of auteur criticism one must grasp certain aspects of the critical background against which it developed. For many years serious film criticism followed the model of literary criticism by concentrating most of its attention on films that could unmistakably be conceived as total

---

1. Of the various general accounts of the *auteur* theory, the most useful are those in Peter Wollen, *Signs and Meaning in the Cinema* and Raymond Durgnat, *Films and Feeling.* The reader should also consult the criticism of André Bazin in *What is Cinema?* and Andrew Sarris in *American Cinema* for discussions of the *auteur* approach. I have also been helped in my understanding of the subject by unpublished papers by Charles Flynn and Christian Koch.

works of art. This meant in practice films that were controlled from inception to final editing by a single artist and that could be viewed as original creations with serious rather than entertaining intentions. Naturally such criticism largely rejected the output of the American film industry where, with the exception of a few rare films like Welles's *Citizen Kane,* the product was the result of many conflicting judgments and the criteria of entertainment commonly played a greater part than the ideals of art. The auteur critics, finding artistic value and interest in the Hollywood film, have created a new mode of analysis based on the individual stylistic characteristics and the thematic interests of the director. Their criticism has demonstrated that despite the commercial orientation and artistic limitations of the American film industry, certain directors of great ability—men like Hitchcock, Welles, Renoir, Lang, Ford, Hawks, and Cukor—have been able to make significant individual artistic statements. The crucial difference in the approach of the auteur critics from that of contemporary critics of literature lies in the way the artistic statement is defined.[2] Where the new critic defines the artistic statement in terms of the total unity and power of the individual work, the essential reference of the auteur critic is to the auteur's complete work; the artistic statement is sought not in the complex totality of the individual work, but in those aspects of the individual film that are clearly related to the overall stylistic or thematic preoccupation of the auteur. Indeed, for the auteur critic, many elements of the work, including some of its most obvious characteristics, may have to be set aside in order to discover the auteur's statement:

> One essential corollary of the theory as it has been developed is the discovery that the defining characteristics of an author's [auteur's] work are not necessarily those which are most readily apparent. The purpose of criticism thus becomes to uncover behind the superficial contrasts of subject and treatment a hard core of basic and often recondite motifs. The pattern formed by these motifs is what gives an [auteur's] work its particular structure, both defining it internally and distinguishing one body of work from another. (Geoffrey Nowell-Smith qtd. in Wollen 80)

An example will clarify what these somewhat enigmatic statements mean. The most obvious defining characteristic of most of the films of

2. Of the *auteur* critics who have written full-length studies of major directors, I have found the work of Robin Wood, who has written substantial monographs on Hitchcock, Howard Hawks, and Arthur Penn, most interesting. Some of the best *auteur* criticism remains unfortunately untranslated from the French such as the excellent study of John Ford by Jean Mitry.

Hitchcock is their thrilling, frequently melodramatic plots presenting situations of international intrigue and crime. These plots are, for the most part, derived from the work of others—many of Hitchcock's films have been based on novels by such writers as John Buchan, Somerset Maugham, Daphne du Maurier, Patricia Highsmith, Cornell Woolrich, and even Joseph Conrad. In turn many aspects of the way these stories are realized in Hitchcock's films relate to popular traditions of the thriller and the romance. Yet, despite all these limitations on his originality, limitations typical of those imposed on any director working in Hollywood, Hitchcock remains a highly distinctive and unique director. In what consists this uniqueness? According to the auteur critics the answer to this question lies along two lines: a) the special technical cinematic competence and unique mastery of visual style and editing that Hitchcock brings to his work and b) the way in which he is able to use conventional materials of many different kinds to explore certain moral and artistic themes that have always fascinated him. Anyone who has seen a Hitchcock film is probably at least unconsciously aware of one recurrent motif: the peculiar intensity of attention, which is focused on particular details or objects. Hitchcock's settings are commonly rather austere; even when they represent lavish ballrooms or luxury hotels, they are almost never cluttered with objects or rich with decor. But within this general austerity certain small details and objects, usually very ordinary things, become highly charged with significance and ambiguity: a glass of milk, which may or may not be poisoned, a key, a newspaper, a man's hand—these ordinary objects have a way of suddenly becoming symbols of something sinister and terrible. This pattern of the innocent becoming sinister or evil is clearly a basic form of Hitchcock's imagination and few of his most successful films fail to embody it both in detail and in the larger patterns of the story. Film after film is based on the plight of an ordinary person suddenly caught up in a web of intrigue and crime and forced to undergo the experiences of guilt and terror. Those incidents from Hitchcock's films that haunt the mind invariably bear this quality of the sudden transformation of the ordinary into the terrifying: the shower murder in *Psycho* where a ghastly murderous figure suddenly turns up in the most banal and ordinary motel bathroom; the crop-dusting plane in *North by Northwest*, which suddenly becomes a murderous instrument, or, to take a much earlier example, the tweedy country gentleman in *The 39 Steps* who is suddenly revealed as the leader of the enemy spies when the hero notices that he has a portion of one finger missing. Or think what Hitchcock has so often made of train journeys, commonly experiences of mild boredom and relaxation. Such examples could be multiplied indefinitely, but these should be enough to suggest the presence of basic patterns derived from stylistic and thematic preoccupations, which Hitchcock is able to impose on the most diverse and conventional kind of story material.

Because it is concerned not with the unity of the total work, but with those elements that show the individual mark of the director, auteur criticism has been very fruitful in dealing with those films that have been created as part of a mass entertainment industry. The auteur approach also has the value of ducking the problematic art-rhetoric distinction by simply ignoring those aspects of films that aim at manipulating audience emotions and attitudes and concentrating on the director's style and themes. Far from distinguishing between "rhetorical" filmmakers like Hitchcock and serious artists, the auteur critics like to insist on the authentic artistry of a Hitchcock and frequently remind us of the analogy between the "commercial" Hollywood cinema and the equally "popular" Elizabethan theater. Robin Wood draws out this comparison in a statement that directly opposes Hardison's comments on the nature of Hitchcock's films:

> Hitchcock's films are usually popular. Indeed some of his best films . . . are among his most popular. From this arises a widespread assumption that, however "clever," "technically brilliant," "amusing," "gripping," etc. they may be, they can't be taken seriously. They must be, if not absolutely bad, at least fatally flawed from a serious standpoint. And it is easy enough for those who take this line to point to all manner of "concessions to the box office," fatal compromises with a debased popular taste: Hitchcock returns repeatedly to the suspense-thriller for his material; he generally uses established stars who are "personalities" first and actors second; there is a strong element of humor in his work, "gags" and "comic relief" which effectively undermine any pretensions to sustained seriousness of tone. To one whose training has been primarily literary, these objections have a decidedly familiar ring. One recalls that "commercial"—and at the same time intellectually disreputable— medium, the Elizabethan drama; one thinks of those editors who have wished to remove the Porter scene from Macbeth because its tone of bawdy comedy is incompatible with the tragic atmosphere. What one does not want either Shakespeare or Hitchcock deprived of is precisely the richness their work derives from the sense of living contact with a wide popular audience. To wish that Hitchcock's films were like those of Bergman or Antonioni is like wishing that Shakespeare had been like Corneille. (9-10)

Like many new, partly developed critical methods, the auteur approach has been highly susceptible to faddism. Some of its judgments can leave those outside the magic circle of conviction gasping: "Charlton Heston is an axiom of the cinema." Apart from its occasional excesses, however, the auteur approach has produced the most interesting and systematic body of film criticism being written today and therefore merits our attention as a possible model for the analysis and interpretation of popular culture generally.

Auteur criticism has effectively widened our range of awareness in the film, because the auteur critic's concept of artistry corresponds with the kind of creativity most successful under the circumstances of popular culture. If we look a little more closely at the concept of the auteur, we will see how this is the case.

According to most proponents of the theory the auteur is not one of those few film directors who insist upon absolute originality, who create their own material, write their own scripts and thus create total works of art without any compromises for the sake of commercial success or mass audience tastes. On the other hand, the auteur is not a mere technician who simply transmits to film the script, which an omnipotent producer hands him. Instead, the auteur is an individual creator who works within a framework of existing materials, conventional structures, and commercial imperatives, but who nonetheless has the imagination, the integrity, and the skill to express his own artistic personality in the way he sets forth the conventional material he works with. In other words, the successful auteur lies somewhere along the continuum between original creation and performance. He is not an original artist because he is an interpreter of materials or of conventional structures largely created by others, but he is more than a performer because he recreates these conventions to the point that they manifest at least in part the patterns of his own style and vision.

Thus, the analogy between Shakespeare and a film auteur like Hitchcock is not totally absurd. Like Hitchcock, Shakespeare worked in a popular, commercial medium and accepted the limitations of that medium. He, too, made extensive use of conventional material; as we know from the many studies of his sources, most of Shakespeare's plays were adaptations of existing stories. His work is full of the stage conventions of his time and emphasizes many of the same popular elements on which Hitchcock has fastened: sensational crimes and international intrigues, madness and violence, mystery and romance. Moreover, it is not inconceivable that like Shakespeare's plays, Hitchcock's films will make the transition from the popular art of one century to the high art of another. Still, I find it a little hard to accept the Shakespeare-Hitchcock analogy with the same conviction as a good auteur critic like Robin Wood. Wood, I think, might agree that Shakespeare does far more to transform his materials and thus to create totally unique works of art than Hitchcock does. But it seems to me there is also something of a theoretic as well as a qualitative distinction here. The distinction I have in mind is a result of the difference between contemporary popular dramatic conventions, and those of the Elizabethan stage. The tradition of the contemporary thriller, in which Hitchcock operates, is a far more specialized and restrictive tradition than that of the Elizabethan tragedy. For one thing, the thriller is the result of a longer process of cultural evolution and is consequently more rigid and refined in its conventional limits. In addition, the thriller is generally conceived of as a form that, for purposes of entertainment, restricts the depth and range of emotion that it arouses. While the Elizabethan theater was also devoted to entertainment, it is evident from the plays themselves—and not just Shakespeare's—that the nature and kind of emotion that could be represented was richer and more complex. Elizabethan tragedy arouses pity and fear and brings them to their fullest expression before dismissing them; the thriller arouses these emotions, but never fully because it restricts their expression by relief when we see that the hero and heroine will be saved from a terrible fate and by a displacement of pity and fear into terror and suspense. Even in a film which verges on tragedy like *Psycho,* Hitchcock is very careful to restrict our sense of identification with the heroine by showing her yielding to a temptation so petty that the viewer pities her plight, but does not feel the tragic sense of identification. Then, in the murder scene, our emotion is displaced from a specific feeling for the heroine to a more generalized sense of terror and the uncanny, a feeling that is immediately powerful but less deep and lasting in its impact. This is, of course, a function of the conception of entertainment as a highly controlled experience, which puts us through an intense series of emotions that immediately dissipate upon conclusion of the performance. Working within the limitations of contemporary conceptions of entertainment, Hitchcock must strive for an artistic effect that is less rich and deep but more tightly focused and controlled than that cultivated by the Elizabethan dramatists.

Thus, there is some validity to the kind of distinction O. B. Hardison makes between Hitchcock and directors like Eisenstein, Bergman, and Fellini. But this is not a contrast between art and rhetoric, but between different kinds of art. The art of the free creator is the making of a unique and integrated work, which in its totality embodies a new conception of art and of the world. The art of the auteur is that of turning a conventional and generally known and appreciated artistic formula into a medium of personal expression while at the same time giving us a version of the formula that is satisfying because it fulfills our basic expectations. As noted earlier, the art of the auteur lies somewhere between creation and performance. It differs from original creation not in being more rhetorical, but in sharing certain of the characteristics of performance. It is this aspect that relates it to popular or mass culture.

Hall and Whannel point out in their interesting book on the popular arts that these are above all arts in which performance plays a central role. They ascribe this fact to two conditions of popular art. First, there is the essential conventionality that makes it widely understood and appreciated and stresses the repetition or performance of something already known rather than the creation of something new. Second, popular art needs a quality of personal style, since among essentially similar versions of a formula the one that manifests most clearly a sense of individual style will be most attractive and gratifying. "Popular art is essentially a conventional art that restates in an intense form values and attitudes already known; that reassures and reaffirms, but brings to this something of the surprise of art as well as the shock of recognition. Such art has in common with folk art the genuine contact between audience and performer, but it differs from folk art in that it is an individualized art, the art of the known performer. The audience-as-community has come to depend on the performer's skills, and on the force of a personal style, to articulate its common values and interpret its experience" (66).

The concept of the auteur has made available to us, at least in terms of the art of film, an effective means of discussing the kind of art that Hall and Whannel describe in the passage just quoted. Though it is just beginning to develop an articulated method, auteur criticism has already given valuable examples of how to define and analyze the personal within the conventional in the work of such directors as Hitchcock, Howard Hawks, John Ford, George Cukor, and many others. It seems to me that with some changes for the different artistic media, the auteur approach should be a profitable one for other areas of popular culture. In popular music, for example, one can see the difference between pop groups who simply perform without creating that personal statement that marks the auteur, and highly creative groups like the Beatles who make of their performances a complex work of art. The methods of the auteur approach—examination of the entire body of work for recurrent stylistic and thematic patterns rather than the isolated analysis of the individual work in its unique totality—should prove a fruitful method for defining those patterns that mark the Beatles as auteurs and thereby make more articulate for us the special values of their art. The same method should prove useful in the analysis of highly conventionalized types of popular literature like the detective story, the western, or the spy thriller. These literary types, like the analogous films, are dominantly repetitions of conventional formulas that have a simple entertainment function but little lasting interest or value. However, there are always a few writers who, without losing sight of the conventional structures of the story type they work within, still manage to create a distinctive personal art. These are the auteurs of popular literature; writers like Raymond Chandler, Ross Macdonald, Dorothy Sayers, and even Ian Fleming, whose personal performances stand out from the mass of mystery fiction. As in the case of pop music and the conventional films, it is not so much the unique totality of the individual work, but the artistic dialectic between auteur and convention, the drama of how the convention is shaped to manifest the auteur's intention, that excites our interest and admiration.

3

Beatles, Batman, and the New Aesthetic

Written and published in 1968 this essay shows something of the creative ferment and the impact on popular culture of what we now commonly refer to as "postmodernism." I didn't know the term at the time, though I believe it had already been used in some forms by critics like Leslie Fiedler. Nor was I familiar as yet with poststructuralist philosophical and critical developments like deconstruction, gender theory, and multiculturalism that would later be associated with the artistic developments of postmodernism. Since the essay's main value is the way in which it reveals the perspective of the time, I have only revised some of the less readable passages and corrected gross errors. I've tried to retain the flavor, the angle, and the limitations of the time in which it was originally written. As an essay in period sensibility it's interesting to me that I treat creators who have proved to be of lasting value, like the Beatles, in the same tone of voice as now largely forgotten sixties fads like *Candy* and the super-poppish television series *Batman*. Of course, the latter still shows up on late night television in the form of a movie based on the TV series so it must have had some lasting appeal. *Candy,* which delivered sex in the guise of comedy has, I guess, been blown out of the water by the increasing acceptance of erotic realism and fantasy of all sorts. I was really wowed by Michelangelo Antonioni's *Blowup* when it first came out, but that, too, seems to have fallen by the wayside. However, I'm still rather proud of the way I interpreted the film as a reflection of the imposture and escapism that I still think is part of the essence of postmodernism. I deal with some of the same issues from a later perspective in "Popular Culture/Multiculturalism" and "Cowboys and Canons: Humanistic Education and Popular Culture."

In 1915, the American literary critic Van Wyck Brooks gave birth to a figure of speech that became, for a time, one of the most popular explanations of American culture. America, Brooks said, was divided between the highbrows and the lowbrows. Highbrows believed that life should be a pursuit of the highest moral and artistic purposes, and they wanted to surround themselves with, in Matthew Arnold's phrase, "the best that has been thought and said in the world." In America this meant that their primary allegiance was to the great European tradition of literature, art, music, and philosophy. Brooks's lowbrow represented the ordinary man and his culture. Though indifferent to traditional cultural values, lowbrows were vigorous, energetic, and practical because they were in direct contact with the everyday problems of life. Brooks argued that since highbrows and lowbrows both represented important cultural energies, it was unfortunate that, in America, they had so little contact with each other. Lacking the vigorous pragmatism of lowbrows, highbrows had become overrefined and too idealistic, standing above the hurly-burly of a democratic culture. However, without the leavening influence of the highbrow tradition, lowbrow existence was animated but crude and purposeless. Brooks hoped that America would eventually produce a mediating middlebrow culture synthesizing lowbrow energy and highbrow ideals. He even believed that he had detected the beginnings of such a literature in the vigorously eclectic poetry of Walt Whitman.

In one way, Brooks's prophecies came true. Popular culture did undergo a considerable transformation in the early twentieth century. The new magazines, the bestsellers, Broadway theater, the movies, radio, and finally TV evolved cultural forms that were much slicker and more sophisticated than the popular culture of the nineteenth century. But this new middlebrow culture, or midcult, as some critics have called it, was not really what Brooks had in mind. Animated mainly by commercial purposes, with marketability as its primary criterion, it was not a synthesis of highbrow and lowbrow, but simply a slicker form of lowbrowism. As such, it quickly became dominant in the new mass media, replacing such older forms of popular art and literature as vaudeville and melodrama. Once exposed to the skillful techniques, the glamorous stars, the elegant settings, and the more sophisticated stories of the movies, the public was no longer willing to settle for a traveling company of *Uncle Tom's Cabin* or a local production of *East Lynne*. However, if this new middlebrow culture tended to drive the older popular forms into a marginal cultural position, it did not satisfy the younger artists and intellectuals who increasingly turned to the European avant-garde for artistic and cultural leadership. During the 1920s, the split between the complex and difficult art of the intellectual avant-garde and the middlebrow-lowbrow culture of the mass media apparently became even greater. By 1950, it seemed to have been institutionalized. A small enclave of avant-garde culture was supported by foundations and universities and appreciated by a small intellectual elite. The rest was mass culture organized by commercial interests and consumed by the majority of the public. If there was any meaningful connection between the atonal serialism favored by most important American composers of serious music and the products of Tin Pan Alley, between the novels of Faulkner or Bellow and the westerns and situation comedies that formed the staple of TV, between the paintings of de Kooning, Pollock, or Kline and the decoration of the average American living room, no analyst of American culture was able to point it out. In fact, critics like Dwight MacDonald and Harold Rosenberg concluded that any attempt to synthesize high culture and the art of the masses could only result in corruption. Their cultural program was to protect high culture and real art from the influence of mass art:"So let the masses have their Masscult, let the few who care about good writing, painting, music, architecture, philosophy, etc. have their High Culture, and don't fuzz up the distinction with Midcult" (MacDonald 73).

But suddenly, in the 1960s, just as it seemed that the avant-garde and mass culture had agreed to ignore each other, we find ourselves in the midst of a whole series of artistic events that have crossed over and obfuscated the brow lines. There is the striking vogue of pop music among intellectuals and avant-garde artists and writers. The Beatles have received the imprimatur of not only *Time* magazine and Leonard Bernstein, but also of the composer Ned Rorem in the austerely intellectual *New York Review of Books*. The Beatles may be unique, but their example has been followed by a multitude of other pop groups. Things have even gone so far that one promising young novelist and poet, the Canadian Leonard Cohen, writes both impeccably post-Joycean novels and extremely successful popular songs. Nor is the art of the pop groups new only in a fashionable sense. Many of the groups, again following the Beatles, have taken over some of the experimental techniques of avant-garde electronic composers, as well as some of the characteristic instruments and sounds of non-Western music. Another kind of cultural line-crossing has appeared in the visual arts. Among widely admired artists of the last decade one became famous for his imitations in various sizes of Campbell's Soup cans. Another modeled his style on the conventions of the pulp-paper comic strip, while a third has created a new type of sculpture with mammoth models in canvas and plaster of hamburgers, ice cream cones, and fancy cakes. [Since pop art is now another historic movement, I'd better explain to the reader that these characterizations referred to Andy Warhol, Roy Lichtenstein, and Claes Oldenberg.] A few further examples: *Playboy* magazine combines the old popular appeal of the girlie magazine with fiction and essays by leading writers and intellectuals. The James Bond movies and TV programs like *The Man from U.N.C.L.E.* and *Batman* have created a large following among intellectuals through their tongue-in-cheek treatment of popular adventure themes and characters. And the new art has given rise to its tastemakers and prophets as well. Susan Sontag, one of the most brilliant young critics, writes polemics against the tradition of modern literary criticism and defends a "camp" taste for pulp magazines, Hollywood musicals of the 1930s, and other mass cultural products once thought far beneath highbrow notice. Finally, Marshall McLuhan has become one of the most widely known and quoted intellectuals of the present day for his analysis of the radical change in consciousness he says is being created by the new mass media. Sometimes it seems as if we're all going hippie. Milton Mayer recently wrote (I hope ironically): "A doctoral dissertation by a University of California sociologist reveals that every hippie in the Haight-Ashbury district of San Francisco has now been interviewed 12–32 times by University of California sociologists" (29).

I believe that these and many other similar trends are not passing fashions but signs of a major transformation in our culture that is rapidly throwing into question not only the brow theory of culture, but also many of our traditional assumptions about the nature and function of the arts. Although the new trends are too diverse to be meaningfully thought of as a single movement, certain tendencies have turned up often enough in the new art that they can help us to characterize and understand it more sharply. I wish to focus my attention on a number of these.

One manner in which the new art crosses the brow lines derives from its concern with life as it is refracted and distorted by mass culture. Terry Southern's *Candy* illustrates this in a most obvious sense. In this novel (if it can be called that), the characters are neither representations of real human beings nor reductions and simplifications of real characters as, for example, in a western or a situation comedy. Instead, Southern creates characters by imitating and parodying the formulas of popular fiction:

> In the fifth row center, Candy Christian slowly closed her notebook and dropped her pen into her purse. She was sitting on the edge of her chair, holding her breath; then she gave a soft sigh and sat back limply. She felt utterly exhausted, yet exhilarated too. A great man, she thought, a truly great man. I'm in the presence of a truly great man. (11)

Here we are in the presence of a heroine and a style that come right out of pulp magazines like *True Romance* or *True Confessions*. In some respects this is similar to what James Joyce does in the Nausicaa section of *Ulysses* when he describes the young Dublin girl, Gerty MacDowell:

> Gerty MacDowell who was seated near her companions, lost in thought, gazing far away into the distance was in very truth as fair a specimen of winsome Irish girlhood as one could wish to see. She was pronounced beautiful by all who knew her though, as folks often said, she was more a Giltrap than a MacDowell. Her figure was slight and graceful, inclining even to fragility but those iron jelloids she had been taking of late had done her a world of good much better than the Widow Welch's female pills and she was much better of those discharges she used to get and that tired feeling. The waxen pallor of her face was almost spiritual in its ivorylike purity though her rosebud mouth was a genuine Cupid's bow, Greekly perfect. (342)

There is an important difference between Joyce and Southern, however. Gerty MacDowell is not simply a formula figure but a rich and many-sided person who is partly defined by her tendency to see life through the rosy haze of sentimental fiction. Popular culture is part of her character, but not the whole of it. Candy, however, never becomes a complex character. Southern places the formula heroine of pulp romance in the unexpected context of overt sexuality. Romance becomes pornography, which is undercut in turn by satire and irony. This focuses our attention on the absurd and distorted perspectives of sentimental fiction and pornography rather than on a fictional projection of human experience. Southern's object of imitation is not human action, but the pseudoreality of mass culture.

Candy illustrates one of the more limited and superficial modes of the new art. Southern's work is more sophisticated but not basically different from *Mad* magazine or the TV version of *Batman*. Joseph Heller's *Catch-22* is much more subtle and complex. Heller uses the World War II Air Force as a metaphor for the pseudoreality of a mass culture that has become absurdly and insanely separated from the true needs and purposes of human life. In the mad Air Force of *Catch-22* characters like the symbolically named Milo Minderbinder become skillful manipulators and thrive mightily. However, their power grows out of absurd and ridiculous actions, which, like the production and distribution of chocolate-covered cotton or bombing one's own air base for profit, are destructive of whatever purposes the organization originally sought. Heller's hero, Yossarian, is caught in this world of absurdity, but he cannot accept it as the final truth about life. In the end, like many another contemporary hero, he realizes that he must drop out.

Such attacks on mass culture pervade the new art—witness such Beatles' songs as "Nowhere Man," "Eleanor Rigby," and "A Day in the Life," for example—but the curious thing is that these attacks do not lead to calls for revolution or for radical cultural changes. Ironically, these critics of mass culture are among its most successful and popular figures. *Candy* and *Catch-22* were enormous bestsellers; the Beatles' latest appeal to turn on and drop out has sold nearly three million copies. The new pop painters and sculptors are among the most famous and successful artists in the country. Moreover, these writers and artists frequently employ the very techniques of mass culture to attack it. What accounts for this paradox?

The main reason, I think, is that, despite their attacks, these artists belong to the first intellectual generation that has really grown up with mass culture. Though they may attack some of its aspects, they accept it as a given of human existence, and they are more interested in understanding and coping with it than in changing it. As artists, they are concerned with the discovery of whatever human values mass culture may have and with the creation of strategies for evading its worst effects on the human spirit. In fact, the new artists, writers, and musicians have gotten much of their inspiration from areas of popular culture outside the basically imitative and banal formulas of TV, Hollywood movies, Broadway, and the slick magazines. By exploring these areas they have discovered and exploited "lowbrow" forms that possess unique expressive powers. For example, there are the lifestyles of minority groups that have not been fully integrated into the majority audience. The popular tradition of African American music is the most important minority cultural form from which the pop writers, artists, and musicians have derived new kinds of expressiveness, but they have also explored and mined such subcultures as that of the hot rod, the motorcycle, the drug addict, the homosexual, and the insane person. The recent fashion for folk music reflects some of the same interests and needs that led to the discovery of minority and marginal subcultures. The common element is the search for authentic popular forms that have not yet been subjected to the smoothing-out and slicking-up processes of the mass media and that therefore still retain a strong flavor of the human beings who created them. ["Authentic" was a keyword of the aesthetic of the sixties. Someday someone will write a history of the concept of authenticity and will find, I think, that it mattered more than anything else to this period that was so deeply aware of and fascinated by the pseudo-realities of popular culture.]

The new art has also made important discoveries in a second area largely ignored by high culture and by the established forms of mass culture. John Kouwenhoven has called this the vernacular. It includes those more or less anonymous and utilitarian products of industry and technology where self-conscious artistry in design has had little influence. An example is the contemporary discovery of the expressive power of industrial machines. For example, if we look at what passed for the finest thing in later nineteenth-century design, we cannot avoid feeling how silly and dated it seems. But if we contemplate the most straightforward and completely inartistic design for a shop machine it looks superb. Some European artists discovered this a long time ago. Even in the twenties, the French dadaist Marcel Duchamp took functional products like bottle racks, urinals, and typewriter covers and showed them as works of art under the generic name of "ready-mades." Andy Warhol's Campbell's Soup cans, and Claes Oldenberg's hamburgers, mixers, telephones, and wall switches, develop this discovery, which has also extended to the exploration of found objects and junk, the used-up residue of industrial production. One of the most striking sculptures of 1965 was Robert Rauschenberg's "Oracle," which consisted of five large wheeled objects made out of junk and vaguely resembling such artifacts as a window frame, a tub and shower, and a control panel. Each of the objects contained a radio receiver and speaker arranged so that noise and fragmentary snatches of music and speech were emitted in a random fashion. From the description, you might well question whether this was a work of art or not. Yet, whatever it was, it had a great evocativeness and seemed to have a striking relevance to one's feelings about the contemporary world.

The seemingly random structure of Rauschenberg's "Oracle" suggests another area of contemporary mass culture in which the new artists have discovered expressive possibilities. Modem culture has many characteristic structures that yoke together strikingly disparate and unconnected experiences and sensations. Marshall McLuhan suggests that the model of this new kind of structure is what he calls the newspaper "mosaic." This pattern represents "the discontinuous variety and incongruity of ordinary life." Yet, at the same time, it involves the reader in a process of giving order to his life by effecting "a complex many-leveled function of group awareness and participation" (*Understanding Media* 207, 216). There are many other examples of such seemingly random but powerfully engrossing contemporary structures: the lights, signs, buildings, traffic, and flowing crowds of Times Square; the experience of driving down a superhighway; listening to a disc jockey program; walking through a large department store. Even high culture can become transformed into structures of this kind as in museum-going, where the individual works become parts of a moving process. Much of the new art seems dedicated to understanding the implications and realizing the expressive possibilities of such structures. Novels like Burroughs's *Naked Lunch* and Leonard Cohen's *Beautiful Losers* are quite discontinuous, juxtaposing events and characters disparate in time and space. Yet they involve the reader in a compelling psychological process. The recent Beatles' album, *Sgt. Pepper's Lonely Hearts Club Band,* is a collection of separate songs in various styles and settings, yet the relationship of the different songs is haunting and effective.

These sources of the new art's content and structure undercut the traditional barriers between mass and high culture. But even more important than its exploration of these sources is that the new art has developed three pervasive stylistic and thematic tendencies that more than anything else define its character. These new artistic modes are: (a) the theme of detached sensuality or the "cool," (b) the strategy of imposture or the "put-on," and (c) transformational form or "work in process." A fuller discussion of these three modes will help us to understand the basic impetus of the new art.

Surely one of the most pervasive aspects of the new art is its sensuality. Sex plays a much greater and more explicit role, particularly in its more exotic forms, but so do many other sensuous effects. Take, for example, the new genre of spy adventures illustrated by the James Bond movies and novels, and by TV's *The Man from U.N.C.L.E.* and its various imitators. While the older western or detective story hero stuck pretty close to his business and could consider himself lucky if he encountered one stray, willing female, the new spy hero not only beds down with a harem full of luscious and exotic beauties of many different ethnic origins, but he also consumes the fanciest foods, drives elegant cars, uses sophisticated mechanical gadgets, and undergoes the most shockingly sensuous of tortures. The hardy and austere Lone Ranger, who evidently ate nothing but cactus, sand, and leftover silver bullets, would be appalled at the sight of James Bond in his Savile Row clothes stepping out of his Aston-Martin and entering the Arizona Hilton, Kissy Suzuki fanning his brow and Honey-Chile Rider caressingly brushing off the desert insects. Moreover, this sensuality of content is intensified by a sensuousness of style. The Bond movies are a kaleidoscope of visual and aural effects. We are bombarded with sensations from the psychedelic title footage through such incredible visual and tactile images as a girl covered with gilt paint or a breathless flight in an open one-man helicopter right up to the cataclysmic explosions and bursting flames that characteristically close out Bondian missions. The kind of kinetic sensuousness I speak of was epitomized for me in the opening sequence of the Beatles' second film, *Help!* The murky opening music that sounded like a primitive ritual was suddenly superseded by the Beatles' singing the title song, "Help!" This was accompanied by an equally striking visual shift from lush colors, exotic costumes, and a cavernous setting to the Beatles in austere black and white. Then, in a dazzling moment, the black and white was suddenly broken by little patches of bright primary colors, which turned out to be darts being thrown at Ringo by the irate priest of the opening sequence. If, as I did, you saw this film along with several hundred teenage girls who began screaming at the top of their lungs when the Beatles appeared on the screen, the sensuous impact of this sequence was overpowering. Such moments inexorably call the theories of Norman O. Brown to mind. Brown, a major prophet of the new taste, argues on the basis of his personal brand of Freudian psychology that modern civilization needs to break through male-female sexuality to a total sensuality, in which all the bodily organs become capable of a richly sensuous involvement with the environment. Brown is simply the most radical of a number of contemporary thinkers who have stressed the unique need for sensuality *in* modern American culture. Psychoanalysts have long pointed out that the Puritanical asceticism in the American character leads to a neurotic mistrust of life. Erik Erikson argues that

> Puritanism, beyond defining sexual sin for full-blooded and strong-willed people, gradually extended itself to the total sphere of bodily

living, comprising all sensuality. . . . The result was that men were born who failed to learn from their mothers to love the goodness of sensuality before they learned to hate its sinful uses. Instead of hating sin, they learned to mistrust life. (293)

Erikson encourages American mothers to modify those child-rearing practices that tend to deprive children of a full and free sensuality on the ground that such deprivation leads to fear and anxiety, restricting the development of the individual ego.

In her attack on the tradition of literary and artistic interpretation, Susan Sontag also insists on the role of the senses in art. She criticizes interpretation for its tendency to set up a screen of ideas and "meanings" between the audience and the work of art, a screen that prevents us from completely feeling a work's sensuous effects. "Interpretation," she says, "is the revenge of the intellect upon art. Even more. It is the revenge of the intellect upon the world. To interpret is to impoverish, to deplete the world in order to set up a shadow world of 'meanings'" (7).

John Cage, Karlheinz Stockhausen, and other avant-garde contemporary composers seem a long way from James Bond and the Beatles. Yet, as Leonard Meyer demonstrates in a fine essay on modern aesthetics, the transformation of music from a structure of tonal relations into pure sensation is one of their intentions. Meyer explains how these composers seek to create an "antiteleological" art that suppresses purposes, goals, and the control of expectations. For example, John Cage tells the composer to "give up the desire to control sound, clear his mind of music (in the ordinary sense), and set about discovering means to let sounds be themselves rather than vehicles for man-made theories or expressions of human sentiments" (qtd. in Meyer, "The End of the Renaissance" 174). In listening to such music, Meyer goes on, "one is not listening to the relationships among the sounds presented, but just to the sounds as sounds—as individual, discrete, objective sensations" (175). As an example of what he means by awareness of sound apart from its relationships, Meyer suggests we imagine a radio that has broken down: "you may recall that when the syntax and grammar became obscured and meaning was lost, you became very aware of sound qua sound—you became conscious of the bleeps, bloops, and squeaks" (175). This example is interesting because it describes almost exactly the character of the random radio noises used in Robert Rauschenberg's 1965 sculpture "Oracle." Similarly, when Andy Warhol took the Campbell's Soup can, reduced it to two dimensions and blew it up to the size of a painting, he was detaching this object from its conventional associations in our mind as a container of food and making us see it as color and form.

But what a strange sort of sensuousness this is. Usually when we think of sensuality, we have in mind the interplay of sensation and sentiment derived from our relationship to the human meaning or use of the objects we see or hear. Thus, a picture of a pretty girl excites us because we are responding to the imagined lover embodied in the forms we see. Generally, in perceiving something, we mentally move toward or away from it, depending on whether we feel it would be pleasurable or a threat to us. But to relate to something in this way changes it by making it part of ourselves, by involving it with our egos. When we do this we lose our "cool" with regard to that object and find that it can no longer be an engrossing source of pure contemplation. We lose the sensuous immediacy of the object. Pure sensation is an experience that some people find in drug-induced states. We have all heard accounts of how under drugs a crack in the wall or a blade of grass became an all-sufficient reality with every microscopic detail alive and vibrant. But the best definition of the cool I know is a short poem by Wallace Stevens imagining how a winter landscape might be perceived as a pure and beautiful sensation, if we could remove from our minds its association with the feeling of cold and its threat to human life.

THE SNOW MAN
One must have a mind of winter
To regard the frost and the boughs
Of the pine-trees crusted with snow;
And have been cold a long time
To behold the junipers shagged with ice,
The spruces rough in the distant glitter
Of the January sun; and not to think
Of any misery in the sound of the wind,
In the sound of a few leaves
Which is the sound of the land
Full of the same wind
That is blowing in the same bare place
For the listener, who listens in the snow,
And, nothing himself, beholds
Nothing that is not there and the nothing that is.

Bond, Batman, and the Beatles by no means go to this extreme. In many ways their sensuousness is sensuality in the old sense. Certainly Bond's exotic harems are simply expansions of the good old mass cultural tradition of cheesecake. Yet there are important elements of detachment, of the cool, which separate these new pop forms from the more sentiment-oriented traditional forms. First, there is the detached style of the hero, his unshakeable cool. Partly this is an intangible matter of personal style—the Bonds, the Solos, and the Ilyas have a way of moving and acting that suggests that they are not really involved in what they are doing. This style reflects their lack of moral commitment to their missions. The old western hero often struggled against involvement, but once he was in, you knew he was in there to the hilt, fighting for truth and justice. But what the Bonds fight for is far from clear—the whole teleological side of their activity is generally underplayed. U.N.C.L.E. and T.H.R.U.S.H. do not embody good vs. evil so much as rival corporations fighting over the patent rights to the latest weapon. For us, the audience, emotional involvement with the hero's mission is reduced because we are not invited to take its moral purpose seriously. Consequently, we tend to focus on action or movement as a thing in itself rather than as something directed toward a goal.

TV's *Batman* illustrates some additional modes of the cool. First of all, we are detached emotionally from the action because we perceive it as a parody, something not to be taken seriously under any circumstances. Within this framework, the villains become more important for their style than their motives. Violent action flowers into a pure ballet of motion, further cooled down by the transformation of its sounds into visually presented words, and sexuality becomes a quality of sound and vision rather than an incitement to lustful fantasies. The Catwoman's sexiness is so obvious that it becomes an object of amused contemplation rather than a source of lustful feeling.

In many ways the new pop music with its driving rhythms and strident sounds is intensely emotional, yet the dance form most closely associated with it is the coolest and most detached of all. The twist and its successors are redolent with sexuality in their body movements, yet absolutely removed from physical contact. Edward Levine has suggested that the twist is pathological because it is so withdrawn and self-centered. That seems a bit extreme to me. Instead, I think these dances embody the same principle we observed in connection with the treatment of sex in *Batman*. Sexual body movements are transformed into kinetic physical sensation and visual form. They become objects of contemplation rather than invitations to lust. Compare the body movements of the twist with those of the traditional striptease. The twist is inherently repetitive and static. The twister tends to do the same thing over and over again, while the striptease is progressive and moves toward a climax. The same observation can be made about much of the new pop music as compared to the traditional ballads and swing. Rock and roll tends to be static rather than climactic. Thus, when at the conclusion of their song "A Day in the Life" the Beatles actually make use of random sounds, their static nondirectional quality doesn't seem in the least bit out of place.

In essence, the cool mode represents a detached and contemplative attitude toward experience that tends to separate emotional or moral commitment from perception. The perception itself is deeply engrossing because one becomes wrapped up in the process of experience itself. However, the level or quality or meaning of the object, which occasions the experience, is not as significant as the purity and intensity of the perception. McLuhan points out one of the consequences of this:

> When lps and hi-fi and stereo arrived, a depth approach to musical experience also came in. Everybody lost his inhibitions about "highbrow," and the serious people lost their qualms about popular music and culture. Anything that is approached in depth acquires as much interest as the greatest matters. . . . Depth means insight, not point of view; and insight is a kind of mental involvement in process that makes the content of the item seem quite secondary. (*Understanding Media* 282–83)

The second pervasive characteristic of the new art is its strategy of imposture, or the put-on. A put-on involves adopting a role or an attitude yet remaining highly conscious that the role or attitude is an artifice. What remains ambiguous is the degree of commitment that is given to the artifice and just how seriously and in what way we are supposed to take it. There are of course degrees and levels of imposture. The original comic strip *Batman* was a study in imposture of the most minimal ambiguity. Bruce Wayne, the millionaire socialite, assumed the guise of Batman, the caped crusader against crime. The ambiguity resided in the fact that Batman, like the other comic-book superheroes, was purely fantastic, while his alter ego, in however far-fetched a fashion, was an imitation of an ordinary person from twentieth-century life. Thus, unlike the traditional fairy tale characters, the comic-book heroes live in a double world—the ordinary world of twentieth-century America and the make-believe world of super powers, super villains, and costumed crime-fighters. There may be children who accept the superheroes as completely real, but the very structure of the stories would seem to militate against this. The presence of the ordinary world is always there as a yardstick of reality, making it difficult to accept the fantastic and the ordinary as parts of the same world. Even the child must be made aware by this contrast that his identification with the superhero's adventures is an artifice, a fantasy. Or, as Jules Feiffer suggests in his study of the comic-book heroes, it is possible to take the even more ambiguous step of imagining that it is Superman who is real and Clark Kent who is make-believe.

I do not wish to suggest that this kind of imposture is completely different from the traditional fairy tale or myth, which was also pervaded by disguises and role playing. In fact, one can find comic-book forms where the contrast between reality and imposture is not particularly played up, as in the animal comics where the fantasy of people-like animals completely supersedes the ordinary world and becomes a coherent reality of its own. But it is interesting to note that the superhero comic, one of the unique popular mythical creations of our time, does play up this ambiguity. Perhaps it is for this reason that the superheroes, beyond all the other comic-book types, have become so important to the imagery of the new pop art.

But if the original Batman imposture was fairly straightforward, what happens if we decide to parody this imposture, and then on top of that we become interested in the expressive possibilities that our imposture of an imposture has as a pure choreography of movement? This is where we reach the TV version of Batman.

Jacob Brackman points out that this kind of imposture is a pervasive feature of modern culture. Is pop art really serious or are those artists pulling our legs? Perhaps the artists themselves don't know. Does John Cage really think he is creating music when he writes a piece that consists of four minutes and thirty-three seconds of silence? Does John Barth intend us to take seriously an eight hundred-page novel in which the hero was apparently sired by a computer that raped a virgin and then left its offspring to be raised among the goats? Is this what Barth means when he says he wants to write "novels which imitate the form of the Novel, by an author who imitates the role of Author" (33)? Susan Sontag suggests that the key quality of contemporary "camp" taste is a purely artificial vision of the world—"Being-as-Playing-a-Role" or "life as theater"—and that its essence lies in a fascination with the difference "between the thing as meaning something, anything, and the thing as pure artifice" (281). When in "camp" fashion one takes delight in "Tiffany lamps, Scopitone films . . . Schoedsack's *King Kong* . . . the old Flash Gordon comics . . . women's clothes of the twenties (feather boas, fringed and beaded dresses, etc.)," to quote a few of Sontag's examples of the kind of thing enjoyed by the new taste, one is delighting in objects that are themselves a kind of imposture. Camp taste is a "love of the exaggerated, the 'off,' of things-being-what-they-are-not" (277–79). Moreover, the adoption of such a taste is itself a form of imposture, because it is not taken with the same seriousness as the commitment to art in the traditional sense. Yet it is not all a joke either. The ambiguity of intent is basic.

Imposture seems to serve two main purposes that are frequently hard to distinguish from each other. One obvious reason for an imposture is to avoid being pinned down, to evade commitment. Brackman gives several examples of the put-on as an evasive device in ordinary social intercourse. A hippie questioned by a curious tourist pretends to agree entirely with the tourist's criticisms of hippie attitudes:

> Yeah, well, you know if we could get jobs we'd lap 'em up, but who'd hire us, man? Like we're dirty. I haven't had a bath since last February. . . . You really got the life, Charlie-kids, a couple parakeets, a beer and a ball game. You don't worry about nothin', hear? You're on the right track. Listen, could you spare a quarter? I haven't had breakfast. (58)

Here the hippie puts down the square, but without risking any direct confrontation of ideas and without committing himself to the defense of anything. Similarly, an admiration for outdated Hollywood trash can be simply a means of evading the necessity of any kind of discrimination.

Evasion, yes, but there are also important associations between imposture and creation. Psychologists point out that we often assume a role in order to create. Novelists and poets have always been partly aware of this. Rarely do they write directly of themselves without adopting some kind of mask or persona. Most of us are familiar with this phenomenon from our ordinary experience. When we sit down to write a paper we often go through an elaborate ritual of cleaning our desks, arranging our pencils, jumping up to visit our friends (though we are not in the least interested in them at this critical moment)—all artifices to get the blocked thoughts to flow freely. On the cultural level, when the artist faces the paralyzing possibility of ultimate extinction and senses the exhaustion of traditional beliefs and forms in this extreme situation, imposture may become a necessity to him. It is worth noting that some of the major artists of our century have found a temporary putting-on of the styles of the past an essential strategy to the creation of their own expression. Witness, for example, Stravinsky's dazzling sequence of stylistic impostures, his recomposition of the history of Western music. Picasso, too, has continually revitalized his art by redoing the work of such past masters as Poussin, Delacroix, and Ingres, and by adopting the gestures of primitive art. In a recent essay, John Barth explains how imposture can help the contemporary artist to overcome his sense of the exhaustion and obsolescence of traditional conceptions of artistic form:

> The imitation . . . is something new and may *be* quite serious and passionate despite its farcical aspect. This is the important difference between a proper novel and a deliberate imitation of a novel, or a novel imitative of other documents. The first attempts . . . to imitate actions more or less directly, and its conventional devices—cause and effect, linear anecdote, characterization, authorial selections, arrangement and interpretation—can be and have long since been objected to as obsolete notions, or metaphors for obsolete notions: Robbe-Grillet's essays *For a New Novel* come to mind. There are replies to these objections, not to the point here, but one can see that in any case they're obviated by imitations of novels, which attempt to represent not life directly but a representation of life. (33)

There are other ways in which imposture serves the cause of creative expression. The put-on can break through established habits of mind, uncovering their limitations by taking a stance outside them. The Beatles' elaborate artifice of *Sgt. Pepper's Lonely Hearts Club Band,* complete with far-out costumes, new hairstyles, a private mythology, and a new set of musical devices, helps them to get outside their earlier role as teenage rock-and-roll idols and to see the world of mass culture from a different perspective. John Cage's presentation of four minutes and thirty-three seconds of silence in the guise of a musical performance seeks to break through our established assumptions about music and to demonstrate their limitations. Robert Rauschenberg's notorious show of large canvases painted a plain white with no content whatsoever did much the same thing for the visual arts. This might be called, after Brackman, the "set-breaking" aspect of imposture.

Imposture is also sometimes employed to create a "cool" response to an object. It becomes a means to that effect of detached sensuality we have already characterized as a vital element of the new art. If we are made uncertain how to "take" an object or a performance because it so obviously manifests its own artificial ascribe meanings or to identify it with our own moral concerns and benature, we find it difficult to liefs. Thus, on the simplest level, the put-on quality of *Batman, The Man from U.N.C.L.E.,* or the James Bond films keeps us from fully identifying with the heroes and makes us more conscious of their actions simply as movements. In a more complex way, John Barth, by blatantly imitating the form and devices of the eighteenth-century novel in *The Sot Weed Factor*, keeps us continually aware of the artificiality of his creation. The result is a continual tension between our tendency to identify with the characters and our sense that they are purely abstract fictions. This tension reflects Barth's own concern with the ambiguous nature of human commitment and responsibility.

Along with the cool and the put-on, the search for means of expression that are continually in process is a basic quality of the new art. "Always present a moving target," advises the hero of Richard Fariña's novel *Been Down So Long It Looks Like Up to Me*, and note the shifting meanings in the very title. The new art replies by transforming hard into soft (as in Oldenburg's soft telephones) and small into large (as in the same artist's mammoth six-foot-long ice cream cones), the static into movement (as in op art) and the kinetic into stasis (as in junk sculpture), noise into music (as in John Cage's composition for six radios) and music into noise (as in the Beatles' "A Day in the Life"). Young women iron out their hair to emphasize the natural look and then dress in wildly abstract clothes or adopt some far-out historical style of manifest artificiality. Nothing stays put. The angle of vision, the emotional force, the "meaning" seem constantly in the process of transformation into something else. Walls turn into psychedelic paintings, graffiti blossom everywhere; even in the most serious works of art, ephemerality, spontaneity, and improvisation take the place of permanence of form through the exploitation of such devices as chance structures or the use of found objects. The very distinction between art and life is being questioned. A young New York artist creates a work of "art" by sending a postcard to a group of friends announcing "the sun will rise tomorrow morning, Another artist asked to create a portrait writes, "this is a portrait of—" on a sheet of scratch paper and hands it over to his client, who pays the artist's fee and has the paper framed. Even such popular artists as the Beatles and Bob Dylan are caught up in a continual process of stylistic transformation. *Sgt. Pepper's Lonely Hearts Club Band* moves from the traditional music hall aura of the title song through a diversity of styles until it reaches the absolute stasis of the final note of "A Day in the Life," a stasis which is so disturbing that it becomes almost frantically kinetic.

The mode of detached sensuality, the strategy of imposture, and the fascination with form in process are common elements in much of the new art. We should not forget, however, that there are still significant differences between avant-garde and popular art, though I hope I have shown how they are moving closer together in many ways. Some elements of the new art show a hedonistic tendency in its most extreme popular forms, as in *Playboy* and the Bond movies, while other developments are more ascetic and mystical.

Some of the new artists are experimental and try to create radically new forms; others, like John Barth, are more conservative and seek to express themselves through the transformation of traditional forms. But these differences seem less consequential at the moment than the similarities I have dwelt upon in this article.

The new art has many prophets and critics, who have given us various explanations of its significance. Leonard Meyer suggests that we may be at the "End of the Renaissance (1963), that the new art reflects drastic shifts in our conception of the world at least equal in scope to those associated with the Renaissance. Marshall McLuhan sees the change in a similarly cosmic perspective, but he attributes it to the basic cultural shift from the technology of print and machinery to the new electronic media. Susan Sontag believes that in response to the needs of the contemporary world, the arts are assuming a new function: "art today is a new kind of instrument, an instrument for modifying consciousness and organizing new modes of sensibility" (296). John Barth and Jacob Brackman see the new developments as the reflection of a deep sense of betrayal and ultimacy, the feeling that traditional cultural values and ideas have brought man to the razor's edge. These interpreters agree that the new art reflects a time of radical cultural transformation and that it derives from a basic rejection of longstanding assumptions about the nature and function of art in society. In varying degrees, they feel that an art of evasion, of discontinuity, and of purposeful purposelessness may well be the only appropriate response to a world facing the prospect of nuclear incineration. Yet they wonder uneasily whether the new art is not just as destructive of human values as the world it reacts to. I wish I could replace this sense of ambiguity with a clear and resounding affirmation or condemnation of the new art, but I cannot. At times, it seems to me to hold out the promise of a revitalization of our culture; at other times, I wonder whether it is not simply an evasion of cultural responsibility. We are confronted, for perhaps the first time in history, with a real and continual choice among such cultural alternatives as the traditional forms and ideals of high culture, the formulas of mass culture, and the complex and evasive strategies of the new art.

The new possibilities represented by the Beatles and happenings have made a single-minded devotion to the best that has been thought and said in the world more ambiguous than ever before, just as our knowledge of the great tradition interferes with a simple and uncomplicated response to the new art of our time. Something of this ambiguity is brilliantly expressed in one of the finest examples of the new art, Michelangelo Antonioni's film *Blow Up*. Antonioni's photographer hero, though involved in the illusory world of mass culture, has tried to evade it through a strategy of imposture and the maintenance of a cool detachment from his occupation as a fashion photographer. Seeking a depth perception of reality, he begins to enlarge the photographs he has taken of two lovers in a park. He discovers that what he had taken for the expression of love was actually an act of murder. Yet, when he confronts this reality, he simply doesn't know what to do with it. In the end, he returns to the park where he had unknowingly photographed the murder and finds that the body has disappeared. Bemused, he wanders over to where a group of strangely costumed and made-up clowns are playing an imaginary game of tennis. As he watches, they gesture soundlessly to him that their imaginary tennis ball has been hit out of the court and has landed near him. After some hesitation, he pretends to pick it up and throw it back to them. The clowns resume their game and suddenly, for the first time, we hear the sound of the tennis ball, though we still can see nothing. The photographer turns away from the game and simply disappears.

This extraordinary parable of imposture and transformation is so ambiguous that it is practically impossible to state its meaning. I have heard intelligent friends argue everything from the idea that the photographer is Antonioni's conception of the true artist to the thesis that he represents the impossibility of art in the corrupt and decadent world of mass culture. However, this uncertainty of interpretation did not prevent anyone I talked to from being deeply moved both emotionally and intellectually by the film. Whether one saw the artist as hero or failure didn't seem to matter very much: the important thing was the power with which Antonioni represented his predicament. This predicament, it seems to me, is very much our own. We are conscious that we cannot live in our world without some commitment. Yet our terrifying historical awareness makes us feel that all commitments are impostures, and we try to protect ourselves from being trapped in our impostures by maintaining our detachment. But acting without deep emotional involvement or implication prevents our commitments from being complete and satisfying. In desperation we turn to pure sensation or some form of mysticism, hoping to escape the sense of imposture. Much of the new art is a strategy of escape—this is the function of *Playboy* on one side and psychedelic mysticism on the other. It is better to use these strategies than to accept the destruction of man, but it is more important to recognize and understand our predicament. The best of the new art tries to use these strategies of evasion to explore and represent our ambiguous relationship to culture. In this the new art is the most authentic response to the desperation of our time.

4

The Writer as a Celebrity: Some Aspects of American Literature as Popular Culture

This essay gave me a chance to combine my training in traditional literary studies with my newer interest in popular culture. James Nagel first published it in 1977 in his journal *Studies in American Fiction*. I have considerably updated it for publication in this volume.

〜

In treating of American literature (by which I take it we mean primarily the canon of our "major authors") and its relationship to popular culture (those cultural forms, patterns, and processes most broadly characteristic of the American people), there are a number of problems worth extended examination. For example, we might consider the interplay between the work of major authors and popular formulaic patterns like the detective story, the western, or the sentimental romance. Such a discussion would explore how popular formulas usually originate in the imitation by other authors of some particularly successful work of a major writer. In time, these imitations produce a standardized genre with conventions well known to writers and expected by an audience, which has come to enjoy this particular kind of story. So the western took shape in Cooper's enormously successful *Leatherstocking Tales*. Cooper's frontier hero and his plots of chase and pursuit through the wilderness became the basis of hundreds of novels and dime novels in the nineteenth century and of innumerable films and television programs in the twentieth. In a similar way the detective story sprang from the Dupin stories of Edgar Allan Poe, while the sentimental romance originated with the novels of Samuel Richardson. We would see, in tracing the relation between popular formulas and serious fiction, how the most long-lasting formulas have undergone many transformations, frequently being revitalized by the influence of more original writers. In such a fashion, the western was given a new lease on life at the beginning of the twentieth century by Owen Wister, the detective story was transformed in the early 1930s by Dashiell Hammett and Raymond Chandler, and the sentimental romance was reshaped by the impact of major authors like the Brontë sisters, to say nothing of the Harlequin style of more recent times.

Our examination of this problem would also touch on the influence of established popular formulas and conventions on those writers we have come to think of as canonic. We might look as William Veeder did at how Henry James exploited the stylistic and narrative conventions of popular romance in creating such major works as *The American* and *Portrait of a Lady.* Or, with Richard Slotkin, Edwin Fussell, and others, we might see how Hawthorne and Melville used the myth of the frontier. Finally, we would want to look very carefully at that increasingly important tradition of American fiction that has employed a parodic or ironic version of popular formulas as the formal basis for complex treatments of American cultural myths. Melville's *Pierre,* with its burlesque of sentimental romance, Twain's treatment of the western formula in *Roughing It* and the detective story in *Pudd'nhead Wilson,* and the contemporary novels of Thomas Pynchon, Thomas Berger, and Kurt Vonnegut would be a few of the landmarks in that terrain.

Another quite different problem is the use of popular culture as a subject for serious fiction. Under this rubric we would need to trace the emergence of popular types and the vernacular as material for serious fiction. Fortunately much of this work has already been done for us by students of American humor like Walter Blair and of style like Richard Bridgman. These scholars have shown how experiments with the American language and a growing array of popular stereotypes like the Yankee peddler, the Davy Crockett frontier roarer, minstrel show blacks, the spinster, etc. developed in the early nineteenth century, reaching an initial literary culmination in the work of Mark Twain. Popular culture as a subject in the twentieth century has been less thoroughly examined.

Also, there is much that needs fuller treatment, such as the role of Hollywood and other institutions of modern mass culture in fiction, the emergence of ethnicity as a subject, the role of sports as subject and symbol, and fictionalizations of popular movements like the counterculture.

Finally, there is the question of the popular reception of American literature and of the way in which the general public's response or lack of response to major American writers has shaped the development of our literature. This involves the relationship between works of literature that became bestsellers in their day and those that we have later come to recognize as the canon of American literature. The study of bestsellers and of shifting popular tastes has been solidly grounded by the work of Frank Luther Mott, James D. Hart, Louis Wright, Russell Nye, Carl Bode, and other scholars, but there is another aspect to this problem that has not, to my knowledge, received much attention. In modern democratic societies, popular interest commonly manifests itself in the complex phenomenon of celebrity. The writer's celebrity, or lack of it, plays an important part in his conception of his role and his relationship to his audience.

Celebrity grows out of public interest in a person beyond or aside from his works or accomplishments and is a major aspect of popular culture. While the original source of fascination may be the celebrity's creations, there is a tendency for public interest to fasten increasingly on the person, rather than, in the case of a writer or artist, on his works. Thus, it often happens that when the process of celebration is well under way, there are many members of the public who are familiar with particular writers or artists, without necessarily having read or seen a single one of their works. In turn, a writer's notoriety may lead members of the public who might not otherwise have done so to read his works. The enormous success of Ernest Hemingway's *The Old Man and the Sea*, published in *Life* magazine and read almost immediately after its appearance by millions of people, testifies to the significance of Hemingway as a celebrity perhaps even more than to his reputation as a writer. Obviously this has continued to be the case with Hemingway's posthumous writing, generally considered by critics to be much inferior to his best work, but still an object of great interest to the public. Probably a considerable portion of those who read *The Old Man and the Sea* in *Life* were reading a Hemingway fiction for the first time. No doubt many persons discovered Van Gogh's paintings after they had heard about him as the mad artist who cut off his ear. The ever-increasing popularity of Van Gogh's work and the immense prices paid for his paintings at auction are certainly as much a result of Van Gogh's celebrity as of the objective merit of his paintings. Great though Van Gogh was, he is certainly not that much greater than the other major artists of his time whose works do not command anything like the prices paid for Van Goghs.

Thus, fame, the poet's spur, is intricately related to celebrity, though it is useful to draw some rough distinctions between them. Fame is the immortality of the poet in his or her work, the fact that he/she is known in and through his or her work to many generations. Because great artists have the fortunate power of injecting their imagination into language and visual form, thereby creating something that men can cherish forever, the quest for fame has always been a central motive of poets and artists. Celebrity is, one might say, a kind of immediate fame. It is largely in the present and its mark is being known as a person. The celebrated artist Andy Warhol used to talk about everyone being entitled to fifteen minutes of celebrity. Fame is, if not eternal, at least beyond any individual lifetime. The test of artistic fame is that one's words or images remain in the minds of men; the test of celebrity is being followed everywhere by a photographer. The dead poet may achieve a greater fame than the living man who wrote the poems. The dead celebrity is usually as important as last week's newspaper. Of course, there are exceptions to this. Many writers have achieved a lasting fame not so much through the permanent importance of their writings, but because of what their lives came to stand for: as instances we might cite Chatterton, Poe, and Wilde. In the first case, the meaning of the writer's life was more important than any of his literary creations. The fame of Poe and Wilde is somewhat more complex in that many of their works are still widely read and some are probably great. Wilde, however, was a great celebrity in his own day and, some might say, a pioneer of public relations until he tragically overreached himself and fell into obloquy because of the scandal of his homosexuality. Poe was rather more obscure in his own life, but became something of a scandal through the mystery of his death, a not inappropriate fate for the creator of the detective story. It seems fair to say that Poe and Wilde's importance to literary history is as much a matter of their tragic and symbolic lives as of the greatness of their works. Here, fame has become a kind of extension of celebrity, something that occasionally happens when the celebrity passes over into fame or legend. In general, celebrity is transient and ephemeral and there is a difference between fame and celebrity both in quality and in object. Celebrity is brief and intense; fame tends to be slower in growing and is relatively permanent. The object of celebrity is the person; the object of fame is some accomplishment, action, or creative work.

It would surely be a mistake to assume that celebrity is a phenomenon utterly unique to modern times. The artist as person-performer and therefore, to some degree, as celebrity has been important since the dawn of literature. Certainly those wandering bards whose tradition led to the great epics of Homer had a kind of celebrity. One can easily imagine a village crowd gathered around one of Homer's grandfathers eagerly questioning him about his work, just as reporters cluster around one of today's literary celebrities. Yet there are certain characteristics of modern societies that give celebrity a particular importance for the artist. In a market society, where the writer is dependent on sales, the temptation to let one's person become an advertisement for one's works is great. But there are other dimensions of modern popular cultures that thrust celebrity into the very heart of the creative process. Many writers, if not all, need to feel some contact with their audience. The writer, in complex modern societies, may have contact with individual members of his public and with the small coteries of his acquaintance, but there is no way for him to have a complex relationship with the large and diverse public that constitutes, at least potentially, his audience. In a culture where so much communication is mediated by newspapers, radio, and television, the only way in which the general public can be present to a writer, and he/she, as person, to them, is through the mechanism of celebrity. The importance of celebrity as a means of contact between writer and audience is further intensified by the degree to which the writer aspires to address him- or herself to the widest possible public. A writer in a culture adhering to a democratic ideology is confronted with a difficult choice. He or she can reject celebrity and accept the limitation of addressing him- or herself to an intellectual or cultural elite, but, in doing so, he or she must confront the ambiguous fate of an elitist creator in a democratic society. If he or she seeks to write for the mass of the people, he or she will almost invariably be caught up in the machinery of celebrity.

Today, for any writer who aspires to bestsellerdom, or even just hopes to sell a respectable number of copies, the book tour is a vital part of the publishing process. Often writers will spend exhausting weeks or months promoting their new works through visits to many cities, interviews on television, radio and in the newspapers, and presentations and book-signings at the major bookstores. Now with the Internet available authors create web sites through which they can answer fans questions and further promote their works. In addition, the Internet gives the fans of writers an opportunity to celebrate their favorite by creating web sites that give other readers information about the writer and add to their celebrity.

By contrast, in the first two decades of the nineteenth century writers were much less concerned with literary celebrity. Apparently, no established set of mechanisms for generating and purveying the writer as person-performer existed. Instead, the relationship between the writer and his public followed the more traditional pattern of the community of taste and interest between an educated, aristocratic public and the writers it patronized and supported. In such a system the writers were known and respected primarily through their works and these were widely known in the limited circle to which they addressed themselves. Perhaps this is a kind of celebrity, but it operated very differently from the mass celebrity of the twentieth century. For one thing, writers had a strong sense of contact with their audience, not only because the audience knew and reacted to their work in personal exchanges, but also because they felt themselves to be a member of the elite group that constituted their public. This pattern still prevailed at the time of Washington Irving, and must, in many ways, have shaped his elegant, educated style, the witty sophistication of his rhetoric, and the European flavor of his form and content.

However, later in the nineteenth century many changes in the artistic situation conspired to make the writer's celebrity an increasingly important issue. Increasing literacy, the fact that through new printing technologies books and periodicals became cheaper than ever, and the ideological emphasis of a democratic culture greatly expanded the size and diversity of the writer's public. By mid-century, many writers no longer felt themselves to be merely spokespersons for a coherent, educated, and sophisticated elite. This generated a need for new forms of mediation between the writer and the larger public. Furthermore, the wider circulation of books and periodicals led to the emergence of new attitudes on the part of publishers that made catering to broader public tastes and interests an economic imperative. The enormous success of writers like Scott, Cooper, and Dickens made it clear that a writer could appeal to the mass public without compromising his own artistic aspirations and interests. At the same time, the more successful he or she became with the general public, the more pressure there was on the writer to become a celebrity. Scott generally chose to stay out of the public eye and confine himself to his novels and poetry. Since he lived a very private life and did not travel to America, there was little chance for him to be known outside of his works. Cooper, however, was drawn into political commentary and even, to some extent, into politics. In prose writings like *Notions of the Americans* and *The American Democrat,* and in many of his later fictions such as the "Littlepage" series and *The Monikins,* we see him trying to address his public—albeit not as successfully as in the *Leatherstocking Tales*—as someone with opinions on morals, politics, and society. Of course, most of these opinions ran sufficiently counter to the general trend of public attitudes that Cooper failed to become the kind of amazing celebrity that Dickens did as a consequence of his notorious American tour in the early 1840s. Dickens was one of the first writers to become a celebrity of one modern type: the writer as spokesman of the common sense and basic goodness of the mass of the people. Though this artistic role has declined, it still partly exists in present-day best-selling author-celebrities like Stephen King, Tom Clancy, and Patricia Cornwell. Dickens had already become such a celebrity by the time he came to America that his tour evoked an outpouring of broad public interest similar to that which greeted his countrymen, the Beatles, when they first came to the United States. The vast American outrage against Dickens' criticisms of America in *American Notes* and *Martin Chuzzlewit* indicated the degree to which the public viewed Dickens as a symbolic person.

Another important model of the writer as celebrity to make its impact in this period was created around Lord Byron. The Byronic celebrity image embodied a number of themes that would be of major importance in the later nineteenth and twentieth centuries. The components of the Byronic person-performer show in rather marvelous fashion that combination of high good fortune and transgression that seem so characteristic of one important variety of celebrity. Of aristocratic lineage and enormous poetic gifts, Byron possessed larger-than-life qualities that could become a dramatic object of public admiration. His youthful success as a poet served to enhance the celebrity potential of his birth and abilities. Byron also possessed another characteristic that would be of importance in an age increasingly devoted to the pictorial and photographic representation of its public figures: he was strikingly handsome in a way highly appropriate to his role. Yet Byron's greatest celebrity developed as be became known for his rebellious political sentiments and actions and for his private life with its rich and complex erotic transgressions. Thus, Byron pioneered that basic celebrity image of the writer as political radical and moral rebel that would become one basic pattern of artistic celebrity in Europe and America.

Apparently, the Byronic image proved too radical for most nineteenth-century American writers, though its potential was evident in the posthumous celebrity accorded Edgar Allan Poe. A few minor figures, such as Fitz-James O'Brien, seemingly attempted to perform a version of the Byronic role, but without great success. The initial failure of the Byronic role as a celebrity model for Americans probably reflected a strong feeling on the part of both public and writers in the nineteenth century that American art should be moral and affirmative, the proper expression for a new democratic society. In Poe's case, as in Byron's, an early and tragic death perhaps enabled a public that cherished its moral principles to allow itself to be fascinated by the creative transgressor.

The problem of celebrity had become a serious difficulty for many writers by the 1840s and 1850s, to judge from the ruminations and perplexities of Hawthorne and Melville. Both achieved some minor celebrity as a result of the popularity of their earlier works. Yet, in mid-career, both apparently endured the sense of having lost touch with the wider public and suffered the frustration of seeing writers they judged vastly inferior gain much wider celebrity. It is difficult to estimate the extent to which Hawthorne's disgust at the way a "damned mob of scribbling women" had become the most celebrated novelists of the 1850s was a factor in the artistic difficulties he encountered in his later career. It would also be a vast oversimplification to claim that the failure to achieve a satisfying response from the larger public was solely responsible for Melville's gradual abandonment of the art of fiction. Yet I am sure that a more careful examination of the careers of these two writers in relation to the roles and mechanism of celebrity available to them would show the failure of effective celebrity as an important factor in the shaping of their later careers.

By the end of the nineteenth century, the basic processes of literary celebrity had become well established. Authors made personal tours with readings to audiences all over the country (Mark Twain, Artemus Ward, and other humorists were particularly successful at this). There were many interviews and reporters published accounts of "visits to the homes of great authors" (cultural journalists like Elbert Hubbard). Reviewers and cultural gossip columnists proliferated and writers often established themselves as public figures through regular columns (William Dean Howells) and through other journalistic enterprises (Stephen Crane, Frank Norris, and Theodore Dreiser.) These practices would be intensified and further developed in the twentieth century through the new media of broadcasting, which gave writers many more opportunities to speak to a broad public. In addition, writers in the second half of the nineteenth century tried out a variety of new public roles: that of the poet-philosopher of democracy and democratic culture along the lines of Emerson and Whitman; that of the comic sage and commentator as developed by Ward, Nasby, Twain, and other later nineteenth-century satirists and comic writers; and that of the genteel man of letters, a more traditional role elaborated after the Civil War by men like Edmund C. Stedman, Richard Watson Gilder, and William Dean Howells. The model of the democratic poet-prophet had great attraction for critics and intellectuals and, in the early twentieth century, was strongly advocated by Van Wyck Brooks and other critics as the proper persona for American writers. It was never very appealing to the public as a whole, however. Whitman had his dedicated followers and disciples, but certainly did not become a poet for the masses and a literary celebrity. Not until, ironically, the twentieth century transformed him into an American classic was Whitman widely read. Emerson was much more successful as a celebrity than Whitman was in the nineteenth century, but Emerson's public figure also embodied many elements of the traditional man of letters. The idea of the writer as spokesman for cultivated taste, responsible social and political opinion, and uplifting sentiment continued to be the most successful pattern for literary celebrity. In this period, Longfellow was apparently the general public's favorite image of the poet, while that group of men of letters anatomized by the writers and critics of the early twentieth century as comprising the genteel tradition, were, apart from the comic performers, the nation's most important literary celebrities.

Yet there were evidently severe limitations to the role of man of letters. His audience was still a relatively small elite of educated readers, subscribers to such cultivated periodicals as the *Atlantic, Harper's*, the *Nation,* and the *North American Review.* The possibility of reaching a wider public, such as the mass audience cultivated successfully by Twain and by popular bestsellers like E. P. Roe, must have tantalized Howells and James. Howells's move from Boston to New York, from the center of genteel culture to the center of commercial culture, and his increasing involvement in political and social causes in the 1880s and 1890s was probably motivated in part by a desire to escape what he had come to feel were the restrictions of the genteel tradition in order to reach out to larger concerns and a broader public. The massive criticism of Howells's courageous defense of the Haymarket activists certainly illustrated the degree to which the respectable public had cast the man of letters in a conservative or politically neutral role and resented his becoming a spokesman for unpopular or controversial causes. Yet his involvement in such controversial issues gained for Howells a broader national celebrity and helped create a model of the writer as social critic and reformer that many twentieth-century Americans would adopt.

Henry James's career suggests another set of insights into the ambiguities of literary celebrity. In his earlier novels and stories James had modeled his work sufficiently on prevailing popular conventions to become a highly successful young writer, while his work as critic and reviewer was beginning to establish a place for him within the ranks of leading men of letters. Like Howells, he set out in the 1880s to write the sort of panoramic social novel with contemporary political and social themes that seemed to reflect the new literary interests of the public. But he failed. *The Princess Casamassima* and *The Bostonians* did not succeed with the larger public and James's early potential as a literary celebrity faded. His response was ambiguous. On the one hand, he evidently accepted his separation from America and from the mass public and turned himself increasingly to the kind of complex psychological fiction for which his interests and artistry were most suitable. On the other hand, the lure of becoming a great public success still attracted him. Many of his tales of the 1880s portray the ironic relationship between artistry and celebrity. In the early 1890s, apparently concluding that he could no longer write the kind of fiction that would appeal to the large public, he turned to the drama, hoping to reestablish connection with a larger audience through a different medium. He failed at this, too, of course, and by this time was evidently ready to cast aside the dream of celebrity and write his remaining masterpieces in a way that would please only himself and his small circle of readers. James's experience indicated both how important celebrity had become for the late nineteenth-century American writer, and how strong an impact the quest for celebrity could have even on the work of a creator so greatly gifted and artistically independent.

The twentieth century has brought with it a proliferation of the possibilities for artistic celebrity, as well as an intensification of its pressures. The development of film, radio, and television has made it possible for the writer to reach an even larger public than he or she could in the nineteenth century. Though book sales of more than a million are extraordinary, movies and television commonly have audiences of many millions. A writer whose work is adapted into a popular film or television program can become an international celebrity overnight. One can think of many obscure writers suddenly catapulted into great celebrity by a highly successful film: Margaret Mitchell *(Gone with the Wind)*, James Jones *(From Here to Eternity)*, and Mario Puzo *(The Godfather)*. Even dead authors can become posthumous celebrities, as in the case of F. Scott Fitzgerald, where the eclat of a new film version of *The Great Gatsby* was accompanied by many new publications offering personal revelations about the author and his life. But the newer media have also proved a rather mixed blessing for writers. The collective nature of film and television production forces the writer into association with directors, actors, producers, and technical people, making it nearly impossible for him to have any effective creative control over the final product. In addition, the organization of film and television production in America has placed the writer in a subsidiary position to the producer and the stars with the producer making the final artistic decisions and the audience likely to perceive the work primarily as the creation of its leading actors. The writer who becomes involved in film and television thus can find himself in a new and frustrating kind of anonymity. Some version of his or her work may be seen by millions of people, but he/she may be even less known to the public than a novelist whose actual readership is only in the thousands. For example, how many people recognize such names as Jules Furthman, Francis Marion, Nunnally Johnson, Robert Riskin, Sidney Buchman, Dudley Nichols, and Frank S. Nugent? Yet these were among the most successful screenwriters in the history of Hollywood and were responsible for large numbers of highly popular films.

Another aspect of the process of celebrity is the increasing visibility of a celebrity society, a cultural elite that brings together certain members of the traditional aristocracy of wealth and high social position with certain individuals from the political, artistic, and mass communications spheres of society. The comings and goings of this celebrity elite, which used to be known as "café society" and is now referred to as "the jet set" or "the beautiful people," are extensively reported in newspapers and magazines. The group furnishes an inordinate proportion of the guests on major television talk shows and is the main object of gossip columns and tabloid journalism. Public interest in the lives and personalities of the celebrity elite intensifies fascination with the writers and artists who become associated with the group. Not only their own creative accomplishments, but their connection with the celebrity elite has made national figures of writers like Truman Capote and Gore Vidal, artists like Andy Warhol, and musicians like Leonard Bernstein.

But perhaps the most interesting twentieth-century development in the relationship between celebrity and literature has been in the way major writers have used their celebrity personas as an integral part of their art. One of the instances of this development is Ernest Hemingway; another is Norman Mailer. After his initial success as a writer had established his literary importance, Hemingway began in the early 1930s to create the celebrity figure of "Papa." Through his hunting exploits, his nonfiction reportage, his dramatic adventure, his position as a war correspondent during the Spanish Civil War and during World War II, and his association with members of the celebrity elite, Hemingway created a public persona that was like a real-life version of one of his central characters. This figure had enormous appeal and influence and made Hemingway well known among a much wider public than those who actually read his novels. Indeed, the Hemingway persona of "Papa" was so attractive and compelling that it eventually began to eclipse that other side of Hemingway that had also been a part of his greatest novels and stories. Much of his later fiction, including *Across the River and into the Trees* and *Islands in the Stream,* was less humanly complex and powerful than the earlier masterpieces because the protagonist had become a version of "Papa." He was now that larger-than-life stoic hero, that master of violence and scorner of death, who peers out at us from the pages of *Life* magazine, instead of the tragically limited but artistically more powerful figures of Jake Barnes, Nick Adams, and Frederic Henry. It is tempting to say that in his later life, most of Hemingway's creative energy went into the creation of his celebrity persona, and that while brilliant as a public performance, this persona was insufficient to the demands of great fiction.

Mailer's case is somewhat different, for beginning with *Advertisements for Myself* he has quite consciously sought to make his personal celebrity directly into art and has found a form appropriate to this intention. Unlike Hemingway, who lived out to the end an ambiguous conflict between celebrity and art, Mailer has tried to make his public performances themselves into a kind of artistic exploration, writing about them in a quasi-journalistic form in which the protagonist as celebrity plays the central role. Mailer's open assimilation of his role as artist into his celebrity persona is certainly one solution to the problematic modern tension between the writer as artist and as celebrity, though probably not one that many novelists will choose or be able to adopt.

However, the intense pressure to publicize in the twentieth century, and the emergence of writers for whom celebrity has become in different ways the center of their art, have made writers in general more conscious of the problem of celebrity and of its potentially deleterious effect on their work. A number of important contemporary writers, Saul Bellow, J. D. Salinger, and Thomas Pynchon prominent among them, have decisively rejected the role of celebrity and insisted on being known wholly through their works. Ironically, it turned out that the role of mysterious recluse adopted by Salinger and Pynchon had a great celebrity potential and very probably has played a role in the large popularity of these writers. Bellow has been much more moderate in his seclusion. However by avoiding the literary and celebrity centers of New York and the West Coast, and by rejecting most of the offers he has received to appear on television, to make public appearances, or to comment on contemporary affairs outside of his fiction, Bellow has resisted the role of celebrity. It is perhaps significant that unlike so many American writers who have found themselves entrapped in the ambiguities of celebrity, Bellow's production and artistry has continued unabated well into his middle years and beyond. He recently published in his mid-eighties a novel called *Ravelstein,* dealing with a relatively obscure academic who publishes a best-selling book that changes his life forever. *Ravelstein* offers many brilliant insights into the ironies of celebrity.

Celebrity is so complex and in many ways so irrational that we may never fully understand it, but I can't resist a few tentative speculations about the causes of the phenomenon. First, as compared to the length and complexity of a work, there is something immediately and more directly communicative about the image of a person. It may take hours to read a novel while one can receive a sense of a person in seconds. Reading a novel is a considerable task, but to watch a writer on a television talk show seems effortless. The personal image thus seems more intense in its impact and simpler in its effect than the printed page. The great importance of performance in almost all areas of popular culture bears out these observations. Most forms of popular culture involve some kind of person, an actor or star, mediating between the linguistic material and the audience. All the modern media of mass communications (movies, radio, television) are strongly oriented toward personalities and performance. The distinctive forms these media have developed in America such as the star vehicle, the talk show, the personally hosted news broadcast, etc., have intensified the personal quality to the degree that this seems to us nearly inherent in these media.

If we ask further why the performer-persona is so important in popular culture we encounter two primary functions, which I will generalize as the interpretive and the representative. As interpreters, performers direct our attention and help us to understand and respond to what they are saying by adding to their words the impact of tone of voice, look, and gesture. News show hosts are trusted authorities who give us the impression that we know and have the proper response to the truly significant events that are going on in the world. By extension, writers as celebrities give us an interpretation of their work by telling us about themselves, their hopes, their background, or their literary intentions. Or by their own actions, they provides us with grounds for a more intense and immediate response to their work. Along these lines, many bestsellers succeed because they are based on historical incidents and persons we already recognize as important. The memoirs of important or notorious political leaders are often bestsellers and if these leaders have been involved in a celebrated scandal like Watergate, or the Clinton imbroglio, the resultant literary popularity is often immense. Such possibilities are rare for the writer of fiction, who does not ordinarily act in a public capacity, though several politicians, including John Erlichman, Spiro Agnew, and John Lindsay, were persuaded to capitalize on their established celebrity by becoming authors of fictional thrillers. In these cases, the public's response to the literary work is intensified by the impression that these writers have a unique personal authority for the underlying reality of their stories. One of the most important aspects of interpretation has always been to establish what is "real" about a story, thereby intensifying our response to it. In this case the personal celebrity of the author serves to guarantee the authority of a story.

Such considerations cannot be fully separated from the important representative functions of the performer-persona. One such function is, if not simple, at least clear and obvious. Performer-personas represent us; they stands in for us and play the role we would play or would like to play at the event. Television talk show hosts interview celebrities for us, asking the questions we would want to ask of them. News commentators help us to feel that we are present at significant events. The stars of an adventure film or drama provide a center of identification, giving us the opportunity to share vicariously in the action. Celebrities are our stand-ins at important events, and the author, playing the role of celebrity, helps to guarantee and reinforce his or her position as our witness of contemporary reality. In addition, he/she represents the significance of his/her book and through his/her public comments we can share in some of the excitement accompanying its publication. Through the author's performance as a celebrity, we stand in at the birth of an important literary work.

But there is another representative function of celebrity that goes beyond enabling our vicarious presence at significant moments. The celebrity also becomes a quasi-mythical figure in the sense that he/she symbolizes patterns of aspiration and value, both positive and negative. Indeed, I might hazard the guess that many fascinating celebrities gain their position precisely to the degree that they embody conflicts of value and aspiration. This certainly seems to be the case with criminal celebrities, who comprise one of the most important categories of person-performer for modern democratic publics. The criminal seems to embody at once a fascination with forbidden and lawless deeds and a commitment to a society of laws and limits. Our interest in the criminal seems to be evoked in proportion to the significance of his crime and the apparent respectability of his background. Patty Hearst was an ideal celebrity. Not only was she a young girl and a rich one at that, the heiress of all the ages, but her crimes symbolized a basic rejection of the society that had apparently offered her all a person could want. Such ambiguities are the essence of celebrity in its mythical function.

Not all celebrity is of this sort. There are less ambiguous figures like athletic victors, people of great wealth, men of power, etc. However, the most striking celebrities are those who manifest some kind of paradox or transgression: Howard Hughes, the reclusive millionaire; Marilyn Monroe, the baby-faced sex queen; Jackie Kennedy, the dark widow of the New Frontier; Henry Kissinger, the swinging diplomat. While the celebrity as mythical figure usually embodies some power or position or action that is larger than life, we are most deeply moved by celebrities who also take upon themselves some of the tragedy and limitation of ordinary human beings. These figures live out for us our deep sense that our aspiration to immortal power is doomed by the reality of mortality. In sum, the true celebrity is a human creation of great power and complexity, which approximates in some ways the great mythical figures of ancient times.

Because of its complex significance, the role of celebrity is fraught with difficulties for creative writers. The energy and emotional investment they give to playing the role of person-performer inevitably detracts from what they can give to their proper work. Should they fail to achieve a significant celebrity, the result can be greatly damaging to their ego and thus a threat to their very ability to create. If they succeed, they face the additional danger of being swallowed up into the myth of their celebrity, of becoming the simplified persona of their public legend. The complexity and importance of the phenomenon of literary celebrity and its influence on nineteenth- and twentieth-century American writers suggests that a careful and thorough investigation of this problem would yield some important insights into the development of both individual writers and American literature as a whole.

5

With the Benefit
of Hindsight:
Popular Culture Criticism

This essay was written for a conference to celebrate the opening of a new Speech and Communications building at the University of Iowa. Since I had my MA and PhD in American Civilization from that university I did my best to write for an audience I didn't customarily address but on whose territory I had poached from time to time. The essay was published in *Critical Studies in Mass Communication* in December 1985. I've added a few notes based on events since that time and have tried to eliminate some of the "howlers" without completely removing the signs of its time.

Humanistic criticism of mass communications and popular culture has been plagued throughout its brief history by a widespread belief in the godlike and/or diabolical powers of its subject. As a consequence, media criticism has often been characterized by a quasi-theological tendency. Instead of analyses and evaluations of individual works, such criticism has frequently devoted itself to commentary on the awesome power of mass communications. This commentary usually revolves around such tenets as the view that mass communications have a greater power for good (or evil) than any media hitherto known to man; that they have brought about a profound change in human consciousness; that they enable the entire population to be mystically "present" at major events; that they now have the power to choose and elect presidents. These and other dogmas of the mass communications gospel share a central characteristic with theological tenets: they are matters of faith. Attempts to prove them by showing these alleged powers in action have failed. What mass communications researchers have actually demonstrated as a result of decades of empirical studies is that the media have surprisingly little influence on the deeper convictions of the public in comparison to family, friends, and other primary groups. Ironically, the only exception to this conclusion seems to be that the public shares some of the critics' awe and reverence for the mass media. This, I take it, is the real significance of the often reported public belief that Walter Cronkite is the most trusted man in America.

To illustrate more fully the problems created by this influential belief in the media's god-like power, I want to examine two major kinds of criticism that have been hampered by this quasi-theology. Then, I will look at some more recent developments that have, at least in part, avoided the holistic, grand theorizing of too many humanistic, academic critics. Finally, I will try to suggest some directions in which popular culture and media criticism should go to expand its strength and significance.

The Critical Tradition

Mass communications have grown and changed with remarkable rapidity in the twentieth century, and this development has both influenced and been shaped by the traditions of popular culture. One of these traditions, particularly strong in democratic America, was the ideal of a new popular culture that would educate the masses and create an informed and intelligent citizenry with higher levels of knowledge and taste than had ever existed before. As they developed, all the media have carried the burden of this ideal model of purveying education, information, and values to the masses. The first school of criticism, then, assumed that mass communications had the potential to become a primary educational institution capable of bringing all sorts of enlightenment to the American public; it was to be, in one of the persistent metaphors of this school of criticism, a "window on the world." On the other hand, proponents of this view were fully aware that this great power might be used for diabolical purposes, to convey false values and immoral attitudes to its audience, to make popular culture, in another famous figure of speech, "a vast wasteland." Critics committed to this assumption wrote largely about the media's successes and failures in living up to this great potential. Usually, as these critics saw it, the view out the window was onto a wasteland. Thus the educational school of criticism anathematized most popular culture as garbage, decried its commercialization, and called for government intervention and censorship to reform the communications industries (Rosenberg and White). Only a few areas were exempt from this opprobrium: documentary films, news commentaries, and educational programs being primary examples.

Apparently it did not occur to many of those who idealized the educational potential of the media to wonder if they could succeed where the enormously complex institutions of schooling in American culture seemed to have failed, even though critics often pointed with a fascinated horror to the fact that some children spent as much time at the movies or in front of a television set as they did in school and implied that an apparent decline in educational standards was somehow a result of such overexposure. Most of the attempts to use mass communications in an educational setting, or to convey educational content, have been dismal failures. While many school systems made large investments in television technology, classroom monitors have fallen into disuse except where absolutely necessary to service large lectures and to teach film and TV courses. Nor have the radio and television courses put on by the extension divisions of many universities and by public stations been other than straggling, generally unsatisfactory experiments. We can and should investigate the reasons why mass communications have been such an educational failure—my guess is what Plato already knew in the fifth century B.C.; that serious education thrives on those complex personal relationships between people for which technology can never be a substitute.

Though computers and the Internet have had an enormous impact on education, not all of this has been positive. Certainly, the interactive character of the computer has made it a more effective educational tool than television ever was. Still, every teacher is now familiar with the phenomenon of student papers copied off the Internet and other misuses of technology to avoid individual learning. Whether the media are a blessing or a curse for the future of education remains, I believe, to be seen.

Though the fervor of those early critics who saw in television a great power for education has declined, attacks on the media as teachers of false values and bad attitudes continue to be a major component of media criticism. This is most notable in the area of attitudes toward sex and violence. An article from the *Sunday Magazine* of the *Louisville Courier-Journal* (1985) is entitled "Fatal Television" with the subheading, "New and exotic kinds of 'killing' have researchers wondering if television isn't whetting, as well as feeding, America's appetite for violence." The article begins with the thesis that "there appears to be a difference in the quality, variety and persuasiveness of today's televised violence," and goes on to claim that this year "violence has been more prevalent . . . largely because there are fewer situation comedies and more action series," that "television violence features the use of machine guns and other sophisticated weaponry more often than it once did," that the violence is represented more "realistically" and connected with jokes or gags, and, finally, that the "distinction between heroes and villains is often less clear, and more violence is committed by people with psychological problems" (14). No doubt cause for alarm were it not that similar attacks were made on the movies by the director of the Payne Fund studies in the early thirties, on horror comics by Dr. Frederic Wertham and others in the fifties, and probablyon Shakespeare in the 1600s. The article goes on to cite new research, which purportedly establishes a definite causal link between the viewing of media violence and "aggressive" behavior—new studies always do that until the next round of studies shows that the research designs were faulty. I imagine that most of my readers can remember encountering many examples of this same critical article identical in design and significance. This is not to say that the portrayal of violence in popular culture is not a serious issue, but that the treatment of the idea that violence and other aspects of content encourage the public to perform immoral actions is vastly oversimplified and misleading.

The idea that media reflect, express, and probably reinforce attitudes and values is a subtler, more flexible, and, in my opinion, more fruitful application of the assumption that the media are involved with values. The problem is how one deals with the relationship between the apparent values expressed in genres of popular culture and the actual values of the public. Can one assume that the values in, say, television crime dramas are the same as those of the audience? To what extent do the conventions of a generic tradition or the artificial constraints of any media format shape the values expressed by any particular program? Communications research has largely given up the idea of a simple one-way causation between media content and audience attitudes and behavior, but humanistic critics still sometimes talk as if the media were corrupting our morals.

The problematic relationship between public values and popular culture remains a central critical issue that needs more careful theoretical examination. A few essays, such as Kevin Ryan's "Television as a Moral Educator" (Adler and Cater 111–28), explore this problem with the seriousness it deserves, but such work is rare. Certainly, critics who attempt to deal with the moral and cultural ramifications of mass communications need to be more aware of the many unresolved questions about the relationship between media content and public values.

A second quasi-theological approach to mass communications develops out of ideas about the nature of the media themselves. The influence of this type of criticism was vastly enhanced for a time by the impact of Marshall McLuhan, a remarkable figure whose ultimate significance is still unclear. McLuhan's books such as *The Gutenberg Galaxy* (1962), *Understanding Media* (1964), and *War and Peace in the Global Village* (1968), his many articles, and the pervasive commentary on his theories made him, for a time, a major international celebrity. However, McLuhan's conception of media determinism has not shown much staying power. Such McLuhanisms as the maxim that "the medium is the message," the distinction between oral, print, and electronic technologies, the idea of media as "extensions" of parts of the human body, the conceptions of "hot" and "cold" media, and the ideal of the "global village" have become widely known, yet the permanent influence of McLuhan's system on television criticism and communications research has been surprisingly small. Without his own particular brilliance, wit, and ability to link together seemingly disparate things, McLuhan's grand theories of media determinism have not been widely accepted.

Perhaps we have misunderstood the nature of McLuhan's achievement. Rereading him, I find that his work still holds great fascination in spite of my doubts about the validity of his theories. McLuhan's view of media determinism remains, in my opinion, a considerable oversimplification. However, reading *Understanding Media* again recently, I was struck by McLuhan's remarkable insights in areas where he was far ahead of me when I first read the book. Most notably, his analysis of the cultural significance of the computer revolution was a remarkably prescient account of developments that have actually taken place since 1964, but that were completely unforeseen by most of us at that time.

I've come to the conclusion that McLuhan's importance is not as a theorist but as a poet, the creator of a major philosophical epic. His work assumes a different character, I think, if we consider it to be in the epic tradition of Dante and Milton. Like Dante, McLuhan creates poetic forms, symbols, and metaphors that present a universal view of human history and its relationship to a cosmic order; like Milton, he sings of a Paradise Lost—the decline of the unity of oral culture—and a Paradise Regained—the new unity of the global village made possible by electronic media. McLuhan's work also shares a number of important characteristics with certain modern epics that have sought through myth to bring order out of the chaotic fragmentation of the twentieth century. He shares with Henry Adams the attempt to create a scientific myth of history; with Sir James Frazer the quest for an archetypal myth and ritual beneath the great diversity of human religious beliefs and practices; with Joyce and Yeats the quest for a universal human myth. This is not to say that McLuhan's achievement is on the level of these artistic giants, but only that we cannot properly evaluate the nature of his achievement without understanding it as a poetic rather than an intellectual construction.

However, though McLuhan's system of media determinism lacks the rigor, clarity, and simplicity to become the basis for extensive criticism and research, the concept of medium remains very important as a critical tool in the analysis of mass communications and popular culture. Some valuable examples of this already exist. Walter J. Ong's discussions of the differences between oral and print media in *The Presence of the Word* (1981) and *Interfaces of the Word* (1977) are both more modest in their claims and more thorough and rigorous in their analyses. In particular, Ong's discussions of the transition between the essentially oral culture of the late middle ages and the new print culture of the Renaissance is based on impressive learning and scholarly mastery. A number of critics have treated television as a medium with excellent results, most notably Michael J. Arlen, whose television criticism for the *New Yorker* is one of the best examples of media analysis. Arlen's discussion of the way in which American attitudes toward the Vietnam War were influenced by the way in which that war was visually presented on television is a recognized classic. In his more recent work, Arlen has continued to develop his basic thesis that "more and more, we see what the cameras see. Our interests become determined by what the cameras are interested in" (7). However, Arlen is too astute to define television as simply a visual medium. Instead, he sees it as still in a state of transition with the future open to several possibilities:

> Television, the most conservative of all the popular arts, the most hidebound, the most deeply rooted in the logic of non-visual information . . . has been moving its great weight into the new [visual] terrain. Right now, it is in midstride: one foot still planted in the Old World, where

visual signs exist mainly to express narrative stories or writerly information, and one foot now pressing into the New World, where visual forms have their own logic.

Is the camera eye but an extension of the human eye, or does it have its own perceptions? Already to a remarkable extent, the television cameras stare out across the world, peering into politics, into space, into back yards, into courthouses, casting their eyes at family life, public life, sports, sex, revolution, war, famine, as well as plenty, while we stay home, also staring-living our lives in terms of what we think the cameras tell us. (8)

The tone of this passage is somewhat more apocalyptic than Arlen's criticism of specific programs. Arlen's central theme is the extraordinary capacity of the visual (and aural) medium of television to create increasingly convincing illusions of reality and the contemporary tendency, enhanced by the power of television, to substitute comforting illusions for the sense of reality. Throughout his criticism, Arlen returns to this relationship between the television image and reality. He is deeply concerned by the substitution of illusory images for the reality of black history in *Roots*, the shaping of news to fit the visual possibilities of TV, and the distortion of literary masterpieces by what he calls the "tyranny of the visual." He also warns about the increasing sophistication of media producers, public relations people, and advertising men in presenting political candidates through visual images. Through his treatment of such critical topics, Arlen produces consistently provocative critiques of television.

To make criticism oriented around a conception of medium still more effective, students of mass communications and popular culture need to become much more sophisticated about existing media theory particularly as it has grown up around the fine arts. The great German critic Walter Benjamin recognized many years ago that newer technologies made possible an unprecedented reproduction of visual images, giving such images a new significance in modern culture. Perhaps because of this, our time has also been one of brilliant developments in the aesthetic theory of the visual. Critics of the media need to know much more about theories of the psychology of perception and the aesthetics of the visual in writers like E. H. Gombrich (1960), Rudolf Arnheim (1969), Jean Piaget (1956). In addition they need to be aware of the development of theories of visual analysis in the work of structuralists and semioticians like Christian Metz (1976) and Brian Henderson (1980).

Popular Culture Studies and Its Impact on Criticism

The critical approach to mass communications as an educational force and as a set of media has been hampered by our tendency to imagine a single all-powerful institution or process of communication unprecedented in human history. However, the conception of popular culture as an expression of values and as a network of different media can become the basis of good criticism if we consider it instead in a complex relation with other forms of artistry and communication that make up our culture. One increasingly important approach to media criticism has, by its very nature, tended in this direction. I refer to the recently developed academic field known as popular culture studies.

Popular culture scholars and critics see the media as one part of culture that includes certain kinds of literature, music, visual arts, film, sports, and other creations characteristically produced for and used by the general public. Popular culturalists see the media both contemporaneously and historically in relationship to other cultural patterns. In other words, they see media like television as a compound of many different kinds of cultural creations, each with its own history, traditions, and conventions. For example, the student of popular culture sees television crime shows not as the worrisome teacher of bad values and attitudes decried by the "sex-and-violence" critics, but as part of a long tradition in the literary representation of crime. This includes such earlier genres as the outlaw ballad, the detective story, the true-crime pulp, the gangster film, etc. With this awareness, the popular culture scholar can make a much more historically valid analysis of the extent to which the representation of crime and violence on television differs or doesn't differ from earlier crime dramas and fictions. This gives us a more responsible basis for investigating its current cultural and moral significance.

Popular culture studies have been particularly associated with two conceptions: that of an aesthetic of popular culture and that of popular genres or formulas as in the work of scholars like Nye, Newcomb, Cawelti, and Kaminsky. In essence, the idea of a popular aesthetic assumes that different modes of evaluation are appropriate for different kinds of artistry. Instead of a single set of aesthetic standards, popular aestheticians hold the view that those creations most typical of popular culture—for example, detective stories and westerns, rock and country music, horror films and science fiction, circuses and sports—cannot be meaningfully analyzed and evaluated by the same standards as those used to analyze and evaluate Henry James's novels, Picasso's paintings, the poetry of Wordsworth, or the music of Beethoven.

Perhaps the most important distinction developed so far by the popular aestheticians is that between the essentially conventional nature of the popular arts and the ideals of originality and unique genius so characteristic of the fine arts, at least since the Renaissance. Hall and Whannel, Deer and Deer, Thornburn, and Cawelti, deal with aspects of this issue. Though the media are frequently criticized for the formulaic character of most of their productions, popular aestheticians have accepted the idea that conventionality is a necessary, perhaps even a desirable, characteristic of a truly popular art form. In support of this proposition, they cite the dominantly formulaic character of many creations of the past now accepted as great art, such as ancient bardic narrative, Medieval liturgical drama, Elizabethan theater, and the Victorian novel (see Thorburn, and Fiske and Hartley). Once one accepts the validity of conventional forms like the detective story, the romance, the popular ballad, or the situation comedy, it becomes possible to recognize many different kinds of creativity and artistry within the limits of these conventions. Detective stories, for example, range all the way from the artistry of Raymond Chandler and Ross Macdonald to the humdrum whodunits of hordes of mystery technicians.

While conventional forms may be limited from some aesthetic perspectives, they do constitute a complex of widely recognized and understood patterns. Broad accessibility is another aesthetic principle valued by popular aestheticians. While Joyce's *Finnegans Wake* is undoubtedly a great literary masterpiece, understanding it requires an effort that few people will ever be able to give. The forms of popular culture, however, perform something like what Fiske and Hartley in *Reading Television* call a "bardic" function: they communicate to nearly everyone in the culture by depending on an repertory of basic stories and other artistic patterns that are commonly available in a fashion analogous to the traditional bard's use of epic formulas and a well-known mythology. These conventional patterns guarantee a high degree of accessibility. Of course mere accessibility is no guarantee of artistic interest. However, there is a sense in which the best popular art is not only fairly easy to interpret, but compels audiences to want to understand it, because it deals in an interesting way with stories and themes that seem important.

Some popular aestheticians would go farther and say that conventional patterns surviving over a period of time contain basic cultural meanings that can only be expressed by invoking these established formulas. The extent to which the narrative formulas of popular culture constitute a true mythology is still a matter of controversy. However, it is interesting that many major writers and filmmakers of the second half of the twentieth century used popular forms like the western and the detective story as mythical materials.

Another important concept of popular aesthetics is the centrality of serial form Radway, and Fiske and Hartley, make important points here. The programming imperatives of mass communications and mass publishing make serial form, either as a continuing narrative or as sets of variations on a single basic pattern (e.g., television soap opera or a series with the same basic form in each episode like *Magnum, P.I.*), a dominant type of creation and production. Though serial works such as dime novels, comic books, or movie adventure serials have marginal artistic pretensions, popular aestheticians insist that both types of serial are legitimate artistic approaches possessing special powers peculiar to this form. Though we are only beginning to understand and explore the aesthetics of serial form, many important twentieth century artists like Arnold Schonberg and Alain Robbe-Grillet have been fascinated by the serial principle.

Finally, popular aestheticians have developed the idea of what might be called the performance-persona principle, which they argue informs much popular art. This principle has two major aspects. First it involves the recognition of nonverbal aspects of performance. We are all familiar with the way in which a great performer can take quite commonplace or even banal material and turn it into a moving and complex experience. However, until the advent of modern visual and aural recording techniques, these aspects of performance were largely ephemeral. Consequently, an adequate critical vocabulary for the analysis and interpretation of performance had never developed. Now, however, performances can be recorded, filmed, or taped. Thus, modern communications technology has given the nonverbal aspects of performance an even greater importance. Indeed, popular culture has been in the avant-garde in new developments of performance techniques and forms. Our critical vocabulary for describing and analyzing these developments is sadly in arrears.

The other important aspect of the performance-persona principle involves the fact that a popular performance is not just a way of presenting a particular work to an audience, but is an act by a persona that relates both to a larger social context and to previous acts by the same persona. A good example of this larger social context is the rock concert. The rock concert has developed into a social ritual that can assume awesome proportions. In the case of such creations as Woodstock in the sixties or the Michael Jackson Victory Tour of the eighties, individual works and performances are caught up in a larger and more complex artistic construction that includes such components as showmanship, promotion, media coverage, etc. From this point of view, what has come to be known as "hype" is an important part of the artistic work as a whole.

The phenomena of stardom and celebrity are good examples of how previous acts by the a persona can influence a particular performance. The creation of stars and celebrities has become a major twentieth-century art form. While showmen like P. T. Barnum and "Buffalo Bill" Cody pioneered the form in the nineteenth century, it developed its own patterns of production in the twentieth. When a star like John Wayne portrayed a character in a film, he brought to that individual performance a whole aura derived from his existing star persona. When Elvis Presley sang a song, it was not just another popular ballad, but a major cultural statement. Here, too, we need to create a new critical vocabulary to describe and analyze such examples of the performance-persona principle.

These popular aesthetic principles lead us toward a pluralistic aesthetics rather than a single set of artistic standards. However, we have yet to deal fully with the problem of how these different sets of standards relate to each other. Some popular aestheticians assume that popular aesthetic principles can still be subsumed in some fashion under traditional aesthetic ideals, while others insist on the aesthetic independence of popular principles. I will attempt to deal in part with this problem in the final section of this essay, though it is still too early in the exploration of popular aesthetics to definitively resolve this issue. Nonetheless it remains important and should be continually on our minds as we explore these newer approaches to the analysis and evaluation of popular culture.

Another important concept of popular culture studies is that of popular genres, an idea that grows out of the basically conventional character of popular culture. Popular genres are those types of story, song, game, dance, sport, etc. that have become widely recognizable as such by writers, directors, publishers, producers, and their audiences. In terms of stories, which will be our chief example here, popular genres are immediately recognizable by certain key features such as a specific type of protagonist, a particular kind of plot pattern and setting, and a distinctive iconography. A story that begins with a crime suggests one genre, while one that ends in a shootout implies another. In many cases, these characteristics are so clear that a glance at a book cover or movie poster is sufficient to indicate the generic type: a cowboy on horseback means a western; a bottle of poison, a detective story; and a young woman with wind-tossed hair, a romance.

The study of popular genres has progressed further and has produced more complex and sophisticated analyses than any other area of popular culture studies. Genres like the western and the detective story have been explored from many different perspectives and with increasingly sophisticated methodologies involving ideas gleamed from recent critical movements like structuralism, semiotics, and reader-response criticism. These theories have helped to refine the definitions of various popular genres and to explore the complex meanings signified by the elements of plot, character, setting, and theme characteristic of such genres.

Another critical approach has proved useful in conjunction with the study of popular genres in different media—that of auteurism. This method adapted to film, and then to television, one of the traditional techniques of literary analysis: the study of a particular author's distinctive artistic personality, usually defined as his literary style, his favorite forms, and his dominant themes and ideas. Adapted to film, auteurism started from the assumption that the director was the true "author" of a work of cinema. This idea quickly took hold in the study of film and produced much first-rate analysis that has greatly enhanced our appreciation of the art of film and, even, I believe, had a very creative impact on younger film directors. In traditional literary studies, the analysis of authors has been in a continual dialectic with the study of genres. Concepts of authorial personality are one way to establish the nature of a particular writer's contribution to a genre. Similarly, the concept of genre has often helped provide a framework for defining an author's unique achievement. This has been equally true in the study of directorial auteurism. Much has been done, for example, with the relationship between John Ford and the western, and Alfred Hitchcock and the suspense thriller.

Three advantages of genre criticism are: (1) it provides a simple method for dividing up the critical work, thereby encouraging a more specific and complex form of analysis; (2) it encourages comparison and synthesis of different analyses of the same genres; and (3) it enables fruitful discussion of the relation between genres as they appear in different media and different historical periods. Just as the genre concept was a basic method in the study of literature since Aristotle, it has become equally important in the study of modern media.

Genre criticism is sometimes thought to be irrelevant or even inimical to our understanding of the social and cultural aspects of art. This may be true of dogmatic genre criticism, but responsible generic analysis makes it possible to use patterns of generic development to make inferences about changing values and attitudes as David Marc does in his analysis of television crime shows. It is the case, however, that the genre approach does not particularly encourage complex analyses of the portrayal of social ideas and values in individual works. In other words, what we usually describe as the "thematic" or "ideological" aspects of art are not central to genre criticism. In fact, to give persuasive analyses of the prevailing themes or ideological patterns of a particular period or culture one must usually make cross-generic investigations. In effect, thematic or ideological analysis constitutes a different approach to cultural and artistic study. It is neither contradictory to nor a replacement for generic analysis but simply another way of looking at the same materials with different questions in mind.

The same thing can be said for certain other approaches that have become particularly important in recent literary criticism: the study of the evolution of individual artistic careers, the exploration of the various "rhetorics" of literature, the analysis of individual style and language, etc. Though genre analysis can serve as an effective method for much of the work of criticism, we must be constantly alert to the need for alternative approaches to the analysis of the media and popular culture.

Toward New Critical Standards

In sum, humanistic media criticism has developed along three main lines: the positive/negative evaluation of mass communications as educational institutions; the analysis of the distinctive character of communications media; and the treatment of the media as popular culture. The last kind of criticism has concentrated on genres, including the characterization and evaluation of the contributions of individual auteurs (writers, actors, directors, producers). I have suggested that, with certain changes, the educational and media approaches could produce more valuable criticism.

However, I have not yet tackled what might be called the $64,000 question: what is criticism, anyway? In one sense the answer to this question is easy. David Littlejohn has provided an exemplary set of "Standards for Good Television Criticism" that could be applied to all criticism:

1. The good television critic can point out lies, errors and serious distortions when he discovers them. . . .

2. The good critic can survey trends and types of programming over one or more so-called seasons.
3. The good critic should also, from time to time, venture radical considerations of the very nature and creative possibilities of the medium.
4. Rather than simply attending to and then evaluating what appears on the television set, the good critic might on occasion inquire into the phenomenon and the social effects of those television programs which have now become either national rituals, or materials that we have come to ingest as naturally and unconsciously as the air through which they are transmitted.
5. The good critic should certainly investigate the commonplace that many people now depend on television for (or accept television in lieu of) the real world.
6. What appears on American television is at once the product of and (in a fuzzy way) a reflection of American society. . . . A social critic possessed of sufficient temerity and self-assurance might well make use of the medium of television to discuss both [the television image and American society]. (Adler and Cater 166–71)

These criteria imply the basic issues of television as educator, as medium, and as a set of genres, and give excellent advice on the sort of topics that might engage a critic concerned with these issues. Littlejohn's prescriptions suggest what might appropriately be the content of many specific critical articles, but there still remains the larger question of the fundamental purpose of criticism. Again, the obvious answer is seemingly simple: criticism should improve the quality of media programs and make viewers both more critical and better able to distinguish truth from illusion, beauty from ugliness, and thereby improve the overall quality of human life. This is a fine idea and few would disagree with it. The problem is how to accomplish these desirable ends. There is little evidence that creators have ever paid much attention to criticism of their works; most authors will tell you that they purposely avoid it because it's either depressing or infuriating. Television producers pay a great deal of attention to the ratings, but one would be surprised to find them carefully noting and following the critical prescriptions of what they view as wooly-minded intellectuals who have never met a payroll. The public, in general, rarely encounters serious criticism and probably would not be much interested if it did. Reviewing, which essentially predicts how much it's worth to make the effort to turn on the set or change the channel, will probably remain the form of criticism used most often by most people. While this may have some effect over a long period of time, one would be foolish to expect noticeable improvements in the level of audience taste to result from the work of reviewers. For one thing, this has certainly not been the case with earlier media; centuries of reviewing and criticism have not done much to raise the mass public's taste in fiction or drama. Though widely scorned by critics, *Gone With the Wind* is still considered by a large majority of literate Americans to be one of the greatest novels of all time.

Yet criticism is terribly important in spite of the fact that it does not seem to have a definitive effect either on the nature of artistic creation or audience reaction. What is it, then, that criticism really does? In my opinion, Matthew Arnold defined its most important aspect when he argued that the function of criticism was the understanding of the best that has been thought and said in the world. While the words are late Victorian and have a somewhat musty air about them, the idea is, I believe, still fundamental. It means that criticism is the embodiment of human curiosity in its exploration of human life and of those acts of the imagination in which that life has been most significantly perceived and expressed. Thus, criticism is the final stage in the creation of culture, that process which makes us coherently aware of ourselves. A fine bit of criticism is a special kind of creative act, one that clarifies and shapes the way in which we understand our lives. Because of this, the influence of criticism is mostly indirect; we cannot point to its immediate influence in creating a public demand for a higher class of art. Instead, good criticism is slowly assimilated into the work of other critics, into the thinking of creative artists and finally into the common understanding. It matures into the ways in which we perceive and understand our lives.

Viewed from this perspective, there are certain things the criticism of mass communications and popular culture should try to do, whether its method is value analysis, media theory, genre study, or some other mode. First of all, criticism must stop treating the media as a unique historical phenomenon and try to understand them more fully in relation to the entire range of culture. Second, critics must begin to face up to the task of defining the "canon" of popular culture; that is, they must start to work on the problem of how we define "the best that has been thought and said" in popular culture and the media. This is an awesome problem given the enormous output of the media, but it cannot be solved by a weak-minded pluralism. We must begin to move beyond the kind of total acceptance that has characterized the popular culture movement. This had an important function when traditional aesthetic standards were used to make a wholesale condemnation of popular culture. Now that the principle of a popular aesthetics is winning more acceptance, it is time to begin discussing the range of quality within these different artistic types and determining which individual works best embody the highest excellence of popular cultural creation. One noteworthy attempt in this line is Leslie Fiedler's *What Was Literature?* Though overly apocalyptic in its rhetoric, *What Was Literature?* gives an interesting account of the personal, historical, and cultural factors that ultimately convinced Fiedler that the traditional canon of great art and literature was the result of a particular cultural ideology. When it comes to defining the critical principles that should replace traditional aesthetic standards, Fiedler is less useful. His major interest is in those popular works that have never met with critical approval because their treatment of certain subjects seemed too oversimplified and stereotypical by accepted critical standards. Using as major examples Stowe's *Uncle Tom's Cabin,* Mitchell's *Gone With the Wind,* and Haley's *Roots,* he argues that the apparent stereotypes in these works are really archetypes. He sees the new "pop critic's" chief function as defining these archetypes:

> In every stereotype, no matter how weary, there sleeps a true archetype, waiting to be awakened by the majority (pop) critic, who, like the majority poet or novelist, screenwriter or composer of popular songs, dares be simple enough, sentimental enough, passionate enough, absurd enough to try. (142–43)

Fiedler's critical aim is related to that of those critics, many of them neo-Marxists, who see the purpose of criticism as the exposure of the ideologies that they believe are in all popular works. Fiedler would characterize the same patterns as narrative archetypes that have persisted because they reflect deeply embedded attitudes. Other critics would view them as capitalist ideologies, the repetition of which helps preserve a bourgeois hegemony. The analysis of ideologies and/or archetypes is close to what critics used to call the analysis of themes and is a necessary aspect of any full exploration of individual works and genres. However, like other aspects of analysis such as narrative technique, plot and character structure and stylistics, ideological analysis does not address the basic question of the popular culture canon.

What Fiedler does imply with respect to the expansion of the canon is that those works that have achieved real popularity—what Fiedler calls "majority art and literature" should be considered part of "the best that has been thought and said." This requires that we distinguish between something that is ephemerally popular, or is merely another instance of a popular genre, and those works that are exceptionally and fundamentally popular. The problem of making such a determination is considerable. One obvious criterion is statistical—for example, bestselling books, high Nielsen ratings, top box office grosses, but this alone is not sufficient. There must also be some test of the work's popularity over a long period of time and of its influence on other works. To some extent, then, the canon of popular culture will have to evolve through time.

Both popularity and such aesthetic principles as conventionality, popular mythology, serial form, and the performance-persona aspect suggest lines along which the canon of the best that has been thought and said can be varied and expanded. But the process of evolving and changing a canon is essentially a collective one and a central part of the ongoing practice of criticism. In effect, critics propose new works for inclusion in the canon along with their reasons for this inclusion and their understanding of how the new work relates to the existing canon and its principles. The new work is then subjected to the scrutiny of others. When such a work has been widely accepted it becomes part of what the culture assumes is the best that has been thought and said and thereby becomes the object of further intensive exploration and analysis. By this means, as T. S. Eliot pointed out in one of the most important critical essays of the twentieth century, a new work changes our understanding of the entire artistic and cultural tradition.

At its worst, this process of canon formation can be like elections to an elite private club, particularly when critics who see themselves as defenders of a canon band together to blackball anything that transgresses established criteria. At its best, however, the creation of canons of excellence is the creation of a responsible cultural heritage, our most important gift to the future. Even if we could technically pass on everything, the limitations of human perception and attention would make it impossible to bring all this to consciousness. The great heritage of the Greeks as it passed to modern times was partly determined by the survival of texts and artifacts through wars, social upheavals, and natural catastrophes. We have the opportunity to make different kinds of choices about our heritage. The exploration of what creations of popular culture should become a lasting part of human culture should have a high priority on our critical agenda.

The fundamental purpose of criticism, then, is to play a leading role in the formation of culture; it is responsible for the shaping of our perceptions, the way in which we understand contemporary existence, and the awareness that future generations have of their heritage. This means, of course, that criticism and education are vitally intertwined. However, where society's educational institutions tend to operate in terms of past awareness and traditional definitions of culture, the special place of criticism is to be concerned with the shaping of culture in the present and for the future. If we wish the continuing formation of culture to be shaped by rational humanistic discourse rather than by the accidents of history or the interests of particular groups, we must make the criticism of popular culture and the media a vital part of the ongoing exploration of literature, the arts, philosophy, history, and those other areas that constitute the major expressions of the human imagination.

6

Masculine Myths and Feminist Revisions: Some Thoughts on the Future of Popular Genres

Written for a conference honoring Ray Browne on the occasion of his retirement from teaching, the original version of this essay appeared in *Eye on the Future: Popular Culture Scholarship into the Twenty-First Century in Honor of Ray B. Browne*. I've expanded the final section on "The Feminization of Popular Culture" considerably.

⚏

Popular Culture, New Criticism, and American Studies

Since the mid-1960s when Ray Browne founded the serious study of popular culture, the analysis of popular genres has come full circle. The most important work of the 1960s and 1970s focused on two aspects of popular culture: the aesthetic characteristics of popular genres and the way in which popular culture embodied or expressed the basic myths of America. These trends reflected the dominant academic literary movements of the time, the New Criticism and American Studies. Both reacted against the critique by many intellectuals of popular culture as aesthetically and culturally worthless because it represented only the

79

conventional stereotypes and ideologies of the culture, or worse, simply reduced cultural and artistic values to the lowest common denominator.

One of the most popular genres of the late 1950s, the western, was also one of the most extensively studied. Analysts of the western during this period were particularly influenced by a few scholars and critics of the 1950s who had suggested that the popular tradition of the Western had a unique importance in the culture because it expressed basic cultural myths as well as possessed its own distinctive artistic qualities. Henry Nash Smith's *Virgin Land* was the most important of those works linking new trends in American Studies with popular culture, while Robert Warshow's often reprinted essay on the western (collected in *The Immediate Experience*) insisted on the serious artistry of films like *High Noon*. It was perhaps the most important single influence in creating an aesthetic approach to popular genres. Smith's work was continued and expanded in such studies as Richard Slotkin's *Regeneration through Violence, The Fatal Environment,* and *Gunfighter Nation,* a major three-volume study of cultural myths embodied in the popular western tradition. Other studies of the 1960s and 1970s explored the formal and aesthetic values of westerns and other popular genres. These studies resulted in an increasingly widespread recognition of the aesthetic potential of popular genres. It also led to the addition to the artistic canon of some popular writers like Dashiell Hammett and Raymond Chandler and of filmmakers like John Ford and Howard Hawks who were less appreciated by an earlier generation of critics because their work was largely in popular genres.

It no longer seems necessary to preface analyses of popular genres with an elaborate justification and apology for the "serious" consideration of such material. In fact, when an occasional article does so, one hears the screams of a long-dead horse hovering ghostlike in the air. Yet the very acceptance of the aesthetic and mythical analysis of popular genres has made these approaches, once so innovative, now seem like the conventional tradition of studies in popular culture. The innovative edge is elsewhere and this has led to a new approach to popular culture on the part of many younger scholars.

This new approach is partly a circling back to something like the more ideology-centered analysis that characterized the critique of the 1940s and 1950s, but it is also very different from the attack on "the vast wasteland" of popular culture, which typified that era. First of all, the new kind of analysis—let's call it "poststructuralist" for simplicity's sake—generally does not make the same kind of distinction between high and popular culture that dominated earlier thinking. From this methodological standpoint there is no significant difference between the analysis of the ideology of a work by a major writer and an item of popular culture: they are both seen as cultural or ideological structures that can be "deconstructed." Barthes has applied the same kind of analysis to the language of fashion as he did to a work of Balzac and Derrida has deconstructed popular texts in much the same way as he has Descartes. The poststructuralist critic often really likes the texts he/she is deconstructing. Jane Tompkins, for example, does not hide her fondness for westerns. In spite of the fact that she finds many of the genre's ideological implications deeply disturbing, she is often able to suggest striking insights into why some western writers, such as Louis L'Amour and Zane Grey, have been so popular and effective with readers.

Second, the poststructuralists have developed a more complex method of ideological analysis than that used by the more reductionistic Marxist critics of the 1950s. Though sometimes its practitioners favor an analytic jargon that seems impenetrable to ordinary minds, their basic assumption that all texts have latent as well as overt meanings and their view that these meanings are frequently in apparent conflict or contradiction with the surface meanings has produced some extremely interesting analysis. There's no doubt but that we can learn a great deal about the layers and levels of meaning in a text from poststructuralist analysis.

Finally, the poststructuralists have expanded the traditional Marxian analysis of ideology as an expression of economic relationships to other ideological areas, most notably gender and race. Not surprisingly, it's in these areas that the most striking reinterpretations of popular cultural texts and traditions have been taking place and these reinterpretations have begun to suggest some possible revisions of the history of American culture as well.

Feminist Critics, Gender, and Popular Culture

One important reinterpretation of popular culture reflected a new interest in popular genres of the nineteenth and twentieth centuries created and read by women, the traditions of the sentimental novel and the popular romance. It's certainly significant that most of the popular cultural studies of the 1960s and 1970s (needless to say written largely by men) had little to say about either the sentimental novel or the romance. In these writings, the major popular genres treated were the western, the detective story, the spy story, the crime or gangster saga, and the bestselling social novel of writers like Harold Robbins, Irving Wallace, James Michener, and Jacqueline Susann. Even in the case of this last genre, some of the most consistently successful women writers like Danielle Steele and Judith Krantz were largely overlooked. I myself look back somewhat guiltily to the mid-1970s when I called a book *Adventure, Mystery, and Romance,* but had almost nothing about romance in it.

Janice Radway's *Reading the Romance* pioneered the academic study of a predominantly female genre and audience. Her work paved the way for many important studies of popular genres such as the sentimental novel, the romance, and pornography from a variety of approaches concerned with the analysis of sex and gender ideologies. These studies have made clear the continuity, the vitality, and the cultural significance of predominantly feminine popular traditions. Radway was one of the first to show that the very act of reading romances was in some ways a female subversion of patriarchal values in spite of the surface content of romance novels with their apparent affirmation of the central values of male-dominated culture. Since then, other critics like Cathy Davidson, Jane Tompkins, and Nina Baym have further studied the popular sentimental novel of the nineteenth and late eighteenth centuries and have shown quite persuasively that Hawthorne's damned mob of scribbling women were not quite the pussycats they used to seem. Such critics have argued that earlier women writers like Susannah Rowson, Susan Warner, Augusta Jane Evans, and Harriet Beecher Stowe were more complex and powerful than earlier analyses would indicate. On the other hand, it's easy to find earlier twentieth-century male scholars who shared Hawthorne's negative, dismissive, and somewhat exasperated view of his successful female contemporaries. For example in James Hart's 1950 study *The Popular Book,* one of the earliest academic surveys of popular literature, Susan Warner is described in highly sexist terms:

> One look at her spare equine face distinguished by a pair of eyes set not quite evenly in her head, a thin determined mouth, and hair brushed tightly behind large ears proclaimed her a spinster by nature. She liked to think of herself as another Jane Eyre, though no Rochester ever came her way. All her emotion was channeled into novels. (95)

The new feminist approach to popular sentimental and romance novels has given us quite a different picture of the ideological and cultural significance of these traditions from the one that sees them as the outgrowth of spinsterish frustration and the channeling of emotions into novel writing instead of domesticity and motherhood. Rather, these analyses present a literature that served as an arena of ideological conflict, a fictional battleground on which the values of evangelical Christianity struggled with an increasingly nonreligious capitalistic and masculinist individualism. As Tompkins puts it, "culturally and politically, the effect of these novels is to establish women at the center of the world's most important work (saving souls) and to assert that in the end spiritual power is always superior to worldly might" (38).

According to this view, the novel of Christian sentiment and domesticity so popular in the mid- and later nineteenth century expressed the conflict between the traditional Christian ideology of sin and salvation that had become increasingly associated with women and the newer ideology of individualism and monetary success. This newer ideology more and more shaped the attitudes of men in the later nineteenth century and, in response to it, women sought to justify and affirm the significance of the feminine sphere. This analysis reflects Ann Douglas's concept of the feminization of American culture, the idea that one of the major cultural developments of the nineteenth century was an increasingly close association between women, domesticity, and religion resulting from the growing importance of business enterprise and the corresponding decline in the social authority of the clergy. According to Douglas, when the clergy became aware of the decline in their status from the pre-Revolutionary period, they turned to women for support of the moral and cultural values associated with the Christian evangelical tradition. Thus, for a time, during the later nineteenth century, women gained a moral authority and a cultural and psychological dominance greater than they had possessed before and in some ways different from and stronger than what they would come to claim even in the twentieth century. The sentimental novel with its powerful and long-suffering female protagonists, who usually succeed through their patience and fortitude in bringing about the spiritual reform of an errant male, symbolized this claim to authority and power.

According to Tompkins, the modem western emerged as a moral counterstatement to this ideology of Christian evangelical reform:

> The Western answers the domestic novel. It is the antithesis of the cult of domesticity that dominated American Victorian culture. The Western hero, who seems to ride in out of nowhere, in fact comes riding out of the nineteenth century. And every piece of baggage he doesn't have, every word he doesn't say, every creed in which he doesn't believe is absent for a reason. What isn't there in the Western hasn't disappeared by

accident; it's been deliberately jettisoned. The surface cleanness and simplicity of the landscape, the story line and the characters derive from the genre's will to sweep the board clear of encumbrances. And of some encumbrances more than others. If the Western deliberately rejects evangelical Protestantism and pointedly repudiates the cult of domesticity, it is because it seeks to marginalize and suppress the figure who stood for these ideals. (39)

At this point, an obvious objection suggests itself. Actually, the popular western is much older than the later nineteenth century, going back to James Fenimore Cooper's Leatherstocking who made his debut in 1823, and who multiplied a thousand-fold through novels, dime novels, and popular theater after the Civil War. However, this objection can be countered by pointing out that the western genre did undergo a radical change just at the turn of the century, the period that Tompkins is really talking about. This was when the modern adult western novel came into being, exemplified particularly by Owen Wister's *The Virginian,* but also by works by other late-nineteenth- and early-twentieth-century novelists like Emerson Hough, Harold Bell Wright, and Zane Grey. These writers were among the leading bestsellers at the turn of the nineteenth century. In fact, Harold Bell Wright is a case in point since we can see an interesting interplay in his world between the traditional Christian evangelism of *Shepherd of the Hills* and the newer western ethos of *The Winning of Barbara Worth.* There also emerged at this time a new kind of western art that went beyond the spectacular landscapes of Thomas Moran and Albert Bierstadt to create a visual world of cowboys and Indians, cavalry, cattle, and horses: the image of the Wild West as we still know it. This was also the apex of the Wild West Show's and the Rough Riders' popularity, when Theodore Roosevelt exploited the myth of the cowboy and the Wild West for political purposes. This period also witnessed the debut of Frederick Jackson Turner's frontier thesis, and of the first western films. Such a large number of contemporaneous developments in the imagining of the West are clearly associated with some major cultural changes.

The traditional way of accounting for these changes has been along lines that Turner set forth in his essay on "The Significance of the Frontier in American History." Basically, Turner argues that as the frontier receded in actuality due to the rapid rise of urbanization and industrialization, it became more and more important in the imagination of American culture because it established a linkage between the present and the past. The western, then, was fundamentally a conservative and nostalgic genre seeking to preserve past values that were being increasingly eroded by the social and cultural changes related to industrialization and the rise of the city. Owen Wister certainly reflected this attitude in his preface to the first edition of *The Virginian:* "What is become of the horseman, the cowpuncher, the last romantic figure upon our soil? . . . A transition has followed the horseman of the plains: a shapeless state, a condition of men and manners unlovely as that bald moment in the year when winter is gone and spring not come, and the face of Nature is ugly" (x). Yet nine years later, when Wister rededicated a new edition, he gave a rather different emphasis to his story by suggesting that it reflects a kind of renaissance of true Americanism rather than nostalgia for the past:

> After nigh half-a-century of shirking and evasion, Americans are beginning to look at themselves and their institutions straight; to perceive that Firecrackers and Orations once a year, and selling your vote or casting it for unknown nobodies, are not enough attention to pay to the Republic. (vii)

Tompkins's explanation of the rise of the modern western as a reaction against the traditional ideology of sentimental evangelical Christianity helps to account for the substantial differences between nineteenth- and twentieth-century westerns. It also points to the way in which the ethos promulgated by the westerns of Wister and other twentieth-century filmmakers and writers connected to a whole constellation of new moral and social values emerging at that time.

With this in mind, we can see that the modern western represented a new mythology departing considerably from the complex of values characteristic of the earlier western. Tompkins indicates one symptom of this change in her analysis of a shift in the treatment of nature from the Edenic Virgin Land of nineteenth-century romanticism to the harsh desert and endless plains more characteristic of the twentieth-century western. In the modern western, nature is not a source of fruitfulness and spirituality as it is in Cooper, but an obstacle course through which the protagonists must struggle in their quest for survival. However, it still remains to be seen how this change in the western relates to gender issues and why it came about at this particular time. Certainly, one of the major characteristics and limitations of the western genre has been the rigidity of its gender roles. Just as the visual background of the typical western emphasizes the binary oppositions of desert and mountain, town and wilderness, church and saloon, light and shadow, so the characters divide with equal rigidity along gender lines. Men are men and women are women and attempts to blur this line or to have women playing a man's role have never worked very well. One of the most fascinating and bizarre western films, Nicholas Ray's *Johnny Guitar*, was one of the few in which women enacted the rites of conflict and violence that are usually the province of men. In this film, a conflict between two women leads up to the climactic shootout. However, the ambiguity of women playing men's roles clearly appears in the strange sequence of costumes worn by Joan Crawford as the female protagonist. When Crawford first appears, near the opening of the film, she wears an elegantly tailored black shirt and pants traditionally associated in Westerns with the gunfighter. However, this is clearly a gunfighter in drag, for before very long, Crawford changes into a low-cut red dress of the sort worn the dance hall girls, and then into a demure white gown, and finally into blue jeans. This set of four costumes runs a gamut of the major male and female roles in the western, but in this case the costume changing is a restless shape shifting perhaps reflecting anxiety about the inverted gender roles.

The gender rigidity of the western tradition becomes even clearer when we compare it to another leading popular genre, the detective story. This genre has readily accommodated itself to women protagonists and, in recent years, with the emergence of hard-boiled women detectives in works by writers like Sara Paretsky, Sue Grafton, and Linda Barnes, males and females have been virtually interchangeable in the leading roles of the detective story genre. Even in earlier periods, though the majority of successful detective characters from the later nineteenth and earlier twentieth centuries were men, there were always a few female detectives. The western has never been able to accommodate such an interchangeability of female and male characters in leading roles because women in men's clothing are somehow inappropriate. It may well be that this lack of flexibility in the portrayal of gender roles is one major reason why, after its heyday from the late 1930s to the early 1970s, the western film and television program has virtually ceased to constitute a significant popular genre. For, in spite of the continued popularity of a few western writers like Louis L' Amour and an occasionally successful western film like *Dances with Wolves*, or a miniseries like Larry McMurtry's *Lonesome Dove*, our current interest in the western seems to be largely a matter of nostalgia.

But why should this particular insistence on the rigidity of gender roles have emerged when it did? Tompkins, as we have seen, thinks that this was primarily a kind of male reaction against the dominant female-centered ideology of evangelical Christianity that gave women and the home the major role in the great life drama of the quest for salvation. It's true that the turn of the century saw major changes in American Christianity, including the rise of the social gospel on one hand and of fundamentalism on the other. However, the new western also reflected other basic social and moral issues. Among them were the increasing mobility of American life, the beginning of the long-term decline of the home and family, and the corresponding emergence of a new ideology of "rugged individualism" that de-emphasized the significance of community and glorified the virtues of male aggressiveness and competition. This is the same constellation of social changes that, in a less popular literary and philosophical form, led to the movement we now refer to as naturalism or social Darwinism of which Ernest Hemingway became the most influential literary exemplar. Significantly, the literary world created by Hemingway bore many similarities to that of the modern western.

Thus, the modern western mythicized the new values of mobility, competitiveness, and rugged individualism that were replacing the more community and family-oriented values of the earlier nineteenth century. It dramatized and affirmed these values by making the struggles of the heroic male western protagonist on the frontier the focus of American history. In different ways, the two main turn-of-the-century schools of western American history, Theodore Roosevelt's "Winning of the West" as Anglo-Saxon conquest and Turner's frontier thesis as the transformation of Europeans into Americans also made this struggle the key to American uniqueness. The rigidity and separation of gender roles in the western related more to the rise of these new values, I think, than to a decline of evangelical Christianity, which in fact adapted rather effectively to the new circumstances.

The heroic male in the western symbolized the new values of individual male competition and aggression, and separation from community and family. The woman represented the values of the past that centered on family, home, and community. Typically, in the modern western, the central female character came to see the necessity of the masculine ethos, and, even, in certain climactic cases, to share in it, as when pacifist Grace Kelly herself shoots one of the remaining outlaws in *High Noon* when she sees her husband physically threatened. Such moments reverberate throughout the western to the degree that we can say there are two archetypal plot structures that dominate the modern western tradition: one is the hero's struggle with nature and outlaws, the other the conversion of the female to the new ethos of violence and rugged individualism. Significantly, this conversion does not mean that the woman becomes interchangeable with the man. On the contrary, in order to affirm the new values of mobility, competition, and individualism, the female must remain feminine while at the same time being forced to recognize that when the chips are down, there is no moral resort but the strength and courage of the isolated individual. In this way the pastoral western became, ironically, a mythic glorification of the new values of modern capitalistic competition and industrial work.

The Feminization of Popular Culture; or, Regendering and Other Transformations of the Late Twentieth Century

Now a century after the emergence of the modern western, another major change in popular genres seems be taking place. The decline of the western and the many important transformations in the mystery story tradition seem to reflect some basic changes in popular narrative structures, values, and ideologies. These changes are fundamental enough that they may be equivalent to those that accompanied the rise of the modern western and such related genres as the hard-boiled detective story and the gangster saga.[1] I've already referred to what might be called the regendering of the hard-boiled detective story through the creation of such tough female investigators as V. I. Warshawski, Kinsey Milhone, and Kay Scarpetta.[2] Another sign of the times is the extraordinary growth of the romance genre. Popular romances have been an important genre since the eighteenth century, but for the most part romance appeared as a plot element in other genres, such as the gothic and sentimental novels. As a genre in its own right romances never dominated the popular paperback publishing industry to the extent that they do now until Harlequin Books first issued mass paperback romances in a new format in the 1960s. Today, romances constitute over 50 percent of the paperback books published and have even begun to establish generic beachheads in the media of film and television.

---

1. I discuss the late twentieth-century decline of the western more fully in chapter four, "The Post-western," of *The Six-Gun Mystique Sequel* and in some of the essays in the section in this volume on "The Mystery of Mystery."

2. I deal with the regendering of the detective story more extensively in "The Question of Popular Genres Revisited" and in some of the essays in the section on "The Mystery of Mystery."

One indication of the contemporary flourishing of the genre is its proliferation into an amazing variety of subgenres including all sorts of historical, gothic, and professional romances. On his web page at About.com, Jim Trent lists romance categories such as Medieval, Regency, English Historical, Futuristic/Paranormal/Fantasy, and Contemporary American/Western Historical with many subcategories in each variety. In addition he points to four areas that new romance series are centering on: Vikings, sports, real and fictional royalty, and pets. These many new subgenres have, so to speak, elbowed their way onto the stage, pushing some of the more traditional popular genres into the wings. One example is the case of the western infiltrated by certain kinds of historical romance, including one that celebrates the love between a Native American (usually a chief of some sort) and a white woman in the nineteenth century. These fantasies about romance in the teepee have flourished as the patriarchal western has declined.[3] In the 1990s, the one successful television series with a western setting was *Dr. Quinn, Medicine Woman.* This series combined elements of the professional romance, the Native American romance, and the traditional western, and was surely a far cry from *Shane, High Noon,* and *The Wild Bunch.*

The rise of feminism and the proliferation of the popular romance have been largely contemporaneous, and this is something of a puzzle. On the surface at least, most popular romances culminate in a presumably happy union of a fairly traditional sort between a man and a woman. In many cases they even eventuate in a return to the sort of masculine dominance and feminine dependence that feminists have so vehemently denounced as sexist and patriarchal. If it were the case that feminists don't read romances and vice versa, we might say that the romance represents a backlash against feminism. But this is not the case

---

3. See Julia Bettinotti, "Race, Gender, and Genre: News from the Indian Romances." Bettinotti's work and that of her students at the University of Quebec at Montreal has been very important in the scholarly study of the popular romance. In addition to Radway's work, other important studies of the genre have been made by Kay Mussell, Carol Thurston, and Jan Cohn. Virgina Brackett's encyclopedia of *Classic Love and Romance Literature* is also useful, as are two anthologies: *The Progress of Romance: The Politics of Popular Fiction* edited by Jean Radford and the indispensable *Dangerous Men and Adventurous Women* of Jayne Ann Krentz, herself a notable practitioner of the genre under such noms de plume as Amanda Quick. The internet bookseller Amazon.com has a whole section devoted to romance, listing an enormous number of romances as well as secondary sources. Many other websites offer reviews, listings, and commentary on romances. Some of them, like Jim Trent's page on romance in About.com, suggest that men are increasingly becoming readers and fans of the genre.

as statements by many women who think of themselves as feminists and also dedicated romance readers indicate. It seems more likely that the apparently patriarchal and sexist themes of many romances imply a certain uncertainty and ambiguity on the part of women who are facing exciting and challenging new roles, but who still cling to some of the traditional patterns of romance in a patriarchal world. Janice Radway has suggested another kind of explanation. The group of romance readers she worked with seemed to feel that the very act of taking time off from other responsibilities to read a romance was a kind of rebellion against a male-dominated world. Perhaps in this case the traditional ending in monogamous marriage reassured readers that their resentment and rebelliousness would not completely subvert established patterns of gender. In addition, more complex writers of romance-centered novels like Danielle Steele and Judith Krantz as well as some of the newer subgenres have increasingly moved away from the traditional romance formulas to explore feminine independence and success in the male world. In a short essay published on the Internet in www.lifesbooks.com, Kay Mussell comments:

> I don't know how you can read many romances today as anything but feminist. To take just one issue: Heroes and heroines meet each other on a much more equal playing field. Heroes don't always dominate and heroines are frequently right. Heroines have expertise and aren't afraid to show it. Heroes aren't the fount of all wisdom and they do actually have things to learn from heroines. This is true of both contemporary and historical romances. I'm not trying to argue that all romances before 1990s featured unequal relationships or that all romances today are based on equality. That's clearly not the case. But in general heroines today have a lot more independence and authority than their counterparts did in earlier romances. I think that's clear evidence of the influence of feminism on romances and of the ability of romance novels to address contemporary concerns that women have.

This great surge in the popular romance goes along with transformations in the horror genre by women writers like Anne Rice and Laurel K. Hamilton that have even further eroded such patriarchal traditions as the division between the sexes and the double standard. Rice's ostensibly male vampire protagonists, like Lestat, are profoundly androgynous and given to what Freudians used to call polymorphous sexuality. In the vampire world created by Rice, gender distinctions become significantly blurred and one senses that it would almost be more appropriate in referring to the characters to put "men" and "women" in quotation marks, as if they were parts one plays rather than biological destinies. In this respect, Rice's creations embody a concept of gender not too different from that of leading feminist thinkers. In addition, with her "Mayfair Witches" series, Rice has toyed with a history articulated by a kind of matriarchal order reminiscent of the prehistoric society postulated by some feminist philosophers.

Hamilton's striking Anita Blake series presents a powerful woman protagonist who brings the skill and toughness of the regendered hard-boiled detective story into a fantasy world that is both quasi-realistic and full of strange creatures like vampires, zombies, and werewolves out of the gothic tradition. In this world, women, like Hamilton's heroine, can be just as powerful and effective as men without losing the powers of nurture and sentiment traditionally associated with them. This kind of experimentation with quite different gender arrangements has also been an important feature of one stream of science fiction. In works like Ursula Le Guin's classic *The Left Hand of Darkness* we encounter a futuristic world in which men can become pregnant and even change their sexuality from "male" to "female." Such hypothetical thought experiments involving gender enable writers to try to free themselves from the ideological limitations of a dominantly patriarchal tradition and to imagine the consequences of a more androgynous culture. We can undoubtedly expect more combinations of this sort using aspects of the horror and science fiction traditions to develop new gender possibilities.

One interesting result of this feminist revisioning of popular genres is a virtual explosion of feminist criticism of the gothic.[4] Since the gothic can be considered the origin of many of today's most important modern popular genres, reinterpreting it casts a significant light across the entire continuum of popular mythology, strikingly revising our view of the treatment of gender roles in it. The conventional view of the gothic is that it is supremely sexist since the main storyline usually is that of an innocent young woman pursued and tormented by a lustful male only, in the end, to be narrowly rescued by a representative of the respectable patriarch. But the new feminist interpretation reads the gothic as strikingly sympathetic to women and critical of patriarchal repression. The

---

4. Among the important texts in this vein are Anne Williams, *The Art of Darkness;* Nina Auerbach, *Our Vampires, Ourselves;* Judith Halberstam, *Skin Shows;* Maggie Kilgour, *The Rise of the Gothic Novel;* and Jacqueline Howard, *Reading Gothic Fiction.* Two books by men, Tropp's *Images of Fear* and Veeder's *Mary Shelley and 'Frankenstein',* also offer somewhat similar readings. Teresa Goddu in *Gothic America* credits Ellen Moer's 1976 essay "The Female Gothic" with initiating this trend.

most interesting aspect of the revisionist interpretation makes the gothic villain into something of a hero, reading him as presenting to women the possibility of a less repressive and more sexually fulfilling life. Applied to its fascinating vampire hero, this argument suggests a very different reading of Bram Stoker's *Dracula* from the traditional one. Anne Williams suggests that Dracula actually "represents the female principle masked by a Terrible Father" (124):

> In an undeniable pattern of allusions, Stoker himself links the monster with examples of female power and perversity. Dracula arrives in England on a ship called the "Demeter" and departs on one called the "Czarina Catherine." His most horrific manifestations occur in the light of the full moon—archetypally feminine—and like the moon goddess Artemis, Lady of the Wild Things, he wields control over beasts and may raise a storm at will. The vampire Lucy's brow is compared to "the coils of Medusa's snakes" (chap. 16), and Devandra P. Varma notes that Dracula shares many of the attributes of Kali, the Hindu Terrible Mother who drinks the blood of her victims. (123)

On the other hand, the heroic but incompetent group—Jonathan Harker, Seward, Van Helsing, and the others—seeking to rescue women from the clutches of the vampire are seen by Williams as symbols of a repressive patriarchy. The stake and the cross with which they try to counter Dracula's power, are, according to Williams, purely phallic and patriarchal. And garlic. Williams's take on that is fascinating. She connects it with the magic herb *molu* that Hermes gives to Odysseus to preserve him from the power of Circe and notes that Homer's use of garlic is in line with ancient tradition in which "garlic was widely believed to be displeasing to the Mother Goddess. The word garlic is derived from two Indo-European roots meaning "spear-leek"—hence it is, like the stake, phallic" (131) and was used to placate the Death Goddess and as "'a supper for Hecate,' whom Neumann [author of *The Great Mother*] describes as 'the snake-entwined goddess of ghosts and the dead'" (131).

This increasing "feminization"[5] of popular culture seems to reflect or at least to relate in some fashion to some very late twentieth-century developments in American culture that many observers have noted.

---

5. I've of course borrowed this term from Ann Douglas's fascinating study of *The Feminization of American Culture*. However, where the nineteenth-century cultural process that she analyzes represented something of a retreat for women, this contemporary feminization seems to represent something more like the return of the repressed.

What seems to be happening is that the traditional institutions and ideologies of community, family, and home that have shaped the lives of ordinary Americans for generations have been eroded. However, the modern ideology of rugged individualism that undercut these traditions has also seemed more and more hollow. Therefore, Americans are rather desperately casting about for ways to build new forms of community and family more viable in the present social and cultural circumstances.[6] In terms of popular genres, one of the most significant contemporary trends is the dramatization of the process by which new family and community groups are both threatened and then created and fostered on a new basis. This may be through a new image of gender in the popular romance, through the threatened and recreated community of the contemporary horror story, through the comic interplay of the regulars at a bar or the adventures of a pair of male or female buddies. The isolated individual hero is no longer the archetypal mythical figure that he was in the western and related genres. Instead, it is the group hero or the ad hoc family that has become the protagonist of the most successful recent popular genres.

I will close with two examples that are, I think, indicative. The first is *Dances with Wolves*, virtually the only highly successful western of recent. This film begins with the isolated individual hero, but is really about his reintegration into a close-knit human community, that of the Sioux. This new myth of the Native American as representing a form of community that the white culture is losing has been one of the few themes that have revitalized the tradition of the western in the last decade or so.

Finally, I would point to what happens in the science fiction movie *Aliens*, which is in many ways the most western-like film I've seen in recent years. I found the shootout between Sigourney Weaver and the alien female in *Aliens* to be the most compelling example of the shootout since the westerns of the 1960s and early 1970s. Significantly, however, the protagonist is a woman and there are no ambiguities about her carrying out a traditionally male action. In fact, Ripley's violence toward the alien creature is a direct outgrowth of the maternal bond she has

6. A recent major study of American values, Bellah et al. *Habits of the Heart*, stresses this aspect of contemporary American culture. It is interesting to compare *Habits of the Heart* with its 1950s counterpart, David Riesman et al. *The Lonely Crowd*, which portrayed an America still deeply rooted in "inner-directed" individualism, but beginning to show an increasing tendency toward "other-directedness."

formed with the young female child she has earlier rescued and not an assertion of her individual courage or an act of revenge—the two primary motives of western heroism. In *Aliens,* what begins as an adventure into the unknown becomes a desperate struggle to preserve the human family against far more powerful and violent alien forces that seek to destroy it. This seems increasingly to be the mythical adventure on which our hopes and fantasies are centered.

7

The Question of Popular
Genres Revisited

It's not often you get a chance to respond to yourself, but in this case Gary Edgerton asked me to revise an early essay on popular genres for a new collection he was planning and this was the result. The original essay appeared in the *Journal of Popular Film and Television* in summer 1985 and then, revised, in the 1997 volume Edgerton edited, *In the Eye of the Beholder*. I hope this still further revision represents a slight improvement.

≈

Some Generic Observations about Genre

Aristotle started it all. His *Poetics,* the earliest recorded work of Western civilization concerned wholly with literary criticism, is also the first example of genre theory. For Aristotle, art is essentially the imitation (mimesis) of life. Genre is the result of strategies of mimesis: (a) the manner or form of representation—lyric (one voice speaking for itself), epic (one voice representing many voices), or dramatic (many voices representing themselves); or (b) the types of action represented—tragic, comic, etc. These two principles of genre classification have been fundamental concepts of literary criticism since Aristotle. In recent times, discussions of the manner of representation must also deal with radio, film, television, and other means of delineation beyond the spoken voice and print. Consequently, new categories introduced by media criticism now compete with the traditional literary classifications of lyric, epic, and dramatic (though the latter still persists in traditional literary criticism and teaching, albeit in a rather residual and attenuated fashion).[1] However, it is the other type of genre theory—genre based on the type of content or, as Aristotle put it, the object of imitation—that I am primarily concerned with in this discussion, since it is this conception of genre that underlies the idea of popular genres.

Genre criticism has long been a standard approach to literature and the other arts, primarily because of its advantages in organizing criticism as a collective enterprise. For one thing, genre criticism provides a simple method for dividing up the critical work: it makes it possible to specialize in one genre, to examine subgenres of a particular type or period, etc. Because these different critical and historical studies can be coordinated, the concept of genre encourages more specific and complex forms of analysis. In addition, genre criticism encourages the comparison and synthesis of different analyses of the same genre—i.e., of different formulations of the generic "supertext"—and thereby increases the sophistication of generic definitions. Finally, the generic approach makes possible the comparison of particular texts in different media and from different periods because they relate to the same genre.

Genre criticism also has its limitations: it tends to lose sight of the genius of individual works and creators. Moreover, it can encourage the kind of proliferating pigeonholing of the arts that Shakespeare satirized in Polonius's famous speech on the varieties of drama. When genre critics forget that their definitions are critical artifacts and start treating them as prescriptions for artistic creation, the concept of genre quickly becomes stultifying and limiting. Finally, genre criticism does not directly address itself to those basic questions of artistic inspiration, impact, rhetoric, and ideology that Plato first defined, and that have been recurrently important in literary discussions, such as at the present time.

In constructing his theory of genre, Aristotle was reacting to Plato, whose ambiguities about art are well known. Plato raised many important questions about art, among which were: (a) the nature and significance of the artist's creation; is it divine inspiration or human artifice? *(Ion);* (b) art's impact on its audience; is it single or diverse, ennobling or corrupting? *(Republic);* (c) the relationship of art to truth; is it a copy of reality or an illusion? *(Phaedrus);* and (d) whether there is a true (serious)

---

1. See Paul Hernandi, *Beyond Genre: New Directions in Literary Classification.*

art, and if so, how it is different from false (popular) art *(Gorgias)*. Aristotle apparently felt he had either resolved or bypassed these questions with his theory of mimesis and genres, but the *Poetics* did not completely answer them and they continue to resurface in the history of criticism, challenging the validity of genre as a critical principle.

The essence of genre criticism is the construction of what, in contemporary critical jargon, might be called a macro- or "supertext." The supertext (genre) claims to be an abstract of the most significant characteristics or family resemblances among many particular texts, which can accordingly be analyzed, evaluated, and otherwise related to each other by virtue of their connection with the supertext. Because it is a consolidation of many texts created at different times, the supertext is one way of conceptualizing artistic traditions. Studying developments and changes in particular texts related to a genre is one way of tracing changes in an artistic tradition, just as studies of the way in which one genre relates to others can be one way of tracing the history of culture. Thus, the supertext can also be treated like an individual text: Its history can be constructed; its impact and influence can be explored; it can be compared with other texts; it can be used as a source for constructing histories and theories of art and culture.

Different genre theories construct their supertexts in various ways. Some do so inductively, creating the genre by generalizing from many individual texts. Others generate definitions deductively from some general theory of art or human nature. Most commonly, genre theories involve a combination of deduction and induction — in the *Poetics,* Aristotle proceeded from the basic assumption that art is imitation to an examination of the elements common to many different Greek tragedies.

These limitations of the genre principle have led to numerous reactions against genre in the history of Western civilization. In fact, genre is commonly associated with the ideals of classicism and their revival in such periods as the Renaissance and the eighteenth-century neoclassical movement. The romantic and realistic movements of the nineteenth century both reacted against the idea of genre, though for different reasons. The romantics were primarily interested in the full expression of individual artistic genius and, to them, ideas of genre seemed debilitating and restrictive. Romantic poets and dramatists rebelled against the neoclassical genres and unities and created forms of poetry and drama that expanded the boundaries of the lyric (e.g., Wordsworth's *The Prelude*) and the theater (e.g., Goethe's *Faust*). Similar rejections of the classical limits of symphonic form appeared in the works of composers like Beethoven and Berlioz. The realists, on the other hand, rejected generic traditions because they sought an ideological goal: the use of literature as a criticism of life. For them, the loose and flexible form of the novel seemed the most appropriate vehicle for the expression of this ideology . These two extra-generic principles—the individual artistic vision and the role of art as ideological expression—have continued to exist in a dialectic with genre criticism and are, in fact, behind many recent efforts in criticism to go "beyond genre."

Genre criticism in the twentieth century was strongly influenced by the idea of popular genres, a concept that made possible the sophisticated analysis of popular culture. The definition of popular genres, formulaic narrative types, or category literature—whatever these new supertexts are called—have made possible more complex critical, historical, and evaluative approaches to the vast output of the modern mass media.

Popular Genres and Popular Culture

The idea of popular genres developed from the assumption that such established categories of popular culture as westerns, detective stories, romances, gothic horror, situation comedies, etc. were comparable in some ways to traditional artistic genres like tragedy, comedy, the social novel, picaresque, pastoral, and satire. Popular genres were assumed to be analogous to these traditional supertexts in that they were authentic artistic types, but different, however, in the kind of artistic principles that governed their construction.

The earliest use of the idea of popular genres appears to have been in the 1920s in the pioneering appreciations of movies and other popular arts in such criticism as Gilbert Seldes's *The Seven Lively Arts*. During the 1930s and 1940s, when treated at all by the critical community, popular genres were mostly anathematized as examples of capitalist exploitation or of the decadence and corruption of mass culture. Only in the late 1950s did a more positive treatment of popular genres begin to appear in works like the British Stuart Hall and Paddy Whannel's *The Popular Arts* and the American Reuel Denney's *The Astonished Muse*. By the mid-1960s, the Pop Art movement in art and literature and the development of popular culture studies were well underway, giving the idea of popular genres additional significance.

The concept of popular genres has been a major basis for the development of an effective criticism of popular culture involving not only the whole range of what used to be called subliterature, but also of film, and, most recently, of television. Film criticism came of age when French and English critics developed the concept of auteurism. Starting from the assumption that the director was the true "author" of works of cinema, the practitioners of this method applied a traditional technique of literary analysis—the study of a particular author's distinctive combination of style, forms, and dominant themes and ideas—to film. As developed by French *cinéastes* like Bazin, Truffaut, and Godard, and by English critics like Robin Wood, auteurism has typically been combined with the concept of popular genres. In fact, much of the most effective film criticism and scholarship of the last half of the twentieth century moved between the analysis of directors and the study of genres with the genres providing a framework for defining a director's unique achievement. Among these were important studies the westerns of John Ford, Sam Peckinpah, Budd Boetticher, Howard Hawks, and others.[2] Similarly, the history of such genres as westerns, crime films, musical comedies, silent comedy, and film noir have now been typically organized around analysis of the contribution of significant directors to each genre. Scholars like Stuart Kaminsky and Thomas Schatz have also made studies of the system of Hollywood film genres. Though the theories of structuralism and semiotics have suggested new ways in which to define the genres of film, these critical theories have thus far been most effective when assimilated into the framework of genre criticism.

Television criticism, too, has been vitally influenced by the concept of genre. Beginning with Horace Newcomb's pioneer work of 1974, *TV: The Most Popular Art*, the concept of genre became an important aspect of television criticism. In anthologies like Newcomb's *Television: The Critical View*, Adler and Cater's *Television as a Cultural Force*, and Kaplan's *Regarding Television*. Though the "cultural studies" approach increasingly pervaded television criticism in the 1990s, genre still remains a basic critical principle.

Another instance of the creative way in which television critics have made use of the concept of popular genre is David Marc's *Demographic Vistas* (1984). Marc adapts the auteurist idea to the analysis of television genres, substituting the producers and the major comic performers as the auteurs of television. In an excellent chapter on the work of Paul Henning, writer-producer of *The Beverly Hillbillies*, *Petticoat Junction*,

---

2. See Jim Kitses, *Horizons West,* and Paul Seydor, *Peckinpah.*

and *Green Acres,* Marc discusses Henning's artistic accomplishments and limitations as a creator in the tradition of rural comedy. Marc skillfully relates Henning's work not only to this genre as it appears in television and film, but to an important American tradition going back to late eighteenth-century popular drama, to southwestern and New England humor, and to Mark Twain. Marc also analyzes the evolution of the crime genre on television through a chronological comparison of the work of several different producers: Jack Webb *(Dragnet);* Quinn Martin *(The Untouchables, The Fugitive);* Roy Huggins *(77 Sunset Strip, Hawaiian Eye);* Aaron Spelling *(Mod Squad, Charlie's Angels);* Stephen J. Cannell *(The Rockford Files);* and Steven Bochco and Michael Kozell *(Hill Street Blues).* Making complex comparisons between genres, auteurs, and cultural backgrounds, Marc constructs an insightful account of the development of the crime show and the cultural significance of its changing patterns. Marc's work showed how the concept of genre could be combined with other critical approaches to develop the historical, artistic, and cultural analysis of television.

Thus, the concept of popular genres seems firmly established in the criticism of popular film and television. In recent years, however, some important new critical theories have challenged the primacy of genre as a basic critical concept. The next important task of genre theory is to examine these objections in order to discover to what extent they require revision of the theory of popular genres and to what extent they may require us to go "beyond genre."

Beyond Genre?

This has been a time of great ferment in critical theory. New European theories—the poststructuralist deconstruction launched by Jacques Derrida, the "hermeneutics" of Hans-Georg Gadamer, the neo-Freudianism of Jacques Lacan, and the neo-Marxian "cultural studies" of British scholars and of Americans like Fredric Jameson—challenge many traditional approaches and make critical theory an important new academic discipline. In the criticism of popular film and television, structuralism and semiotics, particularly as developed in the theories of Christian Metz, have played a more and more important role.[3] Reader-response criticism has become increasingly important in analyses of

3. See Brian Henderson, *A Critique of Film Theory;* John Fiske and John Hartley, *Reading Television;* and E. Ann Kaplan, *Regarding Television.*

popular culture,[4] and last, but not least, there has been the development of feminist gender theory as well as multicultural criticism.

From the standpoint of genre criticism, these new theories restate in contemporary terms those fundamental Platonic questions that have always pointed to the limits of genre criticism: How do we treat the artist's inspiration? (Deconstructionists believe that it is fundamentally self-contradictory, for example); How do we understand art's impact on an audience? (Reader-response criticism is deeply concerned with this issue; so, in another way, are the neo-Freudians and neo-Marxians); What is the relationship of art to truth? (Structuralists and semioticians think that because it depends on the structures of language, art can be best understood not as mimesis but as a wholly artificial construction; thus, insofar as traditional theories of genre assume mimesis, they are misguided). Clearly there are enough cans of worms here to supply a whaling expedition.

While I doubt that these new approaches to analysis and interpretation will ultimately render the conception of popular genres obsolete, there is clearly much room for expansion and further refinement of our generic categories and of the method by which we relate generic conceptions to the study of popular culture. I would like to make a tentative contribution to this reexamination of genre criticism by considering how some of these newer critical approaches can contribute to our understanding of popular genres.

Deconstruction seems to be the new theoretical approach least relevant to the idea of genre. Since genres are abstracted conceptions of structure and the basic premise of deconstruction holds that structures are inherently self-contradictory, the two approaches would seem to be in conflict. Not surprisingly, most deconstructionists have ignored or bypassed the question of genre, preferring instead to deal with individual texts as their primary means of exploring the shifting and ambiguous play of meanings that they assume to be the inevitable result of any attempt to construct a complex linguistic structure. Perhaps there is no way to reconcile the basic assumptions of deconstruction and genre analysis. However, the practice of deconstructive analysis may yet have something to offer the study of popular genres. If we consider that a genre is a sort of text, then genres as texts may be as susceptible to deconstructive analysis as any other sort of text. Certainly, criticism of

---

4. See John Fiske, "Television and Popular Culture: Reflections on British and Australian Critical Practice" and Janice Radway, *Reading the Romance*.

popular genres has often noted that contradiction and ambiguity are central characteristics of such genres as the romance and the detective story. For example, it seems clear that there is a great deal of ambiguity about the sequence of "solutions" that seems to be one primary structural aspect of the detective genre. By presenting the reader with a parade of misleading clues, false suspects, and other "red herrings" the writer sets up a series of false "solutions" that both deceive the reader and prepare him/her for the "real solution" the detective offers at the end of the story. The real solution, by convention, is supposed to give satisfying closure to the whole process. Yet there are inherent problems and built-in ambiguities about this sort of structure that deconstructive analysis may help sort out more clearly than we have thus far.

Cultural studies with its assorted blends of Marx and Freud clearly offers many ideas that have great potential for enriching our understanding of popular genres particularly in relationship to their social and historical contexts. True, the currently dominant concepts of cultural studies—ideology and hegemony—tend to erase generic differences in their attempts to understand how literary or cinematic structures reinforce (or resist) the ideological perspective of the ruling hegemony of a particular society. However, there is no reason that popular genres cannot also be seen as a significant wellspring of cultural values. A number of critical studies have already been undertaken to begin this kind of analysis of popular genres like the crime, detective, and spy story. Frederic Jameson, a leading American exponent of cultural studies, suggests that "genres are essentially contracts between a writer and his readers; or rather, to use the term which Claudio Guillen has so carefully revived, they are literary institutions, which like other institutions of social life are based on tacit agreements or contracts. The thinking behind such a view of genres is based on the presupposition that all speech needs to be marked with certain indications and signals as to how it is properly to be used" (135). Possibly the analysis of the various tacit agreements implied by the "indications and signals" characteristic of different genres can help us understand why a particular genre has been shaped in the way it has by the society that produces and uses it.

Reader-response criticism can be broadened to include the study of audience responses to nonliterary media like film and television as well. This is a rather complex movement, which has developed out of some dissatisfaction with the way that critics have traditionally made assertions about responses to literary works. In particular, reader-response critics have questioned the assumption that everyone reacts or ought to react in approximately the same way to literary works. In traditional critical terms, this reaction can be described as a fairly straightforward understanding by the reader of such aspects of texts as character, plot, and theme. According to the conventional critical approach, the reader identifies these primary elements and then reacts accordingly. The role of the critic and interpreter is to help the reader recognize what the important elements of the text are.

The first reader-response idea was that texts often (or always) not only structure the actions they represent, but the way in which readers encounter and experience the work. Developed particularly by Stanley Fish and his followers, this kind of reader-response criticism tried to evolve a new approach to the analysis of texts by focusing attention on the act of reading. In structuralist terminology, these critics tried to attend not so much to such paradigmatic aspects of a text as character and plot, but to the syntagmatic or diachronic dimension of the text's structuring of the way a reader experiences the process of reading. This involves analysis of the developing perception and understanding the reader has from moment to moment as he goes through the text. Because this approach is an open invitation to the elaboration of purely personal, subjective responses—"at this moment the text made me feel gay, then I encountered this image, which made me unhappy, etc."—it has inspired some of the most dubious analysis in the history of criticism. However, when used by intelligent and well-trained minds, the analysis of the reader-response structure of a text can lead to new and important insights. For example, Stanley Fish famously reinterpreted many seventeenth-century poetic texts as "self-destructing artifacts"— poems whose experiential structure tried to make the reader turn his thoughts away from the delusions of the world to a new realization of God's grace, a feeling that, in turn, made the poem no longer necessary. Whether or not one ultimately agrees with such reinterpretations, they give new insights into the richness of major works like Milton's *Paradise Lost,* just as Levi-Strauss's structuralist reinterpretation of the Oedipus myth gave us a new understanding of the power of Sophocles' play.[5]

In the analysis of popular genres, this idea of reading as an act or process has become an important new approach. As Janice Radway points out in her study of the romance, the reading of a popular book or the viewing of a television program is part of a larger process of experience.

5. See Claude Levi-Strauss, *Structural Anthropology.*

When Radway began talking to a group of women who regularly read romances, she soon discovered that:

> I would have to give up my obsession with textual features and narrative details if I wanted to understand their view of romance reading. Once I recognized this it became clear that romance reading was important to the Smithton women because the simple event of picking up a book enabled them to deal with the particular pressures and tensions encountered in their daily round of activities. Although I learned later that certain aspects of the romance's story do help to make this event especially meaningful, the early interviews were interesting because they focused so resolutely on the act of romance reading rather than on the meaning of the romance. (86)

As Radway's work illustrates, the reader-response idea of analyzing the process of reading a text can also be applied effectively to the supertexts we know as popular genres. Here, however, the act of reading is not only shaped by the way in which the elements of a text are presented syntagmatically, but by the part that the act of reading plays in the whole social and psychological life of the reader. This consideration brings us to the second major idea associated with reader-response criticism — the insistence that different readers make very different interpretations of the same text or supertext and that these various readings have an equal or nearly equal validity. Norman Holland's theoretical approach to the "dynamics of literary response" and his careful studies of the variant interpretations of individual readers have been particularly important in developing this approach to the study of individual readers, but a similar approach to the study of audiences has become an important part of new research and theory in England and Australia where the political philosophy of democratic socialism makes the idea of many different, equally valid audience responses particularly congenial.[6]

This new variety of audience research is refreshingly different from the major tradition of audience research in American sociology with its massive offshoot in advertising, marketing, and mass communications, such as the Nielsen ratings of television. Because its context is primarily that of finding out whether audiences will approve certain candidates or policies in politics, consume certain products, or watch certain movies or television programs, this tradition of audience research defines the public as a monolithic statistical aggregate capable of only three kinds of response: yes, no, or no opinion. More sophisticated forms of such research

6. See Fiske, "Television and Popular Culture."

may offer a scale from positive to negative with five or more positions on it, but the basic assumption remains that audience response is best understood as an abstract generalization based on a one-dimensional range of responses from positive to negative.

The new kind of research assumes, on the contrary, a very diversified audience capable of a multitude of different interpretations of a particular book, show, or film:

> This new audience research does not ask what effect television has on its audience, nor what use does the audience make of television; rather it asks how a particular television work, seen as a polysemic potential of meanings, connects with the social life of a viewer or group of viewers. It is concerned then with how a television text is created out of a work (or program) by the active reading of an audience, and how this activity of reading can be explained in terms of a theory of culture. (Fiske, "Television and Popular Culture" 6)

Moreover, these multiple readings are not simply variants on a general line of interpretation defined by the intended meaning of the text. Audience interpretations can actually run counter to the obvious intentions of the text's producers, and these opposite readings are just as significant as the intended interpretations. This phenomenon has long been apparent to mass communications researchers, appearing in such studies as those of responses to characters like Archie Bunker: while the creators clearly intended to satirize bigotry through him, researchers found that large numbers of the audiences thought bigotry was being portrayed in a positive fashion. This kind of audience response was usually dismissed on the grounds that audience's ignorance or prejudice made it unable to correctly interpret the message. The new audience research denies this kind of conclusion by insisting that variant responses are an appropriate aspect of the communication process.

John Fiske argues that a television text can prefer a reading, but that it cannot impose one on its viewers. Members of the audience, his argument runs, can oppose this reading by rejecting the dominant ideology of the text, and thus produce a reading that serves their interests, rather than that of the hegemony whose interests are structured into the form of the text. Alternatively they can settle on meanings that accept the dominant ideological frame, but find the space within it to negotiate inflections that suit their own class positions (3).

Certain problems still remain with the concept of multiple meanings of texts, problems that are particularly highlighted when we encounter some of the wilder flights of reader-response criticism. The basic issue is whether all possible readings are equally valid, and, if not, what principles determine whether one reading is more valid than another. This becomes a real difficulty in connection with the deconstructionist assumption that all significant texts are inherently self-contradictory. The same concern applies to the interpretation of such supertexts as the western, the detective story, or the romance. When is an interpretation of a genre valid, and when is it not? I encountered this issue when developing my own interpretation of the western genre in *The Six-Gun Mystique* and I resolved it in what now seems to me a partly correct fashion, which, however, completely failed to deal with the key issue. I argued at that time that

> popular formulas like the western [I'd now call it a genre] cannot be understood as the effect of any single factor. However simple the formula may be, the artistic, social and psychological implications it synthesizes are extremely complex. . . . The western's capacity to accommodate many different kinds of meaning has made the formula successful as popular art and entertainment over many generations. (113)

This seems to suggest that any meaning is possible, but I would reject that idea, just as I would oppose the view that any interpretation that a reader arrives at of a particular text is as good as any other.

Reader-response criticism has not yet clearly faced up to the implications of this issue. Insofar as the reader-response approach assumes that all reader responses are equally valid or relevant it raises serious problems. Surely there is something more than off center about the reader who laughs at Quentin's suicide in Faulkner's *The Sound and the Fury*, or who is depressed when the heroine is reunited with the hero at the end of a romance. One cannot deny that there is a wide range of significant differences in the responses of both individual readers and communities of readers to the same texts and genres. The problem lies in how to determine the range of meaningful responses as differentiated from those that are ignorant or perverted.

Let us momentarily leave aside the thorny question of what principles might establish the limits of meaningful individual interpretations, i.e. when and how we can decide that a reader is simply wrong. Nevertheless, it seems to me that one of the most important aspects of recent critical theory lies in the extent to which it has defined new audience communities based on gender and multiculturalism. Radway's work was particularly significant because it not only pioneered a new approach to the analysis of responses to the popular genre of romance, but because it based that analysis on interviews with a community of women. Thereby it gave us new insight into that genre's connection with gender and with the social and cultural situation of women. This new interest in the gendering of generic analysis and the related investigation of subcultural traditions within a multicultural society has led to much of the most challenging recent work in the study of popular genres.

It's hardly surprising that gender would turn out to be a major factor in the history of genre, for the two words have the same linguistic root. Certainly writers, publishers, producers, and critics have always been aware of the intricate connections between gender and genre. Some genres have been thought of as distinctly gender oriented, while others seem to have shifted in their gender orientation during different historical periods. The popular romance, for example, has always been thought of as primarily a woman's genre, just as during the height of the Hollywood studio system there was a kind of production widely known as the woman's film or "weepie." Contrarily, action-adventure genres like the hard-boiled detective story, the western, and the war adventure have been produced with the image of a male audience in mind and have often been characterized by misogynistic themes, symbolic abuse of women, and macho masculinity. In its early phases, the novel was widely thought to be primarily reading for women, and many of the literary and cultural debates about this new genre concerned the issue of whether this was uplifting or corrupting for the "fair sex." Many of the most successful early forms of the novel, such as the sentimental romances and tragedies created by Samuel Richardson, and the gothics produced by Mrs. Radcliffe, had female protagonists and a partially feminine point of view. This practice continued in the highly popular sentimental novels of the nineteenth century, but clearly changed in the course of the nineteenth century. By the early twentieth century men had apparently become as important an audience for novels as women. The rise of the major tradition of the American novel in writers like Cooper, Melville, and Hawthorne culminated in the modern American novel of Hemingway, Fitzgerald, Dos Passos, and Faulkner. Recent feminine scholars have argued that this tradition can be seen as reflecting a move to take the novel away from that famous "mob of scribbling women" that irritated Hawthorne so much.

Clearly, the history of genres needs to be reexamined from a gender-oriented point of view and many feminist scholars are in the process of doing just that. Similar work related to masculinist genres and to male ideologies is needed. A few scholars, like Fred Pfeil in *White Guys,* have made an excellent start on this task. Analysis is also badly needed in the case of other audience communities such as those based on ethnicity and race. This seems particularly important in the case of the history of popular genres, as the interplay between subcultural generic traditions and the mainstream of American popular culture has been perhaps the most dynamic force in the evolution of American culture.

One of the most significant recent phenomena to emerge in connection with these developments is what might be called the regendering and reethnicizing of contemporary popular genres. What I'm referring to here is the tendency of current popular writers to take genres that used to be largely oriented to white male fantasies and to rewrite them with women, African American, and ethnic hero-heroine figures. This has been particularly notable in the area of mystery and detective fiction, where the contribution of women writers has been a major factor in the generic tradition beginning with the first American detective novel, Anna Katherine Green's *The Leavenworth Case.* However, even the most successful women mystery writers of the first half of the twentieth century—heavy hitters like Agatha Christie, Dorothy Sayers, Margery Allingham, Ngaio Marsh, and Josephine Tey—mainly wrote about male detectives. The rare female detectives tended to be highly eccentric amateurs like Christie's Miss Marple. Even Dorothy Sayers noted, in 1928, that "there have . . been a few women detectives, but on the whole, they have not been very successful. In order to justify their choice of sex, they are obliged to be so irritatingly intuitive as to destroy that quiet enjoyment of the logical which we look for in our detective reading" (58–59).

This has changed dramatically since the 1950s. A new type of female detective has emerged in the work of writers like Marcia Muller, Sue Grafton, Sara Paretsky, Patricia Cornwell, Margaret Maron, and Julie Smith. Moreover, the books of these writers involve for the most part a regendering not of the classical rationcinative tale, but of that most antifeminist of mystery genres, the hard-boiled detective story. These woman writers create detectives who are highly professional, as knowing and cynical as Sam Spade and Philip Marlowe, and as physically tough as Mike Hammer. Yet, these detective heroines also manifest qualities of sensitivity and concern for the weak and helpless traditionally associated with women. Currently, there is much discussion among feminist critics about whether these new woman detectives actually reflect feminist ideals and values or simply reinforce traditional masculine ideologies by dressing them up in women's clothes.[7] Whether truly feminist or not, some of these writers have been enormously successful with the contemporary reading public. Paretsky, Grafton, and Cornwell are perennial bestsellers.

What I've called the reethnicizing of popular genres has also been a very significant feature of current detective stories. The fine African American writer Chester Himes who, in the 1960s, created a wonderful series of detective stories describing the adventures of black Harlem police detectives Cotton Ed Smith and Grave-Digger Jones, pioneered this trend. For a time Himes's only significant competitor was a white writer named Ernest Tidyman who created the elegant African American detective Virgil Tibbs. Tibbs, however, was, in most respects, a traditional great detective in blackface. It was not until the 1980s when Walter Mosley published *Devil in a Blue Dress,* his first book featuring Easy Rawlins, that a detective fully immersed in African American life again walked the mean streets of the city and this time he became a highly successful bestseller. The 1980s was also a time when other ethnic groups began to find representation in the detective story genre: there was, for example, Robert Campbell's Irish Jimmy Flannery, James Lee Burke's Cajun Dave Robicheaux, K. K. Constantine's Slavic Mario Balzic, and Les Roberts's Slovak Milan Jackovic.

Regendering and reethnicizing has proceeded much further in the case of the detective story than in other popular genres, and this may tell us something about the detective genre or at least about its contemporary significance. However, there have been attempts to do this to other genres as well. The western has been regendered in the successful television series *Dr. Quinn: Medicine Woman,* though other essays along these lines have not worked particularly well. One movie, *The Ballad of Billie Jo,* was an excellent treatment of gender issues in the wild West, but was not a big hit at the box office. Michael Cimino's epic *Gates of Heaven* was an attempt to ethnicize the western, as was the recent television mini-series *Children of the Dust,* but both were clumsy and unsuccessful. Reethnicizing has flourished more in the case of the western with movies treating Native American cultures in a more sympathetic and complex way. Here, recent films like *Dances With Wolves* and *Geronimo* have tried with some success to transform traditional western formulas like the clash between pioneers and savages, cavalry and Indians,

---

7. See the discussion of these issues in Sally Munt's *Murder by the Book,* and in Glenwood Irons, ed., *Feminism in Women's Detective Fiction.*

into a new perspective on the significance of the American frontier. But whether these new versions of the western reflect a transformation of the myth or its final demise remains to be seen.[8]

Perhaps the ultimate test of the significance of regendering will reveal itself in connection with the popular genre of romance. This genre has had the strongest ties to women and has largely held to fixed traditional formulas over the years. However, there are definite signs of interests in new romance formulas and subgenres, especially those involving a more explicit treatment of sexuality as well as those with new settings and characters. It's still hard to imagine what a regendered romance would be like, but in a culture where so many changes have been occurring in the relationships between men and women, we may even see the emergence of a type of romance catering directly to men.

The study of the regendering and ethnicizing of popular genres is just beginning, just as the trend itself has only recently spread throughout American popular culture. Thus, it is very hard to predict just what direction the analysis should take and what sort of conclusions will emerge. But it is clear that this is one of the most exciting and significant areas now opening up in the study of popular genres.

Two final considerations: we need to recognize that the multiple interpretations that can be offered both of particular texts and of genres are themselves aspects of culture, gaining their significance from the particular groups within a culture that hold them. Thus, the meaning and significance of genres must be understood not only in formal or structural terms but also in a way that produces a better understanding of how particular cultural groups interpret texts and supertexts in the process of making them a part of their everyday lives.

Lastly, the construction and criticism of genres is itself an important cultural process that involves writers, publishers, producers, directors, actors, readers, and many others as well as critics. Thus, a fuller understanding of popular genres requires further investigation of the process by which genres are created and experienced. Some promising work has

8. The most astute and learned student of the myth of the frontier, Richard Slotkin, believes that this myth no longer makes sense of American experience and that we will have to create a new myth of America based on the idea that "our history in the West and in the East was shaped from the beginning by the meeting, conversation, and mutual adaptation of different cultures" (*Gunfighter Nation* 655). In effect, Slotkin seems to be saying that the old myth of the frontier, which involved the white pioneer's overcoming of the savage wilderness, will have be replaced by a new myth of multiculturalism and that the traditional western genre probably cannot be successfully adapted to this new myth.

already begun along these lines, particularly in the analysis of the role of genre in television and film production.[9]

Our discussion of newer interpretive ideas and methods suggested by the various schools of contemporary criticism indicates that we need not abandon the concept of genre, but that there are new directions in which our studies of genre should move. In particular, we need to examine more carefully the relationship between popular genres and broader social and cultural contexts by studying the actual experiences of readers and audiences with genres. This kind of reader-audience research seems to be the most important direction for future analysis of popular genres.

9. See Thomas Schatz, *Hollywood Genres* and Todd Gitlin, *Inside Prime Time*.

8

The Internationalization of Popular Genres

First published here, the original version of this paper was given at a conference in Quebec City, Canada in September 1997. Organized by the Centre de Recherches en Littérature Québécoise around a conference theme calling for "for inquiry into struggles for cultural dominance among 1) the Great European Tradition, as illustrated by the consecrated masterworks that make up the Occidental cultural + canon; (from the Parthenon, through the Mona Lisa, *Hamlet, Der Ring der Nibelungen* to *A la recherche du temps perdu*); 2) the contemporary mass media culture transmitted through the cinema, television and music recording industries that assert transnational corporatist hegemony; 3) various practices of resistance arising from artistic avant-gardes, smaller national configurations or third-world postcolonial nations and ideologies of identity rooted in ethnicity, gender and sexual orientation. Shifting ascendancies among such trends are usually grounded in more or less freely reached consensus rather than in violence or oppression. At issue, then, are the values that determine and legitimate such consensus." I'm very grateful to the director of the center, Denis St-Jacques, for giving me the opportunity to participate in this international conference.

Contemporary cultural debate often assumes that there is an inveterate hostility and separation between the traditional canon and modern mass culture. Such cultural debates have stressed, as one recent conference indicated, the "struggles for cultural dominance [between] . . . the Great European Tradition, as illustrated by . . . consecrated masterworks [and] the contemporary mass media culture transmitted through the cinema, television and music recording industries that assert transnational corporatist hegemony." Many intellectuals align themselves with the canon in what they see as a global struggle between capitalistic imperialism and traditional cultures.

However, even if this conflict exists outside the mind of intellectuals, it is surely less significant than the many creative impulses that have resulted from the increasing confluence of traditional national cultures. Over the course of the last fifty years or so there has been a considerable confluence of national cultures as well as a breakdown of the boundaries that used to exist between majority and minority and between imperialist and subaltern cultures. Similarly, a complex dialectic between the traditional canon and popular culture has developed in recent years.

To begin with, it is important to distinguish between different patterns of internationalization. One pattern is relatively simple and might be called, following Simon During, the global popular. In a 1997 article in *Critical Inquiry,* During points out that there are certain works or stars who seem to achieve popularity in almost every culture where the technology exists to project them. His particular example is Arnold Schwarzenegger and the film *Total Recall,* the impact of which he ascribes to Schwarzenegger's distinctive construction of masculinity and its relationship to themes of nuclear devastation and the clash between empires and subaltern states. There are other works one might deal with under this rubric, such as the American television series *Dallas,* which has also had a remarkable international career. One might likewise point to the worldwide response to the death and funeral of Princess Diana as another example of this kind of global impact.

One of the most striking cultural phenomena of the late twentieth century and the early twenty-first is quite different from that of a single text or person achieving worldwide impact, namely the complex process of cultural engagement and interaction involved in the internationalization of the Euro-American system of popular narrative and dramatic genres. Since World War II, this system has spread throughout the rest of the world with something of the same irresistibility as the global spread of English as the language of air travel. This internationalization may ultimately prove to be a passing aspect of the last throes of Euro-American cultural imperialism or it may herald a new global culture. Whatever the end result, the detective story, the horror film, the adventure thriller, the romance, and the futuristic fantasy are migrating from their original base in Western Europe and America to the shores of the Pacific, the upper reaches of the Ganges, and the steppes of Central Asia.

Yet the study of this complex development is fraught with difficulty and has hardly begun. In fact, this paper is not so much a preliminary report on findings as an attempt to suggest a more systematic approach to the investigation and analysis of the internationalization of the system of popular genres. Given the sheer enormity of the material to be studied along with the difficulties involved in dealing with many different languages and cultures, we badly need a theoretical and methodological framework that will make collective and cooperative research possible. To this end, I will offer a tentative definition of the system of popular genres as well as a few reflections on its historical and cultural significance. I will then follow up with an attempt to define some of the processes of generic transformation that seem to be involved in the internationalization of the system of genres.

Popular genres can be analyzed in terms of their individual history and structure. However, there is also a sense in which the major popular genres taken together constitute a system and we can also try to study the evolution of that system. Each major popular genre—e.g., the detective story, the romance, the horror story, the western, etc.—has a history as well as an authorship and readership of its own, but there are also greater or lesser degrees of overlap among readers and even, to some extent, among authors of the different individual genres. Most of the significant research up to this point has been done on particular genres through histories, author studies, and formal and thematic analyses of the mystery story, the western, the romance, the gothic tale, etc. The very few studies that have been done on the internationalization of popular genres have also tended to follow the lines of individual genres.

However, important as these particular generic traditions are, it is increasingly apparent that these different genres constitute a cultural system, comparable in some ways to the generic system of epic, tragedy, comedy, and satire that dominated western civilization from the Greeks to the nineteenth century. Moreover, certain aspects of the cultural significance of these genres can be investigated only when we consider them in relationship to the larger system of which they are part. It would appear that the system itself originated in the mid-eighteenth century with the rise of the modern romance and the gothic. Then, there was a second major wave of creation in the mid-nineteenth century that led to the development of the detective story and science fiction as well as of some of the major modern forms of heroic adventure, such as the western, the colonial adventure, and the spy thriller. At the same time, the system of genres flowed from country to country, as the crucial interplay among English, American, French, and, to some extent, German popular literatures in the mid-nineteenth century demonstrates. I'm thinking of such things as the influence of French crime literature, such as the memoirs of Eugene Vidocq on Poe and, and then the impact of Poe's Dupin stories in both England and France. Another example is the impact of French romanticism on American visions of the frontier, refracted in Cooper and transferred back across the Atlantic and emerging, among other things, in the Old Shatterhand series of the German writer Karl May. There is also the influence of Dickens and Eugene Sue in creating the modern bestseller and of Jules Verne and H. G. Wells on the origins of science fiction. These conjunctions probably represent the first internationalizing of the system of popular genres, and may have created a number of models for the further spread of this system in the twentieth century.

To construct the history of the system of popular genres from its early stages to the present we will have to draw on the many existing specific historical and theoretical analyses of particular genres like the gothic, the romance, the detective story, and the western that have been produced in different countries, particularly in England, France, America, and Germany. However, when we come to the last fifty years or so, the process of generic elaboration and internationalization becomes so complicated and intensive that some initial theorizing of the problem is desirable in order to spur new research initiatives.

Much of the analysis of the globalization of popular culture to date has proceeded under the rubric of coca-colonization or cultural imperialism. In other words, scholars have been particularly interested in the international merchandising of forms of Euro-American popular culture, which has largely been interpreted as part of the process through which western cultural hegemony has sought to spread itself in order to increase corporate profits and extend the markets for these products. While this has undoubtedly been a major force behind the global spread of fast foods, blue jeans, and cigarettes, portraying this process as unilinear and profit driven is an oversimplification that fails to pay adequate attention to the more complex cultural dialectics that are involved in the situation.

Let me cite just one specific example out of many. In the 1929 novel *Red Harvest,* the American detective writer Dashiell Hammett virtually created a new subgenre of the detective novel by transforming the traditional mystery story of ratiocination into a tale of violent action. He changed the detective from a gentleman sleuth to a tough guy who cleaned up a corrupt town not by solving crimes but by setting criminal gangs against each other. In this way Hammett linked the detective story to the flourishing popular tradition of the western adventure. Some years later, in 1961, Akira Kurosawa helped revitalize the samurai tradition in Japanese films by drawing on the plot of Hammett's novel to create *Yojimbo.* This film in turn inspired a revival of the American western through the tremendous success of an Italian adaptation of Kurosawa's story in the first successful spaghetti western, Sergio Leone's *A Fistful of Dollars* (1964). Finally, Leone's film was readapted into American film using, ironically, an era and a setting very similar to Hammett's original conception in the 1996 Bruce Willis film *Last Man Standing.*

What we have here is not a simple line of influence but a complex and creative interplay among individual artists, genres, and national traditions made possible by the interacting system of popular genres. These acts of adaptation and transformation are not simply a reflection of the imposition of American values onto helpless foreign cultures, but also involve significant transformations of the system itself. The American western was never the same again after the impact of the spaghetti westerns. This change in the American western undoubtedly reflected important cultural and ideological changes in American culture. However, the form that some of these changes took was certainly influenced by the popularity of Leone's image of the West and his hero as enacted by the young American Clint Eastwood (who himself went on to create a very important series of cinematic transformations of popular genres).

The simplest form of cultural exchange is that of translation, a practice that has been of great significance in the history of civilization. One need only refer to the translation of the Bible from Hebrew and Greek into Latin and then the European vernaculars. Another translation of profound significance was that of Homer into the modern European languages. Just such a translation inspired Keats's great sonnet "On First Looking Into Chapman's Homer," a poem that powerfully dramatizes how important an act of translation can be. Translation not only conveys something from one culture to another or from the past to the present, but it can also inspire major cultural transformations. While few translations of popular generic works into other languages have a biblical or Homeric significance, their increasing pervasiveness certainly has some impact. Studying the translation of popular works in systemic terms could be extremely illuminating; though at this level translation might be more a matter of what Simon During calls transnationalization, that true globalism.

Such a study could include several different lines of research. We need to know more about the social and economic process of how translations are commissioned and marketed. What authors are regularly translated into different languages and what genres and ideologies do these authors represent? The history of the translation of popular genres into particular languages would also offer much insight into the way genres developed in different countries. In fact, one can imagine all sorts of studies proceeding from the basic fact of translation and these, at the present time, probably represent the most important sort of fundamental research that needs to be done in terms of the globalization of the system of popular genres.

Though the most common examples of popular generic translation are probably from English into other languages, there are important examples of the reverse. Georges Simenon's crime novels and Maigret stories translated from French into English, have had a definite influence on mystery genres. Even a relatively exotic work such as Peter Hoeg's *Smilla's Sense of Snow* from Denmark had a considerable impact in English translation. It's also interesting to note that some things translate very successfully from one language into another while others do not. Simenon's stories seemed to move almost effortlessly into English. On the other hand the highly popular works of the French Mickey Spillane, hard-boiled writer San Antonio, have never achieved comparable popularity in English translation because they are so full of untranslatable French slang.

This last observation highlights the fact that translation is never just a matter of language, but a matter of culture as well. A successful translation not only has to find the linguistic equivalents, but must also work out many cultural equivalents of the original. This often leads from translation into transformation, as when Kurusawa's samurai film *The Seven Samurai* was translated into the terms of the American western and became *The Magnificent Seven,* a film successful enough that it spawned a number of sequels and imitations like *The Return of the Seven.* In a situation where there is increasing international exchange of genres, retranslation becomes a common phenomenon and another process that needs to be investigated. What, for example, was involved in the translation of the American action film, mainly the western, into the Asian kung fu film, which then was retranslated into a highly successful American TV series starring David Carradine and into the tremendously popular Chuck Norris action films?

The study of retranslation offers the opportunity to discover what sort of narrative patterns can be successfully exchanged between cultures and what sort of exchanges fail. We've just looked at the great success of the retranslation of martial arts as an element in all kinds of action films. There are many kinds of contemporary retranslation. Another was Umberto Eco's *Name of the Rose.* This was a translation of the Anglo-American detective story genre into Italian retranslated in turn back into English and then further retranslated into the form of an American film. A particularly fascinating example of retranslation occurred in 1995 when the Library of America, which specializes in editions of canonic American masterpieces, issued a two- volume collection of the writings of Raymond Chandler, followed by another two-volume edition of *Crime Novels: American Noir from the 1930s to the 1950s.* When most of these novels by writers like James M. Cain, Horace McCoy, Cornell Woolrich, and Jim Thompson were originally published they were briefly popular. Many were then made into classic movies like Billy Wilder's *Double Indemnity* and Tay Garnett's *The Postman Always Rings Twice,* but then forgotten, except for by the French who devoured them in translation after the war. It's not surprising that the French term "noir" is commonly used in connection with these crime and detective novels. It was their passage through French culture in the form of the famous Gallimard "série noire" that elevated this genre from throwaway American pulps to serious popular fiction much admired by French existentialist heavyweights like Camus and Sartre. The success of these writers in French translation not only facilitated their return to America on a new cultural level but a inspired a whole series of new movies based on or exploiting the "noir" style This has introduced these texts to a younger generation.

Another process differs enough from translation that I would suggest the term transculturation to describe it. This occurs when a writer from one culture and language seeks to create a persuasive version of a genre set in another culture. Some of the most interesting examples of this process on the contemporary scene are in the mystery genre. I'm thinking of examples like Nicholas Freeling's Van der Valk series about a

Dutch detective in Amsterdam, Stuart Kaminsky's remarkable Soviet and post-Soviet mysteries, H. R. F. Keating's stories of Inspector Ghote in India, or even Tony Hillerman's Native American detective tales. I suppose we encounter a somewhat similar phenomenon in the popular romance when a writer seeks to reconstruct a historic period or an exotic locale.

In the case of transculturation there is an intersection between cultures taking place in the mind of the writer and the reader that certainly reflects and perhaps reshapes to some extent the understanding that one culture has of another. But there is still another level of transculturation that occurs when a culture adopts an entire genre or system of genres characteristic of another culture. One of the striking twentieth century examples of this process is the adoption by Japanese culture of a large number of western genres including that of the detective story beginning even before World War II in the work of such Japanese writers as the appropriately pseudonymed Edogawa Ranpo. We have already noted the Japanese transformation of the American western into the samurai film and we could also point to Japanese versions of the horror film in the form of the Godzilla series of monster movies. Ian Buruma and other scholars have studied some of these transformations. There is also a sizeable literature on the kung fu film phenomenon, but these studies only scratch the surface of the growing international transculturation of popular genres.

This area of study offers wonderful opportunities not only for important original research into ongoing cultural phenomena, but also for international scholarly collaboration. Only through the work of teams of scholars from different countries can the analysis of the patterns and implications of generic exchanges between different languages and cultures possibly be carried out. It is time to move beyond the simplistic formulations of cultural imperialism and the spread of capitalistic hegemony through the ideologies of popular culture to develop a more accurate understanding of the complex dialectic of cultural meanings being engendered in the world today through the exchange of popular genres.

9

Cowboys and Canons: Humanistic Education and Popular Culture

This is the first publication of this paper. An earlier version was presented at the 1996 PCA-ACA Conference when I was honored with the American Culture Association Governing Board's third annual award for Outstanding Contributions to American Culture Studies. I'd like to dedicate the paper to Ray and Pat Browne, whose encouragement and support to me over a period of over thirty years has been a major factor in my work as it has in that of every scholar of popular culture. I've also added some related material from a talk given at a symposium to honor the retirement of my University of Kentucky colleague, Ray Betts.

＝

1996 was the twenty-fifth anniversary of the first meeting of the Popular Culture Association in East Lansing, Michigan. The American Culture Association had its beginning a bit later in 1978–79. The 1971 meeting was held at Michigan State University where Russell Nye, one of the true pioneers of popular culture studies, was a professor. I remember the meeting well. For some reason the sewer system in East Lansing was in a crisis state and a horrible aroma of ripe putrefaction hung heavily over the city. Whether this symbolized the decay of traditional academe or the rising tide of mass culture depended on whom you talked to. But, in spite of this olfactory obstacle, the meeting was a great success and the PCA was launched for good.

1971 was also a banner year for me. I had just published *The Six-Gun Mystique* and turned 40 without collapsing. I had expected my debut as a scholar of popular culture to at least raise an eyebrow or two among my colleagues at the University of Chicago, but instead of exploding, they promoted me to professor. So it was on a wave of euphoria and pride in my intellectual grasp of the patterns of popular culture that I arrived in East Lansing.

There I attended a session that has remained a deeply symbolic and chastening experience for me. The subject was the art of pulp magazine covers. I've long forgotten the name of the presenter, but I'll never forget his presentation. He came to the podium with a large dog-eared cardboard box from which he extracted one pulp magazine after another, holding each one in turn for the audience to see while exclaiming things like "isn't that great!," "isn't that wonderful!," and "look at the red of that blood!" While we learned nothing explicit about the aesthetic or cultural significance of these texts, the passion and admiration of the fan and collector carried a deep meaning. The very essence of culture lies in the relationship we have with the things we unquestioningly love, enjoy, and choose to involve ourselves in. We sometimes lose sight of this in the attempt to winnow our enthusiasms and order them into patterns that, transcending the pleasure of the moment, can become part of a cultural heritage that is passed on from one generation to another. In the process we lose something of the vitality and immediacy of that original experience.

Yet ordering and winnowing is necessary as well for without it there is no way in which the experience and meaning of a cultural text can be conveyed from one generation to another. Another event might stand for the antithesis of a fan's enthusiastic celebration of pulp magazine covers. In 1995 the Library of America published an edition of the major works of Raymond Chandler. Now Chandler, whose original stories appeared in the very pulp magazines celebrated by the enthusiast in East Lansing, has been apotheosized (or incarcerated depending on your point of view) along with other great American writers like Henry James, Nathaniel Hawthorne, and Ralph Waldo Emerson.

I embarked upon the somewhat ironic career of a "scholar" of popular culture when I acknowledged to myself that I really enjoyed westerns and detective stories as much as and sometimes more than I did the "classics" of literature. Now, three decades later, I still puzzle over their complex relationship. We enjoy popular culture on an everyday basis and in a relatively unreflective fashion, but that doesn't mean that it is without artistic and cultural significance. On the other hand we set out to master the canonic culture or heritage, believing that it embodies those texts and modes of conceiving the world most worth preserving and passing on. Some canonic works may require special effort, but others can be as enjoyable and immediately pleasing as works of popular culture. The line between canonic and popular is constantly shifting.

After more than two centuries as the largely unchallenged basis of humanistic education, the canon has come under heavy attack. Critics argue that the traditional canon is too restrictive and ideological and that, instead of being a repository of excellence, it expresses and reinforces social and political domination of particular elites. These cannoneers against the canon argue that students need to "come to grips with their own identities" by encountering texts that reflect the experiences of their own particular groups whether defined in terms of ethnicity, gender, or subcultural tradition. Today's dominant trend, as reflected in the new structuring of literary survey courses and humanities requirements and in the new anthologies being created to service these courses, is either toward abandoning the canon altogether or toward making it more "multicultural." Unfortunately though it sounds good, multiculturalism seems to mean confusingly different things to different people. To some it points to cultural differentiation and separatism. For example, to many feminists, African Americanists and Native Americanists, multiculturalism means the definition and presentation of a distinctive body of texts and theories expressing a subcultural vision. Other multiculturalists believe that the right approach is to teach everybody something about all the major cultural traditions that are present in contemporary American culture, including popular culture, and thereby to foster a society that supports cultural pluralism. Still others look to new cultural combinations to break down the ethnocentric limits and animosities so characteristic of past cultures.

Such attacks have also inspired some heavy defenses of the canon. The battle lines were most dramatically drawn in 1987, the year in which two major defenses of the traditional canon appeared, E. D. Hirsch's *Cultural Literacy* and Allan Bloom's *The Closing of the American Mind.* Hard on the heels of these came the other Bloom, the polymathic Harold, whose *Western Canon* reasserted and attempted to explain the unique importance of his version of the traditional canon. These works summed up a widespread reaction against several developments in American education since the 1960s. They included the growth of studies in popular culture and the increasing inclusion of popular works in the curriculum; the development of African American studies, women's studies, ethnic and postcolonial studies, and other forms of multiculturalism; the expansion of the historical curriculum beyond the borders of western civilization to include texts and ideas from other world cultures; and finally, a new emphasis on contemporary or modern studies as a means of importing what was thought to be greater contemporary social and political relevance into the process of humanities education.

Hirsch, the Blooms, and other defenders of the canon opposed these developments by reaffirming two major twentieth-century models of canonic education. One was the Columbia University approach of studying the history of Western Civilization through its most important artistic and philosophical products. The other was the University of Chicago model of the Great Books harking back to such later nineteenth-century formulations as Matthew Arnold's concept of culture as the "best that has been thought and said" and President Eliot of Harvard's five-foot shelf of books. Both of these models implied that the only way to become truly educated was through an encounter with that body of texts that most completely embodied the humanistic tradition at its best. Thus, they argued that higher education should be largely based on the study of texts containing the thought and expression of the greatest and most historically influential minds that had appeared in the course of Western civilization. These defenders felt that studies of the traditional canon were the only route to the possession of culture, and the best foundation for further significant thought and creativity.

In turn this view was vehemently attacked by popular culturalists and multiculturalists who argued that the traditional canon confused greatness with exclusivity and mistook for truth a limited ideological perspective, that of powerful White European Males. These anticanonic forces set out to replace what they saw as a fixed and immutable canon with an ever-expanding body of texts reflecting the many different groups and levels of expression within modern culture. In addition, they created alternative ideologies of analysis and evaluation, which they believed would reveal the true relevance and meaning of this variety of texts.

The struggle over the canon proved to be neither as fierce nor as apocalyptic as some of the combatants foresaw. The resistance of the devotees of tradition has not been as adamantine as their rhetoric might have suggested. Nor have the inroads of the anticanonists brought about the wholesale explosion of the canon and the total loss of coherence imagined by the traditionalists. In those bellwether anthologies, whose pattern of selections both reflect and influence the shape of introductory and survey courses, changes have been, on the whole, cautious and relatively minor. The new editions of standard anthologies of English and American literature like those published by Norton, Macmillan, Little, Brown, and Harper/Collins contain more selections by women and writers representing various minorities, but the traditional canon still dominates. The self-consciously multicultural anthology of American literature published by Heath is by far the most innovative. It does offer a higher percentage of nontraditional texts, but certainly does not involve a radical reconceptualizing of the history of American literature. In fact, the teaching of American literature has adapted itself easily to these new approaches, perhaps because the canon of American literature had increasingly been conceived in partly multicultural terms even before the multicultural revolution.

That the traditional canon readily adapted itself to the new multiculturalism came as something of a surprise to the anticanonists, who had expected a more rigid and diehard resistance. In fact, the cautions and alarms raised by Bloom, Hirsch, and others probably had more of an impact on the general public than on the academic community. Hirsch's idea of cultural literacy has become a part of popular culture itself, generating a small self-help industry to service those who desire to become certifiably literate. On the whole the recent changes in anthologies and syllabuses have been peaceful, piecemeal, and constructive, offering not only interesting new materials for study, but also a valuable series of new perspectives on the texts of the traditional canon and the ways in which we conceive and teach them.

That recent developments have not led to a significant subversion or destruction of the canon highlights two aspects of the process of canon formation. The first of these factors is that all human creations are subject to a kind of winnowing process that results from the erosive effects of time and the limits of human attention and memory. In the past, much of the winnowing was determined by accidents of history. Wars and natural disasters took their toll and what survived them was often as much a matter of chance as of the conscious preservation of the best. Who knows but that the greatest plays of the classical Greek theater were lost when the library of Alexandria burned down in 47 B.C.? In recent times, our technologies have made it possible to preserve more and more. Now, the limits of human attention have become a much more important aspect of the winnowing process.

Since we now seem to have much more control over what is preserved and how it is used, the way in which we conceptualize cultural value and significance is increasingly important. This will continue to make the canon an arena of ideological debate, and will inspire further heated arguments about the process of canon formation along with acceptance of the idea that the canon must be continually subject to change.

These discussions have also clarified a second aspect of the canon. Unlike the biblical canon, after which it was named, the literary and cultural canon never became a fixed and immutable body of texts. Studies in the history of humanistic education by Gerald Graff and Lawrence Levine have reinterpreted the specifics of this development and its significance. These studies show that humanistic education has repeatedly and drastically changed since its early nineteenth century beginnings. First there was an emphasis on work in classical languages that gave way to the study of Shakespeare and other earlier English writers. Then, early American and finally modern British and American literature entered the canon. In general, the literary canon and the conceptions of analysis and evaluation it implied changed quite drastically in each generation if not more often. The current struggle over the canon then is part of a long history of canonic transformation rather than an unprecedented attack on a long-established sacred tradition.

The new emphasis on popular culture and multiculturalism is turning out to be not so much an attack on the canon but part of its continuing revitalization. When I began teaching in the late 1950s, American cultural debate widely assumed that there was a great gulf between the traditional canon and modern mass culture. Recent changes in the idea of the canon have seriously questioned the validity of this distinction. Instead, in the second half of the twentieth century boundaries that many intellectuals once postulated between the traditional canon and popular culture, and between historical ethnic and national cultures and the new internationalizing culture of the mass media, have increasingly broken down. The new global popular culture may well have originally grown out of cultural imperialism, but it is now spreading with an impetus of its own through developing communications technology and the increasing influence of the Internet. Many people thought Marshall McLuhan a deluded enthusiast when he spoke of the "global village" but his ideas now seem prophetic.

In the end, if one tries to penetrate the haze of diatribe and argument surrounding the issues of canonicity and multiculturalism one finds a lot more smoke than fire. It may well be that this simply reflects the timidity and conservatism of college curricula and major publishers and that in the course of time anthologies and courses will change more radically. Other actors in the wings, such as computers and the World Wide Web, may further revolutionize humanistic education and our understanding of culture(s). However, I'm not sure that all these new theories and technologies will really change one fundamental reality, the limits of individual memory and attention. These limits make the passing on of culture a highly selective process. Perhaps computers can remember virtually everything and scan huge amounts of data with tremendous speed, but collecting data is not the same as understanding it. We human beings can only remember, learn, and understand a little bit in a lifetime. Many people have already commented about the problem of information overload and the need for new methods of controlling and processing the enormous amounts of information already available. If we are not to be buried in a landslide of data, we will somehow have to decide how to choose the very limited number of works we can hope to pass on as our cultural heritage.

Canons are a way of dealing with the fundamental distinction between what might be called the culture of the immediate present and the culture of permanence. Every area of human life, including popular culture, undergoes a process of selection and winnowing from which a few texts, ideas, and other cultural creations emerge with a relative degree of permanence. Even if we reject the idea that time is necessary to determine true excellence, the creation of a cultural heritage seems to reflect a deep-seated human need for some sort of continuity and identity over the generations, as well as the impossibility of each new generation starting from scratch. Throughout much of human history this process of selection has involved a lot of chance and accident. Today our capacity to record and preserve almost everything in some form or another means only that the cultural heritage will increasingly be shaped by another kind of chance and accident, the quirky limits of human attention. However, because texts are more likely to be preserved in some form, rather than destroyed altogether, we face the additional complexity of texts slipping in and out of the canon. Some will disappear forever but others will periodically go through a sort of cultural reediting—so, for example, modernist writers rediscovered the once nearly forgotten metaphysical poets and contemporary feminists have canonized several nineteenth-century woman writers. Inevitably this creates a much more fluid and continually changing definition of our heritage. Or to put it another way, our heritage has increasingly become not something handed on from on generation to another, but an arena in which many different forces contend to define what is most basic to the culture.

The canon, then, is a temporary and shifting codification, largely for pedagogical purposes, of the cultural heritage. When the culture was dominated by a particular hegemony, as was largely the case in America between the Civil War and World War II, the canon reflected that dominance and seemed fixed and limited. Today, American culture is characterized by much more interplay among different subcultural groups, and the canon itself has become looser, more flexible, and changeable. This has led some to argue that the canon should be abandoned altogether in favor of a curriculum that is completely open, or popular or multi-cultural or pluralistic or postcolonial or postmodern.

However, most multiculturalist or postmodernist curricular proposals are not really open, but imply the imposition of particular ideologies or theories. It's become an all-too-common practice to distinguish between ideologies you reject and those you believe in by calling the latter theories. These "theories" include feminism, postcolonialism, Afrocentrism, new historicism, and many other forms of "political correctness." But it seems to me just as ideological to teach a course on American literature dominated by Native American, African American, and feminist texts as to have a reading list centered on dead white New England writers. Though such courses may be useful correctives to the oversimplifications of the past, they impose new distortions of their own. Somehow the curriculum must be limited, and we must work out some coherent rationale for changing it.

We might try to respond to the ambiguity about the canon by developing a richer and more complex understanding of the way cultural heritages are formed. After all, this is in itself a significant part of popular culture. Actually as noted earlier the cultural heritage was never as fixed nor was the canon as inflexible as it is frequently assumed in current criticism to have been. In America, the canon has been in a constant state of flux. In addition, there has also been tension between the literary-philosophical canon which tends toward a transcultural humanistic vision and the powerful ideologies of national cultures—the American way of life, British Civilization, Deutsche Kultur, etc.—which tend to be much more ethnocentric and hegemonic.

Though there were periods of excessive rigidity when the curriculum lagged significantly behind new cultural developments, the embodiment of our cultural heritage in a canon has always been an ongoing process. Currently, that process has become increasingly subject to several different kinds of influence, which have made it much more complex and contested than ever before. We must examine these new pressures more carefully and try to understand them. This involves a fuller analysis and discussion of such relatively new demands as representativeness, the recognition of cultural archetypes, the affirmation of cultural pluralism and other values, which are currently considered important in the reformulation of the canon.

There's a final aspect of the relationship between popular culture and the canon which takes me back to that dedicated fan of pulp magazine covers at the first popular culture meeting. One problem with the canon is that the works in it tend to be distanced from us because the living cultural context in which they first appeared is not available to us. On the other hand, this distancing actually sets a highly creative process into motion insofar as it allows us to discover all kinds of new and complex meanings that remain hidden from us so long as the text only exists in its original cultural space. Most Elizabethan viewers must have perceived *Hamlet* as a rather strange and fascinating revenge tragedy, not seeing at all the many layers of psychological, moral, and philosophical meaning that later generations have discovered in the play. But canonizing texts also creates a kind of distance between them and later generations, which can, in the end, alienate future audiences. Because of this, a necessary major project of important literary and cultural movements since the Renaissance has been the reinterpretation and revitalization of the canon. The modernist movement struggled hard to give the cultural heritage a new birth by, as Ezra Pound put it, "making it new." This was clearly one of the major artistic and cultural purposes of those massively allusive modernist works like *The Waste Land, Ulysses,* Pound's *Cantos,* the paintings of Picasso, and the music of Igor Stravinsky. But the modernist renaissance ran its course and we now find ourselves in an era when young people seem increasingly distanced from and even suspicious of the works of the past. So do many younger critics and scholars and this feeling is probably one factor in the widespread criticism of the canon.

I do not believe that we should try to fix our cultural heritage in the pedagogical equivalent of bronze, but I am certainly against getting rid of it altogether. Our task as teachers is to help foster in young people both a critical understanding of and a sense of discovery and delight in the great works of the past; and I think that popular culture has a key part to play in this process. Insofar as they have known it at all, today's students have experienced through popular culture the immediacy, the excitement, the passion, the rush of understanding and the momentary sense of self-transcendence that are vital to the deep experience of any kind of true culture. We must help our students come to have this kind of experience with the works that constitute their cultural heritage. This is not an easy task and students can show an increasingly sophisticated and determined resistance to our attempts to make the canon live for them. However, one way of subverting and attacking this alienation is by creating a complex dialectic between popular culture and the canon.

Back in the 1960s when popular culture studies was developing, we used to talk about the need to make the humanities "relevant." However, the notion of relevance pervading that time was an oversimplified one that emphasized the translation of canonic works into contemporary social and political terms. In recent years this version of relevance has been still further straightjacketed into the contortions of "political correctness." Instead, we need to recognize that there are emotional and aesthetic aspects of "relevance" that are just as important and that have become badly attenuated. It is the excitement, the passion, and the sense of commitment associated with popular culture that we must struggle to recreate in connection with the canon. I'm not suggesting here that we carry out some kind of seduction by trying to persuade students to give up trash TV for Shakespeare. This is not only impossible but also deceptive. There are important ways in which the experience of popular culture is distinctive and can never be transplanted into works from the past and vice versa. But we do need to help our students see how these experiences are importantly connected. One cannot fully experience the culture of the past without referring it to the present. At the same time, the culture of the present is shallow and meaningless without a deeper sense of its roots in the past and its relationship to the more timeless world of the cultural heritage. As I see it, the ultimate justification of popular culture studies lies in the contribution it can make to the revitalization of our cultural heritage. Each of us will have our own ideas of how to accomplish this, but the most important thing is that we are all working toward an increasingly creative interplay between popular culture and a more rich and complex conception of the canon.

10

Formulas and Genre Reconsidered Once Again

The reader may well accuse me of not being able to make up my mind and find it intolerable to ramble through still more ruminations on the tricky relationships of formulas, genres, and cultures. I sympathize, but here they are. I may be deluded, but I think they do a better job of clarifying these issues than I have managed before.

—

In her recent paper on developing a more effective narrative theory of popular culture, Barbara Emrys suggests, correctly, I think, that the arbitrary association of the idea of formula with popular fiction has limited the more complex analysis of narrative as well as of popular culture.[1] As this kind of association was at the center of my 1969 essay on "The Concept of Formula in the Study of Popular Culture" I am, I suppose, partly responsible for this association, and, I must confess, I have spent a good deal of my own career trying to think myself beyond it.

As I now see it, the major problem with my original conception was that I defined formula as type or level of literature (i.e., the conventional vs. the original). By asserting that there could be something artistically valuable about formulaic popular literature, I was trying to escape from the high culture/mass culture paradigm that dominated the discussion

1. Emrys kindly sent me a manuscript of this paper.

of popular culture at the time I began my work and that was, I think, the right direction to be going in. However, I was still enough influenced by the idea of different levels or types of culture that it remained implicit in the way I talked about formulaic literature. As a result, I ended up with a real problem dealing with the whole issue of convention vs. originality that lay at the heart of my definition of formulas. Essentially I concluded that formulas were structures of conventions, while what we then called high culture, and are now more inclined to refer to somewhat less invidiously as "canonic literature," was most characterized by originality.

But even as I was writing "The Concept of Formula" I was dimly aware that Shakespeare makes as much use of conventions as a western or a detective story, and that the many of his plots are based on what were then conventional formulas. It's difficult to think of any kind of literature that doesn't have a formulaic aspect of some sort. Even such a unique masterpiece as James Joyce's *Ulysses* depends to a tremendous extent on literary formulas that it inverts, parodies, and plays with from beginning to end. Moreover, *Ulysses* itself established a novelistic structure that has become one of the most widespread formulas of the contemporary novel, that of the story that takes place during a very limited period of time but that nonetheless covers many years by presenting its narrative largely through memories, flashbacks, and other nonchronological devices.

Moreover, if we look at the kind of story that seems almost totally dependent on formulas, i.e., popular genres like the detective story, the western, the romance, the horror story, even there the writers that we most value are those who make their own distinctive uses of the formula or formulas in question. While addicts of a particular popular genre may tolerate a much higher degree of formulaic repetition, even they tend to be most interested in those writers who can be counted on for something unique. To speak for myself, while I have an extraordinary tolerance for ordinary detective stories I am always most content when I find a writer like James Lee Burke, Tony Hillerman, Reginald Hill, Sara Paretsky, Stuart Kaminsky, or Elizabeth George, who is able to do something creative and unique with the formulas of the mystery, and my view is evidently shared by many others since these are the writers whose work appears most frequently on bestseller lists.

Thus, it could be said that there are formulaic aspects to almost any sort of literature, just as there are probably aspects of artistry or creativity in the most tired of standardized romances or mystery stories. We may find neither that an aesthetic analysis of a Harlequin romance is particularly exciting, nor that the formulaic aspects of James Joyce are as interesting as other dimensions of his work, but it is still possible to make such analyses. In brief, I've concluded that formula is not characteristic of a particular level or type of literature, but a feature of all literature, and that to pay attention to formula is simply a specific way of reading and analyzing. Just as we can make an artistic analysis or a socio-cultural analysis of any work of art, so we can also make a formulaic analysis if we choose to do so.

But, is there any particular reason for approaching works through the idea of formula? At one point, I began to wonder whether the concept of formula was redundant since it seemed difficult to differentiate between formula and convention. Couldn't all the phenomena we were interested in under the heading of formula be subsumed under convention? On the other hand, there were other ways in which formula seemed equivalent to form and still others in which it meant much the same as "popular genre." Wouldn't things be clearer if we simply stopped using the word "formula" and based our analyses on ideas of convention, form, and genre, as literary critics had traditionally done?

This puzzled me for some time, but eventually I began to see that however slippery the concept of formula might be and however ambiguous the way we used it was, it still had an important place for it stressed one aspect of literature and culture that was extremely important and that was not quite present in the concepts of convention and genre. To explain this let me develop an analogy with cooking. When you're going to make a dish, you can begin with two things. You may begin with an idea of the kind of thing you want—a pasta dish, steak and potatoes, salad, a stew, etc.—or you may start with a group of ingredients that you happen to have on hand. In the first scenario, the kind of dish you are trying to cook up will require you to assemble certain ingredients; in the second, the ingredients will dictate the kinds of dishes you might make. This relationship between kind of dishes and ingredients constitute the genres and conventions of cookery in a particular culture at a certain time. For example, once in America, it was unheard of to make pasta with anything but hamburger and tomato sauce. Now pasta can be made with all sorts of things—vegetables, seafood, chicken, etc.—that would have been considered beyond the pale thirty years ago. The kind of dish is, in other words, analogous to the genre, while the cooking conventions relate to the relationship between kind of dish and ingredients and among ingredients.

But you still need a recipe, or a set of rules, for combining the appropriate ingredients to produce the dish you have selected. The same ingredients can be put together in a lot of different ways and still end up as pasta, or steak and potatoes, or stew. But a specific recipe is necessary so one turns to cookbooks or one's own experience with this kind of dish. This is the formula and it gives us the rules for making a certain particular dish. Now if we apply this analogy to literature, the kinds are the many different genres, ranging from broad archetypal constructions like tragedy and comedy to more culturally specific genres like the realistic novel, the situation comedy, the romance, the detective story, and the western. The conventions are the ingredients, possible patterns of character, plot, theme, setting, etc. that are associated with various genres. The formulas are the patterns within the genres, such as revenge tragedies, bildungsromans, hard-boiled detective stories, or gunfighter westerns, that have become widely recognized through their frequent use in many different examples of the genre. Most major genres have a considerable number of formulas and often give rise to new formulas for a variety of reasons. In the case of the detective story, for example we have such formulas as the classical story, the hard-boiled story, the police procedural, and the inverted narrative. In addition, a number of other formulas have grown up around certain themes of detection—mysteries involving food, for example, or animal detectives. These formulas proliferate in any genre that lasts over a significant period of time, and yet they continue to bear a certain basic resemblance to one another such that we are inclined to see them as part of a definable genre.

Once we have recognized this we can see that there are a number of reasons why we need to concern ourselves with formulas. For one thing, we probably wouldn't be able to appreciate many aspects of any particular fiction without a kind of implicit knowledge of the formulas the author is playing with. This is obvious in the case of popular genres, like the mystery story, where our awareness of the way in which the author creatively plays with the character of the detective, the criminal, the crime, and the elements of mystery investigation constitute one of our primary sources of delight. And this is true of so-called serious or canonic fiction as well. *Ulysses* wouldn't be the same book for us if we weren't at all aware of the many literary conventions and formulas that Joyce so wittily interrogates throughout his masterpiece. For example, take the so-called Nausicaa episode in which the story is partly told through the mind of the Dublin girl Gerty MacDowell in a style that is a brilliant pastiche of the sentimental and romantic fictions that were and still are so pervasive in modern European and American culture. Or, to take another example, one reason why Shakespeare's comedies don't seem as funny to us today as they must have to his contemporaries is that we don't know many of the formulas on which they depend. One of the most important jobs that traditional literary scholars used to perform for us was one of recovering the major literary formulas and conventions of earlier periods so that we could better understand and enjoy the literature of those times.

Another reason that formulas are important is that they can serve as a sort of shorthand for speeding up the communication between writer and reader. If he or she plugs into a well-known formula for character and action, the writer often does not need to explain it at great length to the reader. This is because formulas work by reflecting values and assumptions shared by a community of readers within a culture. For example, the formula of the hard-boiled detective story calls for an isolated individualistic investigator encountering social corruption in the form of secret alliances among criminals, the police, and the social elite. It clearly embodies the American myth of individualism, which expresses suspicion of large concentrations of political power at the same time that it encourages individuals to create such concentrations. We find a similar pattern echoed in the formula of the gunfighter western. Many American literary formulas from the nineteenth and early twentieth centuries gave fictional manifestation to the racist and sexist ideologies of that time as many recent analysts have shown. A good example here is the Indian captivity or Indian attack western in which the Indians are revealed to be lustful savages determined to rape white women and the women are shown as having to learn that they are vulnerable and dependent on strong males. This racist ideological formula runs through the history of the American western genre from its beginnings in the late seventeenth-century Indian captivity narrative, through Cooper's *Leatherstocking Tales,* down to such twentieth century movies as John Ford's *Stagecoach* and *The Searchers.* A similar formula frequently appeared in the Confederate romance, a popular type of historical novel that culminated in the great bestseller of the 1930s and 40s, Margaret Mitchell's *Gone With the Wind.* In this formula African Americans occupy a place analogous to Native Americans, in the west but women are still represented as dependent on men.

In addition, in response to changing cultural values, writers can try to undercut existing formulas, thus creating new kinds of fiction. In many westerns of the later twentieth century, such as *Little Big Man* and *Dances With Wolves,* the Indian captivity formula was turned on its head and made to show how the Indian cultures were morally superior in many ways to the white savages who were in the process of exterminating them. In *Gone With the Wind,* Margaret Mitchell largely followed the formula of the Confederate romance, but she changed the portrayal of the dependent Southern belle by creating, in the figure of Scarlett O'Hara, a woman who becomes strongly independent. Significantly, however, Mitchell found it necessary to end her novel with hints of a possible return of her character to the role of subservient female.

Because literary formulas are so thoroughly imbued with the patterns of value and belief shared by their audiences, their critical ideological analysis has proved to be a particularly effective tool in revealing how pervasively racism and sexism have permeated American culture in the past. Such analysis can also be helpful in comparing cultures and in tracing changes in cultural ideologies over the course of history. Some of the analyses of this kind published in recent years have been largely limited to the castigation of racism and sexism in popular literature, but not all (and it would be a shame if the critical analysis of formulas were confined to this purpose).

Formulaic analysis can serve another important purpose by articulating the artistic and creative aspects of particular writers and works. The way in which outstanding writers like Raymond Chandler and James Lee Burke or great film directors like John Ford or Howard Hawks use the formulas of the genres they are working in to create powerful works of art can be most effectively explored by comparing their works with others making use of the same formulas in a less original and exciting fashion. Thus formulaic analysis has aesthetic as well as social implications and further development of the methods of this kind of analysis would be extremely helpful.

For the sake of clarity we must often treat the analysis of formulas as structures isolated from the cultural background that creates them. However, in order to synthesize formulaic analysis with other kinds of historical and cultural investigations we need to understand the cultural aspects of formula creation more fully. Formulas are created within a cultural matrix that results from the interactions of writers, audiences, and publishers or producers and changes in media. These give rise to new formulas that may in turn lead to the formation of new cultural patterns having a significant impact on the values and perceptions of certain cultural groups. Studying this dialectic between formulas and culture makes for a very complex kind of criticism and involves much more than ideological analysis, though that is certainly part of it. Just as the French developed so many other kinds of critical theories and methodologies in the later twentieth century, French literary historians and cultural sociologists created the most complex studies of cultural dialectics of this sort. Paul Bleton's remarkable *Western, France: La place de L'Ouest dans l'imaginaire français* examines the interplay among cultural ideologies, changes in audiences, and the different characteristics of changing media as they affected French versions of the American Western and led to the emergence of different literary formulas. Canadian scholar Christine Bold tried a similar less complex analysis of American literary westerns in *Selling the Wild West*. Difficult as it is, however, this kind of analysis is extremely important for it is the most significant way in which the study of literary formulas can be effectively synthesized with other disciplines like history and sociology. Such analyses, along with comparative studies of literary formulas in different cultures, some of them probably requiring collaborative efforts of scholars from different countries, will be one of the most exciting areas in formulaic studies in the coming years.

These reflections may help clarify the perennially confusing relationship between formulas and genres; though I fear areas where the division remains murky will always exist. Clearly, genres are the largest of literary classes or archetypes. They can be virtually universal, playing some role in most historical cultures (e.g., tragedy, comedy, and tales of adventure or of encounters with the unknown). Or genres can be defined in more historically and culturally limited ways (e.g., westerns, detective stories, romances, sentimental novels, horror stories, or realistic novels). To some extent, but probably not altogether genres in this class can be subsumed under archetypal genres. Thus, for example, westerns like *The Last of the Mohicans* or *The Gunfigher* can be seen as forms of tragedy, but that would certainly not be true of all westerns, some of which are more like romances, epics, or even comedies. In other words, historically defined genres can contain aspects of more universal archetypes (how many times, for examples, have we seen popular cultural heroes like the western John Wayne or James Bond compared to classical mythic figures?) but they may not. Despite the frequent comparison with Oedipus, is there really any classical genre that contains the detective story?

Genres will eventually give rise to a large number of formulas. So we understand such different structures as Indian captivity tales, cavalry versus Indian tales, and gunfighter stories as forms of the western, perceiving them as formulas within the genre of the western. These formulas are specific recipes for characters, plot types, themes etc. within a genre that seem to have a particular resonance for still more limited times and places. Cooper's *Leatherstocking Tales* is clearly an important part of the western genre, but requires massive changes to work for today's audiences as in the case of the successful Michael Mann version of *The Last of the Mohicans*. Thus, many particular formulas can be subsumed into a larger genre though it's hard to define just where the boundary line between formula and genre lies. Sometimes the formulas spawned by a genre become so different from the main lines of the genre that they come to constitute a new genre. This is what happened, for example, when Edgar Allan Poe took the formulas of the gothic story and turned them upside down, creating the modern detective story. In general, if a literary pattern is clearly one way in which a larger grouping of such structures can be rendered, we are probably talking about formulas in their relationship to genres.

How formulas arise and flourish and what they mean to the cultural groups employing them are questions that involve the analysis of the cultural dialectics of genres or formulas. This is, as we have seen, a very complex kind of investigation that only a few scholars have been able to carry out. Bleton does it brilliantly in the case of the French western, but the enormous mass of research he carried out to be able to do this is daunting. Fortunately there are many simpler studies that can be effectively carried out if we keep the problem of this larger synthesis in mind. In this way, our narrower studies may, taken together, gradually form a larger synthesis that will increasingly offer useful insights into the complex history of genres and formulas.

For example, the aesthetic analysis of formulas, which we have already touched on in several ways, can be effective within a more limited area and can help us understand the evolution of formulas. The important thing to remember is that these different modes of analysis are all connected to the way in which we perceive (and conceive) things. All these analytical concepts represent approaches to interpretation and analysis, not levels of literature. Thus, one can just as well analyze formulas in "serious" novels as one can "originality" in popular genre fictions. Analytical approaches are modes of reception among many, and which ones we use depend on the different social and cultural matrices within which we, or whatever readers we are talking about, are functioning. A group of romance readers as studied by Janice Radway brings a very different set of reception assumptions to a romance than a male

critic, for example, even if the latter is trying to be sympathetically responsive. Our awareness of the relativism of the critical view is perhaps
about seventy-five years behind the relativity of physics, but it may represent the most important transformation of the theory of criticism in
this century.

Section Two

The Role of Violence in Popular Culture

11

God's Country, Las Vegas, and the Gunfighter: Differing Visions of the West

The American West, a journal sponsored by the Western Historical Association, kindly gave some of my early thoughts on the western a hearing. This article appeared in 1972, two years after the first publication of *The Six-Gun Mystique,* and it represented one of my early attempts after *SGM* to place the western in a cultural and historical perspective. The conclusion clearly predates the major decline of the western as a popular genre that began in the 1980s, though most of the other observations still seem valid to me.

≋

From the very beginning of American history, the West was an idea to conjure with. Since the first Englishman stepped ashore on a new continent, the West has not only been an important historical reality, but a landscape of the imagination, a setting for symbolic dramas that continue to preoccupy many of our most creative as well as our most popular novelists, dramatists, and filmmakers. And the imaginative role of the West, important as it has been in the thinking of westerners and those we commonly think of as western writers, has also generated a vital set of symbols that fascinate easterners as well. In fact, easterners who had never been west of the Mississippi, or in some cases, the Hudson, made many of the most important statements of the myth of the West. Moreover, the American West has always held a fascination for Europeans, from the French Chateaubriand and Gustave Aimard and the English Mayne Reid and the German Karl May in the nineteenth century to the late twentieth-century Italian Sergio Leone and the Japanese Akira Kurosawa. In the twentieth century the lure of the West has cast its spell in Asia and Africa as well, becoming the basis of what may be one of the first truly international popular mythologies.[1]

What is the nature of this mythology, and why has its power over us persisted as the specific historical experiences on which it is based slip further into the past? I'm sure that no single factor can account for this long-term fascination. Many scholars have pointed out the similarities between the western story and the archetypal myth of the hero that has appeared in so many different cultures. Certainly figures like the Lone Ranger with his mysterious origins, his strange disguise, his close association with the spirit of nature, and his symbolic passage through death reflects the pattern of god-heroes like Gilgamesh, Odysseus, Siegfried, and even Christ. Therefore, in some way the western hero partakes of an archetypal power that reflects a seemingly universal human need for heroes of a certain kind. Others have emphasized the violence in the western myth, attributing its fascination to an instinctual or cultural proclivity for vicarious indulgence in aggression and destruction. Still another explanation points to the great dramatic potential of the western story, suggesting that the kind of powerful contrasts and exciting movement built into the western setting provides a compelling background for heady stories, particularly when presented through the visual dimension of the film medium. I am sure that many factors play an important role in the twentieth-century popularity of the western myth. As a result, any complete account of the imaginative functions of the Wild West would include a variety of explanations, some of them overlapping.

One of these factors is certainly the western myth's role in our imaginations as a myth of America or as a set of imaginative statements about the meaning of America. To begin with, the myth of the West is, like

1. Only toward the end of the twentieth century did the myth of the West seem to be losing its power for many Americans. It still remains an important force in Europe, however. There are French fast-draw clubs, German reenactments of Native American cultures, and Wild West theme parks in many countries including a section in Denmark's Legoland presided over by a many times life-size statue of Sitting Bull made entirely out of Legos. Paul Bleton's excellent new book *Western, France* traces the extraordinary pervasiveness of the French interest in the American West.

many classic myths, a story about the founding of a new order. Whether novel, film, work of history, or political speech, any embodiment of the western myth has as its essential backdrop the vision of the pioneers leaving behind an older settled society and moving across the wilderness in search of a new and better life. The myth of the West is the myth of America in this very special sense: that men can leave their history behind and father a higher human possibility on a virgin continent. The power of this imaginative vision, often referred to as the American dream, has survived any sense that there is no escape from history. It's also still competing with our increasing awareness that the European approach to the New World was less analogous to marriage with a virgin than to the rape and murder of a neighbor's wife. We are still struggling to come to terms with this new awareness of our tragic betrayal of the American dream, and this struggle is reflected in the guilt-ridden and ironic undertones of many contemporary treatments of the western myth, such as Thomas Berger and Arthur Penn's *Little Big Man.*

The most cursory look at the great range of statements and actions in which Americans have expressed their feelings about the West makes it evident that it has meant many different things to many different people. Yet I feel that most of these diverse visions can be understood as expressions of two general themes that, as it happens, are in fundamental conflict with each other. The first is the idea of the West as a place where men can construct a new and better society, which by virtue of its superior order and environment will avoid all the mistakes and evils of past history. This might be called the conception of the West as God's country. The other great theme of our western imaginings is in many respects the very contrary of the first: it is the dream of the West as escape, the perennial safety valve not of Frederick Jackson Turner but of Huckleberry Finn. This version of the myth of the West envisions a territory where one can flee from the constraints and responsibilities of civilization, to become free, savage, and natural.

These two grand visions of the true meaning of the West have manifested themselves in one form or another since the beginning of American history. Probably, as a number of scholars have suggested, we inherited them from European hopes and dreams about the millennium even before the discovery of the New World. The conception of the West as God's country has taken many different forms throughout our history. Its first major manifestation was in the seventeenth-century Puritan planning for a godly community in the Massachusetts Bay colony. From that time to the present, the hope of founding a purified religious community in the West has been a continuous thread in our history. It inspired the evangelical migrations of the eighteenth century, the religious utopias and theocratic colonies of the nineteenth century, including the great Mormon movement into the desert, and the California communes of the twentieth century. But this theme has appeared in many other guises as well. One is the myth of the West as ideal agrarian order or garden of the world that Henry Nash Smith analyzes in *Virgin Land* as so compelling a dream of mid-nineteenth century Americans. Another is the vision of a purified renaissance in the West embodied in the Great White City of the Columbian Exposition of 1893 where as one commentator put it, "hither had leaped, across the centuries, . . . all that was beautiful and sacred in the Bride of the Adriatic . . . a Venice resurrected from its crimes and glorified." Furthermore, the twentieth century suburban impulse was, as Richard Sennett suggests in *The Uses of Disorder*, motivated to a considerable extent by the desire to form homogeneous, purified communities apart from the corruption and disorder of our cities. Perhaps the rhetoric used to justify some of our disastrous ventures in the Far East like the Vietnam War reflects this long-standing impulse to move westward in order to create new and more moral communities transcending the errors and evils of history. The vision of God's country in the West runs deep in our culture. Its primary symbol is the morally purified community, redeemed from the mistakes of the past, and set in a hospitable, natural environment where men and women can lead forever a harmonious and happy life. The visual image of the small town often embodies this hope, and thus, it is no accident that the most common setting for westerns is the small frontier settlement, which promises to develop into just such a town if only the forces of disorder and corruption can be purged.

Where the vision of God's country in the West stresses moral order, purification, and a settled society, the vision of the West as "Injun territory" has always seemed equally compelling to our imaginations. Its central motifs are, on the contrary, escape, liberation, freedom from civilized morality along with natural, impulsive behavior, often with strong overtones of violence and eroticism. We apparently need this kind of image of the West just as much as we need the vision of it as God's country. As we look across the history and legends of the West we find that almost every version of the purified community can be paired with an antithetical image of the West as liberation. Every Puritan community seems to have its Merrymount. Similarly, in the late twentieth century, the image of the West as the last bastion of morality and democracy in a corrupt society is paralleled by the countersymbol of Las Vegas, the great American place of liberation from conventional morality. In Las Vegas, one can do openly that which is morally and legally outlawed in most of the rest of America.

The countersymbol to the West as God's country, the settled town with its church, schoolhouse, thriving ranches and farms, was the mythical Indian and the idea of the West as "territory." The mythical Indian was a symbol of natural power and freedom. He was a perennial symbolic certifier of the potency and healthfulness of every sort of nineteenth century medicine and food and the fantasy alter ego of adolescent Americans. At the same time those Americans in actual contact with the Indian seemed to be mainly dedicated to his expropriation and extermination. He represented the ultimate degree of spontaneous action, mobility, aggression, and erotic potency. He was the "fate worse than death" lurking behind the bushes for all pioneer women. It is characteristic of this mythical role played by the Indian that he usually appeared in the popular literature of the nineteenth century as either a noble or a vicious savage and was rarely conceived as a member of a complex culture. In fact, one important sign of change in the western of the 1960s and 1970s was the extent to which the Indian culture as distinguished from Indians as actors in some drama of chase or attack became an important element in the story. Certainly one reason why whites were largely unable to deal with the Indian in a more humane way was the degree to which they projected onto him the wildness of their own fantasies of liberation. It is difficult to carry on a dialogue with a fantasy.

The Indian was not the only figure of liberation associated with the Wild West. Outlaws like Billy the Kid, Jesse James, the Dalton brothers, and Sam Bass also became major western heroes. Along with the glorification of outlaws, there developed a counterimage to the purified town of God's country—the wide-open cow town or mining settlement where the saloon, not the church or the school, was the center of action.

The contrast between God's country and Injun territory as images of the West can also be seen in the legends that grew up around particular western groups, such as the Mormons. In their own view, the Mormons were the ultimate embodiment of the vision of the West as redemption for the purified community. Yet it seemed almost inevitable that for much of the American public, the Mormons became a fascinating symbol of untrammeled violence and eroticism. In *Roughing It*, Mark Twain is clearly a bit bemused by the discrepancy between what he has expected and what he actually sees in Salt Lake City, but he finds it quite difficult to abandon cherished fantasies of Mormon massacres and lascivious polygamy. Other writers preferred to keep the imagining of violence and lechery unqualified like Zane Grey in *Riders of the Purple Sage*, or, one might cite a classic example of the transatlantic potency of this vision of the West in Conan Doyle's treatment of the Mormons in *A Study in Scarlet*.

The Wild West as escape from the moral and legal restraints of civilization has been counterpointed in a rather complex way by another vision of the West as liberation. This could be called the Walden impulse after its richest literary expression in Thoreau's great work. The Walden impulse is not so much a vision of escape but of transcendence and regeneration based on a direct relationship with nature. From James Fenimore Cooper's portrayals of the natural nobility of Leatherstocking through the early twentieth century wilderness ideas that inspired the creation of our national system of parks and recreation areas the Walden impulse has been a vital component of American visions of the West. This impulse still appears in the popularity of camping and backpacking. On the surface this appears to be a very different mythical tradition from the one that runs from the cow town and mining camp down to contemporary Las Vegas. The Las Vegas syndrome presents legitimated indulgence in activities normally considered sinful or illegal. If we consider the ambience of contemporary Las Vegas as the ultimate fulfillment of this idea, it would appear to be the antithesis of nature, a totally artificial environment in which even the diurnal cycle of day and night is overcome. One goes outdoors in Las Vegas only to move from one hermetically sealed and timeless casino to another. The Walden impulse, on the other hand, seems to be a quest for lost simplicity and innocence that can only be found by immersing oneself in the out-of-doors. Yet, despite these fundamental differences, there is an ambiguous connection between wilderness and wildness. Both represent escape from the conventional and the ordinary. Both involve a quest for spontaneity and freedom of action, for the kind of excitement and risk that is absent from the settled and restrained life of the well-ordered community. Because of the curious relationship between these divergent images of liberation in the West they are often combined in western legend. It may be difficult to imagine Henry David Thoreau playing the wheel at Caesar's Palace, but at a more popular level our myth of the cowboy contains elements from both Walden and Las Vegas. The cowboy is a figure who spends most of his time in communion with the wilderness and animals. His code of courage and loyalty and his love for the outdoors represents a morality of natural simplicity and innocence that transcends the artificialities of civilization. Yet, the cow town, the saloon, the gambler and the dance-hall girl are also a vital part of the cowboy myth. His goal, after the heroic passage of the cattle drive, is to be the hardest drinking and fighting and wenching man in Dodge City and Abilene, though somehow he is able to indulge in these conventional sins without losing his natural purity and innocence. Today this patterns recurs in the stream of campers, many of whom work their way from camp to camp in specially designed vehicles until, having played at Walden, they arrive in Las Vegas and the games become blackjack, roulette, and burlesque.

Just as the cowboy unites in his mythic persona and actions the Walden impulse and the fantasy of escape from law and social convention, the western story has always in its richest and most successful versions sought a synthesis of the conflicting visions of God's country and Injun territory. As it took shape in the popular imagination through stories, Wild West shows, radio, movies, and finally TV, the western story developed those central symbols of dramatic antithesis expressing the conflicting images of the purified community and the liberated individual: town and wilderness, pioneers and Indians, settlers and outlaws. And, as these antithetical symbols moved inevitably toward their explosive conflict, there emerged the figure of the heroic and reluctant gunfighter whose role was to create the purified community by purging the denizens of Indian territory, whether outlaws or Indians. But the gunfighter's shootout was a complex and paradoxical act. Though it mythically brought into being the redeemed community it was in itself a supreme act of individualistic aggression. Around this ambiguous heroic act, the western legend, story, and film evolved.

The legend of our first true western hero, Daniel Boone, clearly illustrates the paradoxical relationship between the West as new community and as escape from society. Boone occupied the ironic position that western heroes were to find themselves in time after time: a leader in the settlement of Kentucky, he led the pioneers across the Cumberland Gap. However, once the new community had grown up and the territory was pacified and settled, Boone himself found that he could not stand it, and lit out for the wilderness. At least, that is the way the Boone legend goes and we are not concerned here with whatever actual and probably more complex motives led Boone to leave Kentucky. Boone's first and greatest literary avatar, Cooper's Leatherstocking, finds himself in precisely the same situation. Though he uses his skills in violence to help the pioneers clear out the Indians, there is no place for him in the new community. Like Boone, he keeps on moving West until his age at last overtakes him.

These early versions of the western hero figure indicate the beginnings of an imaginative struggle to at once affirm the distinctive ideas of the purified community and of individual liberation while still establishing some unity between them. But the unity remained problematic. In fact, for Cooper, it became more and more so. From his first written Leatherstocking tale, *The Pioneers* (1823), to the final *Deerslayer* (1841) the sense of irreconcilable conflict between the new community and the values of the open wilderness life grows deeper and deeper. At the end of *The Pioneers,* the Leatherstocking's protégé, young Oliver Edwards, has become domesticated and has been integrated into the leadership of the new settlement, which has been purged of disruptive conflicts and is clearly on the way to becoming an ideal social order. Though Leatherstocking chooses in the end to return to the wilderness, this is not so much a function of conflict between the values of the settlement and of the wilderness, but rather the result of the fact that "the hero has become too old to change his ways. In *The Deerslayer,* however, things have gone sour in the settlement. The new community has become perverted and, in defending the pioneers, the Leatherstocking feels almost like a murderer. His flight from civilization has increasingly taken on the quality of a moral stance, while Cooper's view of the advance of settlement has become darker and more pessimistic. For him, the ultimate reconciliation of the new American community and the free individual had become increasingly questionable.

In many ways, the evolution of the western film in the twentieth century parallels this development of Cooper's Leatherstocking saga, though for different reasons. The western film came together in the early twentieth century essentially out of a combination of the traditional spectacle of the Wild West show and the literary western romances of men like Owen Wister, Emerson Hough, and Zane Grey. Up until the 1930s, the structure of the western typically involved a regeneration and purification of the community and a domestication and integration of the hero after he had destroyed the forces of anarchy and savagery in the climax. In Wister's *The Virginian* of 1903, more than any other work the origin of the modem western, the cowboy hero is caught between his individual code of honor, which requires him to face the villain Trampas in a shootout, and his eastern schoolmarm sweetheart's ideals of law and order. She tells him that if he meets Trampas, she will never speak to him again. Fortunately, however, it turns out that her love for the Virginian is greater than her commitment to these conventional notions. When she actually sees him in danger her heart takes charge of her head. And because Trampas is a rustler and the rustler gangs have corrupted the legal machinery, the Virginian's action is actually a purification of the community. Thus, everything ends happily with a final integration of the liberated individual into the purified community. This purging of the community and domestication of the wild hero became the basic subjects of W. S. Hart and Zane Grey, the two most popular western creators of the early twentieth century.

In harmonizing our conflicting western myths in this way, the western novel and film of the early twentieth century was, I think, in tune with the upsurge of moral optimism that seemed to be shared by much of the American public during this period of confident progressivism. It seems appropriate that Wister dedicated his *Virginian* to Theodore Roosevelt, for that dashing president was not only famous as a lover of the West, but the novel can be interpreted as a progressive parable in which courageous individual leadership drives the rascals out and regenerates the community. In this way, the spirit and the code of the West could be seen as pointing the right way for the effete and decadent East. This particular version of the western myth became something of a specialty for Zane Grey. His novels are filled with tired, jaded Easterners—mainly attractive and wealthy young ladies who are restored to moral and spiritual health and discover the true meaning of love—through their encounter with a wild westerner. By the end of the story these two are ready to march off hand in hand into the sunset, prepared to found the purified community. It is not too hard to see in these stories a popular romantic version of the Turner thesis, which also hypothesized that the western experience stimulated a continual moral and political regeneration of the East.

But this vibrantly optimistic feeling about the moral future and rich human possibility of American life was deeply shaken by many factors in the late twenties, thirties, and forties. If it was to survive, the western had to develop a new kind of imaginative orientation. It not only continued to flourish but also, in the late 1930s, entered into what we will probably view in retrospect as its greatest period. This is a testimony to how deeply the images of the West had become meaningful to the public as an expression of something important about America.

The new version of the western was foreshadowed by the emergence in the 1930s of the Lone Ranger. In spite of the fact that the Lone

Ranger was essentially a creation for children and greatly resembled certain traditional dime novel figures like Deadwood Dick, there was an important new emphasis in the legend of the Lone Ranger. In a more sophisticated form, this new theme would become increasingly significant in the great classic westerns of John Ford, Howard Hawks, Anthony Mann, and other major western filmmakers of the forties and early fifties. Though he was all good and his enemies were all bad and though he always acted as the ally of the pioneer community—the man who brought law and order to the West by purging the community of evildoers—the Ranger remained curiously isolated and separated from the community. His symbolic garb as outlaw and his penchant for disguise were perhaps perennial features of popular folklore. However, in the case of the Lone Ranger they symbolized a self-elected separation from the pioneer community. When the chips were down, the Ranger evidently preferred the company of Tonto and Silver, and at the end of each adventure he lit out for the territory. No doubt this was a very convenient device for keeping a serial going, but it also suggested that audience no longer preferred to see their western heroes finally integrated into the regenerated community. This ambiguous relationship between western hero and the pioneer community he was called on to save became more and more the dominant subject of the serious westerns of the forties and fifties. From the great era of the cowboy hero exemplified in the Virginian, the figure of the melancholy and isolated gunfighter became increasingly the center of the western film. And it was usually the gunfighter's fate that after he had carried through the shootout, there was no longer a place for him in the community.

The final confrontation between the hero and some savage, outlaw, rustler, or land baron who represents the West as liberation from moral and social restraint became an increasingly poignant as well as a violent moment. In casting his lot with the redeemed community, the hero was also destroying someone who stood for an important side of his own nature. For the first three decades of the twentieth century, the ambiguous nature of this moment was less evident in the popular western. The Virginian killed his former associates, got his eastern schoolmarm, and settled down to become a leader of the redeemed community. The reformed gunfighter of W. S. Hart, Zane Grey, and Max Brand typically purged the town of outlaws, burned the saloon, and became happily domesticated. But the accumulating crises of the twentieth century made Americans more and more uncertain of the meaning of the American dream; the central symbols of the western became darker and more complex. The purified community of pioneers became the hypocritical, corrupt, and mendacious townspeople of *High Noon*, the helpless farmers of *Shane*, or the narrow-minded ladies of the law and order league in John Ford's *Stagecoach*. These townspeople are always in need of the heroic individual, but when he appears and reluctantly saves them, they have no real place for him. Instead of becoming one of the pioneers, the typical western hero since the forties is either destroyed or finds that even his heroic success is a kind of defeat.

The demise of the western as a primary American art form has been often prophesied, but it has always managed to revitalize itself by discovering new cultural meanings for the great dramatic triangle of pioneers, outlaws, and gunfighter heroes. The western today is clearly a mythical form in search of a new set of cultural meanings. The dialectic of social redemption and individual freedom grounding the popular western has given way to a more enigmatic and pessimistic view of the meaning of America. If anything the vision of the West that dominates such recent films as *Little Big Man, Soldier Blue, Bad Company,* and *The Wild Bunch* is almost a reversal of the traditional moral universe. In these films, it is the pioneers who are corrupt and savage and who bring unrestrained violence and destructiveness to the wilderness. Many western fans are unhappy with these new trends in the western, yet if the myth is to remain a vital one, it cannot simply continue to repeat the old patterns. In an age when the vision of America has changed as drastically as our view of the American dream seems to have been transformed in the last two decades, the western must confront our new understanding of ourselves. It must somehow begin to articulate and explore the conflicts of value and meaning that now dominate our lives. If not, it will become at long last, a truly dead myth, living only in the flickering half-light of nostalgic television reruns.

12

Myths of Violence in American Popular Culture

This essay appeared in *Critical Inquiry* in 1975. It explores the idea that violence is embedded in several different mythical patterns in American culture.

⇒

One of the "big issues" of the late 1960s was the question of violence in the mass media. Actually public concern about the portrayal of violence and crime in the media rises and falls in a distinctive cycle. The agitation usually reaches its peak in a time of considerable social upheaval and in response to the emergence of a new popular genre centering on violence and crime. In connection with the general clamor, new scientific studies purport to show a definite causal connection between violence in the media and criminal behavior. Moral pressure groups of various sorts pick the issue up and there is an outbreak of censorship episodes, prosecutions, and legislative inquiries. Finally, two developments usually lead to a lessening of tension and, for a time, the public agitation dies down. First, the medium under attack announces with great éclat a program of self-regulation resulting at least temporarily in a reduction in the level of violent content or in a more conventionally acceptable mode of presentation of violent themes. Second, a further series of scientific inquiries are carried out that cast some doubt on the causal claims of the earlier studies. These suggest that the relationship between the media portrayal of violence and violent behavior is more complex than was thought and cannot be understood in terms of a simple cause-effect equation. These two developments tend to defuse the issue until it is raised in relation to a new generic development. The attack on the gangster film in the 1930s, the agitation about horror comics in the 1950s, and the concern about television violence in the 1960s exemplified this cycle. The discussion will doubtless break out again when new developments in the representation of violence appear.

Like many big issues, such as corruption in government, about which the public becomes agitated from time to time, the discussion of media violence has been frustratingly repetitive in its cyclical character. The same issues are aired over and over again, while new versions of "expert" testimony lead to the same ambiguous conclusions as before. [In 2001 as I reread this, the cycle seems to be well underway again particularly in response to new forms of violence available through the Internet and on video games. Socially, the spread of violence to the suburbs, to schools, and workplaces is a kind of upheaval that has stimulated a new wave of public concern. For a time it seemed as if this new wave might actually focus attention where it belongs—on the nearly universal availability of firearms in America (see the essay "Violence and Apple Pie" later in this collection). However, there are already signs that new research will draw attention away from this to the "media." The National Rifle Association is happy to blame our frequent outburst of meaningless violence on something other than the ready availability of guns.]

The apparent failure to "prove" the effects of represented violence is at least partly due to the way this "issue" has been formulated. I would like to try to develop an approach to the problem of violence and literature that may enable us to gain some new insights into the significance of this complex phenomenon. The chief difficulty with most social and psychological studies of violence[1] lies in their assumption that violence

1. In 1975 the most useful and provocative brief survey and critique of studies of media violence and their theoretical assumptions was André Gluckmann, *Violence on the Screen*. The 1930s agitation, which focused particularly on the impact of the newly popular gangster films and that led eventually to a new formulation of the motion picture production code, was accompanied by the first major studies of the impact of film, a series of investigations supported by the Payne Fund. These were reported in a number of books and summarized—quite inaccurately as Garth Jowett points out in a recent review of a reprint edition of the Payne Fund Studies—in Henry James Forman's Our *Movie Made Children*. The Payne Fund studies and other early research into the impact of media violence were exhaustively and rather devastatingly criticized by Mortimer J. Adler

is essentially a simple act of aggression that can be treated outside of a more complex moral and dramatic context. This may be the case with news reports of war, murder, assault, and other forms of violent crime, but it is certainly not a very adequate way to treat the fictional violence of a western, a detective story, or a gangster saga. It is true that one can count and catalog the number of violent acts that occur in a day or a week of television and produce distressing statistics about the number of murders and assaults per minute on the typical television show. One can, like the redoubtable Dr. Wertham, amass specific instances where a young person has imitated or thinks he has imitated an act of violence he or she saw on television. However in doing this we should not forget that it can also be said without much fear of contradiction that the literary work that has directly caused more violence in the history of Western civilization than any other is the Bible. One can also construct laboratory experiments in which various groups are shown short films of violent acts and demonstrate that in certain circumstances this experience will cause further aggressive behavior.[2] With procedures such as this, the evidence of a correlation between media violence and aggressive behavior becomes more and more persuasive. But do such studies tell us anything more than that this is a violent age and that there is probably some connection between the violence of actuality and the presence of represented or play violence throughout our culture?

However, the degree to which people may imitate acts of violence or be stimulated to aggressive behavior of their own by an overdose of

---

in his *Art and Prudence*, which remains the most solid philosophical study of the questions surrounding the moral and political impact of the arts. The attack on the crime and horror comic books in the 1950s, which led to the temporary elimination of the genre and a new comics code, was most vividly mounted in the articles, books, and legislative testimony of the psychiatrist Dr. Fredric Wertham (see his *Seduction of the Innocent*). The most effective defense of the media and critique of research in that period was Joseph T. Klapper, *The Effects of Mass Communications*. The execution of the crime and horror comics, like that of the gangster film, was short-lived. A number of elements of the genre went right on in *Mad* magazine and its imitators, while the full-scale panoply of the horror comics surfaced in the 1960s in the various underground comics and in slicker, more expensive comic publications like *Vampirella*. More recent investigations of the impact of violence can be found in Otto N. Larsen, ed., *Violence and the Mass Media;* Leonard Berkowitz, *Aggression: A Social Psychological Analysis;* and David M. Rein, "The Impact of Television Violence," which reports on the extensive series of studies commissioned by the Office of the Surgeon General.

2. This has been the approach commonly adopted by the most careful laboratory students of media violence, Bandura and Berkowitz. See the reports of their experiments in Berkowitz.

violent fantasy is only one dimension of the problem. In fictional works, acts of violence appear in a complex context established by generic conventions, cultural stereotypes, and the specific treatment of motive, act, and emotion in the story in which the violence occurs. While it may be true that a certain proportion of the audience may be so disturbed or unsophisticated that they experience, say, the shootout in a western, as an isolated act of violence without a moral or dramatic context, this is surely a pathological extreme. I would assume, until there is persuasive evidence to the contrary, that most people experience their media violence in the moral and dramatic context provided by individual stories and by the generic conventions that underlie these stories. Unfortunately, only one experiment that I am familiar with dealt even tangentially with the extent to which children experienced violence in film in such a context and that experiment seemed to indicate that generic convention was a dominant part of the experience.[3] Clearly, inquiries into the significance of media violence should address themselves in a more complex way to this dimension of context in the fictional representation of violence because it is from the contextual patterns in which violence is portrayed that acts of aggression gain their meaning and significance.

American culture has long been defined by books, films, and television programs in which violence plays a central role because there has always been a large public demand for violence. Much as one can point to the indispensable place of violence in the whole history of literature from savage, fighting Achaians through murdering Macbeths, American writers and filmmakers have been exceptionally prolific in the invention of stories and even whole genres of violent action. This began in the seventeenth century when early tales of Indian wars and captivity were among the first bestsellers. It continued through the nineteenth-century fascination with bloody sagas of the western frontier and gothic thrillers about the cities down to the violent gunfighters, private eyes, gangsters, and gangbusters of twentieth century film and television. For many years, the American public has made its legends of violence a primary article of domestic consumption and of export. So potent and pervasive have been these American images of violence that it is through

Violence through the years!

3. F. E. Emery, "Psychological Effects of the Western Film." Himmelweit et al. in *Television and the Child* noted that children were less disturbed by violence in genres they were familiar with than in adult dramas, but did not systematically explore the effect of generic conventions.

them that Americans have been imaginatively known in much of the rest of the world.[4]

However, in spite of this penchant for imagined violence, Americans have traditionally thought of themselves as a nonviolent law-abiding people. Our rhetoric of manifest destiny in the nineteenth century taught that America was the great redeemer nation, bringing peace, democracy, and the rule of law to the world. Though much of this rhetoric is obsolescent and even seems, to some, obscene, the basic belief in America's role as a peace-bringer still retains its hold, as can be seen from the way former President Nixon and his supporters tried to use the idea that he was a peacemaker to justify his actions. Indeed, the Watergate situation mirrored in microcosm the complex ambiguities that so often seem to characterize the American way of relating peace,[5] violence, law, and crime. In trying to understand how Nixon and his aides were motivated, I find myself drawn to a paradoxical supposition about a deep-lying American attitude. Why were these burglaries carried out in the first place? Why, after their discovery, was the even more dangerous and far-reaching cover-up decided upon? An air of irrationality still hovers about the original Watergate burglary. I find it difficult to understand except in the light of the assumption that these men believed that, in their crusade to bring peace and law to America and the world, a certain degree of violence and crime was not only permissible but also morally necessary. Would a group of practical, experienced politicians have embarked on such a destructive and absurd course of action as Watergate and the cover-up unless driven by the feeling that their goals necessitated such actions? Could it be that they needed to test their dedication to law and peace by their willingness to commit criminal and even violent actions in support of their crusade?

I may be completely wrong in imputing such motives to the president's men. However, its clear that, on the evidence of the large body of our literature devoted to violence and crime, Americans have a

4. For the literary and cultural background, see Leslie Fiedler, *Love and Death in the American Novel*; David Brion Davis, *Homicide in American Fiction, 1798-1860*; Richard Slotkin, *Regeneration through Violence*; W. M. Frohock, *The Novel of Violence in America*; National Commission on the Causes and Prevention of Violence, *To Establish Justice, To Insure Domestic Tranquility*; John G. Cawelti, *The Six-Gun Mystique*.

5. In a column in the *Chicago Sun-Times*, Vic Gold observed as so many have that "we, as a people are guilty of conducting a prime time love affair with crime and violence. In the daytime, we talk law-and-order morality. But after hours, we take vicarious pleasure in lawlessness and violence."

deep belief in the moral necessity of violence and that this belief accounts for the paradox of an ostensibly peace-loving and lawful people being so obsessed with violence. It also, I think, helps explain certain aspects of the actual character of violence in America, in particular that which grows from our inability to control the spread of firearms throughout our society. The gun is our prime symbol of moral violence. Until we can eliminate the imaginative connection between possession of guns and the moral stature of the individual in our society, we will remain in the thrall of what I have called, in another place, "the six-gun mystique." A fuller understanding of the imaginative meaning of violence in our society is not only a matter of seeing how violence in our media reflects certain fundamental cultural attitudes, but a necessary base for any serious attempts to change these attitudes.

I will examine the portrayal of the moral necessity of violence in several pervasive literary formulas. The formulas I have in mind are those of the western, the hard-boiled detective story, the gangster saga, and the police melodrama. While these genres by no means encompass the totality of American popular culture, they are the popular genres in which crime and violence are the central themes. Presumably the way in which these genres represent the world is sufficiently close to the public's sense of what is significant, interesting, and plausible to be satisfying as a fictional experience. We can hardly claim that these genres fully coincide with the public's attitudes, but they must present at least an acceptable picture of the world for the purposes of entertainment and escape. We can assume, then, as a preliminary hypothesis, that the themes appearing in all these popular genres are of compelling interest to their audiences. And of such themes, the most obvious and recurrent is that of the moral necessity of violence.

A few examples will clarify the general outline of this theme. In the highly popular, western film *Shane* (1953), based on Jack Schaefer's novel, the heroic protagonist is a gunfighter who rides out of a mysterious past into a newly settled Wyoming valley. There he finds himself in the midst of a conflict between a group of homesteaders and the tyrannical old rancher who seeks to drive them out. Throughout the first part of the story, Shane attempts to escape from his violent past. He settles down on a farm with the Starrett family, hides his guns, and never speaks of his history. At first, he takes no part in the struggle between farmers and cattlemen. However, when the rancher's attempts to persuade the farmers to leave the range fail, and he turns toward violence, Shane is increasingly drawn into the conflict. The rancher hires a professional gunfighter, the notorious Stark Wilson, to help him drive the settlers out. Wilson tricks one of the farmers into drawing his gun and then shoots him down in cold blood. By this time it is evident that appeals to legal process or morality will not stop the rancher from driving the peaceful farmers out of the valley. Shane buckles on his guns, knocks out Joe Starrett to prevent him from facing the professional killer, and rides into town, where he shoots both Wilson and the villainous rancher. Shane's killings are presented in such a way that violence is not only seen to be inevitable in relation to the plot—since the rancher will not give up his open range except over his dead body—but morally right and even transcendent. In the novel, the young boy who narrates the story describes Shane's act in the following terms:

> I would think of him in each of the moments that revealed him to me. I would think of him most vividly in that single flashing instant when he whirled to shoot Fletcher [the rancher] on the balcony at Grafton's saloon. I would see again the power and the grace of a coordinate force beautiful beyond comprehension. I would see the man and the weapon wedded in the one indivisible deadliness. I would see the man and the tool, a good man and a good tool, doing what had to be done. . . . I would see him there in the road, tall and terrible in the moonlight, going down to kill or be killed, and stopping to help a stumbling boy and to look out over the land, the lovely land, where that boy had a chance to live out his boyhood and grow straight inside as a man should. (101)

The combination of moral, aesthetic, and psychological values united in this passage is a striking formulation of the theme of the moral necessity of violence. Shane's killings are an essential precondition of the young boy's "chance to live out his boyhood and grow straight inside." But the act is not only morally justified in terms of its social end, it is a moment of beauty and power in its own right, one in which the hero becomes one with himself and his weapon, a moment of supreme fulfillment. As narrator Bobby Starrett observes earlier when he sees Shane buckle on his gun: "These were not things he was wearing or carrying. They were part of him, part of the man, of the full sum of the integrate force that was Shane. You could see now that for the first time this man who had been living with us, who was one of us, was complete, was himself in the final effect of his being" (101).

Another example from a different genre. Mike Hammer, the hardboiled private investigator of Mickey Spillane's widely popular *I, the Jury,* finds his best friend has been brutally murdered. His quest for the killer leads him to uncover a vicious drug racket operated by a beautiful, wealthy psychiatrist who uses her situation as a doctor to hook her patients on drugs and as a cover for her operation. This woman, the appropriately named Charlotte Manning, attempts to betray Mike by pretending to be in love with him. At the end of the story, after Mike has discovered her guilt, Charlotte tries to kill him. She seductively strips before him to distract his attention from a gun she has hidden. Instead, Mike waits for the climax of her striptease and shoots her himself. Here the killing of the evil one is obviously a matter of self-defense, vengeance, and the righteous execution of a vicious killer who endangers society. But the killing is given further moral overtones as an appropriate response to an immoral use of feminine sexuality for the purpose of betrayal. It becomes a purification of the obscene as well as the destruction of a killer. The moral necessity of this act of violence is so clear—at least to Mike—that when the dying Charlotte asks him how he could have shot her like this, he can reply, "It was easy" (174).

In *The Godfather*, Mario Puzo treats violence in a more complex fashion, in part because he is not working in the tradition of heroic adventure that dominates the western and hard-boiled detective genres, but in the more morally ambiguous genre of the gangster saga. Nevertheless, the violent actions Michael Corleone progressively engages in are presented to us as morally necessitated by the endemic corruption and brutality of a fundamentally unjust society. Michael's first act of violence, the murder of police Captain McCluskey and his criminal associate Virgil Sollozzo, is an attempt to preserve the security of his own "family." However, it is also a just revenge for the attempted assassination of Michael's own "good" father and is further justified as an attack on criminal gangs who seek to enter the vicious drug traffic. Throughout the story, the Corleone family is presented to us in a morally sympathetic light, as basically good and decent people who have had to turn to crime in order to survive and prosper in a corrupt and unjust society. Even the climactic series of assassinations planned by Michael to destroy rival gang leaders and consolidate his own power are presented to us in conjunction with a complex of moral and religious symbols. In the end, Michael Corleone stands out just like Shane does as a man who has achieved complete self-integration by sacrificing himself to violence for the sake of the peace and prosperity of those he loves and feels responsible for. [It should be noted that Coppola also undertook to deal with the tragic results of these acts of violence in the two sequels to the original *Godfather* film. Since the 1970s and perhaps inspired by revulsion against the meaningless carnage of the Vietnam War, more writers and filmmakers have presented stories dealing with the ironic way in which violence returns upon itself. However, these are still not the majority of films and for every attempt to make a serious critique of violence, there are three Schwarzenegger, Stallone, Segall, Chuck Norris, or Jackie Chan films that revel in it.]

Finally, there is Michael Winner's film *Death Wish* (1974). This film might be characterized as a modern urban western. In this story, a successful New York real estate planner of liberal inclination, who abhors violence to the degree that he served as a conscientious objector in the Korean War, becomes a one-man vigilante force. He is motivated to do this because his wife is beaten to death and his daughter driven into psychosis by a gang of muggers. When a business associate from Arizona gives him a gun, our hero goes for an evening stroll in the park and is accosted by a mugger, whom he shoots. Though his initial reaction is horror (he rushes home and vomits in the toilet), he soon overcomes his squeamishness and embarks on a one-man crusade to destroy the rampaging muggers who seem to be everywhere in Fun City. In this particular film, there is no question about our basic sympathy and moral support for our hero's killings. Vicious barbarians and nasty-looking thugs against whom the law is utterly helpless overrun society. To drive the point home, our hero reminds his grieving son-in-law that the pioneers would never have allowed things to come to this point and that it is perhaps time for Americans to become pioneers again. As to the good social consequences of our hero's crusade, we are told that not long after the actions of "the vigilante" had made the headlines, the rate of mugging in New York City sank drastically. Even the police turn out to be sympathetic to the hero. When the police inspector in charge of the investigation discovers the vigilante's identity, he only insists that the hero leave town and move to another city. At the end of the film, we leave our hero in Chicago, obviously ready to continue his crusade there.[6]

This narrative pattern, a protagonist placed in a situation where some form of violence or criminality becomes a moral necessity, is one of the basic archetypes of American literature. It is certainly an important

---

6. *Death Wish* is a more sophisticated version of a genre that might be called the enforcer. This genre has gained great contemporary popularity in the form of pulp paperback series like "The Destroyer," "The Executioner," "The Butcher," "The Enforcer," etc., which can be seen in large quantity at any paperback bookstand.

element in Cooper's *Leatherstocking Tales,* whose hero inspired D. H. Lawrence to his well-known observation that "there you have the myth of the essential white America. All the other stuff, the love, the democracy, the floundering into lust, is a sort of by-play. The essential American soul is hard, isolate, stoic, and a killer" (71–72). Some scholars, like Richard Slotkin, have traced this pattern back as far as the very beginnings of the American imagination in the seventeenth century. It comes down to us today in a relatively unbroken tradition through the followers of Cooper, like Robert Montgomery Bird. It appears in the dime novel, in the adult novel in the late nineteenth-and early twentieth-century western adventures of writers like Owen Wister, Emerson Hough, and Zane Grey, and then in the uncountable twentieth-century books, films, and television serials involving gunfighters, private detectives, gangsters, and policemen.

But observing the pervasiveness of the story pattern of morally necessary violence does not carry us very far into an understanding of the imaginative significance of all these shootouts and heroic killings. Indeed, the treatment of heroic violence as morally justified has been an almost inevitable accompaniment of stories of heroic adventure since the epics of Homer. To have a truly splendid hero we must have a man who faces the ultimate challenge of life and death and emerges triumphant. And if the hero becomes involved in violence, his action must be justified in some sense, if only because a hero performs it. Why modern American culture seems to need so many different sorts of adventurous heroes is a good question. One wonders whether this penchant for adventurous heroics is a more or less universal constant in human nature or whether some cultures tend to require heroic archetypes more than others, but such a complex inquiry exceeds the limits of my knowledge at the present. Instead, I want to look into the more specific sorts of interpretations given to the pattern of morally necessary violence in American popular media. How, in other words, do American stories of violence tend to justify their culminating acts of violence?

As I see it, these justifications are typically built into the stories themselves in the form of patterns of circumstances and choice that enforce upon the hero the necessity of acts of violence. There are, I think, at least five of these patterns, which I shall refer to as the "myths of violence." They are to some extent interrelated, and while some stories emphasize only one of these myths, it is more typically the case that two or more will be involved in the development of any given story.

The Myth of "Crime Does Not Pay," or "As Ye Sow, So Shall Ye Reap"

In the more overtly moralistic 1930s, such explicit statements as these used to appear at the beginning and ending of many gangster films, including *Little Caesar* (1931), *Public Enemy* (1931), and *Scarface* (1932). This myth reflects one of the oldest and simplest human conceptions of justice, the lex talionis, or "eye for an eye," principle of retaliation that most civilized societies have rejected. However, there is something profoundly satisfying and morally neat about this kind of justice, which flourishes in the area of popular literature. There, unlike in life, circumstances can be manipulated to insure a moral and poetic equivalence between the criminal act and the hero's vengeance. To some degree, this myth is embodied in most examples of the literature of violence, particularly in those forms especially designed for the younger and the less sophisticated portions of the public. The lex talionis is the dominant moral principle informing the writings of Mickey Spillane, the most broadly read of hard-boiled detective writers, for example. The more sophisticated private-eye adventures of Dashiell Hammett and Raymond Chandler are usually critical of this myth of justification, even if some of the satisfaction to be derived from their stories comes from our seeing the criminal meet an appropriately violent end. Perhaps the pervasive presence of this myth in so many of our stories of violence reflects a deep underlying commitment to a primitive sense of justice latent in all of us under the veneer of civilization. This feeling may be especially intense in those who face the most frustration and powerlessness in their actual lives, the young and the poor. In any case, this hypothesis might merit empirical testing by examining the attitudes of audiences and inquiring into the comparative patterns of distribution of films and books that place the most immediate stress on this particular myth.

However, even in the case of the relatively simple and straightforward myth of "Crime does not pay," we encounter a complexity. While this myth does provide an obvious moral justification for the killing of gangsters or murderers by G-men, detectives, or policemen, it becomes more ambiguous in films where the gangsters themselves are clearly the protagonists as in the three early 1930s films mentioned above. Here, "Crime does not pay" was an official motto, a bit of publicly acceptable moralism. The actual sympathies of the audience were probably as much with the gangster who initiated the violence as with the lawman who retaliated against it.

The same ambivalence is reflected in the popular genre that embodies the myth of "Crime does not pay" in its simplest, most abstract form—the saga of the superhero. Tales of caped crusaders, supermen, and Lone Rangers have in common their portrayal of an inevitable nemesis or transcendent force that automatically responds to criminal activity with perfect justice. The hero's own violence tends to be somewhat muted in these stories. Superheroes rarely kill the criminals they overcome; instead they knock them out and turn them over to the police, or, like the Lone Ranger, they shoot the gun out of the villain's hand with silver bullets or some other mystical weapon and then call the sheriff. For all his dazzling capacities, marvelous weapons, and fantastic disguises, the superhero is a transcendent agent of society. In fact, in his other identity, he is generally some respectable member of that society. As superhero, he gains no personal advantage or satisfaction from his heroic deeds beyond his basic and automatic concern to make justice prevail. Thus, he is purely reactive, a symbolic embodiment of the general principle that the criminal is certain to meet his nemesis. No wonder that in such stories the villains are often more interesting, various, and enjoyable. As in the classic gangster film, I am inclined to believe that in superhero stories we secretly root for the villain. The official conventionality of the myth and the certainty of the superhero's ultimate triumph enable us to delight in the villain's criminality without having to worry about its consequences.

The Myth of the Vigilante Avenger

The myth of "Crime does not pay" emphasizes the evil deeds of the antagonist, the admirable motives behind the hero's violence, and the inevitability of the process through which bad acts of violence beget retaliation. Another myth, that of the vigilante, dwells on the weaknesses and corruption of society. In this myth the hero is typically reluctant to use violence. Only after it has become absolutely clear to him that the legally constituted processes of society cannot bring about justice does he step in and take the law into his own hands. Sometimes the hero's family or friends become victims of an act of criminal violence that the law is unable to avenge. When it becomes evident that the police, the courts, and society in general cannot either protect the innocent or avenge acts of criminal violence, then the vigilante must himself become the law. Since he is only an individual (or a small group without legal authority), his only possible means of securing justice is counterviolence.

With no court but his own judgment, his only choices are either to destroy the antagonist or let him go. Since failure to destroy the villain will only free him for further evil deeds, the community being either helpless or in some way supportive of the criminal, the hero must confront and destroy the criminal through violence, usually with a gun, which he uses with considerable skills.

Unlike the superhero in the myth of "Crime does not pay," the vigilante does kill. Probably to satisfy our thirst for vengeance against the evildoer and our feeling of frustration at the weakness and corruption of society in general, his violence is dramatically climactic. It either represents an escalation of the villain's acts of violence or it is performed with some striking skill or style. In *Death Wish*, Charles Bronson develops a distinctive style of cool and humorous nonchalance in dispatching the villains. In *Dirty Harry*, another recent film, Clint Eastwood plays a police officer who rejects the legal process to destroy a maniacal killer, who threatens many lives, but who apparently cannot be stopped by regular police procedures. In this film the principle of dramatic climax is one of escalation. In the first phase of his extralegal attack, the vigilante hero beats the killer to a bloody pulp to make him confess. Then when he is released from jail on the basis of legal technicalities and returns to his maniacally violent ways, the hero tracks him down and shoots him in a lavishly brutal scene.

The western *High Noon* (1952) was a much more complex elaboration of the vigilante myth. The hero, persuaded to retire from his post as sheriff by his new Quaker wife and about to depart on his honeymoon, discovers that a vicious killer is about to arrive in town with his gang in order to kill the sheriff and wreak vengeance on the town. Advised to run away, the sheriff decides that it is his obligation as a man to face up to the situation. He asks for support from the community, but out of cowardice, weakness, and corruption, the townspeople leave him to face the outlaws alone. The dramatic climax comes when, after killing most of the gang, he is about to be shot by the one survivor; his pacifist wife, in a sudden burst of action, shoots the villain in the back.

The myth of the vigilante is often traced to the actual social phenomenon of vigilantism in the nineteenth- and early twentieth-century South and West. Yet, there is a distinctive difference. Vigilantism was invariably a collective phenomenon, the result of mob action or of organizations like the Klan and the quasi-legal vigilante committees of some early western communities. These organizations or mobs, tacitly supported by the community, were as often directed against an unpopular minority and were frequently the expression of racial or social prejudice, as they were against criminal violence. In the myth of the vigilante, however, the hero is generally an isolated individual who must cope with the weakness and corruption of the community as well as the violence of criminals and outlaws. Moreover, the vigilante myth appears to be more characteristic of twentieth- than of nineteenth-century stories of violence. While there are elements of the vigilante myth in later nineteenth-century dime novels, these stories were more characteristically focused on such superhero characters as Buffalo Bill and Deadwood Dick and therefore constitute forms of the "Crime does not pay" myth. The first major adult version of the vigilante myth I am familiar with is Owen Wister's *The Virginian* (1902).[7] But in recent years, the vigilante myth has seemingly become the most pervasive pattern of the literature of violence. It dominates urban action films, both black and white, and pervades many western and gangster films. *The Godfather*, for example, can be seen as a particularly complex form of the vigilante myth, with the Corleones taking the law in their own hands to establish justice in the face of a totally corrupt and unjust social order.

Both novel and film begin with a group of people appealing to the Godfather for justice that has been denied to them because of social prejudice, government inflexibility, or the corruption of men of power. The Don uses his extralegal power, based on his willingness and ability to use violence, in order to accomplish justice for these petitioners whom society would deny. Later in the book, Michael kills a police captain to avenge an attempt on his father's life because the police are themselves corrupted allies of his enemies. In every case, the Corleone family brings order and justice to decent people, and punishes evildoers society is unable to deal with. When the family moves its headquarters into an outlying area,

> Long Beach became the most crime-free town in the United States. Professional stickup artists and strong-arms received one warning not to ply their trade in the town. They were allowed one offense. When

---

7. In *The Virginian*, vigilantism is not only a major element in the dramatic action but is explicitly rationalized and defended as an important American moral and political tradition: "When your ordinary citizen sees . . . that he has placed justice in a dead hand, he must take justice back into his own hands where it was once at the beginning of all things. Call this primitive, if you will. But so far from being a defiance of the law, it is an assertion of it—the fundamental assertion of self-governing men, upon whom our whole social fabric is based" (340–41). Wister's spokesman, Judge Henry, sharply differentiates between this western vigilantism and southern racial lynching, which he condemns.

they committed a second they simply disappeared. The flimflam home-improvement gyp artists, the door-to-door con men, were politely warned that they were not welcome in Long Beach. Those confident con men who disregarded the warning were beaten within an inch of their lives. Resident young punks who had no respect for law and proper authority were advised in the most fatherly fashion to run away from home. Long Beach became a model city. (227–28)

This is perhaps the ultimate fantasy embodied in the myth of the vigilante: the use of individually controlled violence to create the ideal suburb. In such an expression, the vigilante myth perhaps comes closer to reality than is entirely comfortable, for the unrestrained use of personal and community security forces has always played a significant role in protecting the American upper classes in their walled-off estates and housing developments. In a sense, *The Godfather* projects a democratization of this sort of power by self-constituted vigilantes.

The Myth of Equality through Violence

This myth centers around stories of how lower- or lower-middle-class individuals use their skills in violence to achieve a level of equality with persons of established wealth and power. In *The Godfather*, the account of the early life of Don Vito Corleone is organized around this myth. It is a tale of how an Italian immigrant, despised and exploited by those above him in the social structure, used his willingness to engage in acts of violence to win a position of equality and even superiority in the society.[8] Many of our gangster stories portray the gangster's rapid rise from obscure poverty to power and affluence as a variation on the Alger story, the protagonist's technique of success being not pluck and luck but his free and easy manner with a .45 or submachine gun. Equality through violence is also an important pattern in hard-boiled detective stories. The private eyes of Dashiell Hammett and Raymond Chandler, though men of relatively low social status, prove in the course of their adventures that they are more than equal to the corrupt men of wealth and high status whom they usually encounter in the course of their adventures. Curiously, this does not appear to be a particularly significant myth in recent westerns, though many earlier tales, like Wister's *The Virginian* or W. S. Hart's *The Return of Draw Egan*, present heroes who

8. For a brilliant account of this myth as an aspect of American organized crime, see Daniel Bell, "Crime as an American Way of Life.

rise from low status to positions of leadership in society through their skills in violence.

The myth of equality through violence relates to the conception of America as a frontier society in which violent confrontations are part of the ordinary course of life. This is a pervasive vision in our popular literature and films, whether set in the Wild West or the jungle of the modern city. In the western, attacks by Indians or outlaws are an everyday occurrence, just as in the city of contemporary police, detective, and gangster stories, the threat of criminal violence is the dominant characteristic of life. In such a setting, violence is normative rather than exceptional, and the hero who can use it for just and valuable purposes is inevitably a leading citizen. But, in this context, the mere achieving of equality or status is rarely treated as a sufficient justification for the hero's violence. Rather, the hero's action is seen either in terms of the myth of the vigilante, which we have already discussed, or that of the hard-boiled hero and his code.

The Myth of the Hard-Boiled Hero and His Code

For the hard-boiled hero, violence is a test of honor and integrity, a means of proving an individual code of morality that transcends both the law and the conventional morality of society. He is prepared to risk his life in man-to-man confrontations with the criminal, but it is also significant that he uses his violent abilities with extreme moral restraint. The classic western shootout is one key symbolic dramatization of the hero's responsibility to act in accordance with a rigorous moral code in his use of violence. The shootout usually occurs only after the most extreme provocation by the antagonist. It is a ritual ceremony in which the hero waits for his opponent to draw first and then with the most extraordinary grace and discipline pulls his own gun and sends a bullet through another dastardly heart. The hero's controlled and restrained demeanor under pressure and his adherence to the ritual structure of the shootout are external signs of the inner discipline and moral integrity he gains from his absolute obedience to the Code. Though the Code is an unwritten law, engraved only on the hearts of its adherents, it is, nevertheless, a stringent set of moral rules concerning, above all, the proper uses of individual violence. The Code assumes that neither written law nor the conventional standards of society are adequate guides to moral conduct. True morality can be judged only by a man who is prepared to face extremely violent situations with trust in his own individual judgment backed up by a willingness to place his life on the line at the proper moment. The tough private investigator and the heroic policeman are both usually presented as being deeply concerned with the moral conditions of their acts of violence. A substantial part of their special tough-guy heroism results from their willingness to bend or break the law when it seems right to do so. The hard-boiled detective is often shown in conflict with a legalistic police officer who insists on following the letter of the law, but is incapable of stopping unrestrained criminal violence. In contrast, the heroic policeman is more often than not a maverick who finds that to preserve law and order he must step outside the constitutional limits. The justification for this rejection of legally constituted processes is the individual's superior moral concern and judgment. The hard-boiled hero's acts do not derive from an unrestrained delight in violence or from a willingness to use violence for personal ends of wealth and power. This is the immoral mode of criminal and outlaw. The hard-boiled hero's violence must be accomplished in such a way as to prove the validity and propriety of his personal code. He is a curious sort of crusader who wanders through the endemic criminality, violence, and corruption of the frontier West or the urban jungle attempting not so much to save society as to preserve the honor and integrity of his character. As Raymond Chandler eloquently expressed this myth:

> Down these mean streets a man must go who is not himself mean, who is neither tarnished nor afraid. The detective in this kind of story must be such a man. He is the hero, he is everything. He must be a complete man and a common man and yet an unusual man. He must be, to use a rather weathered phrase, a man of honor, by instinct, by inevitability, without thought of it, and certainly without saying it. He must be the best man in his world and a good enough man for any world. I do not care much about his private life; he is neither a eunuch nor a satyr; I think he might seduce a duchess and I am quite sure he would not spoil a virgin; if he is a man of honor in one thing, he is that in all things. He is a relatively poor man, or he would not be a detective at all. He is a common man or he would not go among common people. He has a sense of character, or he would not know his job. He will take no man's money dishonestly and no man's insolence without a due and dispassionate revenge. He is a lonely man and his pride is that you will treat him as a proud man or be very sorry you ever saw him. (qtd. in Haycraft, 237)

Or as Robert Warshow puts it:

> What [the western hero] defends, at bottom, is the purity of his own image—in fact his honor. This is what makes him invulnerable. When

the gangster is killed his whole life is shown to have been a mistake, but the image the Westerner seeks to maintain can be presented as clearly in defeat as in victory: he fights not for advantage and not for the right, but to state what he is, and he must live in a world which permits that statement. The Westerner is the last gentleman and the movies which over and over tell his story are probably the last art form in which the concept of honor retains its strength. (94)

The Myth of Regeneration through Violence

In this myth, the justification of moral violence derives from its treatment as a necessary act of purification and regeneration. A classic example in relatively pure form is W. S. Hart's movie *Hell's Hinges* (1916). In this film, a young minister and his beautiful sister arrive from the East at the frontier town of Hell's Hinges. Here, a small group of decent pioneers have established a church to oppose the town's unrestrained outlawry and sensuality, centering on the saloon operated by villainous "Silk" Miller. The young minister is weak, however, and is easily seduced by a dance-hall girl in Miller's entourage. Inspired by this victory over the forces of God, the saloon crowd marches to the church, determined to burn it to the ground and drive out the good pioneers. However, the area's most courageous gunfighter, Blaze Tracey, has fallen in love with the minister's sister and in the process has converted to religion. Outraged at the course of events, Tracey single-handedly constitutes himself an angel of vengeance and purification and, in the film's climactic moments, he attacks the saloon and purges it with fire. Out of the burning ashes of Hell's Hinges, the nucleus of a new, moral community marches forth led by Tracey and the minister's sister, now fully united in Christian love.

In *Regeneration through Violence*, Richard Slotkin traces this myth from what he argues are its origins in seventeenth-century Puritan Indian captivity and war narratives down through its complex elaboration in the nineteenth-century figure of Daniel Boone, the frontier hunter. As Slotkin sees it, the myth of regeneration through violence grew out of the deep conflicts and ambivalences Americans felt as they underwent the "initiation into a new world and new life that is at the core of the American experience" (179). These conflicts grew out of a confrontation between two cultures, the Christian English and the Indian, that embodied two distinctly different phases of mythological evolution, two conflicting modes of perception, and two antagonistic visions of the nature and destiny of man and the natural wilderness. In the imaginative elaboration of the confrontation among settler, Indian, and wilderness, there emerged two basic mythical patterns, both of which tended toward a resolution through violence. The first myth, Slotkin argues, was that of the captive, a story of the white Christian captured, tormented, and tempted by Indians. The captive's faith was tested by this challenge and he then destroyed the diabolical Indians and returned, regenerated, to the Christian community. The violence in this myth, Slotkin feels, was related to the settler's imaginative tendency to project onto the Indians his own latent desire for freedom, sensuality, and escape from the spiritual rigors of the Christian community. Thus, in the myth of the captive, the ultimate rescue and destruction of the Indians is also symbolically a destruction of the captive's own feared desire for lawlessness and the lascivious freedom of the wilderness.

However, the appeal of the wilderness and the fascination of the Indian way of life were strong enough that a second myth developed presenting a symbolic union between the white man and the wilderness. This was the myth of the hunter in which, through the tracking and killing of an animal (or an Indian), the hunter entered into the spirit of the wilderness and was reborn. Here, the violence of the hunt "is an initiation and a conversion in which [the hero] achieves communion with the powers that rule the universe beyond the frontiers and acquires a new moral character, a new set of powers or gifts, a new identity" (551). This myth was elaborated, according to Slotkin, in the variety of legends and stories that grew up around Daniel Boone and was then given significant literary expression in Cooper's Leatherstocking series. It is also, Slotkin feels, the myth that underlies the more complex and profound explorations of Thoreau's *Walden* and Melville's *Moby Dick*.

Yet as Slotkin sees it, the myth of the hunter was rarely expressed without ambivalence for it contained tendencies that, from the point of view of the Puritan tradition, were morally dangerous: the hunter, in achieving his quest, runs grave moral risks. He has broken the family circle by his own act. He becomes partly assimilated to the world whose ways he is learning, the world of the Indian; and he may partake so much of the flesh of wild, hunted things that he becomes like them. Or he may so delight in the exercise of his newly acquired skills and powers that his pursuit of them becomes a calling or profession, an activity that he regards as self-justifying or as a substitute for civil religion (552).

Slotkin sees the myth of the Code as one imaginative means of allaying the fear that the hunter's wildness will subvert and destroy civilized morality. Another mythical means of insuring that the hunter does not give way to wilderness urges is to place his actions in juxtaposition with the captivity myth, as Cooper did with his Leatherstocking:

> Participation in the captivity myth alters [the hero's] relationship to the wilderness. For the sake of the captive and the values of society and Christianity that she represents, the hunter must exterminate the Indians who have taught him his skill and establish a safe refuge for the captive by opening the wilderness to settlement. He may not merge his identity with the wilderness so far that he is truly of it. Hence his acquisition of the powers of the wilderness creatures has disastrous consequences: he will use those powers, not to sustain the wilderness world, but to destroy it in the name of something higher. (552–53)

Though Slotkin does not carry his analysis of the myth of regeneration through violence down to the present day, it is clear that it continues to inform the popular tradition of the western at least as recently as *Shane* and John Ford's *The Searchers* (1956). In *Shane* the hero's return to his role as heroic gunfighter is clearly represented as an act of revitalization and redemption through which he saves the captive homesteaders and becomes one with himself. In a different way, in *The Searchers*, an epic hunt for a girl captured by the Indians leads the two heroes to become more and more like the Indians they pursue until, in the culminating battle, the Indian chief is destroyed and the captive are restored to the Christian community. Whether this myth in a somewhat different form also plays a major role in other contemporary genres of violence, such as the hard-boiled detective story and the gangster saga, will require further inquiry. It is possible that the myth of regeneration through violence constitutes, as Slotkin would argue, the basic American way of dealing imaginatively with violence and that the other myths we have analyzed can be seen as versions of it. Certainly the myth of the hard-boiled hero and his Code has many points of connection with the archetype of regeneration through violence.

Conclusion

The definition of different myths of violence suggests a variety of provocative lines of inquiry that should give us much fuller insight into the role of fantasies of violence in American and other cultures. What are the relationships between different myths of violence? Almost certainly different cultures and subcultures stress different myths in their presentation of fictional violence.[9] Are there certain subcultures that seem to prefer one myth to another? Are the different myths of violence equally distributed throughout the culture or are some more dominant than others? Does each culture have a basic myth of violence or do those myths I have discussed suggest some conflicts in values? As we set out to analyze the presentation of violence using more complex and specific methods such as those I have tried to follow in this paper, we shall doubtless have to add further categories and to redefine some of the myths I have treated here. In addition, where I have focused my attention on the protagonist's violence and the various story lines that serve to justify it morally, we will also need to examine the antagonist's violence to see whether it reflects the same mythical patterns or implies something else.

But this is certainly enough to show that violence in popular culture is not simply a mindless representation of aggression that can be understood in simple quantitative terms. Perhaps that is true of video games, but certainly not of more complex stories. Further studies should consider the variety and complexity of the mythical patterns involved in the representation of violence in popular culture. If they do not, they will continue to oversimplify this complex phenomenon to the point that conclusions about the causal effect and significance of media violence will be as open to doubt as they have in the past. With a more complex and specific conception of the various patterns of media representation of violence, we may be able to arrive at the answers to some of our questions about its impact.

9. For example, a very interesting study could be made of the significant differences between English and American detective and crime fiction as they relate to different cultural attitudes toward violence. For British attitudes toward violence, see the historical study by T. A. Critchley, *The Conquest of Violence*.

13

The Gunfighter and the Hard-Boiled Dick: Some Ruminations on American Fantasies of Heroism

This essay has always been a favorite of mine and I'm grateful to *American Studies* for publishing it in 1976. What especially interested me in the rereading was how I try to define toughness or the hard-boiled as a central theme of American culture. I've always been fascinated by this, perhaps because I am the least tough person imaginable. I'd like to be tough, but I haven't the strength, the indifference, or the wit. Richard Nixon was quoted as saying, "when the going gets tough, the tough get going." But I don't think he was really tough, just obsessed and paranoid. I think he really wanted to be hard-boiled because he recognized this as a central virtue in American culture. The essay was another attempt to go beyond the limits of *The Six-Gun Mystique* and shows its connection to *Adventure, Mystery, and Romance* of the same year by dealing with comparative genres. I've never pursued the theme of toughness in American life and its strangely paradoxical relationship with American optimism much further. I hope somebody will. I think that de Tocqueville's observation about American melancholy with which I end the essay is one of the most brilliant things ever said about American culture.

≡

Outlaws suddenly beset the thriving little frontier settlement. Coming out of nowhere they viciously attack, beating the citizens and killing the old sheriff. Desperately the citizens gather in the church. After prayer for divine guidance, a debate breaks out between those who would leave the town to the outlaws, and those who think they should tough it out. The braver element prevails and the townspeople determine to stay. They petition the governor for a new sheriff. In the nick of time, a heroic figure, beautifully dressed in fringed buckskin and riding a magnificent stallion rides out of the desert. With his help the townspeople successfully defend themselves against the outlaw bands until, in a final confrontation, the hero exposes, tracks down, and out shoots the corrupt politician who has tried to drive the people out and take over their land. With law and order restored, the hero leaves grateful townsfolk behind and rides off into the desert (and the sunset) with his faithful partner.

Sound familiar? It should, since with minor changes this could be a plot description of any of a hundred western films ranging from an episode of the Lone Ranger through John Ford's *My Darling Clementine,* George Steven's *Shane* and Fred Zinneman's *High Noon* to Clint Eastwood's *High Plains Drifter.* Actually the film I was more or less describing in this summary is Mel Brooks's total send-up of the western, *Blazing Saddles. Blazing Saddles* is hilarious and has become one of the most popular westerns of all time. It brilliantly follows the Hollywood archetype of the western hero, with certain incongruous details that enable Brooks to keep his audience in stitches while he reduces the great myth of the western gunfighter to a shambles.

The fact that the new sheriff in *Blazing Saddles* is black constitutes the most pervasive burlesque of the mythic tradition. Though there have been a few black heroes in western films, particularly of more recent vintage, the heroic lawman of the Hollywood myth has traditionally been white in more than his hat. However, the satire of *Blazing Saddles* does not result simply from setting a black man in a traditionally white heroic role. It is not just his blackness, but also his style that makes Cleavon Little's portrayal of the new sheriff so incongruous with the tradition. The external characteristic of blackness and Little's subtle qualities of manner, attitude, and gesture expose to our sense of the ridiculous certain basic assumptions that have always dominated the portrayal of the western lawman-hero in American films.

First of all, there is the fact that the western lawman is almost never presented to us as a man of law. Though the vast majority of western films work toward that climactic moment in which a heroic figure redeems the law by destroying the outlaws who would deny it, this character is rarely a man of the law by profession or career. In *Blazing Saddles* this convention is burlesqued by making the new sheriff a black railroad worker who is dragooned into serving as sheriff in order to save his skin. Even in *High Noon,* one of the few films in which a professional sheriff plays the role of hero, the action takes place after the sheriff has determined to retire from office. In most westerns, the heroic lawgiver is not a sheriff or marshal at all, but a cowboy, a reformed outlaw, or a mysterious gunfighter. In the list of 106 representative western films from 1903–1966 that I assembled for the appendix of *The Six-Gun Mystique,* only 11 clearly and unmistakably have professional sheriffs or marshals as heroic protagonists. In several of these the hero is not a sheriff at the beginning or ending of the film. Most westerns do have a sheriff or marshal present as a minor character, but he is likely to be old and helpless, confused or corrupt; often enough he has been suborned by the outlaws or by the evil tycoon.[1]

The hero's ambiguous relationship to law embodies, among other things, a traditional American notion of individualism. The western hero acts out the myth that society and its organized processes of law, however necessary, are incapable of bringing about true justice. Society and law exist not as a fountainhead of what is just, but as a set of rules controlling the action of individuals who are the true source of morality and justice as well as of injustice. Because the law is only a set of shifting rules it can readily be bent by those who are strong or unscrupulous enough to do so. Thus, for Americans, the individual who can mold society and the law to his own ends is as much admired as condemned. There's a slight edge of contempt in our attitude toward the conscientious and law-abiding citizen, as if some weakness or impotence prevented him from acting aggressively for himself.[2] On the other hand,

---

1. See *The Six-Gun Mystique,* 110–13.

2. Every western has its contingent of decent law-abiding citizens who eschew violence and depend on the law to secure justice. They are nice, but foolish, and they invariably need the violent hero. The same thing is true of the hard-boiled detective story. Even in the situation comedy, the kind of foolish terror the good citizen feels when confronted with the law is a perennial source of laughs, as if those who accept the rule of law are somehow ridiculous. One discovers, I think, the same sort of attitude in the ambiguity American parents so often demonstrate when confronted with that classic situation of the bullied child. Should the child be advised to use violence on his

Americans are clearly not prepared to extend this view of individualism to its logical conclusion of a war of all against all, for there are other, different values that are also important to us, in particular the ideals of equality and community. These, too, must somehow come into play if justice is to be accomplished. The grasping tycoon, the egocentric rancher, or the lawless outlaw, these favorite western villains may be partly justified in their ignoring of the law, but when their aggression threatens the community or harms the innocent farmers, something must be done. The community must be redeemed and the unjust individualist purged. In the western, society's law cannot do this, since it has not yet been established, or has broken down. At this point, the hero must appear, and he must have the same aggressive force and skill in violence that the villain commands. To carry out his mission, he must be a lawman, not a man of society's law, as society's law is useless in such situations. Instead, he is obedient to an inner code of his own—"a man's got to do what a man's got to do"[3]—that happens to coincide with the needs of the community. Thus his act of aggressive violence is legitimated, the excessive individualist threat to the community is purged, and the ultimate harmony between individualism and justice is mythically reaffirmed.

These considerations indicate why the sheriff-hero of *Blazing Saddles* comically exposes the Hollywood myth of the lawman not only through his blackness but also through his style. The black sheriff of *Blazing Saddles is* a super cool dude. He is elegant and urbane, a connoisseur of fine wines and good food; he is sensuous and erotic and something of a dandy; he prefers trickery to an open fight; most shocking of all he is even, perhaps, just a wee bit gay in his inclinations. These characteristics of style, so antithetical to the tight-lipped austere dignity and puritanical rigor of Gary Cooper or John Wayne, provide a mocking commentary on the traditional myth of the lawman. But why does the super cool style undercut the myth so effectively? I think because it exposes the degree to which the role of heroic lawgiver portrayed in the western is a construction of fantasy, and thereby self-contradictory and even absurd. Because he is a superior man of violence, capable of purging

---

oppressor or to turn the other cheek or to seek justice either from his peers or an authority such as the teacher? Most parents seem to feel their child is a little foolish and might even feel contempt for him if he refuses to "stand up," i.e. to use violence, in pursuit of his interests.

3. The *locus classicus* of this western cliche is Owen Wister's *The Virginian* where the hero asks his genteel law-abiding schoolmarm sweetheart "Can't yo' see how it must be about a man?" (371).

whole bands of outlaws, the mythical lawman has to be a heroic outsider like the Lone Ranger. After all, if we felt it appropriate for the
community to do the job through its duly constituted legal agencies,
there would be no need for the myth in the first place. However, having
invented this potently aggressive hero to symbolize the ideal individualist, we also need to be assured that he is using his force in a just and
moral fashion for the benefit of we, the people. Consequently, though
he is trained and dedicated to killing, the heroic lawman must also be a
man of great restraint and morality, even of gentleness. He must be an
outsider, but also in a very deep sense one of us. This, I think, is why the
blackness of the sheriff in *Blazing Saddles* constitutes such a comic
shock. The hero must be wonderfully potent, but also ascetic and pure
in his habits; he must avoid erotic entanglements in order to put his
whole force into his moment of violent redemption. In comic contrast
to this image of western heroism, Mel Brooks's sheriff is richly sensuous
and obviously interested in sex. Finally, though the Hollywood lawman
is characterized by his austerity toward the opposite sex, there must
never be the slightest question of his total and unquestioned masculinity. Even if he prefers the company of men and horses, and is something
of a dandy, we must never see a hint of effeminacy or homoeroticism.
This, too, becomes an object of mockery in the running commentary of
gay gestures and jokes in *Blazing Saddles*.

That the heroic western marshal is so ripe and hilarious an object of
parody in *Blazing Saddles* suggests how important he has been as a figure
in the American imagination.[4] In fact, we can probably go so far as to say
that, at least in the period of his peak popularity, the late fifties and early
sixties, the western hero was considered by many to be the archetypal
American. Unfortunately, the more archetypal a heroic figure becomes,
the more he is likely to mean a great variety of things. In a complex, pluralistic society, popular heroes and their myths probably perform an important integrative role by providing common objects of vicarious identification and admiration for people with very diverse attitudes and
backgrounds. However, for the mythical hero to function in this way he
must be susceptible to many different kinds of interpretation; he must

4. It may also suggest that he is a little past his prime, though this is not necessarily the case,
since parody and burlesque do not invariably indicate a loss of power in the object or figure being
satirized. The western hero was richly burlesqued by Bret Harte and Mark Twain in the later
nineteenth century, long before he became one of the central figures of twentieth-century film and
television.

be, in effect, a container into which various meanings can be poured without breaking or changing the basic shape of the container. The archetypical western hero is clearly a figure of this sort, since he has been the inspiration not only of a great variety of interpretations, but of a number of different versions of the western myth.[5] For example, in his recent book on the subject, Philip French suggests that the westerns of the last two decades can be classified into fairly distinctive "Kennedy," "Johnson," "Goldwater," and "Buckley" versions of the basic western story.[6] Whether or not one agrees with this particular anatomy, the western obviously encompasses a considerable ideological range and, depending on the perspective of the viewer, can be seen as expressive of either conservative or liberal attitudes, sometimes simultaneously. Indeed, the doughty John Wayne, survivor of so many imaginary gunfights, has managed in recent years to become something of a cult figure among young radical movie fans without his having ed in any significant degree the reactionary stance he has taken on most public issues. This is presumably because in his various roles as western hero he transcends political controversy and embodies something that is at once more vague and more archetypal.

Because of this archetypal or mythical dimension, the western is extremely difficult to interpret in specific ideological terms. One reads the various critics who have attempted such interpretations and tends to agree with all or none of them. Each interpreter offers a more or less persuasive account of what the western is all about, but it seems very difficult to demonstrate that one interpretation is more correct than another except in the case of individual works. We can more or less agree about the lines of interpretation relevant to Owen Wister's *The Virginian*, Jack Schaefer's *Shane*, or Thomas Berger's *Little Big Man*, but when it comes to the western myth as a whole, which somehow includes these three very different works along with several thousand others, it is increasingly difficult to be specific about just what it means. The more versions of the western myth our inquiry includes the more difficult it is to state what political or social attitudes if any are implied by its popularity. One solution to this problem is to take a broad structural approach to the analysis of the myth, seeking to define those basic elements and relations that are invariably present in all versions of the

5. Some indication of the diversity of interpretations the western myth has inspired can be found in Jack Nachbar, ed. *Focus on the Western*.

6. Philip French, *Westerns*, 28–42.

western. This is the method I attempted in *The Six-Gun Mystique* where I tried to describe the basic opposition of pioneers and outlaw-savages mediated in some fashion by the hero that permeates all instances of the western I am familiar with. However, though this provided a useful framework for viewing the western as a popular artistic genre, and led to interesting speculations about the cultural meaning of the Western myth, the treatment remained at a high level of generality. I was never fully satisfied that I had established the cultural significance of the basic structural elements. In particular, I found it too difficult to separate the cultural and artistic imperatives involved in the creation of westerns to be sure which themes were present because they embodied important cultural meanings and which were simply part of the conventional artistic structure.

In this paper, I propose to approach the inquiry into the cultural significance of the western in a slightly different way by attempting to sort out the most important cultural themes of the it as they relate to another genre of contemporaneous popularity. My basic assumption is that those common elements or patterns that we find in related but different popular genres reflect basic cultural themes. In other words, when a certain kind of character, or situation or pattern of action appears in more than one mythical structure, we have grounds for believing that this pattern is of basic cultural importance and not simply the reflection of the attitudes of a particular creator. I have chosen for this purpose the popular genre commonly known as the hard-boiled detective or private-eye story.[7]

Many previous scholars and critics have noted the relationship between the hard-boiled detective and the western hero. Lewis Jacobs, in his *Rise of the American Film,* describes the gangster cycle of the 1930s as an urban version of the western. Robert Warshow, in his two brilliant essays "The Gangster as Tragic Hero," and "Movie Chronicle: The Westerner," draws similar comparisons. But neither of these writers,

---

7. The hard-boiled detective story had not received as much attention as the western until recently, but there are a number of useful studies including the essays on the hard-boiled genre in David Madden, ed., *Tough-Guy Writers of the Thirties,* George Grella, "Murder and the Mean Streets"; John Paterson, "A Cosmic View of the Private Eye"; Philip Durham, *Down These Mean Streets a Man Must Go;* William F. Nolan, *Dashiell Hammett;* and most recently William Ruehlmann, *Saint with a Gun.* I have also profited from a recent University of Chicago doctoral dissertation on Ross Macdonald by Ms. Johnninc Hazard and from Raymond Chandler, "The Simple Art of Murder," Ross Macdonald, "The Writer as Detective Hero," and Dashiell Hammett, "Memoirs of a Private Detective" which have been reprinted in a number of places.

nor anyone else so far as I am aware, has attempted a systematic comparison between the two genres as a basis for discovering the cultural themes that they may embody. That is the purpose of the following discussion. The results, as the reader will doubtless note, cannot be considered definitive. Even when one has established common patterns between two popular genres, it is difficult to be sure of their relationship to popular attitudes.

Moreover, when two literary genres have much in common, it's possible that the artistic necessities of a certain kind of story are as influential in shaping similarities in character and theme as the expression of cultural attitudes. Thus, the results of our comparison remain in the area of the speculative and the possible. Nonetheless, I would argue that there are enough differences between the hard-boiled detective story and the western to suggest that the similarities are at least in part the result of a cultural need to represent the same fantasy in different garb. In addition, there is much to be said for the point that when a culture creates and consumes so much literary material of the same fundamental sort, it is expressing something about itself. Tentative as they are, the results of this comparison suggest the existence of a tradition in American popular culture worth further investigation.

At first glance, there are a number of striking differences between the hard-boiled detective story and the western. The setting of the two genres is almost antithetical. The western takes place on the edge of the wilderness or in a frontier settlement and with the exception of a distinctive subgenre set in the present (which includes such films as *Lonely Are the Brave, The Misfits,* and *Bad Day at Black Rock*) represents a historic moment in the past. The private-eye genre is almost always set in the city and takes place in the present. In line with this difference in setting, the cast of characters in the two story types seems at first to bear little relationship to one another. The western centers upon the sort of people likely to be found in the rural West. It has ranchers, small-town merchants and farmers, a banker, possibly a doctor and a newspaper editor, the sheriff, the schoolmarm, the dance-hall girl, the boys down at the saloon, and, of course, a complement of outlaws or Indians to generate the excitement and danger of the plot.

The hard-boiled detective, on the other hand, typically has to thread his way through the manifold social levels and complexities of a modern city: rich businessmen, mobsters and their gangs, the district attorney and the police, the middle-class, and, sometimes, bejeweled glamour girls and women of the night. Within the first few chapters of Raymond

Chandler's *The Big Sleep* private investigator Philip Marlowe encounters the millionaire General Sternwood and his two wild and beautiful daughters, a pornographer named Arthur Gwynn Geiger, a cheap hoodlum and his moll, a seductive bookstore salesgirl, an old friend from the district attorney's office, and a miscellaneous cast of policemen and grifters. Such a variety of types are impossible in the simpler environment of the western.

The pattern of action also differs between the genres. The hard-boiled detective is, above all, involved in the investigation of a crime. The climactic point in his story usually revolves around the unmasking of a criminal or a conspiracy. The western is generally a tale of conflict—between townspeople and outlaws, ranchers and rustlers, cattlemen and farmers, or pioneers and Indians—leading to a shootout between the hero and the antagonist that resolves the conflict, usually through the destruction of the antagonist. Beyond these contrasts in setting, character and action, the western and hard-boiled detective genres have innumerable differences in symbolic detail: horses vs. cars; six-shooters and Winchesters vs. .45 automatics and Tommy guns; boots, spurs, and chaps vs. business suits; smoke signals vs. telephones, etc. Finally, there is frequently a contrast in narrative structure between these two genres. The hard-boiled story is usually a first person narrative, told to us by the detective-hero, while the western almost never adopts this form of storytelling.

Despite these many differences, however, there are certain fundamental patterns that the western and hard-boiled detective stories have in common, which, if our initial assumption is correct, embody important American cultural themes. First of all, the two heroes have very similar characteristics. Each is a skilled professional man of violence, and, while the hard-boiled detective story ends less often in a shootout than the western, the hero is always prepared for this eventuality. However reluctant he may be to use them, he is skilled with guns and fists. This connection between hard-boiled detective and western heroes becomes even more obvious when we compare the American detective with his English counterparts. Sherlock Holmes, Hercule Poirot, Lord Peter Wimsey, or Mr. Campion possess great powers of inference and deduction, but are almost never called upon to engage in violent confrontations with guns. In America, even the relatively pacifistic Lew Archer knows how and when to handle a gun, while the more vehement and vengeful Mike Hammer usually climaxes his investigations by shooting the criminal. Readiness for violence is one important common characteristic of hard-boiled detective and western heroes, but many also share another aspect of their persona: reluctance to use their skills in violence, often related to a sense of ambiguity about their involvement in the situation in which they find themselves. These are typically heroes who do not initiate their heroic actions. Instead, they are forced into them.[8]

The hero's reluctance seemingly results from two aspects of his situation. First, as a skillful man of violence his actions are likely to bring about someone's death. Consequently, his commitments cannot be entered into lightly. Secondly, the hero has a penchant for becoming committed to other persons in such a deep emotional and moral fashion that his actions not only affect the lives of others, they have a deep impact on him. The model of these circumstances is the situation of Sam Spade in *The Maltese Falcon.* Sam is initially drawn into the case when a woman asks him to investigate the disappearance of her supposedly missing but actually fictitious sister. This has become a favorite opening for the hard-boiled detective story. For example, the recent film *Chinatown* begins when a woman impersonating the wife of an important Los Angeles official asks the detective to secure evidence of the official's supposed liaison with a younger woman.

As in the case of Sam Spade, this initial mission is purely a matter of business for the detective. He has no personal interest or concern in the outcome of the case, except as a matter of doing his job. However, this apparently insignificant initial mission is soon revealed to be a cover for something much more serious, and dangerous complications gradually draw the detective into a web of emotional and moral commitments. Sam Spade finds himself falling in love with the woman whom he must, in the end, expose as a vicious killer. Something of the same sort happens to Polanski's J. J. Gittes as his purely businesslike connection with the case develops into a deeply personal involvement with his client.

---

8. Some qualification of this generalization needs to be made. Spillane's Mike Hammer and his more recent descendants such as "The Enforcer," "The Destroyer," and "The Butcher" are far less reluctant about using violence than Philip Marlowe, Lew Archer, and the Continental Op. Similarly, in the case of the western, there are few heroes with the gentleness and reluctance displayed by Gary Cooper in *The Virginian, Man of the West,* and *High Noon;* Alan Ladd in *Shane;* James Stewart in *Destry Rides Again, The Man from Laramie,* and *Winchester 73.* In general, the less sophisticated a version of the myth, the less ambiguity there is about the hero's violence. Undoubtedly, this reflects some difference in the level or segment of the public at which a particular version of the myth is directed. It probably also reflects differences in meaning of the myth for different subgroups within the culture but we need more information about the social and psychological makeup of audience groupings to deal adequately with these differences.

The same sort of commitment typically occurs in the case of hard-boiled heroes as different as Philip Marlowe and Mike Hammer, though their ultimate reactions to their involvement are quite unlike.

This is one of the structural features that most sharply differentiate the American hard-boiled hero from the English ratiocinative detective protagonist. Sherlock Holmes, Hercule Poirot, and Dr. Gideon Fell who typify this brand of detective story generally maintain a rather cool detachment from their clients, focusing their energies on the unraveling of intricate puzzles through inference and deduction from clues. The private eye, on the other hand, either becomes more personally interested in the crime or has such an interest from the very beginning. In Mickey Spillane's *I, the Jury* one of the detective's friends is murdered while in Raymond Chandler's *The Long Goodbye* a friend is pegged as one of the prime suspects.

In this respect, the private eye resembles the western hero much more than the classical detective. Though the westerner is only tangentially involved in detection, he is characteristically caught up in a violent action through personal involvement that he cannot escape. One of the common motives ascribed to western heroes is revenge. Just as Mickey Spillane's Mike Hammer sets out to avenge the murder of a close friend, John Ford's Wyatt Earp in *My Darling Clementine* accepts the job of marshal in Tombstone in order to avenge the murder of his younger brother. In other instances, like Jack Schaefer's *Shane* or Anthony Mann's *The Far Country*, the hero is reluctantly drawn into violence to protect a group of people for whom he feels a moral responsibility.

Whatever the specific motives may be, and these can range from a desire for revenge to a feeling of moral obligation toward a particular group or community, the hard-boiled and western heroes both have personal codes of morality that transcend the written law and the conventional morality of society. This code appears to be both a matter of style and of moral behavior. In terms of style, the most obvious similarity between westerner and private eye is their laconic, understated, and tough manner of speech. These heroes are men of few words. Above all, they rarely attempt to justify or explain in words the morality of their actions, as if prepared to stand or fall by actions alone. Or to put it another way, these heroes are so unwilling to submit their behavior to the judgment of others that they refuse to give any explanation or justification for what they do. Only those who themselves participate in the code really understand why the hero does what he does, and they do not need to put it into words.

Sometimes, on climactic occasions, the hero is forced to explain himself. The heroine of Wister's *The Virginian* threatens to leave the hero forever if he fights the villain Trampas and he feels he must tell her why he has to. Sam Spade feels he must explain to Brigid O'Shaughnessy why he is going to turn her over to the police. But, even in these circumstances, the hero usually finds that words are not very satisfactory and finally resorts to gnomic generalization like "A man's got to do what a man's got to do," or "I won't play the sap for anybody."

Even when, as is generally the case with the hard-boiled detective genre, the hero tells the story to us, we still retain the impression of a man of few words, who is willing to tell only the smallest portion of what he knows and feels. The narrative tells us with great precision what the detective does and where he goes and, in the case of skillful writers like Dashiell Hammett and Raymond Chandler, is studded with humorous and lyrical observations about the people he encounters and the places he visits. But the hero rarely comments directly on his feelings, his motives, and his moral judgments. Even Mickey Spillane's Mike Hammer, the crudest and most overtly moralistic of the private eyes, tends toward a style of tough, if garish, understatement. In the case of more sophisticated writers like Raymond Chandler, the detective holds so much back that we are often unclear through the middle of his stories just why he is carrying on his investigation in the way he is. No doubt this is partly a result of the need for mystification about the detective's inquiry that characterizes any mystery story. However, in the hard-boiled story the enigma often extends beyond keeping the reader in the dark about the facts of the crime to the point where he is also forced to guess at the motives and morality of the detective, a situation that rarely arises in the classical detective story.

Because the hero's code is so personal, it is difficult to analyze it into component elements. Like all heroic codes, it places strong emphasis on a concept of honor. Yet this is not the traditional aristocratic conception of honor, or the epic principle of glory, both of which require social validation. For the epic hero it is of primary importance that his deeds become part of the legend of the tribe so that the memory of his glory will be preserved from generation to generation. For the aristocrat, honor involves preserving and adding to the greatness of his family name. However, hard-boiled and western heroes are preeminently private persons, as is perhaps appropriate for the heroic archetype of a democratic society. They spring from no noble lineage, but are, in effect, self-made men. Instead of seeking publicity for their deeds, they seem more inclined to resent even the temporary local fame their acts inspire.

Here we see another dimension of the laconic, tight-lipped style. Where the Homeric hero loves to tell of his feats of valor, this American figure seems to seek instead the deepest recesses of individual privacy. Like the Lone Ranger, once he has accomplished his mission, he prefers to ride off as quietly as possible. It should be noted that in this, as in a number of other respects, there are important differences between earlier and more recent avatars of the western hero. Wister's Virginian parlays his heroic accomplishments into a position of importance in society, as do many other western protagonists of the early twentieth century. However, since the development of the hard-boiled hero in the early thirties, the western hero has become increasingly alienated from the society for whose sake he performs his deeds, just as the hard-boiled detective is more commonly criticized than applauded by the society in which he operates. Thus, the concept of honor espoused by hard-boiled detective and western gunfighter is a very personal and private thing. He fights, as Robert Warshow puts it, to maintain the purity of his image of himself, rather than to gain social prestige or status.[9]

Other aspects of the hard-boiled and Western hero's code include great physical courage and endurance as well as highly developed skills in the use of guns and in hand-to-hand combat. These heroes are extremely tough and dangerous men, a toughness that they frequently manifest as much in their ability to endure physical punishment as to shoot quickly and with great accuracy. The hard-boiled detective is knocked out and beaten up regularly before he arrives at the solution to the mystery. Similarly, a bruising fistfight is almost de rigeur for the western hero, though he usually accomplishes the final shootout through his skill at the fast draw. In fact, it has become increasingly common in westerns to subject the hero to an extended ordeal and even, on occasion, a considerable humiliation, before he finally defeats his antagonists. The tough-guy hero, then, must always be prepared for violence, because this is what he expects of his world.

The hero's code cannot be considered in complete isolation from the world he inhabits. We noted earlier that the western and hard-boiled detective genres had quite different settings, one usually taking place in the contemporary city and the other on a past frontier. However, beneath the surface these settings have two fundamental characteristics in

9. Robert Warshow, "Movie Chronicle: The Westerner." Warshow also deals brilliantly with some of the central themes of the present essay: the hero's reluctance; the sense of melancholy and defeat that accompany his deeds; the peculiar concept of honor.

common. They are on the edge of anarchy, and within their societies, legitimate authority tends to be weak and corrupt. The wildness of the western town is obvious enough, since it is typically on the edge of a wilderness where there is nothing but savage Indians and outlaws. At any time an Indian attack, an outlaw raid, or a gunfight down at the saloon may occur and it is far from certain that law and legitimate social authority will suffice to restore order and bring about justice. This is the conventional western situation that *Blazing Saddles* burlesques as the archetypal moment of our western fantasies. But essentially the same situation exists in the hard-boiled detective story despite its more recent urban setting. For the hard-boiled detective confronts a situation in which as, Raymond Chandler puts it:

> Gangsters can rule nations and almost rule cities . . . a world where . . . the mayor of your town may have condoned murder as an instrument of moneymaking, where no man can walk down a dark street in safety because law and order are things we talk about but refrain from practicing.[10]

For Indians and outlaws the hard-boiled detective story substitutes gangsters, for the frontier, the dark and dangerous streets where no man or woman can go in safety. Legitimate social authority is even more obviously weak and corrupt in the typical hard-boiled detective story. It usually turns out that the rich and respectable pillars of society are implicated with the criminal underworld, while in relation to this corrupt alliance of wealth and criminal power, the police and the courts are either weakly incompetent or actively on the take. In westerns this corrupt alliance is sometimes represented as a tie between an overbearing and tyrannical rancher and outlaws he hires to run out the homesteaders.

Also there is the corrupt alliance between a greedy Indian agent and a group of renegade Indians, or between a dishonest banker or railroad tycoon and killers he engages to take away an honest farmer's land. Sergio Leone saw this as the basic American western situation and he used it as such in his *Once upon a Time in the West*. Occasionally, as in *High Noon*, the entire town is too cowardly or avaricious to confront the outlaw gang. Or, there is a conflict between the good townspeople and the saloon crowd. But despite these variations, the western town and the city of the hard-boiled detective story are places of lawlessness, violence,

---

10. Chandler, "The Simple Art of Murder," in Howard Haycraft, ed., *The Art of the Mystery Story*, 236.

and inadequate social authority. Indeed, the kinship between the two genres was clear from the very beginning of the hard-boiled detective story, since Dashiell Hammett's first major hard-boiled novel, *Red Harvest*, was actually set in a western city not far removed in time from its days as a frontier mining settlement. Moreover, in terms of the characterization of the hero and the portrayal of the weakness and corruption of social authority, the western and the hard-boiled detective story have been growing more similar in recent decades. In his style and manner, in his cynicism and the moral ambiguity of his conduct, the western hero played by Clint Eastwood in so many recent films bears a far greater resemblance to Dashiell Hammett's Sam Spade than he does to Tom Mix and W. S. Hart.[11] And of course, Eastwood went on to play Dirty Harry, the ultimate hard-boiled cop.

Against the lurid background of a savage and corrupt society, the hero's code stands out as a beacon of disinterested morality. Because of his readiness for violence, his skepticism, and his unwillingness to play the sap for anybody, the hard-boiled hero is a figure capable of moving freely "down these mean streets" and surviving.[12] Yet as a man with a profoundly personal sense of honor and feeling of obligation to his role, this figure is never content to be a mere survivor. Reluctantly, but inexorably, he finds himself drawn into the quest for justice.

When the hero becomes committed to the cause of some other individual or group, the problem of his moral relationship to his code and to society becomes more complex and ambiguous. Because society is presented as wild and corrupt, its law and police machinery are at best inadequate and at worst unjust. The hero's code, however, rests primarily on a personal sense of honor and rightness, which is outside both law and conventional morality and, being primarily concerned with the individual's own image, does not contain a clear conception of the social virtue of justice. Thus, the hero appears in the rather paradoxical position of one who acts outside the law in order, supposedly, to more fully uphold it by bringing a just retribution to those criminals that society is

11. The television series *Have Gun, Will Travel* was an interesting reversal of the *Red Harvest* situation. There, a western hero showed all the characteristics of a hard-boiled detective. In the film *Coogan's Bluff* and its television spin-off *McCloud*, a cowboy lawman is transplanted from the West to New York City where he encounters a typical hard-boiled social setting. Such variations suggest that the western and the hard-boiled detective genre may evolve into some kind of a synthesis, though at the present time they still retain a fairly distinct generic differentiation.

12. The quotation is from Chandler's essay "The Simple Art of Murder."

unable to expose and punish. This paradoxical and ambiguous act—the stepping outside of the law in order to make manifest a more perfect justice is, I should say, the central myth shared by the western and hard-boiled detective genres, and, as such, suggests the existence of deeply-lying moral and cultural patterns in American society.

One of the most striking things to me about this myth of the hard-boiled, bitter, and reluctant hero moving through a corrupt and chaotic society is the degree to which it seems, at first, to be at odds with the generally optimistic, moralistic, and progressive tone of the mainstream of American popular culture. Where do Sam Spade, Mike Hammer, and Shane fit into the procession of Horatio Algerish self-made men of nineteenth-century popular novels and plays, or the noble, dedicated, and problem-solving doctors, lawyers, and teachers who provide much of what passes for heroic action on our television screens? How does the corrupt and decaying society of the hard-boiled hero relate to that sense of the "smiling aspects of life," as William Dean Howells put it, and the faith in progressive individual and collective betterment that seemingly characterized the popular vision of America at least until the 1960s? Of course, scholars like Leslie Fiedler have long argued that the mainstream of American literary creation has been more dominated by a pervasive gothic pessimism and an overpowering sense of evil than by optimism and a sense of boundless American potentiality for good.[13] Still earlier, D. H. Lawrence argued from his reading of Cooper that the true American soul was not the dauntless civilization-bringing pioneer but a bitter, alienated hunter—"hard, stoic, isolate, and a killer."[14] But such a vision of America seems more typical of major writers like Hawthorne and Melville or of alienated intellectuals such as Henry Adams than of our popular mythology.

Possibly, the hard-boiled detective and the more recent western gunfighter represent something new in American popular mythology. The hard-boiled detective story, the gangster saga, and the new tougher style of western hero exemplified by the gunfighters of the 1940s and 1950s developed around the time of the depression and world war. These hard-boiled heroes became popular at a time when the depression created large-scale disillusion and skepticism about American society,

13. See Leslie Fiedler, *Love and Death in the American Novel.*
14. D. H. Lawrence, *Studies in Classic American Literature,* 72. The original hardcover edition was published by Viking in 1923.

while World War II and the atomic bomb left a legacy of global insecurity and anxiety. It makes some sense to see in the hard-boiled protagonist a collective fantasy: the heroic figure immersed in the world of violence, corruption, and anarchy he inhabits, capable not only of personal survival but of imposing something of his sense of rightness and order on that world.

Thus, one might see the emergence of the hard-boiled hero as the adaptation into popular formulas of the more ambiguous vision of the world developed earlier by writers in the pessimistic and critical literary tradition of naturalism. The early stories of Hemingway seem to be one major source of the style and ethos of the hard-boiled detective writers, though that has been questioned. In any case, the more despairing naturalistic view of life so brilliantly articulated by Hemingway came to seem more plausible and exciting to the general public than the optimistic religious and moralistic vision that characterized most nineteenth-century popular genres.

Yet the special power of the hard-boiled hero may also stem from deeper sources in the American past than the particular anxieties and doubts of the twentieth century. The theme of the violent hero and the quest for salvation through violence certainly reaches back through American history to the seventeenth-century myths of Indian captivity. In *Regeneration through Violence*, Richard Slotkin shows how fear of corruption by the Indians was a threat felt so deeply and ambiguously in the Puritan imagination that it could be resolved only in fantasies or real acts of destructive violence.

Perhaps the deepest source of the twentieth-century fantasy of the hard-boiled detective lies in the Puritan sense of pervasive evil to be overcome, but only by the most sustained and austere self-discipline, and, finally by an act of violence. In this connection, the embodiment, or perhaps perversion would be a better word, of Puritanism was in the act of detection, both in sniffing out one's own sins and in the hunting down and destruction of witches, which might be viewed as one historical prototype of the hard-boiled detective story. Like Sam Spade, the Puritan witch hunters ruthlessly pursued the tiniest clues until they had uncovered and proved the guilt of the evil women who had become the chief source of sin through their trafficking with the devil. Many of the most striking hard-boiled villainesses—Brigid O'Shaughnessy of *The Maltese Falcon*, Carmen Sternwood of *The Big Sleep*, and Charlotte Manning of *I, the Jury*, for example—have a witch-like aura and must be captured or destroyed by the detective to prevent the corruption of others.[15] Moreover, the witch-hunt situation also contains in embryo another social theme of the hard-boiled hero saga—the failure of a secularized law to cope with pervasive evil and corruption. In the Puritan community in its earlier phases, moral, religious and secular law, were one and the same. In the twentieth century Western and hard-boiled detective story, this is, of course, not the case. The secular law has become separated from the moral law and the function of the detective or gunfighter is to enforce the moral law in the face of the weakness and corruption of the secular law. The difficulty of moralizing the law is one major source of the isolation, loneliness and frustration of the hard-boiled hero and in this, he differs from the witch hunter, who, like the vigilante, was not a lone individual but the agent of an aroused community.

Possibly, then, the Puritan witch hunter was the first example of that image of the ruthless pursuer of transcendent crimes who would later develop into the hard-boiled private eye and the gunfighter. In any case as this figure developed in the nineteenth century, he no longer had the explicit religious overtones of the witch hunter. Cooper's Leatherstocking and the Daniel Boone legends on which he was based added a number of new dimensions to the conception of an American hero. The Leatherstocking hero was more completely separated from society; he was of obscure origins; and he possessed great skills in violence and woodcraft. One particularly haunting version of the western hero—the Indian-hater who so fascinated major writers like Melville and Hawthorne—seems in his peculiar isolation and despair, as well as in the obsessive nature of his commitment to the destruction of evil, to be even closer in spirit to the contemporary hard-boiled detective than the more benevolent Leatherstocking.

By the later nineteenth century, the myth of the heroic tracker and hunter, able to move through a corrupt and chaotic world without being sullied by that corruption, had evidently become part of the legend of the American city. The occasional memoirs of later nineteenth century police detectives often include characterizations of the detective that bear a striking resemblance to the later fictional figures of Hammett, Chandler and Spillane. For example, George S. McWatters, a New York police detective from 1858 to 1870 remarks in his memoirs that

---

15. This figure of the femme fatale or bitch-villainess, so common to the hard-boiled detective story, rarely appears in the western. This may reflect both a generic difference and a difference in mythic tradition.

[the detective] is as bad in these days as was his prototype, St. Paul in his, 'all things to all men' but like him he is defensible, in that his rogueries and villainies are practiced for other people's salvation or security; and aside from the fact that the detective, in his calling, is often degraded to a sort of watchman or ordinary policeman, to help the big thieves, the merchants, etc. protect themselves from the small thieves, who are not able to keep places of business . . . his calling is a very noble one, and a singularly blessed one, inasmuch as it is the only one which I call to mind, by which hypocrisy is elevated into a really useful and beneficent art. ("Beneficient Roguery")

Such a statement seems to imply that the mythos of the heroic tough-guy prepared to use all the dirty tricks and amoral and lawless skills he knows to accomplish justice in a corrupt society was already well developed by the 1880s. I would speculate further that this hard-boiled ethos had very important cultural consequences at the end of the nineteenth century by providing a dramatic self-image for a number of the muckrakers. Lincoln Steffens, for example, tells us that he acquired his new view of the basic corruption of American society from his association with police detectives. Until he later converted to socialism, Steffens' conceived of the heroic muckraking reporter as another version of the lone hunter who prowls the mean streets of the corrupt city, immersing himself in its evil ways in order to expose the deeper crimes the law prefers to ignore. It certainly seems no accident that the world through which the fictional detectives of Hammett, Chandler, and Spillane hunt their evil prey seems very close to the shameful cities of the muckrakers with their corrupt alliances of business, politics, and crime.

Thus, the particular twentieth-century resonance of the myth of the hard-boiled hero may well have an even deeper source than the special anxieties of the twentieth century. The hard-boiled hero, the gunfighter, and their worlds of evil and corruption are contemporary versions of a myth of the isolated hero in a pervasively corrupt society and have welled up out of a strain of pessimism and despair in the American tradition that has been a part of our popular as well as intellectual culture. This strain is certainly a different one from the complex of ideology and feeling ordinarily associated with the popular vision of the American Dream. It suggests that there may have always been doubts about the American Dream among the public as well as among more skeptical intellectuals. One of the most perceptive observers of American life in the early nineteenth century, de Tocqueville, gave a striking characterization of that strange melancholy which often haunts the inhabitants of democratic countries in the midst of their abundance, and that disgust at life which sometimes seizes upon them in the midst of calm and easy circumstances. . . . In democratic times enjoyments are more intense than in the ages of aristocracy, and the number of those who partake in them is vastly larger; but, on the other hand, it must be admitted that man's hopes and desires are often blasted, the soul is more stricken and perturbed, and care itself more keen. (de Tocqueville, II, 147)

14

Chinatown and Generic Transformation in Recent American Films

This essay was originally written for the late Gerald Mast, who published an anthology of articles on film theory with Marshall Cohen in 1979. It's been one of my most often reprinted essays so I couldn't resist doing it again. It places Polanski's *Chinatown* in two related contexts: one is the tradition of the hard-boiled novel and film, or the roman and film noir as it is sometimes called. The other is emergent postmodernism with its complex relationship to such earlier traditions.

~

Roman Polanski's *Chinatown* (1974) invokes in many ways the American popular genre of the hard-boiled detective story. Most of us, I suppose, associate this tradition primarily with two undoubted film masterpieces, both of which starred Humphrey Bogart: John Huston's *The Maltese Falcon* (1941) and Howard Hawks's *The Big Sleep* (1946). But these are only the two most remembered and perhaps most memorable versions of a narrative formula that has been repeated in hundreds of novels, films, and television programs. Next to the western, the hard-boiled detective story is America's most distinctive contribution to the world's stock of action-adventure stories, our contemporary embodiment of the drama of heroic quest that has appeared in so many different cultures in so many different guises. Unlike the western, the epic quest on the frontier that can perhaps be traced back as far Indian captivity narratives of the late seventeenth century and certainly to Cooper's Leatherstocking saga of the early nineteenth century, the hard-boiled detective story is of quite recent origin. It developed through the medium of short action stories in pulp magazines like the famous *Black Mask*. By 1927, Dashiell Hammett had created in *Red Harvest* the first significant hard-boiled detective novel. Before he lapsed into literary silence in the mid-thirties, Hammett had created a core of hard-boiled adventure in his Continental Op stories and *The Dain Curse, The Maltese Falcon, The Glass Key,* and *The Thin Man*. In very short order, the hard-boiled detective made the transition from novel to film. *The Maltese Falcon* appeared in two film versions in the early thirties, before John Huston made the definitive film with Humphrey Bogart in 1941. *The Glass Key* was produced in the mid-thirties and in the forties; *The Thin Man* became one of the greatest movie successes of the later thirties, so popular that it led to a number of invented sequels. And as the hard-boiled detective flourished in film, Hammett's example inspired novels by writers whose literary skills ranged from the subtlety and depth of Raymond Chandler and Ross Macdonald to the sensational—and bestselling—crudity of Mickey Spillane. Radio and television also featured many series based on the figure of the hard-boiled detective. If a myth can be defined as a pattern of narrative known throughout the culture and presented in many different versions by many different tellers, then the hard-boiled detective story is in that sense an important American myth.

Chinatown invokes this myth in many different ways. Its setting in Los Angeles in the 1930s is very much the archetypal "hard-boiled" setting, the place and time of Hammett's and Chandler's novels. Hard-boiled novels and films are set in different places and times such as Spillane's Mike Hammer stories in New York City and John D. Macdonald's Travis McGee saga in Florida. However, the California city setting of Hammett and Chandler and the approximate time of their stories, memorialized in the period furnishings, visual icons, and style of the great hard-boiled films of the 1940s, have become for us the look and the temporal-spatial aura of the hard-boiled myth. It is this aura that Polanski generates, though there is something not quite right, something disturbingly off about it. In this case, it is the color.

The filmic world of the hard-boiled myth is preeminently a world of black and white. Its ambience is that compound of angular light and shadow enmeshed in webs of fog that grew out of the visual legacy of

German expressionism in drama and film, transformed into what is now usually called film noir by its adjustment to American locales and stories. Polanski carefully controls his spectrum of hue and tone in order to give it the feel of film noir, but it is nonetheless color with occasional moments of rich golden light—as in the scene in the dry riverbed. These moments of warm color often relate to scenes that are outside the usual setting or thematic content—for example, scenes in the natural landscape outside the city—that are themselves generally outside the world of the hard-boiled detective story. The invocation of many other traditional elements of the hard-boiled myth, the film noir tone, and the 1930s setting cue us to expect the traditional mythical world of the private-eye hero. But the presence of color, along with increasing deviations from established patterns of plot, motive, and character give us an eerie feeling of one myth colliding with and beginning to give way to others.

The established narrative formula of the hard-boiled story has as its protagonist a private investigator who occupies a marginal position with respect to the official social institutions of criminal justice. The private eye is licensed by the state, but though he may be a former member of a police force or district attorney's staff, he is not now connected with such an organization. In the course of the story, he is very likely to come into conflict with representatives of the official machinery, though he may also have friends who are police officers. His position on the edge of the law is very important, because one of the central themes of the hard-boiled myth is the ambiguity between institutionalized law enforcement and true justice. The story shows us that the police and the courts are incapable of effectively protecting the innocent and bringing the guilty to appropriate justice. Only the individual of integrity who exists on the margins of society can solve the crime and bring about true justice.

The marginal character of the private-eye hero is thus crucial to his role in the myth. It is also central to his characterization. We see him not only as a figure outside the institutionalized process of law enforcement, but as the paradoxical combination of a man of character who is also a failure. The private eye is a relatively poor man who operates out of a seedy office and never seems to make very much money by his exploits; he is the most marginal sort of lower middle-class quasi-professional. Yet unlike the usual stereotype of this social class, he is a man of honor and integrity who cannot be made to give up his quest for true justice. He is a compelling American hero type, clearly related to the traditional western hero who manifests many of the same characteristics.

The story begins when a client gives the hard-boiled hero a mission. It is typical that this initial mission is a deceptive one. Either the client is lying, as Brigid O'Shaughnessy lies to Sam Spade in *The Maltese Falcon,* or the client has been deceived and does not understand what is really at stake in giving the detective the case, as with General Sternwood in *The Big Sleep.* Often the detective is being used as a pawn in some larger plot of the client's. Whatever his initial impetus to action, the detective soon finds himself enmeshed in a very complex conspiracy involving a number of people from different spheres of society.

The ratiocinative English detectives of authors like Dorothy Sayers, Agatha Christie, or Ngaio Marsh investigate crimes by examining clues, questioning witnesses, and then using their intellectual powers of insight and deduction to arrive at the solution. The hard-boiled detective investigates through movement and encounter; he collides with the web of conspiracy until he has exposed outlines. The crime solved by the ratiocinative detective is usually that of a single individual. With this individual's means and motives for the criminal act rationally established, he or she can be turned over to the law for prosecution. But the hard-boiled detective encounters a linked series of criminal acts and discovers not a single guilty individual, but a corrupt society in which wealthy and respectable people are associated with gangsters and crooked politicians. Because it is society that is corrupt, and not just a single individual, the official machinery of law enforcement is unable to bring the guilty to justice.

The hard-boiled detective must decide for himself what kind of justice can be accomplished in the ambiguous urban world of modern America, and he himself must, in many instances, undertake to see this justice through. There have always been two different strains of the hard-boiled myth. Some writers, like Mickey Spillane and his many current followers, place their emphasis on the hero playing the role of executioner as well as detective and judge. More complex and artistic writers, like Hammett, Chandler, and Ross Macdonald, develop instead the theme of the hero's own relationship to the mythical role of lawman-outside-the-law. Their versions of the story rarely end with the detective's execution of the criminal; they prefer instead either to arrange for the criminal's self-destruction, as in Chandler's *Farewell, My Lovely,* or simply to bring about the criminal's exposure and confession, as in *The Maltese Falcon.*

This latter trend may have produced greater literature, but is perhaps best understood as a humane avoidance of the true thrust of the myth, which is essentially toward the marginal hero becoming right-eous judge and executioner, culture hero for a society that is profoundly conflicted between its commitment to legality and its belief that only individual actions are ultimately moral and just. One further element of the hard-boiled myth needs to be particularly noted: the role of the feminine antagonist. In almost every case, the hard-boiled hero en-counters a beautiful and dangerous woman in the course of his investi-gations and finds himself very much drawn toward her, even to the point of falling in love. Sometimes the woman is his client, sometimes a figure in the conspiracy. In a surprising number of cases (*The Maltese Falcon, The Big Sleep, Farewell, My Lovely, I, the Jury*, and many others) the woman turns out to be the murderess and, in Spillane at least, is killed by her detective-lover. This murky treatment of the "romance" between detective and dangerous female is occasionally resolved hap-pily, as in the Bogart-Bacall relationship at the end of the film version of *The Big Sleep* (in the novel this romantic culmination does not take place). However, such an outcome is rare. Even if the beautiful woman does not turn out to be a murderess, the detective usually separates from her at the end to return to his marginal situation, basically unchanged by what has happened to him and ready to perform more acts of Justice when the occasion arises.

We can see from this brief résumé of the hard-boiled formula how close a resemblance *Chinatown* bears to it. But the film deviates increas-ingly from the myth until, by the end of the story, the film arrives at an ending almost contrary to that of the myth. Instead of bringing justice to a corrupt society, the detective's actions leave the basic source of cor-ruption untouched. Instead of protecting the innocent, his investiga-tion leads to the death of one victim and the deeper moral destruction of another. Instead of surmounting the web of conspiracy with honor and integrity intact, the detective is overwhelmed by what has hap-pened to him.

True, the action of *Chinatown* increasingly departs from the tradi-tional hard-boiled formula as the story progresses; however, there are, from the very beginning, a number of significant departures from the standard pattern. The choice of Jack Nicholson and Faye Dunaway as leading actors is a good instance of this. Nicholson and Dunaway bear certain physical and stylistic resemblances to Bogart and Bacall, and these are obviously played up through costume, makeup, and gesture. Indeed, there is one early scene in a restaurant that is almost eerily rem-iniscent of the famous horse-racing interchange between Bogart and

Bacall in *The Big Sleep*. But much as they echo the archetypal hard-boiled duo in a superficial way, the characters played by Nicholson and Dunaway differ considerably from those created by Hammett and Chandler.

Dunaway has a neurotic fragility, an underlying quality of desperation, that becomes even more apparent as her true situation is revealed. She never generates the sense of independence and courage that Bacall brought to her hard-boiled roles or her qualities of wit and sophistication. Those characteristics that made Bacall such an appropriate romantic partner for the hard-boiled detective are quickly seen in the case of Dunaway's character to be a veneer covering depths of anguish and ambiguity. Nicholson also portrays, at least early on, a character who is not quite what he seems. His attempt to be the tough, cynical, and humorous private eye is undercut on all sides; he is terrible as a wit, as his attempt to tell his assistants the Chinese joke makes clear. Nor is he the tough, marginal man of professional honor he pretends to be at the beginning; actually, he is a successful small businessman who has made a good thing out of exploiting the more sordid needs of his fellowmen. One of the most deeply symbolic clichés of the traditional hard-boiled formula is the hero's refusal to do divorce business, in fact one of the primary functions of the private detective. By this choice the traditional private eye of the myth established both his personal sense of honor and his transcendent vocation, distinguishing himself from the typical private investigator.

However, from the beginning of *Chinatown*, it is clear that the accumulation of evidence of marital infidelity is Jake Gittes's primary business. He is, indeed, drawn into the affairs of Noah Cross, his daughter, and her husband by a commission to document a supposedly clandestine affair between the husband and a much younger woman. The name, J. J. Gittes, which Polanski and Robert Towne, the screenwriter, chose for their protagonist, is a good indication of this aspect of his character. Think of the names of the traditional hard-boiled detectives: Sam Spade, with its implication of hardness and digging beneath the surface; Philip Marlowe, with its aura of knightliness and chivalry; Lew Archer, with its mythical overtones. Gittes, or "Gits," as Noah Cross ironically keeps pronouncing it, connotes selfishness and grasping and has, in addition, a kind of ethnic echo very different from the pure Anglo of Spade, Marlowe, and Archer.

Yet, qualified and even "antiheroic" as he is, Gittes is swept up into the investigation of a murder, which in turn leads him to evidence of a large-scale conspiracy involving big business, politics, crime, and the whole underlying social and environmental structure of Los Angeles. Like the traditional hard-boiled detective, Gittes begins as a cynical and alienated individual. However, in the course of the action he becomes committed moral agent with a mission At the same time he becomes romantically involved with a character deeply implicated in the web of conspiracy, the mysterious widow of the man who has been murdered. By the middle of the film Gittes is determined to expose the political conspiracy that he senses beneath the surface, and also to resolve the question of the guilt or innocence of the woman to whom he has been so strongly attracted. Thus far, the situation closely resembles that of *The Maltese Falcon* and *The Big Sleep*. It is at this point, however, that the action again vastly departs from that of the traditional hard-boiled story. Instead of demonstrating his ability to expose and punish the guilty, Gittes steadily finds himself confronting a depth of evil and chaos so great that he is unable to control it. In relation to the social and personal depravity represented by Noah Cross and the world in which he can so successfully operate, the toughness, moral concern, and professional skill of Gittes not only seem ineffectual, but lead to results that are the very opposite of those intended. At the end of the film, Noah Cross is free to continue his rapacious depredations on the land, the city, and the body of his own daughter-granddaughter; and the one person who might have brought Cross to some form of justice—his daughter-mistress—has been destroyed.

Gittes's confrontation with a depth of depravity beyond the capacity of the hard-boiled ethos of individualistic justice is, I think, the essential significance of the Chinatown motif in the film. Chinatown becomes a symbol of life's deeper moral enigmas, those unintended consequences of action that are past understanding and control. Gittes has been there before. Sometime earlier in Chinatown his attempts at individual moral action led to the death of a woman he cared for. It is apparently this tragedy that motivated him to leave the police force and set up as a private investigator. Now he has been drawn back into moral action, and it is again in Chinatown that his attempt to live out the myth of individualistic justice collides with the power of evil and chance in the world. The result is not heroic confrontation and the triumph of justice, but tragic catastrophe and the destruction of the innocent.

Chinatown places the hard-boiled detective story within a view of the world that is deeper and more catastrophic, more enigmatic in its evil, more sudden and inexplicable in its outbreaks of violent chance. In the end, the image of heroic, moral action embedded in the traditional private-eye myth turns out to be totally inadequate to the task of overcoming the destructive realities revealed in the course of this story. Not only is the revelation of depths beneath depths made increasingly evident in the film's relentless movement toward Chinatown, the symbolic locus of darkness, strangeness, and catastrophe, but it also appears in the film's manipulation of action and image. The themes of water and drought, which weave through the action, not only reveal the scope of Noah Cross's conspiracy to dominate a city by manipulating its water supply, but also create a texture of allusion that resonates with the mythical meanings traditionally associated with water and drought. Polanski's version of Los Angeles in the 1930s reveals the transcendent mythical world of the sterile kingdom, the dying king, and the drowned man beneath it. This is the world of, for example, T. S. Eliot's *The Waste Land* and before that of the cyclical myths of traditional cultures.

Another of the film's mythic motifs is its revelation of the rape-incest by which Noah Cross has fathered a daughter by his own daughter and is apparently intending to continue this method of establishing a progeny through the agency of his daughter-granddaughter. This is another of the ways in which the hard-boiled myth is thrust into depths beyond itself. Though traditionally an erotically potent figure, the private eye's sexuality seems gentility itself when confronted with the potent perversity embodied in the figure of Noah Cross. Cross is like the primal father imagined by Freud in *Totem and Taboo*. Against his overpowering sexual, political, and economic power, our hero—Oedipus in the form of J. J. Gittes—proves to be tragically impotent, an impotence symbolized earlier in the film by the slashing (castration) of his nose and the large comic bandage he wears throughout much of the action.

Manipulating a traditional American popular myth to reveal its profound inadequacy when confronted by a world that is deeper and more enigmatic in its evil and destructive force, *Chinatown* is brilliant. In fact, it is one of the richest and most artistically powerful instances of a type of film of which we have seen many striking instances in the last decade. It is difficult to know just what to call this type of film. On one level, it relates to the traditional literary mode of burlesque or parody in which a well-established set of conventions or a style is subjected to some form of ironic or humorous exploitation. Indeed, many of the most striking and successful films of the period have been out-and-out burlesques of traditional popular genres, such as Mel Brooks's *Blazing Saddles* (westerns), his *Young Frankenstein* (the Frankenstein horror cycle), and his *High Anxiety* (Hitchcock's psychological suspense films).

However, burlesque and parody involve a basically humorous thrust unlike many of the most powerful generic variations of the last decade or so. Films like *Bonnie and Clyde* (Arthur Penn), *The Wild Bunch* (Sam Peckinpah), *The Godfather* (Francis Ford Coppola), and *Nashville* (Robert Altman) though based on established popular genres tend like *Chinatown* more toward tragedy than comedy in their overall structures. It seems odd to speak of a tragic parody or a doomed burlesque. Therefore, one is at first tempted to conclude that the connection between *Blazing Saddles* and *The Wild Bunch* or *The Black Bird* (David Giler) and *The Long Goodbye* (Robert Altman) is only superficial. Yet it is clear that in many of these films the line between comedy and tragedy is not so simply drawn. What, for example, of the extraordinary combination of Keystone Cops chase scenes and tragic carnage in *Bonnie and Clyde,* or the interweaving of sophomoric high jinks and terrible violence in Altman's *M*A*S*H* (1970)?

This puzzling combination of humorous burlesque and high seriousness seems to be a mode of expression characteristic of our period, not only in film, but also in literary forms. It is at the root of much that is commonly described as the literature of the absurd or of so-called black humor, and is characteristic as well of the style of major contemporary novelists like Thomas Pynchon. By adopting this mode, American movies have, in a sense, become a more integral part of the mainstream of postmodernism. In addition through their frequent allusions to the conventions of American film, contemporary novelists and dramatists have created a new kind of relationship between themselves and the traditions of popular culture.

The linkage among these many different kinds of contemporary literary, dramatic, and cinematic expression is their use of the conventions of traditional popular genres. Basically, they do in different ways what Polanski does in *Chinatown:* set the elements of a conventional popular genre in an altered context, thereby making us perceive these traditional forms and images in a new way. It appears to me that we can classify the various relationships between traditional generic elements and altered contexts into four major modes.

First, there is the burlesque proper. In this mode, elements of a conventional formula or style are situated in contexts so incongruous or exaggerated that the result is laughter. There are many different ways in which this can be done. The formulaic elements can be acted out in so extreme a fashion that they come into conflict with our sense of reality, forcing us to see these aspects of plot and character as fantastic contrivances. A good example of this is the burlesque image of the gunfighter in *Cat Ballou* (Elliott Silverstein, 1965). In this film we are shown how, by putting on his gunfighter costume, a process that involves strapping himself into a corset within which he can barely move, an old drunk can become the terror of the bad guys. Or, in a closely related type of altered context, a situation that we are ordinarily accustomed to seeing in rather romanticized terms can be suddenly invested with a sense of reality. This is how the famous campfire scene in *Blazing Saddles* operates. The cowboys sit around a blazing campfire at night, a scene in which we are accustomed to hearing mournful and lyrical cowboy ballads performed by such groups as the Sons of the Pioneers. Instead we are treated to an escalating barrage of flatulence. Anyone familiar with the usual digestive aftermath of canned wilderness fare is likely to be delighted at this sudden exposure of the sham involved in the traditional western campfire scene. Sam Peckinpah's *Ride the High Country* (1962) offers another instance of the humorous effect of the sudden penetration of reality into a fantasy when one of his aging heroes attempts to spring gracefully into the saddle and is suddenly halted by a twinge of rheumatism.

In addition to these sudden confrontations with reality, conventional patterns can be used to humorous effect by inverting them. A good example of this is the device of turning a character with all the marks of a hero into a coward, or vice versa. A favorite manifestation of this in recent films and novels is what might be called the hard-boiled schlemiel, the private detective who turns out to be totally unable to solve a crime or resist villains except by accident. This type of burlesque is even more effective when the inverted presentation actually seems to bring to the surface some latent meanings that were lurking all the time in the original convention. Mel Brooks is a particular master of this kind of burlesque. In his *Young Frankenstein*, the monster attacks Frankenstein's fiancé, Elizabeth—a moment of tragic violence in the original novel—and the result is complete sexual satisfaction on both sides, something most of us had suspected all along.

These two primary techniques of burlesque, the inversion of conventions and their undermining by the intrusion of reality, have frequently appeared in the history of literature as a response to highly conventionalized genres. So the Greek tragedies gave rise to their burlesque counterparts in the plays of Aristophanes. The western, one of our most formally distinctive genres, has been the inspiration of parody and burlesque throughout its history from Twain and Harte's assaults on James Fenimore Cooper to Brooks's send-up in *Shane* and *High Noon*. Thus, there is nothing particularly new in the penchant for humorous burlesque so evident in recent films. What is more striking in the films of the last decade is their use of these techniques of generic parody less for humor than for ultimately serious purposes.

The second major mode of generic transformation is the cultivation of nostalgia. In this mode, traditional generic features of plot, character, setting, and style are deployed to recreate the aura of a past time. The power of nostalgia lies especially in its capacity to evoke a sense of warm reassurance by bringing before our mind's eye images from a time when things seemed more secure and full of promise and possibility. Though one can, of course, evoke nostalgia simply by viewing films of the past, a contemporary nostalgia film cannot simply duplicate the past experience, but must make us aware in some fashion of the relationship between past and present. Attempts to evoke nostalgia merely by imitating past forms, as was the case with the television series, *City of Angels,* do not generally work because they seem simply obsolescent. A truly successful nostalgia film, like Henry Hathaway's *True Grit* (1969), succeeds because it sets its highly traditional generic content in a slightly different context, thereby giving us both a sense of contemporaneity and of pastness In *True Grit,* this was done in a number of ways. First of all, the central character played by Kim Darby represented an extremely contemporary image of adolescent girlhood. She was independent, aggressive, and full of initiative, a shrewd horse trader, and a self-confident, insistent moralist, unlike the shy desert rose of the traditional western. John Wayne, aging and paunchy, did not attempt to cover up the ravages of the years and pretend to the vigorous manhood of his earlier films. Instead, with eye patch, unshaven face, and sagging flesh, he fully enacted his aging. Similarly, the film's images of the western landscape were in many ways deromanticized. But out of this context of contemporaneity there sprang the same old story of adventure and heroism culminating in an exuberant shootout that seemed to embody everybody's best dreams of Saturday matinees. The same kind of nostalgic reinvocation of the past played an even more powerful role in Peckinpah's *Ride the High Country,* in which two tired, aging, and obsolescent heroes ride again. A hard-boiled example is Dick Richards's recent version of Raymond Chandler's *Farewell, My Lovely* (1975), where a sagging Robert Mitchum moves out of the malaise of modernity and reenacts once more the ambiguous heroic quest of the hard-boiled detective of the 1930s and 1940s.

The difference between nostalgic reincarnation of an earlier genre like *Farewell, My Lovely* and the more complex ironies of *Chinatown* and Robert Altman's *The Long Goodbye* is considerable. It is a difference similar to the one between *True Grit* and a neo-western like Altman's *McCabe and Mrs. Miller* (1971) or Arthur Penn's *Little Big Man* (1970). In the former case, nostalgia is the end result of the film. In the latter nostalgia is often powerfully evoked, but as a means of undercutting or ironically commenting upon the generic experience itself. This brings us to the third and, in many respects, the most powerful mode of generic transformation in recent films: the use of traditional generic structures as a means of demythologization. A film like *Chinatown* deliberately invokes the basic characteristics of a traditional genre in order to bring its audience to see that genre as the embodiment of an inadequate and destructive myth. *Chinatown* sets the traditional model of the hardboiled detective's quest for justice and integrity over against Polanski's sense of a universe so steeped in ambiguity, corruption, and evil that such individualistic moral enterprises are doomed by their innocent naivete to end in tragedy and self-destruction.

The work of Arthur Penn has also explored the ironic and tragic aspects of the myths implicit in traditional genres. His *Night Moves* (1975), another transformation of the detective film was, like *Chinatown,* the ambiguous enactment of a reluctant quest for the truth about a series of crimes. As the detective approaches a solution to the crimes, he becomes morally and emotionally involved in the quest, making it more and more difficult for him to integrate truth, feeling, and morality. In the end, like Polanski's Jake Gittes, he is more dazed than fulfilled by the catastrophe his investigation has brought about.

In other films, such as *The Left-Handed Gun* (1958), *Bonnie and Clyde,* and *Little Big Man,* Penn created versions of the western and the gangster film in which traditional conventions were inverted, but the effect was tragic rather than humorous. In *Little Big Man,* for example, the conventional western opposition between Indians and pioneers, which embodies two of the most powerful of our western myths, the Indian captivity and the massacre, serves as the basis of the plot. However, the conventional renderings of these myths pit the humanely civilizing thrust of the pioneers against the savage ferocity and eroticism of the Indians and thereby justify the conquest of the west. Penn inverts this pattern. In his film it is the Indians who are humane and civilized, while the pioneers are violent, corrupt, sexually repressed, and madly ambitious. By the end, when Custer's cavalry rides forward to attack the Indian villages, our sympathies are all with the Indians. From this perspective, the conquest of the West is demythologized from the triumph of civilization into a historical tragedy of the destruction of a rich and vital human culture.

Despite its many virtues, the film version of *Little Big Man* was less artistically successful than Thomas Berger's novel, on which it was based, primarily because as the film proceeds, Penn loses the ironic detachment that Berger successfully maintains throughout the novel. Penn's portrayal of Custer as a lunatic symbol of aggressive American imperialism is overstated, and toward the end the cinematic *Little Big Man* tends to fall back from the serious exploration of mythical meanings into melodramatic burlesque.

This is an artistic problem common to films that try to demythologize traditional genres. Penn was far more successful in *Bonnie and Clyde,* which will remain one of the major masterpieces of recent American film. Taking off from the traditional gangster film with its opposition between the outlaw and society, *Bonnie and Clyde* established a dialectic between conventional and inverted patterns that is powerfully sustained throughout the film. In the traditional gangster film, a powerful individual, frustrated by the limitations of his lower-class origins, is driven to a life of crime. Initially the audience is inclined to sympathize and identify with this character, but as he becomes involved in criminal actions, he overreaches himself and becomes a vicious killer who must be tracked down and destroyed by the representatives of society. The underlying myth of this genre affirms the limits of individual aggression in a society that tolerates and even encourages a high degree of personal enterprise and violence. The gangster becomes a tragic figure not because he is inherently evil, but because he fails to recognize these limits. The myth assures us that society is not repressive or violent; instead it shows how criminal violence evokes its own inevitable doom. It is this comforting myth of proper and improper violence that Penn demythologizes in *Bonnie and Clyde.* As in *Little Big Man,* conventional patterns are inverted. Instead of representing a limit to aggression and violence, society is portrayed as its fountainhead, while the outlaw protagonists are seen as victims of society's bloodlust. Throughout the film, we are shown a depressed and chaotic society that yearns for action and that satisfies this yearning by vicariously enjoying the robberies and murders of the Barrow gang. Penn effectively develops this theme through his representation of the newspapers that so avidly report the gang's adventures and by the reactions of witnesses to the gang's attacks on banks. Finally, its lust for the hunt aroused, society itself takes up the pursuit in packs and posses, and, in a final ambush that set a new level in explicit screen violence, the doomed Bonnie and Clyde are shot to pieces. But the inversion of generic conventions is still more complex, for Penn refuses simply to reverse the opposition between gangster and society as he does in *Little Big Man*. The protagonists of *Bonnie and Clyde* are not just victims of society. They are themselves very much a part of the society they are attacking. They share its basic aspirations and confusions, and they yearn above all to be reintegrated with it. In many respects, their actions reflect a desperate and misconceived attempt to achieve some measure of the status, security, and sense of belonging that ought to be among the basic gifts of a society to its members. Instead of simply reversing the meanings conventionally ascribed to the opposing forces of criminal and society in the gangster genre, *Bonnie and Clyde* expressed a complex and dark awareness that this basic opposition was itself a mythical simplification. Thereby, it showed us the deeper and more difficult irony of the twisted and inseparable fates of individuals and their society, acknowledging, in its way, that skein of ambiguous inevitability which Polanski summed up in the symbol of Chinatown and which Francis Ford Coppola developed through the fateful intertwining of individuals, "families," and society in *The Godfather*.

Though the demythologization of traditional genres has been primarily evident in the work of younger directors, it has also had some influence on the later work of some of the classic filmmakers, most noticeably perhaps in the later westerns of John Ford, particularly *The Searchers* (1956), *Cheyenne Autumn* (1964), and *The Man Who Shot Liberty Valance* (1962). In *Liberty Valance*, Ford symbolized the conquest of the West through a story in which the territory's last major outlaw was supposedly killed in a shootout by a man destined to lead the territory into the "blessings of civilization." In fact, the legend of Senator Stoddard's heroic deed was a myth, the actual shooting of Liberty Valance having been done by another man. Toward the end of the film, the newspaper editor to whom Senator Stoddard confesses the truth says simply "when the legend becomes a fact, print the legend." But is this an ironic comment on the falsity of legends and newspapers alike, or is it some kind of affirmation of the significance of myth in spite of its unreality? Ford was apparently inclined to the latter interpretation, for he once told Peter Bogdanovich, "We've had a lot of people who were supposed to be great heroes and you know damn well they weren't. But it's good for the country to have heroes to look up to."

This brings us to a fourth and final mode of generic transformation that might be described as the reaffirmation of myth for its own sake. In films in this mode, a traditional genre and its myth are probed and the fantasy of the myth exposed, but then the myth itself is at least partially affirmed as a reflection of authentic human aspirations and needs. This is the element that becomes dominant in Ford's later westerns, in which he seems to see the heroic ethos of the West in critical terms and become more and more sympathetic with the Indian victims of the westward movement. Yet, at the same time that he becomes more cynical about the reality of the western myth, he seems to feel even more strongly the need to affirm its heroic ideals.

Thus, in his powerful late film *The Searchers*, Ford turned to the old western theme of Indian captivity, portraying the mad, obsessive hatred with which a white man pursues a band of Indians who have captured and adopted his niece. Yet Ford also changed the ending of the original novel—in the novel, the mad Indian-hater was finally destroyed by his obsession, but Ford redeems his protagonist and makes him answer in order to reaffirm the heroism and self-sacrifice of this obsessive quest. *The Searchers* is a powerful and beautiful film, yet one feels, in the end, that Ford's sense of historical reality and his feelings about genre and myth have come into collision.

Sam Peckinpah's *The Wild Bunch*, for all its ugliness and violence, is a more coherent example of the destruction and reaffirmation of myth. Throughout the film, Peckinpah undercuts the conventional western's heroic struggle between pioneers and outlaws and his pioneer lawmen are despicable bounty hunters in the employ of the railroad, and they kill the guilty and the innocent indiscriminately. His outlaws are not much better; they are brutal, coarse, and quite capable of leaving a wounded comrade behind. Moreover, their type of criminal operation has become absurdly obsolescent in the early twentieth-century west of the film. In the end, Peckinpah's outlaw protagonists are drawn into a ridiculously destructive shootout with an entire Mexican village full of troops and are completely wiped out in the process. Yet the film also leaves us with a sense that through their hopeless action these coarse and vicious outlaws have somehow transcended themselves and become embodiments of a myth of heroism that people need in spite of the realities of their world.

While I have separated the four modes of generic transformation—humorous burlesque, evocation of nostalgia, demythologization of generic myth, and the reaffirmation of myth as myth—into categories in order to define them more clearly, most films that employ one of these modes are likely to use another at some point. Probably the best films based on generic transformation employ some combination of several of these modes in the service of one overriding artistic purpose; *Chinatown* uses both humorous burlesque and nostalgic evocation as a basis for its devastating exploration of the genre of the hard-boiled detective and his myth. Some directors seem to have a predilection for one of these modes; Brooks is primarily oriented toward burlesque, Bogdanovich toward nostalgia, Penn toward demythologization, and Peckinpah toward reaffirmation. Some directors—Robert Altman springs particularly to mind—have, in their best films, worked out a rich and fascinating dialectic among different modes of generic transformation. In films like *McCabe and Mrs. Miller, The Long Goodbye, Thieves Like Us* (1974), and *Nashville* it is quite difficult to decide at the end whether Altman is attacking or reaffirming the genre on which he has based each particular work. In fact, until the last two or three years, Altman's filmography had looked almost as if he had planned a systematic voyage through the major traditional film genres. That generic transformation has been so important a source of artistic energy to the most vital younger directors suggests that it is a key to the current state of the American film.

There are probably many reasons for the importance of these modes of filmmaking in the last decade, but in conclusion I will comment briefly on what seem to me the most important factors involved in the proliferation of this kind of film. I think it is not primarily the competition of television. Though television has been somewhat more conservative in its use of generic transformation than film, the same modes seem to be turning up with increasing frequency in television series. Instead I would point to the tendency of genres to become exhausted, to our growing historical awareness of modern popular culture, and finally, to the decline of the underlying mythology on which traditional genres have been based since the late nineteenth century. Generic exhaustion is a common phenomenon in the history of culture. One can almost make out a life cycle of genres as they move from an initial period of articulation and discovery, through a phase of conscious self-awareness on the part of both creators and audiences, to a time when the generic patterns have become so well-known that people become tired of their predictability. It is at this point that parodic and satiric treatments proliferate and new genres gradually arise. Our major traditional genres—the western, the detective story, the musical, the domestic comedy have, after all, been around for a long time. They may have simply reached a point of creative exhaustion.

In our time, the awareness of the persistence of genres has been intensified by an increasing historical awareness of film. A younger generation of directors has a sense of film history quite different from many of their predecessors who, like Ford and Hawks, were involved with the art of film almost from its beginnings. Similarly, audiences have a kind of sophistication about the history of genres different from earlier film publics because of the tremendous number of past films now regularly shown on television and by college film societies.

But I am inclined to think that there is more to it than that. The present significance of generic transformation as a creative mode reflects the feeling that not only the traditional genres, but also the cultural myths they once embodied are no longer fully adequate to the imaginative needs of our time. We may eventually see emerging out of this period of generic transformation a new set of generic constructs more directly related to the imaginative landscape of the next millennium. The present period of American filmmaking will then seem in retrospect an important time of artistic and cultural transition. Like many transition periods, it may also turn out to be a time of the highest artistic accomplishment.

15

Violence and Apple Pie: Reflections on Literature, Culture, and Violence in America

This previously unpublished essay was yet another unsuccessful attempt to deal with the paradoxical tragedy of violence in American culture. In essence it explores the cultural background of American violence in connection with the mythic tradition of the frontier and the impact of Puritanism and racism in America. There's nothing particularly original about these ideas, but I think I give them a few interesting twists.

Harrodsburg is a normally quiet little town on the edge of the prosperous Bluegrass, but it is one of Kentucky's earliest settlements whose founding goes back to 1774 and evokes memories of Indian warfare and the frontier. In fact, one of the town's major features is a reconstruction of old Fort Harrod, where pioneer settlers struggled to survive the rigors of the wilderness and the hostility of the Native Americans and succeeded, usually through violence, in expropriating the Indians and reducing the forest and canebrakes to farms.

Not long ago, six young men from Harrodsburg gathered together in a field near the town and one of them, for reasons that are still not clear, pulled out a gun and shot four of the group, killing two and severely wounding two others. Thus Harrodsburg joined the growing list of small towns and cities shocked by the sudden eruption of violence among young people: Littleton, Colorado; Paducah, Kentucky; Tunica, Mississippi, Eugene, Oregon and many others. While Americans have become familiar with and even largely indifferent to violence among young people in the inner city, this rash of killings among high-school students and teenagers is making gun control, almost for the first time, a serious political issue. It has also led to a renewal of the perennial struggle to understand the prevalence of violence in America.

Along with the horrors of school violence, the American public has been shocked by an apparent upsurge in "hate" crimes, and in random shootings by disgruntled workers. Young white Texans brutally dragged an African American man behind a truck until he was virtually decapitated; Jewish children in California were shot in a day care center; a gay young man in Wyoming was tied to a fence and beaten to death. Angry workers in places as diverse as Chicago, Illinois, Atlanta, Georgia, and Honolulu, Hawaii have shot and killed many fellow workers as well as bystanders. Violence has apparently erupted not only in the inner city, but in what many consider the very center of American experience — the public school and the workplace.

The history of violence in America is pervaded by racism and the violence associated with the protection of white male supremacy. Instances of violence due to ethnic, racial, and moralistic hatred have recurrently marked American life, since the first settlers began killing Native Americans in order to take over their land. In fact, one can easily discern a cycle of violence that has been enacted in many ways in American history. This cycle began when members of the dominant white Euro-American classes crossed a frontier in search of property and profit. Their incursion against the original inhabitants provoked defensive violence that was then used to justify further violence on the part of the "pioneers" and the eventual destruction, expropriation, or domination of the original inhabitants. A similar cycle manifested itself in the relationship between American white owners and African American slaves. The fear of slave revolt, provoked by the violent domination exercised over the slaves, was then used to establish the need for even harsher and more repressive methods of control. An extension of this cycle characterized relations between southern whites and emancipated African Americans during the Reconstruction era and well into the twentieth century, the fear of rape and miscegenation being invoked to justify the thousands of lynchings and other forms of violent action that terrorized African Americans in the south.

Thus, even before Turner formulated his frontier thesis, Americans perceived their history in relation to the white Anglo-Saxon conquest of the continent and the "winning of the West." Turner's thesis gave a kind of intellectual coherence to this "epic of America" and established the view of American identity that would dominate the writing of American history through much of the twentieth century. However, few Americans at any time actually went through the frontier experience. It was the mythicizing of this experience as a narrative of the relationship between white American males and wilderness that became crucial to the formulation of the American identity.

The narrative went something like this. Since the original condition of America was wildness and savagery, the founding experience involved crossing the boundaries of civilization and entering into a realm of disorder and lawlessness in which the only possible recourse was violence. Since the wilderness was populated with savages determined to resist the establishment of "law and order" violence became the sacred duty of heroic individuals bent on reducing chaos to order, savagery to civilization.[1] Through the courage of heroic individuals the savages were destroyed or forced onto reservations where their destructiveness could harm only themselves. Thus, the myth sanctified the act of heroic individual violence as the foundation of a new order and, in the dramatic form of the western, this heroic moment was immortalized as the shootout between pioneers and Indians, or lawmen and outlaws.

Though this mythic and ideological narrative of justification and "regeneration through violence" (Richard Slotkin's useful phrase)[2] was

---

1. History, as is often the case, is very different from the myth. In most cases, it was the aggressive invaders who instigated violence against the native occupants in order to take land and resources away from them. Then, when the natives belatedly reacted against their expropriation their resistance was characterized as savage violence that justified further violence to bring about a permanent order (i.e. solidify the political, social, and economic hegemony of the invaders). Those natives who were not exterminated were then restricted to reservations where any violence was directed against themselves. A related pattern is clear in the case of African Americans whose resistance to slavery was used to justify further repression and restriction. In the twentieth century, prisons have served much the same function as reservations, containing those whose violence might pose a threat to the middle and upper classes.

2. Richard Slotkin's great study of the frontier myth beginning with *Regeneration through Violence* has greatly influenced my own thinking on these issues.

first used against the Native Americans and Hispanics expropriated by the new white Americans, it was soon adapted to other purposes. After the Civil War southerners used it to deal with the challenge of newly emancipated African Americans. It also played an important role in white protestant American resistance to newly arrived ethnic minorities in the later nineteenth century. One can even make the argument that it was used against women's demands for equality. Undoubtedly the mythology of frontier conquest was reflected in the twentieth-century significance of the western as an American popular art form. Finally, Richard Slotkin persuasively suggests that the latest embodiment and final disaster of the frontier myth was in American foreign policy during the Cold War, a policy that led to the crossing of one frontier after another with horrendous results.

The lasting power of the myth of heroic violence on the frontier helps explain the remarkably paradoxical attitudes toward violence prevalent in nineteenth- and twentieth-century America. Americans view their country as a peaceful one where internal conflicts are resolved through the democratic process and whose major role in the world is to bring freedom and peace to all human beings. At the same time, Americans commit more murders than any other democratic people and possess the millions of weapons that make this possible. Moreover, since the 1860s, when as historians often point out, Americans virtually invented modern total war in their own Civil War, American history in the world has been one of massive wars in which, however justified, American soldiers have killed great numbers of other people including each other.

The myth of frontier conquest became a fundamental component of the American ideology by subsuming a number of other important American themes. One was the right of revolution, which proclaimed that the possession and use of arms was a fundamental political right of the individual citizen. Another was the American myth of equality, which not only limited equality to white males, but also seemed to accept a large amount of economic inequality among these males so long as the individual had the symbolic power of violence and the right to possess weapons. Not surprisingly the Colt Revolver was known as the "great equalizer."

Closely related to the myth of frontier conquest, the ritual of the hunt was a primary rite of American masculinity throughout the nineteenth century and, in many areas, is still a major sport and an ideological justification for the ownership of guns. The myth of the hunt pits the lone individual against nature's powers often in the form of a gigantic beast who can be seen as a substitute for the dangerous savages after their disappearance or their restriction to a reservation. The hunt thus became and remains an annual reaffirmation of the heroic individual's right to violence in the conquest of wilderness, even though in most cases the actual target of the hunt, a deer or a duck, hardly poses any significant threat to the hunter. The power, as well as the ambiguities, of the myth of the hunt are amply revealed in American literature and film. Many of our most powerful works of literature, from Cooper's *Leatherstocking Tales* and Melville's *Moby Dick,* down to Faulkner's "The Bear" and to important late twentieth-century films like *Deliverance* and *The Deer Hunter,* treat the myth of the hunt as an archetypal American narrative and a symbol of the destructiveness inherent in the drive to conquer wilderness.

Finally, American myths of violence also grew out of the puritanism that made the American drive to conquer the wilderness a quest for redemption and purification. This, I think is the primary source of that strange aura of religion and moralism that so often accompanies American violence. American religiosity has always been deeply imbued with violence and in the major protestant denominations and evangelical ministries that dominate the spiritual climate of America there is little evidence of the pacifism of many Christian traditions.

The Puritans justified their violence against Native Americans as a moral crusade against diabolical savagery and this tradition continued in the great religious revivals on the frontier that had such an important influence on the shaping of American religiosity, particularly in the South and parts of the Midwest. Much of American Christendom has turned a blind eye to the violence used against Native Americans and African Americans and has done little to expose and remedy violence within families most commonly resulting from the anger of men against women and children. American Protestantism, on the whole, allied itself during the settlement of the West with the sometimes hysterical struggle to maintain white supremacy as a moral crusade against the threat of savagery and frontier chaos.

Many have commented on the powerful connections among American religion, racism, and violence against minorities, but one of the most eloquent statements of this connection can be found in William Faulkner's *Light in August,* a powerful novel about racism, religion, and lynching. Hightower, a defrocked minister, hears music coming from a church near where he lives, and

[l]istening, he seems to hear within in it the apotheosis of his own history, his own land, his own environed blood: that people from which he sprang and among whom he lives who can never take either pleasure or catastrophe or escape from either without brawling over it. Pleasure ecstasy, they cannot seem to bear: their escape from it is in violence, in drinking and fighting and praying; catastrophe too, the violence identical and apparently inescapable. *And so why should not their religion drive them to crucifixion of themselves and one another?* (367–68)

Faulkner is speaking here of southern American culture, but the pattern is by no means limited to the South. This attitude also extended to an affirmation of the violence of the mythical western hero who cleans up the town or the self-righteousness of the hard-boiled detective shooting the criminal. It also appears in the endemic religiosity and violence of the so-called right-to-life movement, and other late-twentieth-century politico-religious movements like the many private "militias" that dot the countryside with their stockpiles of arms and explosives.

Violence is so deeply ingrained in basic American ideologies and institutions that it is not surprising that even schools and workplaces are no longer free of mortal danger from outbursts of individual rage. The possession by Americans of guns has long been considered a sacred right, and even by some, a duty. Studies suggest that nearly 50 percent of American homes have guns on the premises, while *Time* magazine reports that there are at least 235 million guns in the United States, almost enough for every one of the approximately 290 million Americans to have at least one. The "right to keep and bear arms" written into the second amendment to the Constitution and increasingly construed as the right of every nonfelonious adult American to have as many guns as he or she wishes has often been criticized but not yet effectively challenged. One result of this is the peculiarly deadly character of violence in the United States is that, according to a recent report by the Milton Eisenhower Foundation, "in 1995, handguns were used to kill 2 people in New Zealand, 15 in Japan, 30 in Great Britain, 106 in Canada, 213 in Germany, and 9,390 in the United States."

The one hopeful sign in this murky history is that the recent concern about violence in schools and the workplace has inspired an antigun movement that is beginning to demand more effective gun control legislation. In addition, some states have begun lawsuits against gun manufacturers modeled on the class-action litigation that has had such a powerful impact on the tobacco industry. Moreover, just as the anti-tobacco movement has led to great changes in America's smoking habits, it appears that more than two thirds of the American population is in favor of action against guns.

Thus, the powerful myths and ideologies that have long made America a culture in which individual violence of a certain kind has been not only widely justified but also considered by many to be a test of manhood look as though they are being challenged. Perhaps, then, this would be a good time to reexamine these myths and to try to trace their patterns and their development in the course of American history. The contemporary concern with violence challenges the powerful combination of myth and ideology that has long justified the sacred right of gun ownership and the acceptance of extraordinarily high levels of individual violence in America. It remains to be seen whether it will finally undercut centuries of American myths of individual violence.

Section 3

Multiculturalism and Popular Culture

16

Symbols of Ethnicity and Popular Culture

The growing interest in ethnicity and multiculturalism naturally made me wonder about the role the popular culture played in relation to these aspects of American life. The standard account of this was that by using ethnic and racist stereotypes, as it certainly did, popular culture supported racism and attacked multiculturalism. However, as I thought about it, it dawned on me that in some ways popular culture was more open to members of ethnic groups and minorities than much of high culture and so I started to think that maybe there was another side to the story. The present essay explores both the positive and negative sides of the relationship between popular culture and multiculturalism.

≋

Throughout the nineteenth and twentieth centuries, American popular culture was involved with issues of ethnicity and race to a far greater extent than "classic" "canonic" American literature.[1] Indeed, one could

1. A few examples illustrate the point. While William Dean Howells wrote one novel about an octoroon, race is otherwise largely absent from his work and ethnicity appears only in such portraits as that of Dryfoos and Lindau in *A Hazard of New Fortunes*. Race is almost completely absent from Henry James though ethnicity is present in his ominous fulminations about the decline of the lower East Side in *The American Scene*. Melville did do a brilliant parable of racism in *Benito Cereno*

almost say that the more popular the medium or genre, the more intense the involvement. Nineteenth-century American novels, with a few notable exceptions like *Uncle Tom's Cabin*, tend to ignore ethnic groups and racial minorities except as background to the trials and triumphs of white protestant heroes and heroines. Popular genres and entertainments, however, show a pervasive, if often negative, awareness of ethnic and racial groups in American culture. Not only does the content of these popular forms reveal the diversity of cultural groups in America, but the popular arts also offered some members of ethnic and racial minorities access to audiences, the opportunity to display their talents and even, more recently, the chance to become rich and famous.

The contribution of ethnic and racial minorities to American popular culture is unique and rich. Here, more than in any area of American life, much more so than in the realms of business, social life, and the fine arts, the ideal of the melting pot came closest to reality. Popular theater shows the first relatively sympathetic and complex characterizations of ethnic and racial groups, while some of the first instances of ethnic and racial integration can be found in the world of the popular performer in drama, the mass media, music, and sports. Many ethnic Americans have found in the world of popular culture a route to the success denied them in most spheres of American culture.

This is the positive side. American popular culture has also been instrumental in the persistence of negative stereotypes of racial and ethnic subcultures. Though it is difficult to assess the degree to which the drunken Irishmen, grasping Jews, and childish African Americans

---

and there are several men of different races aboard the Pequod, but this is his only treatment of the issue; Hawthorne has almost nothing to say about race or ethnicity. Cooper creates some comical black stereotypes, but has no significant Irish, Jewish, or German characters. Whitman shows great sympathy with runaway slaves as do Thoreau and Emerson, but African American characters or culture are absent from their work. The stock comic Irishman appears as an incompetent servant in Brackenridge's *Modern Chivalry*, but there is certainly no treatment of Irish American culture. Even in the early part of the twentieth century, only southern literature has much to say about race. Though F. Scott Fitzgerald was an Irish American, there is little about ethnicity except perhaps implicitly in the unfinished *The Last Tycoon*. Race appears mainly in the silly apocalyptic racism of Tom Buchanan in *The Great Gatsby*, though there are a few other mentions in *Gatsby* and in *Tender is the Night*. One should also acknowledge Toni Morrison's argument in *Playing in the Dark* than even when race is not explicitly present it is often symbolically pervasive in the intensity that hangs about images of whiteness and blackness. I'm persuaded by her suggestion that the emotions surrounding race are so murky that the absence of black characters is no indication that the writers do not share the prevailing racist attitudes.

portrayed in the popular media are symptoms or causes of prejudice, they are nonetheless there in full measure. In addition, though popular culture has exploited ethnic materials and assimilated immigrant performers and producers, its primary symbol of American life until World War II was the WASP. For example, Louis B. Mayer, Jewish movie tycoon, was fascinated with the Andy Hardy pictures and their idealization of WASP small-town life in America.

There is, then, a paradox at the root of the relationship between popular culture and race and ethnicity in America. On the one hand, popular culture seems more open both to the representation of ethnic experience and to members of ethnic and racial groups than the official culture, but, on the other hand, it has preserved some of the most negative aspects of American culture's response to its minority groups.

Two related structural characteristics of American popular culture are its high degree of commercialization and its broad accessibility. Though popular culture everywhere tends toward commercialism, several features of the American situation intensified the importance of profitability in the production and distribution of popular culture. For one thing, the relative ambiguity of the class structure in the United States, particularly when it came to matters of taste, encouraged cultural entrepreneurs to direct their products to the widest and most diverse audience possible, rather than, as in other countries, concentrating their attention on particular classes or segments of the public. In nineteenth-century England, for example, distinctions in entertainment were drawn along class lines to a degree that never happened in America. Of course, respectable nineteenth-century Americans rarely attended the theater, but this was more a matter of religious and moral taboos than of class prejudice. Since class ideologies and tastes were less significant in the development of the popular arts in America, it was possible for profitability became a dominant concern.

The greatest profit lay in attracting the largest and most diverse audiences, and cultural entrepreneurs quickly learned how to tailor their product to an audience made up of people from many different cultural and class backgrounds. By the 1870s, the ethnic diversity of major urban centers, particularly New York City, had made ethnic groups a significant part of the audience for popular theatricals. The great success of performers like Harrigan and Hart indicated that ethnic materials could draw a large and diverse audience to the theater. Even earlier than this, there were minstrel shows, Tom shows, and stereotypical ethnic characters in comic theater and their popularity paved the way for the extensive use of such materials in later nineteenth-century theater and vaudeville.

Regional stereotypes in earlier American popular culture may well have been a precedent for the later development of ethnic characters. As early as 1787 in Royall Tyler's play *The Contrast* the figure of the stage Yankee was introduced. The first half of the nineteenth century saw a procession of Yankee peddlers, southern rapscallions, and western hell-raisers making their way across America through the pages of numerous periodicals.[2] Characters like Sam Slick, Jack Downing, Simon Suggs, Sut Lovingood, Davy Crockett, and Mike Fink embodied what were thought to be the distinctive characteristics of different regional subcultures. They presented to the American public the image of diverse cultural styles. In addition, these regional stereotypes often displayed an ambivalent mixture of positive and negative characteristics not unlike those later ascribed to such ethnic stereotypes as the brawling Irishman, the Jewish mother, and the Italian gangster.

The commercialism of American popular culture also fostered the development of new media and methods of distribution. The use of new methods gave a certain advantage to cultural entrepreneurs and creators who were not bound by traditional modes of cultural production. In addition, because the popular arts were considered morally and religiously suspect by many members of the established cultural elite, members of these groups did not ordinarily seek careers in the popular arts. Without their competition, bright and inventive entrepreneurs from ethnic backgrounds, who were effectively barred from successful careers in such traditionally respectable enterprises as banking or manufacturing, had easier access to a career in the popular arts. First the Irish and then Eastern European Jews moved into popular culture on a large scale. Irishmen like Boucicault and Harrigan ended up dominating the popular New York theater in the later nineteenth century while the new even more popular medium of movies quickly became a fiefdom of Eastern European Jews like Laemmle, Selznick, Mayer, Goldwyn, and Lasky.

Because of the imperatives of mass distribution, popular culture became increasingly centralized and urban-oriented. Even in the mid-nineteenth century, when America was still both demographically and ideologically centered in the small-town and rural areas, the major media of popular culture, traveling theater troupes, story and sporting

---

2. These developments are chronicled in Rourke, *American Humor*, Blair, *Native American Humor*, and Blair and Hill, *America's Humor*.

periodicals, and minstrel shows were organized and dispatched from the cities into the hinterlands. Because the larger cities had more concentrated ethnic populations, it was more likely that members of these groups would drift into the popular cultural professions, a trend intensified by the prejudice against ethnic Americans in so many other areas. Moreover, since most popular productions were first put on in major cities, the presence of a potential audience made the introduction of ethnic materials a profitable thing. Both of these factors shaped the later nineteenth-century development of popular theater and made Irish performers and producers a notable feature of popular culture. From the 1870s on, men like Dion Boucicault, Edward Harrigan, and George M. Cohan introduced Irish themes, settings, songs, and characters. Their success was mirrored in other areas such as newspaper humor culminating in the great success of Finley Peter Dunne's "Mr. Dooley." Large cities were also center of constant tension between ethnic groups, and this, too, found expression in the interplay and rivalry among ethnic stereotypes in popular theater and vaudeville.

Another important factor in the relationship between ethnic groups and American popular culture was the impact on the immigrants themselves of the cultural uprooting involved in moving from Europe to America. While most immigrants tried to bring their customs, traditions, and institutions along with them, the arrival in America created wholly new cultural situations for most of them. People who had been peasants in the old country found themselves becoming urban factory laborers in the New World. Men who had been farmers became businessmen; laborers became clerks. People accustomed to the isolated homogeneous life of a small village were suddenly thrust into the midst of chaotic cultural diversity. The force of culture shock must have been great and the strength of traditional institutions like the church, the extended family, or the village community inevitably weakened, particularly as the second generation sought greater assimilation into the new country. The decline of traditional institutions and the rebellion of young people against the attempt to impose traditional customs created a particularly tense situation in difficult areas like courtship. Rejecting the rigidity of Old World codes regulating relations between the sexes, younger members of ethnic groups found a different and more flexible mode of encounter and courtship in conjunction with popular amusements like the theater and the new amusement parks. John Kasson insightfully describes the way in which Coney Island offered a new kind of courtship institution for ethnic young people:

Though traces of class and ethnic backgrounds still clung to Coney Island's amusement seekers, in arriving at the resort they crossed a critical threshold, entering a world apart from ordinary life, prevailing social structures and positions. . . . Sidewalks, public parks, dance halls and amusement parks offered opportunities to meet and enjoy the company of the opposite sex away from familial scrutiny. At Coney Island in particular, unattached young men and women easily struck up acquaintanceships for the day or evening. According to Coney Island folklore, some couples even married on the spot. The freedom of anonymity together with the holiday atmosphere of the resort encouraged intimacy and an easing of inhibitions and permitted couples to display their affection in public. (41–42)

In this way, popular culture was a very important educational and ideological influence on American ethnic groups. The increasingly large-scale spectator entertainments, sports, and places of amusement brought members from different ethnic groups into more or less peaceful contact with each other; they also inculcated a new ethic of personal enjoyment and fun that could be shared by people of diverse religious and social backgrounds. This new ethic not only permitted, but also encouraged and rewarded, the pursuit of individual pleasures and the delights of consumption. It stressed the more immediate and ephemeral gratification of needs for relaxation and escape as opposed to self-denial, saving to carry out future responsibilities, and the long-term pursuit of religious salvation.

The amusement park, the dance hall, the circus, the Wild West show, and other forms of late nineteenth- and early twentieth-century mass entertainment offered to ethnic Americans not only a temporary release from cares, but the chance to try on new roles and develop new aspirations. For these entertainments created worlds of fantasy and encouraged various modes of participation in them ranging from the vicarious enjoyment of the Wild West to direct involvement in the artifice of luxury, glamour, and eroticism generated by the amusement park and the dance hall. Because these palaces of mass entertainment were places of fantasy different from the urban world with its burdensome realities, they became modes of transition between ethnic tradition and newer styles of behavior and morality. The amusement park was a frame for experimentation with looser and more playful modes of action, with more open expressions of sexuality and affection, where impulsive spending and various forms of gambling were possible.

In such environments people of different levels and backgrounds could associate without it completely overturning the religious and social traditions of different ethnic groups. Frequenting the institutions of popular culture, younger persons from immigrant backgrounds learned how to live in different worlds, to play a variety of new roles, and to try out new forms of belief and behavior.

The new ethic of pleasure and consumption fostered by popular amusements grew so rapidly in the late nineteenth century that many feared it would subvert traditional American Protestant values as well as the customs of immigrant groups. Because it stressed spending rather saving, pleasure rather than self-discipline, release and relaxation rather than the pursuit of salvation, the new ethic of popular culture encouraged young Protestants to participate in a similar cultural rebellion against the mores and tastes of the older generation. Thus, the phenomenon of conflict between generations, so characteristic of twentieth-century America, was both created and expressed through the medium of popular culture. The bonds of common experience that participation in popular amusements gradually began to forge between native and immigrant young people, did not, of course, immediately eclipse the deep feelings of ethnic hostility and prejudice felt by most Americans. Yet, insofar as participation in the institutions of mass amusement encouraged younger Americans to leave their ethnic identities behind and try out new possibilities of casual association with members of other groups, popular culture created new forms of self-reference, particularly in identifying with an age group.

Twentieth-century popular culture continued to intensify the phenomenon of age grouping, especially in the area of popular music. New technologies of broadcasting and recording made possible the mass distribution of popular music. Gradually, the recorded performance replaced the local group of musicians as the primary method of transmission of popular music. This led to a second phenomenon, the rapid and regularly changing fashions and fads for particular songs, musical styles, and performances.

These two trends came together with the generation phenomenon in twentieth-century American culture. A particularly intense relationship between individuals and popular music developed during the years of courtship. This pattern probably related to the central role that institutions like the dance hall and the amusement park had come to play as a frame for the development of erotic relations between young people.

From the 1930s on, the broadcasting and recording industries imprinted each successive generation with its own repartee of songs, styles, and performers, creating a linkage among members of a particular generation that has increasingly transcended the boundaries of class, ethnic group, and, in recent years, even that of race. The tremendous generational impact of performers like Frank Sinatra, Elvis Presley, the Beatles, and the Rolling Stones indicates how popular culture can subvert traditional social patterns and foster the development of new cultural groupings and attitudes.

Another popular cultural institution, mass spectator sports, was also very important in diffusing traditional ethnic identities and creating new patterns of association. An afternoon at the ballpark was, like a visit to an amusement park, an entrance into a different world where traditional identities and current anxieties could be momentarily left behind while the individual blended into the larger mass of spectators. At highly climactic moments, the individual self was absorbed into the collective concern for the fortunes of the home team. During a baseball game or a horse race, the individual was partly swallowed up into the mass, with his or her single voice absorbed into the hum and roar of the crowd, the individual gesture of excitement swept up into a mass ballet of motion. In such situations, the individual member of an ethnic group could sense a new kind of belonging, a participation in collectivities that transcended the limits of neighborhood and subculture. In addition, the powerful loyalty that so many sports fans gave to their favorite teams indoctrinated immigrants in the idea of new centers of identification. To become a Yankee, a Giant, or a Dodger fan, a status available to anyone willing to attend an occasional game or even to follow the team through newspaper reporting, and later, through radio and television, offered ethnic Americans a sense of participation in the mainstream of American culture.

This sense of belonging was further intensified when members of ethnic groups or minorities became leading sports heroes. Generally, mass spectator sports played a role for members of ethnic communities similar to that ascribed by Albert F. McLean to American vaudeville:

> Vaudeville took over a function of the historical church through its inculcation of the people with some sense of common humanity, a feeling for community which transcended the boundaries created by ethnic origins, specialization and the impersonalism of urban life. (217)

Popular culture, then, was a positive factor in the process of adjustment and adaptation to American culture that confronted immigrant groups. The entertainment and sports organizations of popular culture were more open to talented members of immigrant groups than many other social and economic institutions, providing access to wealth, status, and celebrity for particularly gifted and lucky members of minority groups. Popular theater and vaudeville provided a kind of education and indoctrination in American values and attitudes for immigrant publics. Popular places of entertainment, such as dance halls and amusement parks, introduced ethnic Americans to new lifestyles and ethical ideas, helped create new patterns of courtship and association among the young, and, to some extent, took the place of traditional institutions and customs.

Other forms of popular culture, in particular the increasingly important mass spectator sports generated new objects of personal and group loyalty and helped create new patterns of community within the large urban centers. Finally, many forms of popular culture stimulated new kinds of self-identification and awareness, most significantly in the creation of generational identities and conflicts that crossed subcultural lines. Whether one judges the end result of these various processes to be good or bad, they all worked in the direction of easing the immigrant's adjustment to a new way of life.

However, like most other areas of American culture, popular entertainment's relation to ethnic and racial minorities was deeply divided and ambiguous. What it offered with one hand, it took away with the other. While more open to ethnic and racial groups than most areas, the same patterns of prejudice and segregation characteristic of the culture as a whole also dominated popular amusements.

In spite of the fact that the minstrel show was one of the primary genres of nineteenth century entertainment, this form not only perpetuated negative stereotypes of black American characters, but it also offered few opportunities for black performers. Even the Tom shows deriving from Harriet Beecher Stowe's powerful indictment of the oppression of black people in America more often than not used white actors in blackface. Irish music and the stereotypical comic Irish men and women had long been a staple of American popular entertainment, but it was not until the 1880s that Irish performers and cultural entrepreneurs began to break into the popular theater in large numbers. Yiddish theater was a thriving ethnic tradition in New York City throughout most of the later nineteenth and early twentieth centuries.[3] However, Jewish entrepreneurs moved into powerful positions in popular culture only in the twentieth century with the new technologies of film, radio, and television. And only in the 1930s were Jewish performers widely accepted in media like radio and the movies. The difficulties faced by black producers, directors, and performers as they struggled to make their way in the film industry has been carefully documented by Thomas Cripps in his excellent chroniclse, *Slow Fade to Black*. Not until after World War II did talented performers and entrepreneurs from the whole range of American minorities and ethnic groups begin to gain access to positions of power and importance in popular culture.

Perhaps the most destructive aspect of popular culture's relation to race and ethnicity was its tendency to develop and perpetuate negative stereotypes of racial and ethnic minorities. These stereotypes probably helped shape prejudices toward minorities on the part of many people whose awareness of ethnic groups was largely mediated through the images of popular culture. Negative stereotypes such as the shiftless Negro, the drunken Irishman, the greedy Jew, and the sinister Oriental maintained and justified the cultural ascendancy of the white Protestant majority by characterizing other groups as morally, psychologically, and culturally inferior. These images not only bolstered the majority's self-esteem but also intensified the sense of insecurity and inferiority of minority group members. Philip Roth's Alexander Portnoy speaks bitterly of his childhood fascination with the white Protestant children he encountered on the radio, in comic books, and in movies:

> The kids whose neighbors aren't the Silversteins and the Landaus, but Fibber McGee and Molly and Ozzie and Harriet, and Ethel and Albert and Lorenzo Jones and his wife Belle, and Jack Armstrong! Jack Armstrong, the All-American Goy!—and Jack as in John, not Jack as in Jake, like my father—Look, we ate our meals with that radio blaring away right through to the dessert, the glow of the yellow station band is the last light I see each night before sleep—so don't tell me we're just as good as anybody else, don't tell me we're Americans just like they are. No, no, these blond-haired Christians are the legitimate residents and owners of this place, and they can pump any song they want into the streets and no one is going to stop them either. (16)

Many stereotypical images of ethnic and racial character not only asserted the inferiority of minority groups, but, in addition, served as

3. See Irving Howe's superb evocation of New York's Yiddish culture in *World of Our Fathers*.

projective fantasies for modes of behavior Protestant mores condemned, but that many individuals yearned to indulge in. By projecting this behavior onto ethnic or racial stereotypes, it was possible to give a vicarious expression to forbidden impulses and, at the same time, to dissociate oneself from them. This is probably one reason why the minstrel show enjoyed such a long-term popularity not only as professional but also as amateur entertainment. Manic exuberance, comic eccentricity, and clownish larking were expressions of the carnival spirit deeply needed in a country as religions and serious in its surface mores as Protestant America. Thus, in the minstrel show, the desire for the liminal experience of carnival was projected onto stereotypical black characters. Burnt cork came to symbolize a kind of license.[4] The power of this symbolism is evident not only in the wide popularity of the minstrel show and of its various Irish analogues such as Harrigan's Mulligan Guards series, but also in the impact of blackface on individual performers. Donning the black persona released a powerful energy in the performances of white entertainers, and, ironically, sometimes had a similar effect on black performers. Robert Toll points out,

> Blackface—a comic mask that minstrel endmen wore even when the rest of the companies shunned it—liberated Bert Williams the (black) comedian, as it had many others, both black and white. "Then I began to find myself," he recalled of the first time he blacked up. "It was not until I was able to see myself as another person that my sense of humor developed." As "clown white" did for some performers, the black mask allowed Williams to act differently than he otherwise could have. But Williams was not just another clown. He was a black man wearing a black mask, a mask that had come to symbolize the stereotyped, simpleminded black fool, a symbol of racial inferiority in race-conscious America. The mask liberated Williams as an entertainer, but it stifled him as a man. (123)

The complex mixture of fascination and repulsion embodied in such projective stereotypes has been a dominant element in the portrayal of such groups as African Americans, the Irish, Jews, and Native Americans in popular culture. Such uses of stereotypes reinforced the fear and hostility that so often characterized relationships between white Protestants and ethnic and racial minorities.

---

4. In *Rabelais and His World*, Mikhail Bakhtin discusses the significance of carnival as an aspect of life and literature. On liminality and carnival see the work of Victor Turner, especially *Dramas, Fields, and Metaphors*.

In spite of these destructive stereotypes, which have persisted in many ways, the basic tendency of popular culture, particularly in recent years, has been toward a more positive and sympathetic treatment of ethnic and minority subcultures. There has also been an increasingly broader acceptance of performers and producers from these groups. This has included, as well, a growing appreciation for the cultural styles actually created by these groups, as opposed to the earlier popularity of more artificial, white-mediated popular genres like the minstrel show. Several different trends of the last two decades are part of this general pattern.

Throughout much of the nineteenth century, the artistic styles created by ethnic and minority groups were taken over and transformed by white performers. Not only were black and ethnic performers discriminated against, but also the original styles of their creations were altered to conform to the expectations of white audiences. This is most obvious in the area of popular music. Jazz was primarily the creation of black performers, but it did not gain wide popularity with the white public until white bands like Gene Goldkette and Paul Whiteman took it up in the 1920s. Indeed, the first successful jazz recording was by a white group, the Original Dixieland Jazz Band.

Throughout the 1930s and 1940s it was the big bands, largely directed by white leaders like Ben Goodman, Glenn Miller, Harry James, Tommy Dorsey, and Artie Shaw that were most popular among white audiences. These bandleaders were usually much less racially prejudiced than their fans, and recognized and continually drew upon the work of black musicians. They used black talent, like the great arranger Fletcher Henderson, in unobtrusive ways, though great white and black jazz musicians rarely played together in public until the famous Carnegie Hall concert of 1938 that brought together members of the Benny Goodman and Count Basie bands. During this period a few black swing bands, most notably those of Count Basie and Duke Ellington, began to be successful with white audiences.[5] By the 1950s, the intermixing of white and black musicians in both swing and jazz was increasingly accepted.

However, the transformation of jazz and the blues into white-styled swing left many talented black musicians and enthusiastic black audiences out in the cold. There developed among these largely black circles

5. For example, a recording survives from 1940 when Duke Ellington played a concert in Fargo, ND, for a very enthusiastic and largely white audience. Basie and Ellington both toured extensively in the 1940s playing for increasingly mixed, though still predominantly white audiences.

a new musical style known "Rhythm and Blues," which had a distinctively different style from traditional jazz and swing. R and B, created largely by black musicians, was recorded on so-called race labels, and sold separately in black areas of the major cities.

As in the case of jazz, more adventurous white musicians and audiences discovered R and B. It was eventually transformed, primarily through the impact of Elvis Presley and other white musicians, into rock and roll. This time, however, the transformation was far closer to the spirit of the black original and as rock and roll developed and there was more and more interplay between black and white musicians and audiences. The broad success of Motown records, a label specializing in developing black performers like Diana Ross and the Supremes along stylistic lines that would be successful with both black and white audiences, became increasingly the wave of the future. Today, the complex spectrum of popular music involves a continual interplay between white black performers. New stylistic ideas are likely to be picked up and developed by both black and white musicians regardless of their origins. An example of this can be seen in the rapid spread of the rap style of music, which emerged from a black tradition, but which was very quickly picked up by performers of all sorts. Not only in music, but also in dance, the same pattern occurs, as with the black style of break- and dirty-dancing, quickly adapted by white dancers and then recreated by other black dancers.

A similar development has taken place in the area of comedy. For a considerable period, the more profane and "dozens"-centered style of black comedy featured by such traditional black performers as Redd Foxx and Moms Mabley was known to white audiences only through a few rebellious white comics, most notably Lenny Bruce. In the seventies, however, Redd Foxx started to develop a large white following through his more sanitized work in the television series *Sanford and Son*. Even though the more overt profanity of Foxx's nightclub performances was cleaned up here, the funky rascality of his comic persona still shone through. Younger black comedians, like the tremendously popular Eddie Murphy and Chris Rock, have made the public accept and even cherish some of the roughest aspects of the black comic tradition. On the other hand, Bill Cosby has become one of the most successful (and wealthy) performers of our time through his adaptation of essentially white traditions of situation comedy and family to a black setting.

The second trend also seems to relate to a more favorable attitude toward ethnic and minority groups. This is the development of more positive stereotypes and of attempts to present more complex and realistic portrayals of the life and histories of racial and ethnic minorities. Positive stereotypes like the heroic black detective, the warmhearted Jewish mother, and the witty and irreverent Irishman have flourished in recent films and televisions series. Thomas Berger's *Little Big Man* and the film adaptation by Arthur Penn treated the culture of the Cheyenne Indians with considerable depth and sympathy. Mario Puzo's *The Godfather*, along with the enormously successful Coppola films it inspired, in spite of perpetuating a stereotypical association between Italian Americans and organized crime, offered a very positive and striking picture of some aspects of Italian American culture. Michael Cimino's film *The Deerhunter* made the members of a working-class ethnic community into a moving symbol of the perplexities of America in the Vietnam Era. And Alex Haley's television mini-series *Roots* showed how black families had histories and a heritage as strong and significant as that of whites though questions were later raised about the book's authenticity.

These novels, films, and television series are part of a trend in recent American culture that seeks to reaffirm cultural pluralism. This favorable attitude toward ethnic identity and distinctiveness has been evident in such diverse phenomena as the Black Power and Black Aesthetic movements of the 1960s and in what Michael Novak has characterized as "the rise of the unmeltable ethnics." These new ideologies of ethnic and racial separatism and identity seem, on the surface, to be a final repudiation of the "melting pot" ideal of assimilation of minorities. Indeed, recent sociological and historical studies have shown that despite changing levels of income and status, many members of minority groups have tried very hard to hold to traditional subcultural patterns. But the new more positive ideologies of ethnic separatism may be, in the American context, more subversive of ethnic traditions than one might expect. It is typical of American life that when one group claims to have a special quality of its own, other groups will hasten to imitate and adopt some portion of its values and cultural patterns. In the nineteenth century, it was the dominant white Protestant majority that claimed to have the mission of defining what was most valuable in American life. But, in recent years, representatives of ethnic and racial subcultures have become increasingly important in popular culture and the arts and as spokespersons for American values. If this trend continues, we may well see an increasing decline in the cultural authority of nonethnic Americans as the American middle class becomes fascinated

by ethnicity and seeks to adopt some of the patterns and attitudes characteristic of ethnic and racial minorities.[6]

This third trend is already apparent in the area of food and entertainment with more and more Americans experimenting with different
culinary traditions and attending "heritage weekends" and other festi-
vals and ceremonies that spring from ethnic traditions. The complex relationship of ethnicity to American popular culture may well be entering a new phase in which distinctive identities of ethnic communities
become an object of emulation and a source of positive values. If this
happens, the paradoxical result may be further attenuation of the very
cultural distinctiveness on which an ethnic racial identity is based.

On March 17 of every year, rain or shine, sun or sleet, the city of
Chicago holds its annual St. Patrick's Day Parade. On this day, the Chicago River, already a bilious olive drab, is dyed a bright Kelly green.
Some say this is by the application of an orange dye, but I cannot vouch
for that. The St. Patrick's Day Parade was once an assertion of the ethnic pride of Irish Americans, and it was a major Chicago event because
of the large Irish American population in a city dominated, since the end
of the nineteenth century, by Irish American political leaders. However,
in recent years, the parade has become celebration of all ethnic and racial groups in the city. One will see blacks dressed as leprechauns, and
Polish Americans wearing T-shirts stenciled "Kiss me, I'm Irish!" There
are likely to be floats representing nearly all the city's numerous ethnic
groups, Jews, Poles, Lithuania Ukrainians, Serbians, Mexicans, Germans, and Italians as well as the Irish. It has become a sort of United
Nations parade, a symbolic testament to cultural pluralism. To me,
this parade is deeply representative of the contemporary relationship
between ethnicity and American popular culture, but whether it foreshadows a renewed affirmation of ethnic subcultures or an attenuation
of ethnicity as a real force in American life, only the future can reveal.

---

6. Michael Novak, *The Rise of the Unmeltable Ethnics*. For black power and the black aesthetic
see, Robert Lee Scott, *The Rhetoric of Black Power* and Addison Gayle, *The Black Aesthetic*. Werner
Sollors's *Beyond Ethnicity* is a very interesting treatment of the whole issue of ethnicity in American
culture. See also Norman Mailer's famous conception of the "white negro."

17

Literature, Race, and Ethnicity in America

This essay tried to deal with literature in something of the same way that I discussed popular culture and ethnicity in "Symbols of Ethnicity and Popular Culture." It also reflects my interest in what I see as a very important cultural trend in post–World War II American literature, the emergence of a number of important Jewish and African American writers and their growing influence on writing in general. I prepared it originally for a conference at the University of Groningen in Holland, and I'm grateful to my friend Wil Verhoeven for inviting me.

~

> So don't tell me we're just as good as anybody else, tell me we're Americans just like they are. No, no, these blond-haired Christians are the legitimate residents and owners of this place.
>
> Philip Roth, *Portnoy's Complaint*

> Who knows but that, on the lower frequencies, I speak for you.
>
> Ralph Ellison, *Invisible Man*

These two quotations seemingly express very different things about the relationship between the speaker and his audience. One suggests that "we," in spite of what anyone says to the contrary, are not the "legitimate residents and owners of this place [America]." The second states, on the other hand that "I" might speak for "you" or to translate it into the terms of the first quote, that "we" could be feeling the same thing "on the lower frequencies." Both meanings are important to the topic of this essay, which is about how, in recent decades, creative artists from groups excluded from the American dream, have produced some of the most important artistic and cultural representatives of America. In American literature, the most influential trend of the last several years has been a basic transformation in how we view our literary and cultural heritage. At the beginning of the twentieth century, most people thought the major American writers, aside from the colonials and the founding fathers, were the nineteenth century New York and New England poets and essayists—Irving, Cooper, Bryant, Emerson, Whittier, Longfellow, Lowell, and, somewhat marginally, Hawthorne. One remembers the gallery of their portraits on the cards of the once popular Authors game. As sterling representatives of what became known in the second decade of the modern century as the "genteel tradition," this phalanx of literary greats dominated what was taught in the schools about American literature.

This version of what we now refer to as the "canon" of American literature was challenged and expanded in the 1920s by literary and cultural modernists insisting on the greater significance of Poe, Melville, and Whitman. Significantly, however, these newly "canonical" authors, though highly ambiguous about established American ideologies themselves, still represented what, even in the 1920s, remained the dominant American hegemony of the white, male, Protestant, middle class. It was not until the aftermath of World War II that the cultural dominance of this hegemony came into question. One significant exception to this generalization was several southern writers who, in many ways, were a creative center of American literature from the late 1920s through the 1940s. These writers, unlike most other Americans, were well aware of the legacy of slavery and racism and reflected it in their works. William Faulkner and Richard Wright were the most important of these writers, but there were a number of others of considerable influence on the next generation, such as Robert Penn Warren, Alan Tate, Donald Davidson, Erskine Caldwell, and Lillian Smith. Faulkner and Wright were in turn the two most important influences on Ralph Ellison, whose *Invisible Man* became the fountainhead of a new black fiction.

In the 1950s, a new era in American literature and culture began and issues surrounding the revision and expansion of the canon has been a significant part of the study of it ever since. In the last two decades of the twentieth century canonic changes largely reflected a conscious intention on the part of scholars, critics, and teachers to democratize an institution that many had come to see as an overly elite area of American culture. College and university study of American literature would never be the same again.

The new scholars and critics sought to undercut the idea of a limited canon of literary excellence and to set in its place a broadly pluralistic concept of American literature in which every significant group within the culture had some representation. However, even before the development of feminist, multiracial, and multiethnic movements to redefine the canon of American literature, another set of events was already bringing about a major change in American literature. This was the influence, beginning in the 1950s, of a new literary vision of America that radiated partly from historical upheavals like the Civil Rights movement and partly from novels by African American and Jewish American writers. Some dates: Ralph Ellison, *Invisible Man* (1952); Saul Bellow, *The Adventures of Augie March* (1953); James Baldwin, *Go Tell It on the Mountain* (1953); Brown vs. Topeka Board of Education (1954); Rosa Parks refuses to stand up on a Montgomery, Alabama bus (December 1, 1955); Bernard Malamud, *The Assistant* (1957); Norman Mailer, "The White Negro" (1957); Philip Roth, *Goodbye, Columbus* (1959).

This new cultural and artistic vision has had a powerful influence on the contemporary American intellectual's sense of his or her literary and cultural heritage. The changing sense of the American heritage not only helped generate a great explosion of creative force from black and Jewish American writers in the 1950s but, in turn, prepared the way for the more organized programs of canon revision that characterized the 1980s. The special situation of African and Jewish American writers is indicated by our difficulty in arriving at some consensus about what name to call these writers and the literature they have created. The term Jewish novel is sometimes used, but is terribly vague since Jewish can describe a religion, a culture, a nationality, or some combination of two or more of these. Jewish American is a widely accepted term, but it also has its problems. Is a Jewish American writer who converts to Catholicism or becomes an atheist still a Jewish writer? What about someone like J. D. Salinger who has apparently become some sort of Buddhist? Or what about an American black like Sammy Davis Jr., who converts to Judaism?

What to call American writers with African ancestry is even more problematic. Afro-American, though once preferred by such leading black scholars as Henry Louis Gates Jr. and by Civil Rights historians like Harvard Sitkoff, is an artificial coinage that many have now replaced with African American, which, however, has some of the same problems as Jewish American and some of its own. For example, it fails to acknowledge the extraordinary diversity of African cultures and their transformations in America. The difference between a recent immigrant from Ghana and an American black whose family has been in this country since the seventeenth century is, after all, considerable. In the fullness of time Americans with African ancestry may revert to the term Negro American to express their pride in the great subculture they have created in America. Some important scholars like John Hope Franklin have argued for this usage, but too many negative connotations have clustered around the term Negro in the recent past for that to be widely accepted.

This ambiguity of names reflects the conflicting attitudes toward race and ethnicity that are endemic in American history and culture. It is clearly related to the important theme of ambiguous identity in Jewish and African American fiction from Cahan's *The Rise of David Levinsky* to *Invisible Man*. Though the ideal of the "melting pot" has long been an important ideology of American culture, America has also been a society based, in many ways, on the oppression of racial and ethnic minorities. Indeed, racism and anti-Semitism have been part of the dirty underside of American culture since the seventeenth century and the dialectic between melting pot and minority oppression is still unresolved. In the twentieth century a new concept of cultural pluralism affirming a multiethnic and multiracial America developed, ironically in response to the tremendous incursion of Spanish-speaking ethnic groups into certain areas of the United States. I hope that my analysis of race and ethnicity as vital sources of artistic creativity in contemporary America may point to some of the positive qualities we might expect to find in a culturally pluralistic democracy of the future.

The importance of Jewish and African American writers in the recent history of American literature is immediately apparent in their influence on most contemporary white American writers. Not all are like the poet John Berryman who, in his *Dream Songs*, gives his white protagonist a black persona and imparts to him a version of black dialect as one aspect of his identity. Though Berryman treats this "blackface" persona with considerable irony and makes clear its origins in the white minstrel show tradition, it made some African Americans uncomfortable. The black poet Michael Harper noted this in his moving elegy for Berryman, "Tongue-Tied in Black and White:"

> Now I must take up our quarrel:
> never dangerous with women
>   though touched by their nectared hair,
> you wrote in that needful black idiom
> offending me, for only your inner voices
> spoke such tongues, your father's soft prayers
> in an all black town in Oklahoma; your ear lied.
>
> (10)

But the styles, myths, themes, and visions created by African and Jewish American writers and other artists have become a central part of the stream of influences that any serious contemporary American novelist or poet must reckon with. The title and the subject of Norman Mailer's famous essay "The White Negro" is one indication of the degree to which, in the 1950s and 1960s, black styles and themes had become powerfully compelling to white intellectuals and artists. A more satirical account of the fashion for black ideologies and styles can be found in Tom Wolfe's *Radical Chic and Mau-Mauing the Flak Catchers*.

As a further example, let us look briefly at one novelist who many would consider the most important contemporary American writer who is not Jewish, black, or female. Thomas Pynchon's ancestry is as white Anglo-Saxon protestant as one could imagine with a family that can be traced back to seventeenth-century Puritan New England. Yet, it is clear that Pynchon's masters, aside from the classic European and American modernists, are mainly black and Jewish writers like Ralph Ellison and Saul Bellow as well as figures from American popular culture also of predominantly black and Jewish origin. It is impossible to imagine Tyrone Slothrop of *Gravity's Rainbow* without the great Jewish popular tradition of the schlemiel. Moreover, one of Slothrop's first intimations of his special mission in life comes when he is chased down a toilet by the Negro shoeshine boy Red Malcolm (later the Black Muslim leader Malcolm X) in the men's room of the Roseland Ballroom. *Gravity's Rainbow* is, like all of Pynchon's work, packed with allusions to black and Jewish folklore and popular culture.

To understand this pervasive contemporary literary influence, we must first try to define the special perspective on life that has emerged from the black and Jewish cultural situations in America. In some ways, blacks and Jews have had related cultural positions in America, a circumstance symbolized historically and economically by the fact that it was often Jewish merchants who operated the most important stores and other commercial agencies in the black ghettos of northern American cities. Jews have also traditionally been among the most committed supporters of civil rights agitation and legislation. For example, Harvard Sitkoff, the leading historian of the Civil Rights movement, participated in the protests of the 1960s as a Jewish student from New York City.

In other respects, these two subcultures are profoundly different, and this has led in more recent years to considerable friction between African American and Jewish writers. Yet this peculiar combination of similarities and differences has enabled these two subcultures to exert an influence on contemporary American culture as a whole much greater than their numbers in the population would suggest was possible.

First, let's look at several similar ways in which Jewish and black subcultures have been related to American culture as a whole. Both have been minority cultures, viewed by most other American ethnic groups as negatively "different," blacks on account of race and Jews for their differences in religion and culture and for other traits alleged in the tradition of anti-Semitism. Many of these putative traits, such as the Jewish male's allegedly insatiable sexual appetite for gentile women and the supposedly promiscuous tendencies of Jewish females, are very similar to characteristics ascribed to blacks. An ironic twist on this stereotype is the striking scene in Saul Bellow's *Mr. Sammler's Planet* in which a large black pickpocket forces the terrified Mr. Sammler to inspect his gigantic penis. One might interpret this moment as signifying the passing on to blacks of the stereotype of sexual potency and danger once projected by whites onto Jews.

This linking through bigotry also appears in the ascription of greater "blackness," i.e. non-European genetic and cultural characteristics, to both blacks and Jews. In addition, Jews and African Americans both came to America trammeled by already existing prejudices against them that had developed in the various European countries from which most of the American population had originated prior to the twentieth century. Until the twentieth century, neither group could point to an "old country" or national homeland in the way that most other American ethnic groups could. This historical circumstance was reflected in the distinctive kind of language that both groups developed in America.

In the case of African Americans this was a distinctive form of English that grew out of the Creole dialects, making it possible for Africans of different tribal backgrounds to communicate with each other. Jews, on the other hand, spoke Yiddish, a dialect of German reflecting the influence of many different European languages, especially Russian. Thus, blacks and Jews were among the few American subcultures whose mother tongues were dialects rather than national languages. In the twentieth century, the strong back-and-forth between these dialects and American English had important cultural and literary consequences. In addition, dietary differences, religious in the case of Jews and based on economics in the case of blacks, further reinforced the sense of cultural differences. In short, the combination of actual cultural differences and racial prejudice operated to make both African and Jewish Americans the two major subcultural groups in America who could not opt for the route of "passing" or assimilation into the mainstream of American life. This is what Philip Roth probably means when he suggests that Jews can never really feel at home in America and will always be outsiders, in spite of their strenuous pursuit of such American values as success and self-improvement.

Inability to assimilate into the mainstream was not the only cultural circumstance shared by blacks and Jews. Because of their enforced separateness these two groups tended to develop or retain distinctive folk cultures of their own. Among blacks this took the form of a largely oral culture that was especially creative in the areas of music and dance. Since most slave masters did not want their slaves to become literate and teaching slaves to read or write was illegal in most of the slave states, the slaves' only permitted forms of relaxation and entertainment were music and dancing. In addition there were African traditions of music and dance passed on by the slaves. Jews had a much more literary folk tradition because of the great emphasis placed on literacy by the self-defined people of the Book. A vital Yiddish literary culture with international roots resulted in distinctive theatrical and journalistic traditions. Irving Howe in *World of Our Fathers* presents a fascinating account of this Yiddish culture.

The popular nature of these distinctive traditions gave an ironic advantage to both blacks and Jews in the rapidly changing world of popular culture of the twentieth century. Jewish entrepreneurs dominated the early American film industry while black performers and creators were increasingly important in twentieth-century popular music and sports. Both groups also played a vital role in the twentieth-century development of American comedy. These developments foreshadowed the increasing postwar influence of these groups on American literature. Here, however, another important difference between Jewish and African American subcultures emerged. In spite of the force of anti-Semitism, Jews became, in the early twentieth century, very powerful in the major cultural institutions of publishing, artistic management, philanthropy, and finally, in the universities in a way that blacks never had the political or financial power to match. This cultural power and influence has grown so much in the postwar period that it is not much of an exaggeration to say that Jews have not only come to dominate Hollywood, but more traditional cultural institutions like symphony orchestras and museums as well. African Americans have yet to achieve this kind of cultural power. Their influence has depended on their creativity and on the impact of what Leon Forrest calls the "yeasty energy of black life with its throbbing rage for freedom."

In spite of their many differences, the postwar literary influence of blacks and Jews reflects considerable congruence between the perspectives of black and Jewish writers and the way in which these attitudes helped shape the new imaginative needs of Americans in the decades after World War II. Why was it, then, that these two minority perspectives now came to seem a more meaningful way of looking at the world than traditional American ideologies?

In contrast to the traditional American myths of success, progress, and increasing abundance through the conquering of an infinite succession of new frontiers, the vision of Jewish and black subcultures was shaped by their own sense of victimization and vulnerability. As a consequence they had a strong sense of limitation, of failure, of frustration, and of irony. Among other things, the sense of vulnerability and the expectation of failure were particularly important in the development of black and Jewish humor. This led, in turn, to a strong feeling for what we call "the absurd" or "black humor" and to the cultivation of irony, particularly as a tactic of secretly attacking the oppressor. In the case of black oral culture this helped encourage the development of the ritual of "signifying" or scoring points against an oppressor in ways in which he cannot retaliate. Jews, on the other hand, have been prolific in the invention of such genres as "Polish jokes" to satirize their Christian persecutors. Few great American writers before the emergence of the major black and Jewish novelists of the postwar period had anything like this sense of comic irony and absurdity. When we come across exceptions to this generalization, most notably Twain and Faulkner, we usually find writers who were concerned with racism and therefore aware of black cultural traditions.

However, racism and anti-Semitism have had quite different trajectories. Until recently, blacks were largely denied access to political and economic opportunities except within the black subculture. Thus, their relationship to the American dream has been largely ironic, as the title of Richard Wright's novel about the destruction of a young black, *Native Son,* would suggest. Jews have usually been able to find economic opportunities though often only in industries for which they alone had the acumen to sense the possibilities, such as the garment industry and mass communications. Thus, the Jewish relationship to the American dream has been rather more ambiguous. For them, as for Alexander Portnoy in Philip Roth's novel, the dream has been both real and unreal. Portnoy is able to become a highly successful lawyer and a rising power in politics, but his quest for sexual fulfillment, warped by his mother's ambitions and repressions, and his own obsession with non-Jewish women as the symbol of his fulfillment, leads him to the brink of psychological chaos.

The important differences between black and Jewish social circumstances and the cultural and artistic styles these circumstances have fostered are fascinating. Black life in America has been marked above all by the constant necessity of re-creating a culture and protecting it from total white control and domination. In slavery, blacks had to improvise a culture by synthesizing many different African tribal traditions with the culture of white protestant America. They had to re-create this culture again after emancipation, again after the great migration to the industrial North, and once again after the partial successes of the Civil Rights movement had brought about a new kind of integration of blacks into American life. In addition, these cultural re-creations had to be carried out without significant access to many of the major white-dominated institutions of cultural transmission like the press, publishing, advertising, and the media. One result of this is that blacks became profoundly gifted at improvisation and transformation, at taking elements from white culture and remaking them into meaningful expressions of black life.

Leon Forrest, an important African American writer, has developed this point in several essays and novels. In "In the Light of the Likeness—Transformed" and "FAULKNER\Reforestation," he shows how the cultural genius at improvisation manifested itself in black mastery of music, of dance, and of oral genres such as in sermons, oral poetry, and taletelling. Particularly important were those oral traditions of a comic nature in which patterns of white culture could be used to "signify" against it. Henry Louis Gates Jr. offers a particularly interesting discussion of "signifying" in relation to African cultures and the development of a slave culture in American in *The Signifying Monkey*. One of the great black folkloric inventions is the poetry of "the signifying monkey," which uses white stereotyping of blacks as monkey-like to take revenge in fantasy against the oppressor. A similar pattern can be seen in the traditional animal tales of American blacks such as those used by the white writer Joel Chandler Harris in his Uncle Remus stories.

The black gift for improvisation has been prominent not only in the tremendous influence of black music in America, but in the increasing adoption into standard American dialects of black linguistic inventions and, along with this, some of the values and styles that such basic concepts as "cool," "hip," and "rapping" imply. This quality of improvisation and re-creation is also evident in the style of major black writers like Ralph Ellison, Ishmael Reed, and Toni Morrison in that the way that black traditions of oral and musical improvisation have influenced the forms and themes of their work. Forrest gives us a brilliant sense of this quality of re-creation when he describes the jazz improvisations of one of his characters as

> bathing, baptizing, purifying Sound into the shape of the softly jangling tambourine in his left hand—washed pure in the Cross—fretful, blissful innocence, lamblike in the skins of baying tide-tossed Sound, as the three bags of wool, singing ballooning, kiting into nine circles, encompassing the voice of Styx and Niobe and now with bellowing steel-making resonance of a nine-pound hammer; lining track out the projected Soul, Ironwood flourished inside of an invisible moldering, or a stirring wakefulness, as the rib of Adam dancing into new singing shape, reshaped out of the valley of dry bones. (*Bloodworth* 297)

When Ralph Ellison's Invisible Man talks of speaking for us "on the lower frequencies" he refers, I think, to another aspect of black culture that is a direct result of the experience of white oppression. Because the legacy of slavery and racism was an ongoing victimization of blacks through erotic exploitation and violence, African Americans have had to deal with some of the most terrible kinds of rape and terror that human beings can face. The result has been that, as Ellison puts it one of his essays:

> The white American figuratively [forces] the Negro down into the deeper level of his consciousness, into the inner world, where reason

and madness mingle with hope and memory and endlessly give birth to nightmare and to dream; down into the provinces of the psychiatrist and the artist, from whence spring the lunatic's fancy and the work of art. (qtd. in Gates 109)

Jews, too, have often known this sort of terror, but their response to it has been shaped by their sense of themselves as a chosen people and as the keepers and followers of God's word as set forth in the Old Testament and interpreted by centuries of Talmudic disputation. Unlike the improvisation and re-creation that is characteristic of black artistic and cultural styles, Jewish culture has been above all one of interpretation. This is connected to the traditional Jewish respect for learning, and is probably why so many of the leading American literary, artistic, and cultural critics of the postwar period have come from Jewish backgrounds. It also helps explain why the Jewish American novel has been particularly concerned with the world of scholarship and the arts, as well as the world of the ghetto.

But if the traditional Jewish heritage was profoundly shaped by the need to interpret the text of God's word in all its complexity, the modern American Jewish tradition has been equally influenced by that great European Jewish creation, the interpretive practice of Freudian psychoanalysis. In a way, Freud's extrapolation of the Talmudic tradition into a method of interpreting the different levels of the psyche in all their complexity might have been created for America with its traditions of individualism, individual success, and self-fulfillment. Under the double influence of the older Jewish and modern Freudian traditions, Jewish writers have created a richer vision of the ambiguities and paradoxes of the individual's quest for self-realization. This meant, among other things, a fuller and more complex treatment of male feelings and emotions. This theme ran counter to the repression and control of feeling that had traditionally been an important part of masculine American individualism. In contrast to Hemingwayesque understatement and the code of toughness, the Jewish novelist proposed to "let it all hang out" in order to "let go." In his very first novel, Saul Bellow flung down the gauntlet to the American tough guy tradition:

> For this is an era of hard-boiled-dom. . . . Do you have feelings? There are correct and incorrect ways of indicating them. Do you have an inner life? It is nobody's business but your own. Do you have emotions? Strangle them. To a degree, everyone obeys this code. And it does admit of a limited kind of candor, a close-mouthed straightforwardness. But on the truest candor, it has an inhibitory effect. Most serious

matters are closed to the hard-boiled. . . . If you have difficulties, grapple with them silently, goes one of their commandments. To hell with that! I intend to talk about mine, and if I had as many mouths as Siva has arms and kept them going all the time, I still could not do myself justice. (*Dangling Man* 7)

These, then, are some of the distinctive qualities of American black and Jewish subcultures: being more deeply aware of the inescapability of victimization and vulnerability in life, they have a particularly well-developed sense of comic irony. Their historical traditions have forced them to recognize some of the darkest and deepest themes of the human condition. They have learned to respect these complexities of feeling and emotion and they have developed styles of improvisation and interpretation that reflect these historical experiences.

On the surface, the 1950s were a period of complacency and optimism for most Americans. The election of 1952 had brought General Dwight Eisenhower to the presidency with the promise of a return to "normalcy" (a promise somewhat similar to that made by Harding in 1920). Moreover, as the supreme commander of the European theater in World War II, Eisenhower symbolized America's rise to predominance as a world power. The American economy was thriving because of postwar consumer demand, employment was high, and more Americans were moving away from the cities and into mushrooming new suburban developments like Levittowns in New York and New Jersey, Park Forest outside of Chicago, and the ring of suburbs around Los Angeles. Affluent consumption, and freedom from the growing problems of the decaying inner cities, seemed a possible fulfillment of the American dream for the average white American family. This ethos was reflected and reinforced by the kind of salesmanship through which consumer products were presented to the public and the optimistic family comedies dominating the television screens of the period.

On the international scene, America ended World War II as the predominant power, its technological superiority guaranteed by its sole possession of nuclear weapons, and its economic strength and democratic idealism manifested in the reconstruction of Europe through the Marshall Plan and the successful establishment of the United Nations, which, for its first few years was virtually an American hegemony. Yet, this high degree of optimism and complacency was rapidly undercut by events of the 1950s that generated a new sense of vulnerability among Americans. The frustrating stalemate of the Korean War raised questions about American omnipotence and combined with the trauma of the Russian seizure of Eastern Europe and the fall of China to the Communists to make America's world power seem dangerously vulnerable. When the Russians developed their own nuclear weapons and rocketry, Americans began for almost the first time since the early nineteenth century to be seriously apprehensive about devastating foreign attacks on the American mainland. Some Americans in the 1950s hastened to add bomb shelters to their suburban homes while school children were drilled in responses to nuclear attack.

These events made many Americans fearful that their culture was being betrayed from within. Anticommunist crusades broke out all over the country and culminated in the frantic charges made by Senator Joseph McCarthy, the Alger Hiss trial, and the execution of Julius and Ethel Rosenberg. The result was a new sense of distrust and uncertainty, fed by fears of wholesale Communist subversion, which added to the average American's deepening sense of vulnerability and insecurity. Other Americans, shocked at the vehemence and hysteria of the anticommunist movement and its attack on basic democratic freedoms of speech and association, became increasingly skeptical about the traditional values of American culture and more open to alternative definitions of democracy. Among young people, this was the origin of the broader cultural revolt that exploded in the 1960s. The beat movement of the 1950s already contained many of the new thrusts of the sixties as one beat anthem, Allen Ginsberg's *Howl*, clearly indicates.

The revolt of the beat generation in the 1950s was one sign of growing discontent among American young people. Another was an increasing militancy among blacks and Jews. Jews, horrified by the revelations of the holocaust in Europe and inspired by the founding of the new state of Israel, became committed to the elimination of anti-Semitism. They were also moved to participate more fully in the growing Civil Rights movement and its agitation for an end to segregation in public accommodations, transportation, and education. The aftermath of the 1954 Supreme Court Brown vs. Topeka Board of Education decision revealed how entrenched segregation and inequality were in American life, and further increased a younger generation's sense of the deep hypocrisy and injustice characterizing the history of race relations in America.

Up until the beginnings of the Cold War, the primary mood of American culture had been optimistic and most Americans firmly believed in the ideologies of progress, individual success, and the infinite frontier. Though some American writers had expressed a much more pessimistic view of the world, they tended to express their pessimism in a tragic rather than comic fashion. When we turn to Hawthorne, Melville, Howells, James, Fitzgerald, and Hemingway we find a despairing recognition of the failure of the American dream. Yet, this tragic sense that America had betrayed its great promise was the other side of American optimism and innocence. Against this vision of betrayed innocence black and Jewish writers presented the more comic and ironic view that man is inevitably limited in his possibilities, that success and failure are more matters of luck than of character, and that we are all potential victims of human folly.

We can see this clearly, I think, if we compare two major black and Jewish works of the postwar period, Ellison's *Invisible Man* and Saul Bellow's *Herzog*, with a great American novel from an earlier period, F. Scott Fitzgerald's *The Great Gatsby*. *Gatsby* was, above all, a tragedy about the failure of the American dream. Jay Gatsby is obsessed with a past time when he and Daisy loved each other. Believing that anything is possible for him, he thinks he can return to this past. His obsession is a powerful commentary on the tragic hubris of the American dream of a New World. On the other hand, Tom and Daisy Buchanan's petty, sordid lives amid the trappings of wealth and affluence reflect on the individual level the tragic American failure that turned the "fresh, green breast of the New World" into an ash heap

As he later made explicit in some of the central scenes of *Tender is the Night*, Fitzgerald was not unaware of the significance of racism. In the opening dinner scene of *Gatsby*, Tom Buchanan raves on to Nick about his currently fashionable fears of a rising racial threat to white civilization. However, the one significant black person who appears in *The Great Gatsby* is a "pale well-dressed negro" who witnesses the accident in which Daisy runs down Myrtle Wilson and is able to describe the car to the police. This may symbolize Fitzgerald's sense of black people as witnesses to white society's tragic betrayal of the American dream. Yet, though we have failed to live up to our dream, there is something tragic and powerful about that betrayal, just as Gatsby's misguided life and death rises above the shallowness of the others to suggest the majesty of his illusion.

Though very different from each other in many ways, Ralph Ellison's *Invisible Man* and Saul Bellow's *Herzog* share a sense of life as comic, ironic, and absurd very different from those of *The Great Gatsby*, or for that matter from *The Scarlet Letter, Moby Dick, Portrait of a Lady, An American Tragedy*, or *A Farewell to Arms*, all powerful stories about the tragic failure of quests for happiness or significance.

The basic patterns of *Invisible Man* and *Herzog* are those of flight rather than of quest and their mood in spite of the often violent nature of the action is comic and ironic. In *Invisible Man,* the protagonist seeks happiness through an escape from the racism of the Deep South where he has been raised. Even in the North, however, he only discovers anew that he cannot run from the vulnerability and victimization of the social position he thought he was escaping from. His flight from the South to the North begins with the delusional belief that through education and a willingness to work hard, he can escape his invisibility, but once he arrives in the North he only discovers ever more subtle, complex, and oppressive forms of racism that reinforce the bars of the complex prison of his invisibility. Though he fruitlessly pursues success in work and in politics he does not realize until near the end of the novel that the symbolic letters he carries as recommendations have sabotaged all his efforts and confirm his true fate and his inescapable condition as victim, saying essentially "hope him to death and keep him running" (194).

For help, the Invisible Man can only turn to those elements of his folk heritage that he has previously tried to escape. It is, in particular, his dying Grandfather's troubling words from which he runs: "Son, after I'm gone I want you to keep up the good fight. I never told you, but our life is a war and I have been a traitor all my born days, a spy in the enemy's country, ever since I give up my gun back in the reconstruction" (16).

Time and again, the Invisible Man tries to articulate an optimistic and hopeful sense of his fate as a black man in opposition to his grandfather's cynicism only to discover that the manipulative symbols of white society and its black allies have blinded him. Finally, he learns that it is only through those traditions he has hitherto believed to be symbols of his victimization that he can find anything to sustain him.

Herzog, too, goes through a process of flight and discovery that has a similarly ironic outcome. Like the Invisible Man, Herzog tries to escape his ghetto background and its vulnerability, symbolized by the homosexual rape he suffers as a small boy. Herzog uses his intelligence and his patrimony not only to enter into an academic career, but also to try to write (i.e. control) the history of the modern world. However, a disastrous marriage and a complete inability to carry through his hopelessly ambitious scholarly project causes him to have something like a nervous breakdown. In this state, he writes letters to his imagined tormenters, private and public, hoping to persuade them and himself that he knows the real truth about his life and the discontents of modernity. Though he still pursues invulnerability through his impressive knowledge of modern philosophy and history, his letters are also a desperate cry for help and lead him increasingly to the realization that he, like all human beings, cannot escape the fate of being a comic victim. In the novel's climactic scene Herzog has an absurd traffic accident and is arrested. In this ultimate state of seeming hopelessness, he, like the Invisible Man, finds strength in his heritage as a Jew.

In the end, both the Invisible Man and Herzog complete their flights by retreating temporarily from life into the contemplation of their vulnerability and their hope of reintegration with their true heritage. The Invisible Man in his underground cellar and Herzog in his decaying country house are not sure of the terms on which they can reenter life, but each knows that at some point he will, and with a new understanding and acceptance of the truly limited and ironic nature of his existence.

These comic portrayals of the failure of the American dream are very different from the portrayal of it in white male tradition of Hawthorne, Melville, James, Fitzgerald, Faulkner, and Hemingway. These writers treat the betrayal of the American dream as a great historical and cultural tragedy. Fitzgerald, for example, sees the Waste Land of the ash heap as the tragic outcome of the failure of the sense of wonder with which Dutch sailors responded to the "fresh green breast of the New World." The black and Jewish attitude is more mocking and, at the same time, accepting of the inevitability of failure.

The ability to laugh in the midst of suffering and disaster, even to make of suffering a source of laughter, is the special genius of much contemporary black and Jewish literature. It pervades Ellison's *Invisible Man,* as Ellison himself noted in his introduction to the thirtieth anniversary issue of that novel:

> After such knowledge, and given the persistence of racial violence and the unavailability of legal protection, I asked myself, what else was there to sustain our will to persevere but laughter? And could it be that there was a subtle triumph hidden in such laughter that I had missed, but one that still was more affirmative than raw anger? A secret hardearned wisdom that might, perhaps offer a more effective strategy through which a floundering Afro-American novelist could convey his vision? (xii–xiii)

Disillusioned by the high expectations that once clustered around the American dream, Jewish and African American novelists have been able to use their comic and ironic sense of lower expectations to create a new sense of possibility. Again, as Ellison puts it, the novel "could be fashioned as a raft of hope, perception and entertainment that might help us keep afloat as we tried to negotiate the snags and whirlpools that mark our nation's vacillating course toward and away from the democratic ideal" (xvii). Though one would expect the failure of the American dream in the face of pervasive racism and anti-Semitism to make Jewish and black fiction more despairing, it is actually on the whole more optimistic and more confident of the future; rebirth is one of its primary themes. While Thomas Pynchon's *Gravity's Rainbow* is, at times, a very funny book, it ends in catastrophe and there is no sense of possibility beyond that.

The black and Jewish vision of the comic irony of human life and man's inescapable fate as a victim grew out of the historic experience of racism and anti-Semitism and the unspeakable inhumanity of slavery and the holocaust. This perspective came to seem more meaningful to many Americans than the traditional vision of the American dream in the aftermath of the Second World War. At that time, America seemed to have become the most powerful nation on earth and was happily preparing to fulfill its ultimate world historic mission of imposing the American dream on the rest of the world. However, in one of those grand ironies characteristic of human history, America's moment of greatness seemed increasingly to reveal not its strength, but its weakness. The constant anxiety generated by the Cold War, the internal turmoil of the anticommunist hysteria of the fifties and the protests of the sixties, the military failure of Korea and the catastrophe of Vietnam put America face-to-face with the limitations of power. Thus America's political and historical experience in the fifties and sixties increasingly led to a realization of the vulnerability of greatness, and a fear of national humiliation.

The seeming victory of American technology in the Persian Gulf War may have temporarily restored American confidence in its international power, but the domestic scene remains a shambles with the catastrophes of AIDS, drugs, crime, and violence infringing more and more on the average American. All this has brought into serious question the assumption that Americans who work hard enough can share in the dream of success and an abundant life. If this were not enough, there hovers in the background the constant threat of nuclear holocaust and the devastation of apocalyptic war. The American continent's great ocean barriers are no longer a significant protection. In this time of uncertainty and chaos, America's black and Jewish writers with their powerful sense of irony and vulnerability, as well as their equally wonderful sense of the comedy of our fate, can, as Ralph Ellison's Invisible Man puts it, speak on the lower frequencies, for all of us.

18

Popular Culture/ Multiculturalism

When Ray Browne invited me to give a talk at the first meeting of the Pacific Rim Popular Culture Association in Hawaii, I thought the intersection of popular culture and multiculturalism would be an appropriate topic. Basically I try to synthesize the material in the two previous essays and to bring the story down to the present, detailing the proliferation of new writing representing different American groups.

⇌

More than a hundred years ago, Walt Whitman noted that culture is the word of the modern. Not one of his more original pronouncements, since this was the chorus of most major nineteenth-century critics from Carlyle to Arnold, as Raymond Williams indicates in *Culture and Society*. Culture, in both normative and descriptive senses, continued to be a dominant concept of Western intellectual life right up to the beginning of the second half of the twentieth century. Normatively, the concept of culture was a unifying ideal, centered on a vision of Western civilization as the climax of cultural progress and synthesis. This vision inspired the idea of the humanistic curriculum as pedagogy, leading the student to acquire a significant proportion of the artistic and philosophical canon thought to define this civilization.

On the other hand, used descriptively by the new late-nineteenth-century disciplines of anthropology, sociology, and social psychology, culture was a concept that articulated the multiplicity of behaviors characteristic of actual human beings in different places and times. Ambiguous and confusing as this double meaning of the word could be in practice, the two senses of culture worked out a complex dialectic with each other. Together they expressed an ideal of human society as "liberal," that is as both broadly tolerant of religious and cultural diversity and also as dedicated to the idea of progress toward increasing cultural integration and transcendence of the limitations of past cultures. This ideal was most powerfully symbolized by the idea of America with its great motto: *e pluribus unum.* Some optimists even dreamed of a world civilization embodying the best that had been thought and said. They imagined that this would eventually synthesize individual cultural heritages into one grand stream of civilization.

Alas, too often this cultural ideal really meant the imperialistic domination of some national culture, whether the American way of life, British hegemony, Deutsche Kultur, or the Communist International. Two world wars and a half-century of other conflicts have made the progress of civilization seem more like an appointment with Armageddon than the emergence of a transcendent world culture. Growing doubts about the value or even the possibility of a unified culture have increasingly led critics and scholars to use the word "culture" with qualifying adjectives—popular, working-class, ethnic, folk, high, low, and middle, global, etc. The word of the postmodern is no longer culture but hyphen-culture. Two of the most significant of these hyphen-culture constructs are popular culture and multiculturalism. As ideas they emerged around the same time historically and shared a number of central themes, but in the last two decades they have diverged more and more so that they now seem like quite different ideas.

Three main factors caused this divergence between popular culture studies and ideas of multiculturalism. First of all, scholars developing multicultural approaches concentrated on the materials associated with their particular hyphenated culture. Second, multiculturalists developed complex theories and methodologies to protect and to foster the perspectives and the historical experiences of their particular cultural groups. Thus, in recent years, both African American studies and women's studies have created many theories and analytical approaches that offer a distinctive angle not only on their own materials but on other aspects of culture as well.

Many of these new approaches have been extremely interesting and have enriched our understanding of all sorts of texts and cultural patterns. However, these approaches have also been restrictive insofar as they exclude alternate approaches to the material. Therefore they have resisted synthesis with other modes of analysis. Moreover, this theoretical separatism has sometimes led particular groups devoted to multicultural analysis to claim that only members of particular hyphenated cultures can really understand and apply these analytical methods—that only women can produce a successful feminist analysis, only African Americans can interpret African American culture, etc. Finally, while several multiculturalists have made important contributions to popular culture, most have been mainly interested in constructing their own canons by highlighting the most powerful, complex, and aesthetically interesting works in their traditions.

Popular culture studies, on the other hand, has embraced a very wide definition of culture, has resisted any particular set of theories and methodologies, and, above all, has tried to expand, or, perhaps more accurately, to abandon, the notion of a cultural canon altogether. Unfortunately, because of its insistence on vagueness, inclusiveness, and synthesis, popular culture studies has failed to provide an effective framework for studying the cultural situation of most importance today, the complex interplay in modern societies and in the world at large of many different cultural traditions. While it is fascinating to talk in prophetic and McLuhanesque terms of global villages and international popular culture, or, in more negative terms, about the corruptions of cultural imperialism and coca-colonization, the actual interplay or dialectic of cultural traditions in modern culture is really very complex.

To explore this interplay more fully, I'd like to offer a preliminary sketch of the interaction between popular culture and multicultural traditions in America from the mid-nineteenth century to the present. By 1850 Americans had successfully suppressed and sequestered one alternative to European cultural traditions—that of the Native Americans—and had enslaved and tried to dehumanize the descendants of another—the African. Still remaining cultural enclaves, particularly in the northern states, tried to pass on cultural traditions differing in language, religion, or pattern of behavior to new generations. There were large areas of German and Spanish speakers, and smaller areas where Scandinavian, Dutch, Jewish, and other traditions of European origin persisted.

In the 1840s a large Irish immigration had brought in people similar in language, but very different in other ways to Anglo-Americans. Later in the nineteenth century there would be waves of immigrants from very different cultural traditions, including Southern and Eastern European and Asian. However, at mid-century, one thing was common to most of these diverse offshoots of European traditions—their "whiteness." In the context of a nation deeply obsessed with the relationship between "colored" and white, this factor encouraged the mutual accommodation and assimilation of these diverse groups into a broader concept of white Americanism. From the middle of the nineteenth century to the time of World War I, popular culture increasingly played a significant part in this process of assimilation, a process based essentially on the assertion of Anglo-American or what used to be called WASP dominance or cultural hegemony.

One can easily see how the popular culture of that time fitted into this pattern. As scholars like Albert McLean and John Kasson have shown, popular entertainments like vaudeville, theater, and amusement parks enabled members of different ethnic groups to come together, and to socialize in arenas free from the constraints of ethnic traditions. Presumably in such a venue Abie met his Irish Rose and determined to marry her in spite of parental opposition. In addition, positive and negative stereotypes such as those found in the ever popular racial, ethnic, and gender jokes of this period taught hyphenated Americans the values and mores of Anglo-Americanism and the shortcomings, absurdities, and outright badness of alternative traditions. One learned through popular culture that being an American meant turning away from traditional attitudes and accepting the political and cultural leadership of the Anglo-American middle class. It was here that one could learn, if one was white and Irish, for example, how to move from the status of "No Irish need apply" to that of "lace-curtain Irish" in a generation.

However, the role of popular culture as the major promoter of assimilation and Anglo-American hegemony began to change significantly around the time of World War I. In the 1920s—later referred to as the Jazz Age by some—popular culture entered a decisively new phase marked by several changes. For one thing, popular culture became conscious of itself in a new way. In the mid-nineteenth century, the line between what we would today call popular culture and canonic culture was by no means clear. Hawthorne thought the novels of the "scribbling women" he complained about whose work sold more than his were bad, but did not think of them as being on a different cultural plane than his own. However, Lawrence Levine and others have shown that the last decade of the nineteenth century and the first decade of the twentieth brought about a major reconfiguration of American culture.

In response to the rise of a new industrial elite seeking to recreate in America many aspects of the European tradition of high culture, people began to think in terms of some sort of opposition between "high culture" and popular entertainment.

At the same time, the growth of a mass audience and the emergence of new media like the movies, sound recording, and broadcasting created tremendous new opportunities for entrepreneurs to develop an industrialized popular culture. Out of this emerged the theory of the "brows." The highbrow, the middlebrow, and the lowbrow as symbols of different cultural levels expressed the sense that American culture was now significantly divided between a high culture with roots in European artistic traditions and a popular culture more responsive to the everyday needs of Americans. The beginning of popular culture studies also resulted from this major shift in the patterns of American culture. Gilbert Seldes's *The Seven Lively Arts* brilliantly analyzed such major phenomena of the new popular culture as jazz, the comic strip *(Krazy Kat),* and the silent comedy (Charlie Chaplin). Seldes probably deserves to be called the pioneer of popular culture studies, though he was certainly not alone. Many intellectuals of the tens and twenties were fascinated by the new phenomenon of popular culture and even such highbrows as T. S. Eliot and Edmund Wilson wrote about it. This new configuration of American culture was solidified at the same time that America's traditionally strong and relatively separate ethnic cultures were being rapidly eroded. By the early twentieth century, the use of European languages like German, Italian, and Swedish in homes, newspapers, books, religious services, and other places was being discouraged by growing nativist suspicion of foreign influences. This process intensified during World War I, when anti-German feeling swept the country and made the widespread use of languages other than English increasingly suspect. Even the thriving Yiddish culture that had long been a major feature of New York City began to decline.

But these ethnic cultures did not simply fade away. Actually, the growth of the new popular culture created opportunities for talented musicians, actors, writers, dancers, and entrepreneurs from the ethnic traditions. Everyone has noticed what an important Jewish presence there was in the movies, in popular music, and in comedy. This could also be said about the Irish. And it was in the area of popular culture that African Americans for the first time broke down the walls of segregation and discrimination that had been constructed to reenslave them after the Civil War. Jazz, the blues, spirituals and other musical creations from the rich African American heritage began, during the early twentieth century, to enter the mainstream of American popular culture.

The continued production and widespread popularity of racist myths like *The Birth of a Nation* as well as the widespread use of other antiethnic and anti-Semitic themes and stereotypes indicated that in many ways the new popular culture would continue to foster white Anglo-American hegemony as it had traditionally done. Yet, there were increasing signs of change in areas like the movies, radio, and popular music. Popular music showed perhaps the most significant and important changes. The big band era was an extraordinary confluence of musical traditions, black, white, and ethnic. Through their grueling schedules of one night stands across the country and their radio broadcasts and records, white bands like Paul Whiteman, Benny Goodman, Glenn Miller, and Artie Shaw and black bands like Duke Ellington, Fletcher Henderson, Louis Armstrong, and Count Basie played widely to both black and white audiences. As time went on their music became more and more interrelated. An important symbolic moment of this era, almost accidentally preserved for us by the new technologies of radio and sound recording, represents the synthesizing and transforming tendencies within the new popular culture. This was the great 1938 Carnegie Hall Concert of the Benny Goodman orchestra. Playing in Carnegie Hall, the great center of classical music, indicated a new respectability for popular music and symbolized its breaking across the highbrow-lowbrow barrier. Even more significantly this concert involved both white and black musicians and thus openly revealed the mutual influence that had long been part of the development of jazz. Benny Goodman, a Jewish American bandleader, whose white musicians were a very diverse ethnic lot, played together with musicians from the Count Basie band, one of the great black aggregations of that era. The concert symbolized, in a highly public fashion, the confluence of black and white musical traditions that had shaped the development of swing.

One other major cultural shift played a vital role in the development of this new phase of popular culture. Sometime in the later nineteenth century youth became something very different than it had been. Once it had been a brief period of apprenticeship during which young people learned the skills they would practice as adults. By the ages of fifteen or sixteen many young people had virtually become adults. With the rise of public secondary education and of a more affluent middle class in the later nineteenth century, youth became a much more protracted phase of life. At this time, adolescence was discovered, and young people were increasingly socialized into the expectation that they would live in a way different from their parents. This created the phenomenon of generational revolt, so characteristic of twentieth-century America. The generation coming of age in the twenties exemplified perhaps for the first time the patterns that would become so characteristic of succeeding generations: rebellion against the past; the quest for liberation; experimentation with new mores and patterns of behavior; and a new kind of immersion in popular culture. The impetus of successive younger generations, which tended to be increasingly affluent, fueled the development of twentieth-century popular culture in a new way, particularly emphasizing its transformational aspects and increasingly subverting its role as agent for the traditional Anglo-American hegemony.

Thus, in the period between the wars, popular culture became more and more the expression of a new cultural synthesis in America foreshadowing the post–World War II trend toward the integration of women and minorities into American culture. The major characteristics of this new phase in popular culture were confluence, synthesis, and transformation. The media, driven by the profitability that resulted from attracting larger and larger audiences, including the newly affluent young people, developed new modes of organization such as Hollywood studios, radio-television networks, and publishing syndicates that could produce and distribute material to the largest possible audiences. These media developed content that was more responsive to the interests and values of this increasingly diverse audience by inventing generic traditions that could be tailored to a great variety of interests. In addition they created new genres with a special appeal to such important components of the audience as women and young people. The new media also produced many synthesizing images of American culture, the most obvious being those multiethnic bomber crews or infantry squads so important in movies of World War II. These sought to place the diverse minorities of America in a new unified constellation. This new unity became more and more different from the Anglo-American hegemony that had played the leading role in the first phase of popular culture. The history of the complex dialectic between new images of multicultural unity and the traditional Anglo-American hegemony is one of the central areas in the history of popular culture that needs to be more fully researched.

When the popular culture movement developed in the late 1960s and early 1970s, its thrust was at first primarily to acknowledge popular culture as synthesizer and transformer of American culture. In fact, most of the early leaders of the popular culture movement—like Ray Browne, Russell Nye, Marshall Fishwick, and Leslie Fiedler—came out of American studies or American literature. But even as such forums as the *Journal of Popular Culture* and the Popular Culture Association flourished, popular culture, itself, was beginning to undergo another fundamental shift. It was during this time that such ideas as multiculturalism, cultural pluralism, and bilingualism began to gain increasing currency. During the 1960s and '70s, multiculturalism became associated with a powerful thrust toward cultural separatism among African Americans as the Black Power and Black Arts movements, the rise of black studies programs in the universities, and the growth of the Black Muslim movement and the legend of Malcolm X suggest. Accompanying this was an growing awareness of aspects of ethnic separatism in America such as those described in Michael Novak's *Rise of the Unmeltable Ethnics*. Native Americans, Asian Americans, and Chicanos and other Latinos increasingly rejected the illusion of the melting pot and sought to revitalize their own cultural traditions, by, for example, demanding bilingualism in the public schools. In addition, these forces of cultural fragmentation were expressed in a rapidly developing feminism that made gender separatism an important part of its agenda.

Committed to the ideologies of civil rights, integration, and equal rights that had dominated ethnic and gender politics since World War II, liberals were initially taken aback by the vehemence and force of this separatist reaction. For a time, the idea of cultural pluralism became itself a contested area: did cultural pluralism mean increasing tolerance and acceptance of cultural differences or did it mean separation among different cultures? Throughout this time the popular culture movement retained its openness and hospitality to divergent views. However, many younger feminist, African American, and Native American scholars did not want openness and they rejected the framework of popular culture to pursue their work in the context of gender studies, African American history and culture, and ethnic studies. At the same time and for somewhat different reasons, various kinds of media studies and cinema studies also started pursuing different paths. In this context popular culture lost its claim to universality and synthesis as well as its position in the vanguard of cultural studies.

To some extent, the trend toward separatism is still strong. However, in the last decade or so, another important development has taken place in the shifting dialectic of American culture. During this time the separatist impulse has diminished considerably and hitherto separate ethnic traditions to have begun to mix and overlap. Something of the same sort has happened in the area of gender with the development of new concepts of masculinity and the emergence of "queer" studies, which stand not so much in opposition to but more in a dialectical relationship with feminism. One of the most knowledgeable observers of this new phenomenon, the English scholar A. Robert Lee, describes the contemporary cultural scene in terms of what he calls the "ethnic postmodern." Lee describes this as a style "in which the vocabulary is one of hybridity, borderland, margins which have moved to the center, in every way a new order of cultural self-positioning and reference. This, indeed, might be called the ethnic postmodern. It entails not only an extrication out, and beyond, essentialist or one-note identity politics, but a cultural stance . . . which, with uninhibited reflexivity, plays upon, contemplates, actually vaunts, its own imaginative self-mirroring."

Lee's discussion is primarily concerned with avant-garde postmodern writers like Ishmael Reed, Maxine Hong Kingston, and Gerald Vizenor, but much of what he says applies on a different level to contemporary popular culture. With the development of cable, videotape, and now Internet and CD-ROM, new means of production and distribution make possible types of diversity and recombination that would have been unimaginable during the 1950s and 1960s. Correspondingly, the unifying structures of the traditional mass media like networks, movie studios, and publishing syndicates have considerably eroded. While these changes have also led to huge media consolidations like the Disney-ABC and Time Warner–Turner Broadcasting mergers, these megacorporations are conglomerations of many media enterprises. They may foster increasing diversity as much as they do homogeneity and standardization.

The popular cultural scene itself seems more and more attuned to recombinations of traditional heritages. There is, for example, the way in which new combinations of white, African American, and Latino musical traditions are continually creating new genres of popular music, such as Afro-Celtic. Moreover, this kind of interplay is spreading to other areas of popular culture like movies and cable television. Contemporary popular culture has also become much more responsive to the international scene than ever before. Recombinant lifestyles are becoming more the norm than the exception. Imagine the very model of a modern urban dweller; dressed in cowboy boots and a dashiki, she nibbles on sushi while listening to the latest country music. No doubt much of this is superficial and a way of rebelling against the dullness of contemporary corporate culture, but there are signs that the ethnic postmodern has a more profound significance. I was particularly struck a few weeks ago by news reports about a parents' movement that wants the public schools to change the way they record the ethnicity of students in order to register multiple backgrounds. These parents are not satisfied with the standard white, African American, Native American, Latino, and Asian categories used by the schools, and have sued to make the schools list their children as African American *and* white *and* Native American, for example. This suggests a basic transformation of attitudes in a culture, which, despite its official melting pot ideology, has long been deeply split by racial and ethnic divisions.

American popular culture has often expressed the racism, sexism and white Protestant ethnocentrism so deeply ingrained in our history, but it has also been more open to cultural transformations and alternatives than most of our highbrow and middlebrow culture. In the later nineteenth and early twentieth centuries America was largely a white Anglo-American cultural hegemony pervaded by a revitalized racism. Yet, popular culture in areas like vaudeville, popular theater, and music still developed more multicultural motifs than the traditional literary areas dominated by white elites. Even more avant-garde literary movements like naturalism showed relatively little awareness or interest in the burgeoning cultural pluralism of American society until the 1920s, when American critics and intellectuals began tentatively to acknowledge the vitality and significance of the new popular culture.

During the last quarter of the twentieth century a renewed tide of neoconservatism led ethnic and gender groups increasingly to define themselves *against* the rest of the culture. Partly this was a response to the way in which a residual Anglo-American "silent majority" of "Christian conservatism" has tried to reestablish its hegemony. However, popular culture continued to subvert such hegemony and to break down cultural boundaries. Ironically, while the continued effect of capitalism on the social and economic level seems to be leading to growing class division between rich and poor, a capitalist popular culture industry seems to operate more in the direction of undercutting and obfuscating these divisions. It seems to me that this increasingly complex and volatile cultural situation opens up a host of new questions and inquiries for students of popular culture and multiculturalism.

Section 4

The Mystery of Mystery

19

Faulkner and the Detective Story's Double Plot

Since I first discovered Sherlock Holmes and Dorothy Sayers's wonderful *Omnibus of Crime* in the Winnetka Public Library over sixty years ago I've been a devoted, occasionally compulsive, reader of the literature of mystery. The literature of mystery has been more central to my work in popular culture than even the western. Discussions of mystery stories dominate my *Mystery, Adventure, and Romance,* for example. I've also been interested in the pervasive influence of the mystery genre on modernist and postmodernist literature, and this essay was one result of that interest. It compares Faulkner's use of mystery themes and structures with that of three postmodern writers, Nabokov, Borges, and Pynchon.

━━

The humble detective story has been a significant source of both structure and theme in modernist and "postmodernist" fiction. William Faulkner read detective stories avidly, and when in need of fast cash, he wrote them as well (Blotner, *Faulkner* 605). But more importantly, the concept of the detective story with its curiously duplicitous and doubled structure informs many of his major novels.

Though Faulkner often affected scorn for popular fiction and films, he was nonetheless a skilled and imaginative craftsman in the major popular genres and his work was much sought after by major directors and film producers. Howard Hawks, for example, considered Faulkner's contributions an indispensable ingredient in such brilliant popular films as *To Have and Have Not* and *The Big Sleep*. Faulkner's dabbling in popular culture began as early as 1925 when, while working on *Soldier's Pay*, he published a series of O'Henryesque sketches in the *New Orleans Times-Picayune*. It continued in the late 1920s when Faulkner started what he apparently conceived of as, in Blotner's phrase, "a spectacular mystery-detective-gangster story" (606) in the spring of 1929.

Not at all coincidentally, this kind of story was rapidly becoming one of the most successful genres of fiction and film of the period. Box office successes like *Underworld*, based on a Ben Hecht story, and *The Racket*, adapted from a Broadway play, had already appeared, and such smash hits as *Little Caesar*, *Public Money*, and *Scarface* would come out in the early 1930s concurrently with *Sanctuary*. Faulkner continued to contribute to popular entertainment through his work in movies in the 1930s and early 1940s and the many stories he published in the *Saturday Evening Post*, *Scribner's*, *Harper's*, and other magazines.

Faulkner also worked from early on within the specific patterns of the detective story genre. "Smoke" which was submitted to the *Post* in early 1930 (and refused) not only used the standard formula of mystery, clues, and dramatic solution, but also introduced a character in the mold of the classical detective, brilliant lawyer Gavin Stevens, who would become an increasingly important figure in Faulkner's later fiction.[1]

Harper's finally bought "Smoke" in 1932. It was followed by several other Gavin Stevens detective stories including "An Error in Chemistry," which won second prize in *Ellery Queen's Mystery Magazine's* annual contest in 1945. The series culminated in 1948 with the novel *Intruder in the Dust*, which has the basic structure of a detective story, and in 1949 with the collected Gavin Stevens stories published as *Knight's Gambit*.

Faulkner's growing reputation and sales after the late 1940s rendered the need to keep the pot boiling less urgent. However, the structure of

1. Blotner suggests, no doubt correctly, that Gavin Stevens was based in large part on Faulkner's friend Phil Stone. However, there is another pretty obvious source for the character, which comes right out of the popular detective literature of the time. Arthur Train's Ephraim Tutt, one of the first lawyer detectives, is very similar in character to Gavin Stevens and the courtroom focus of many of his stories is likewise a feature of the Gavin Stevens stories. Train's work appeared regularly in the *Saturday Evening Post* from the early 1920s on and was collected in several anthologies. While I cannot prove that Faulkner read Train, it seems unlikely that he would have missed noticing a highly successful *Post* author. In addition no less than three of the Mr. Tutt's collections were purchased by Phil Stone in 1926 and 1927, just before Faulkner began work on "Smoke" (125).

the detective story clearly had more than merely financial interest for Faulkner, since he continued to use the character of Gavin Stevens and the characteristic patterns of mystery, clues, and solutions throughout the Snopes Trilogy. We can only guess what it was about the detective story that so fascinated Faulkner, but he shared that fascination with many other modern writers. However, the way in which Faulkner used the formulas of the detective story is very different from their use by writers such as Borges, Pynchon, and Nabokov.

Richard Wilbur has suggested in a brilliant essay on Poe's detective stories that the theme of doubling has been a part of the genre from the beginning. Wilbur points particularly to the mirror-like relationship between Dupin and the Minister D in "The Purloined Letter." In fact, strangely compelling parallels between detectives and master criminals abound in mystery literature. Sherlock Holmes and Professor Moriarty, Dennis Nayland Smyth and Dr. Fu Manchu, Sam Spade and Brigid O'Shaughnessy are three immediately obvious instances. Wilbur's insight that the criminal is in some way the dark side of the detective seems clearly borne out. John Irwin has shown how important a part this doubling of characters played in Faulkner's work, but there is another sort of doubling in the detective story that may be even more significant. I refer to the double, or duplicitous, plot that is integral to the detective story formula. The plot is double because the story is first narrated to us as it appears to the bewildered bystanders who observe and are threatened by the crime but cannot arrive at its solution. Finally, through the detective's explanation of the crime, the true story of the events is revealed. This doubling is duplicitous, because, in the first presentation of the story, the writer tries to tantalize and deceive the reader, while, at the same time, inconspicuously planting the clues that will eventually make the detective's solution plausible. It is, I think, this double plot that most fascinated twentieth-century writers about detective fiction, perhaps because it reflected their own highly self-conscious awareness of the artificiality of narration and the ambiguity of plots.

There are a number of ways in which both modern and "postmodern" writers have employed this aspect of the detective story, and they all express a different vision of the world. Vladimir Nabokov's use of detective story structures and motifs was certainly as pervasive as Faulkner's but his exploitation of the double plot is particularly crucial in two works: *The Real Life of Sebastian Knight* and *Pale Fire*. Since Nabokov's use of this pattern seems to be the most different from Faulkner's, I will begin with a few observations on these novels.

In both *Sebastian Knight* and *Pale Fire* an investigator works through a set of clues in order to discover the "real" truth about the object of his investigation. In one case, this is the life of the investigator's brother, a novelist who has recently died, and in the other, a poem left behind by the investigator's "friend" who has been suddenly murdered. As his research proceeds, the investigator's perversity and egotism become more and more obvious to the reader, who comes to realize that, rather than discovering a hidden truth, the "detective" is projecting his own needs and obsessions into the clues he is examining. Thus, we end up with what appears to be almost a total reversal of the detective story's double plot. It is the detective's "solution" that is false while the original clues in their relative opacity and mystery must contain whatever there is to be known of the truth. Unfortunately, it seems impossible to unravel the meaning of these clues.

To some extent, Nabokov provides the reader with hints that can lead to alternative interpretations. These hints are implicit in the character of the investigator and in the clues or "texts" he is examining. Most readers probably arrive at an alternative solution to that of the investigator, at least to the extent of concluding that the "detective's" solution is totally off track and also, probably, off the wall. One finishes *Pale Fire* with at least a partial conviction that John Shade's attitude toward Charles Kinbote is not one of respect, as Kinbote thinks, but rather impatience at having to deal with a perpetual bore and meddler. Similarly, readers usually decide that the narrator of *The Real Life of Sebastian Knight* has completely misunderstood, or at least persistently misrepresents, the relationship between himself and his brother. However, these conclusions remain fairly tenuous and are themselves a matter of interpretation on the reader's part. They are not truths clearly established for us by the author. Perhaps Shade was fascinated by Kinbote's lunatic claims; perhaps Sebastian did feel some sort of affection for his brother.

There is still a further complication in Nabokov's use of the double plot structure. Though the reader realizes that there is little, if any, truth to the investigator's fantasies about his texts, it is also the case, particularly with Charles Kinbote's Zemblan mania, that the investigator's perverse misinterpretations and projections have imaginative intensity and depth that gives them a strange sort of truth, as if the investigator had been able to impose his perverse obsessions on a recalcitrant world and a reluctant reader.

Thus, the double plot structure in Nabokov becomes the source of an incessant play of meanings and ambivalences, a field in which gaudy butterflies of many different shades flitting to and fro, forever eluding the lepidopterist's net. Nabokov's ironic reversal of the detective story's double structure of mystery and solution becomes, then, an expression of a world in which we continually search for certainty and meaning but find only the evanescent fluttering of "Transparent Things." Our only security in face of this supreme mystery is the delight of aesthetic play as we attempt to give a temporary shape and form to the shimmering surfaces of objects and language.

Jorge Luis Borges's most striking use of detective themes and structure is in the story "Death and the Compass" (*Ficciones* 129–41). In this tale, detective Erik Llonrot, "who thought of himself as a pure thinker, an August Dupin" is lured into a trap when he pursues a series of clues planted by his archenemy, gangster Red Scharlach. Scharlach uses an unrelated murder committed by someone else as the first in a series of clues and sequential murders that, when logically interpreted by Llonrot's supposedly brilliant mind, leads him to the scene of a final crime, which turns out to be his own murder. He comes to a decaying villa filled with images of doubles:

> The house on the estate of Triste-le-Roy was seen to abound in superfluous symmetries and in maniacal repetition: a glacial Diana in one lugubrious niche was complemented by another Diana in another niche; one balcony was repeated by another balcony; double steps of stair opened into a double balustrade. A two-faced Hermes cast a monstrous shadow. (9)

Here, Llonrot confronts his own double, the criminal Scharlach. In true detective fashion, Scharlach carefully "solves" for Llonrot the way in which he has set up the sequence of clues leading Llonrot to this lonely and fatal rendezvous.

For Borges this inversion of the double plot of the detective story exposes the delusion of rationality fostered by the traditional detective story. It shows how the appearance of rational order can easily be transformed into a labyrinth of deceit that completely entraps its human victim. Significantly, the final clue enticing Llonrot into the labyrinth is delivered in a letter signed by one "Baruj Spinoza" presumably an imaginary descendent of the great seventeenth-century philosopher of reason. Unlike Nabokov's incessant play of meanings, Borges' version of the detective story stresses the fatal disappointment inherent in any quest for rational solutions in this world. Like Nabokov, Borges developed his own perverse version of the detective story as a means of dramatizing the ambiguity inherent in the quest for truth or meaning.

Thomas Pynchon tells us that, as a child, he loved the spy stories of John Buchan (*Slow Learner* xxviii). Much in the mold of Conan Doyle's Sherlock Holmes, Buchan's stories were replete with mysterious clues, strange happenings, and master villains. In Pynchon's first novel *V.*, Herbert Stencil's long-term pursuit of the mysterious V is a fantastic detective investigation that spreads out over decades. In his *magnum opus Gravity's Rainbow*, Pynchon hangs his plot, such as it is, on Tyrone Slothrop's attempt to solve the mystery of a secret German rocket device, the Schwarzgerät. But it's his second novel, *The Crying of Lot 49*, in which Pynchon gives us his most straightforward use, or rather, perversion of the double plot structure of detection.

In this novel, the heroine, Oedipa Maas, a California suburban housewife, receives news that she has been appointed executrix of the will of a former lover, the mysterious millionaire business tycoon Pierce Inverarity. Her attempts to deal with this charge are soon sidetracked by her apparently accidental discovery of what seems to be a mysterious conspiracy that may or may not be related to Inverarity. Oedipa's investigation and interpretation of the mysterious clues she finds lead her to believe that she may have discovered a secret society hidden behind the facade of high-tech suburban America, a society that possibly has existed for centuries, secretly conspiring against and functioning as a significant alternative to Western civilization. In the end, having come to see the "Tristero" as centered around an alternative postal system or means of communication, Oedipa goes to an auction where Pierce Inverarity's famous stamp collection will be sold. There she awaits some resolution of the mystery, which is, of course, not revealed to us.

As in Nabokov and Borges, there is no certain truth to be found at the end of the investigation. As Pynchon develops Oedipa's investigation, we find ourselves as readers quite unable to be sure whether the Tristero is real or a figment of Oedipa's fevered imagination, and, if it is a reality, whether it is diabolical or benevolent. Pynchon plants clues with such skill that we find we cannot resolve these basic questions. It seems quite possible to interpret Oedipa's Tristero theory as a projection of her own inner needs (as with Kinbote in Nabokov's *Pale Fire*) except that there are so many clues and some of them have such apparent palpability that we cannot wholly reject the interpretation that argues that

Trsitero is real either. This is apparently just the sort of experience Pynchon wants us to have and it relates to a conception that he later, in *Gravity's Rainbow*, labeled "creative paranoia."

Pynchon believes modern Western civilization is probably doomed to nuclear destruction by its inhumane dedication to rationality, its proliferation of technology, and its sadistic violence, and suggests that only by radical transcendence and the creation of new alternatives in history can mankind be saved. In this belief Pynchon reflects the radical ideology of the 1960s but where that was optimistic and optative, Pynchon tends to be pessimistic and skeptical. As he sees it, the imagining of real change may not only be, but also necessitate, a kind of madness, at least from the perspective of the dominant rationalistic scientific ideology. This visionary madness he envisions as a kind of creative paranoia, the development of a capacity to see mysterious forces and structures operating beneath the surface of things. Unlike the psychosis of paranoia, which sees enemies everywhere and is deeply destructive, "creative paranoia" represents a capacity to transcend the dominant ideology and to imagine the possibility of alternatives in history. It is to this kind of experience, at least vicariously, that Pynchon wants to bring his reader, hoping against hope that this might help bring about the "anarchist miracle" that could redeem history. Thus, for all his comedy and craziness, Pynchon has a deeply serious political purpose and in this he differs from Nabokov and Borges. His use of the double structure of the detective story sets up for the reader the experience of "creative paranoia" by forcing us into the impossible but inescapable quest for solution.

It should now be clear why "postmodernist" writers such as Nabokov, Borges, and Pynchon make such extensive use of detective story structures and themes. Nabokov and Borges are skeptics; they believe that the hope of arriving at some clear sense of truth, reason or meaning is a snare and a delusion. For Pynchon, truth would mean a revolutionary transcendence of history and the emergence or discovery of significant social and political alternatives, and he is dubious that such a thing could happen.

Finally, the three use the traditional detective story structure of investigation and solution as the very antithesis of their own visions. By perverting or inverting the detective story these writers engage their readers in an investigation that has no solution except the recognition that, as Pynchon puts it (quoting Wittgenstein), "the world is all that the case is."

These different but fundamentally similar uses of the double structure of investigation and solution help us to see how different Faulkner was both in his vision of the world and in his use of detective story patterns to articulate that vision. Though, as we have noted, the influence of the detective story was pervasive throughout Faulkner's career, I will limit my discussion to three works: two that are not on the surface detective stories, and one that is at least a quasi-detective story, *The Sound and the Fury, Absalom, Absalom!,* and *Intruder in the Dust.*[2]

The Sound and the Fury seems, at first glance, the furthest possible thing from a detective story. It has no character playing anything like a detective role and no significant sort of investigation. However, if we look at the novel from another angle, the double structure of investigation and solution is central. The writer and reader are detectives and Benjy, Quentin, and Jason are the suspects or witnesses whose monologues provide the clues which must be interpreted to arrive at a solution to the mystery of the disastrous fates of the Compson children and to an understanding of the significance of those fates. Indeed, one important aspect of the traditional structure of the detective story gives us considerable insight into the role of the fourth or "Dilsey" section in the overall form of the novel. There has always been some question about this section. Does its "objective" third-person narration mean that we are getting the whole truth after the partial and subjective accounts of the three first-person sections? Sometimes Faulkner talked about the book as if this were the case, but he also sometimes hinted that the fourth section is only another of many possible versions of the Compson story.

Neither of these statements seems quite right. There is too much of a sense of finality about the fourth section for it to be only another version; yet, at the same time, it does not offer a perspective on the Compson family that is any more total or privileged than the first three sections. Rather, this is analogous to the traditional detective story structure requiring a crime, an investigation, a solution, and a denouement. In the solution section, the detective explains the crime and puts

---

2. While *The Hamlet, The Town,* and *The Mansion* are not in their overall structure detective stories, many of the individual episodes — the murder of Houston, the treasure hunt at the old Frenchman's place, the investigation of Flem Snopes's brassy thefts, the murder of Flem himself, and the final pursuit of Mink Snopes — involve basic conventions of the detective story genre. And, of course, the continued presence of Gavin Stevens in his capacity as flawed but brilliant observer and resolver of mysteries also echoes the form.

the events surrounding it in their proper perspective. Then, as denouement, the criminal is apprehended and justice is meted out. What we have in *The Sound and the Fury* is an account of a crime, the tragedy of the Compson children's disastrous growth to maturity culminating in Quentin's suicide, Caddy's flight, and ultimately in the doubling disappearance of Caddy's daughter, and an investigation with the writer and the reader's pondering of the accounts of Compson family life in the first three sections. But Faulkner leaves out the solution section that would have ensued in the traditional detective story and passes directly to the denouement in which Benjy grieves, Jason receives a kind of poetic justice, and Dilsey dreams of the hope of resurrection. The structure works emotionally in a compelling way, but the solution is left to the reader. If, as seems likely, Joyce's *Ulysses* was a major model for *The Sound and the Fury*, Faulkner's sense of the formal possibilities implicit in the detective story formula may have helped him to differentiate his own use of multiple perspectives and the internal monologue from that of *Ulysses* where there is little evidence of the double plot pattern.

Whether or nor this is the case, Faulkner's use of the double plot pattern in *The Sound and the Fury* clearly foreshadows how he would later use this pattern even more explicitly in *Absalom, Absalom!* and *Intruder in the Dust*. First, it is clear that *The Sound and the Fury* does not "signify nothing" in spite of the allusion of the title. On the contrary, the novel is full of profoundly human truth and significance. Faulkner himself hinted at this in what he probably said most often about the book, that it had originated in the haunting image of a little girl in a tree with muddy drawers and that the various sections of the book are attempts to understand the meaning of this image or, as we might call it in the present context, this "clue." As Faulkner later put it in his Nobel Prize speech, the writer should seek for "truths of the human heart," which are perhaps the most important things of all since they contribute not only to the survival but also to the possible redemption of man.

Second, *The Sound and the Fury* uses the double plot structure to show that these truths are never easy to discover. Moreover, they cannot be formulated in a permanent and fixed way because they must be perceived and understood through the conflicting truths of individuals. The process of coming to understand, to assimilate, and even to transcend these conflicting individual truths is one of the most important of human activities. It may be that the continued struggle to arrive at truth is as important as the "solution" itself. At least this is what Faulkner involves his reader in through the use of multiple perspectives in such works as *The Sound and the Fury, As I Lay Dying,* and *Light in August*. It is also the most essential subject of *Absalom, Absalom!,* sometimes considered Faulkner's greatest novel. The double structure of the detective story is even more obvious in *Absalom* than in *The Sound and the Fury*. There is a pair of detectives, Quentin Compson and Shreve McCannon. They become involved with a series of crimes, the murders of Charles Bon and Thomas Sutpen and the fire that destroys the Sutpen mansion. Finally, there is an investigation and solution built into the very structure of the novel. Chapters I–V represent an afternoon and evening in September 1909 when Quentin hears the Sutpen story from Miss Rosa and his father and then goes out to the mansion with Miss Rosa to see the dying Henry Sutpen. This is the investigation. Chapters 6–9 take place on a winter evening in 1910 in Quentin's room at Harvard. They show Quentin and Shreve seeking to arrive at a solution to the Sutpen mystery in response to Mr. Compson's letter about Miss Rosa's death and the fire that has consumed Sutpen's Hundred along with Henry and Clytie Sutpen.

In *Absalom, Absalom!,* the multiple perspectives of *The Sound and the Fury* are transformed into a multiplicity of storytellers, legend makers, and witnesses who have something to say about the Sutpen history. To the problem of conflicting individual truths, Faulkner adds the complexities of history, memory, and myth, which also embody the perspective of the community, adding a further level of difficulty to the understanding of truth and meaning. In addition, *Absalom, Absalom!* dramatizes the role of imagination and the human capacity for empathy and identification as vital resources in the quest for truth and understanding. Shreve and Quentin become more and more intuitively identified with Henry Sutpen and Charles Bon as they come closer to the ultimate solution to the murder. Yet, despite the difficulty of their discovery and the uncertainty of the evidence supporting them, Faulkner never seems to doubt that there are truths. There is absolutely no firm evidence that the solution Shreve and Quentin arrive at is the truth. As Cleanth Brooks and others have shown, we cannot be sure that Charles Bon was either part Negro or Thomas Sutpen's son (301–28). Yet, to doubt Shreve and Quentin's interpretation of Henry's motivation as a fear of miscegenation rather than incest seems difficult for it would belie the world of the novel and of the Yoknapatawpha County saga of which it is a part. Truth is precarious, never fixed, and always elusive, but it is there and seeking for it is perhaps the most important of human activities.

Another important Faulknerian use of the double plot structure is to show that, in the quest for truth, one may discover important truths other than the solution one seeks. This is made most clear in *Intruder in the Dust,* the closest thing to a straight detective novel Faulkner ever wrote. As he becomes a reluctant partner in the detective team investigating the murder of Vinson Gowrie, Chick Mallison helps, at first reluctantly, prove Lucas Beauchamp's innocence and the guilt of Crawford Gowrie. He also comes to a number of very important discoveries about his community, its heritage, and his responsibility for it, which, for Faulkner, are a most important part of the process of growing up. Chick's experience is an instance in which the process of investigation into truth leads to a kind of transcendence of the ideological limits that blind most individuals.

Quentin Compson, with Shreve's help, arrives at the closest approximation to truth one is likely to find about the Sutpen tragedy, but he is neither able to assimilate nor to transcend this truth. His own ambivalent feelings about himself, his sister, and his family prevent him from embracing a very important truth that has emerged in the process of his investigation: the meaning of Shreve's friendship and his capacity for empathy with Quentin and his dilemmas. Evidently his problems with his own sexuality make it impossible for Quentin to fully accept Shreve's friendship and, as we see in *The Sound and the Fury,* the two have drifted somewhat apart, perhaps unable to handle the taunts and accusations of homosexuality that they have received from their classmates. Unlike Chick Mallison who arrives at a new perception of his heritage, Quentin is finally unable to face the truth and to become reconciled to his life.

Thus, unlike most "postmodernist" writers, Faulkner used the double plot structure of the detective story to portray a meaningful search for truth. He was, of course, not interested in the simple and uncomplicated truths of whodunit but in the infinitely more complex, difficult and ever-changing truths of the human heart. In his supreme accomplishments such as *The Sound and the Fury* and *Absalom, Absalom!* he may well be said to have written two of the greatest detective stories since Sophocles' *Oedipus Rex.*

20

Canonization, Modern Literature, and the Detective Story

This essay was originally written for a conference at Hofstra University celebrating the 100th anniversary of the birth of Agatha Christie. It appeared in a selection of essays from that conference edited by Ruth Prigozy and Jerome Delamater entitled *Theory and Practice of Classic Detective Fiction*. In it, I continue discussion of the relationship between detective fiction and canonic literature as well as some of the important ways that the mystery story evolved at the end of the twentieth century.

⇌

In recent years, the far-reaching and often acrimonious debate about what has become known as the "canon" of English and American literature has dominated literary scholarship and criticism. Much of the debate has involved whether to give literature created by women and minorities, especially African American, Spanish-speaking, and Native American groups, greater emphasis in the accepted literary canon. Supporters of "canon revision" have tried to generate more positive critical analyses and evaluations of literature by women and minority groups, have attacked the exclusion of these groups from the canon, and have argued that the canon itself has been strongly influenced by sexist, racist,

276

and class ideologies. The end result of this activity has been the increasing inclusion of literary creations by women and minority groups in both literary histories and in the text anthologies that are the basis of most introductory literature courses. In this way what we know as literature is being reshaped through education and scholarship.

However, there is another important way in which our thinking about literature has been changing in the last two decades. This is the gradual assimilation into our idea of literature of popular genres that used to be sharply separated from the literary mainstream, most notably the detective story. Now, not only are certain practitioners of the detective story such as Dashiell Hammett and Raymond Chandler frequently included in those classroom anthologies that effectively define the literary tradition, but also the genre itself has achieved a new cultural centrality, both in America and in the world. Some of the more significant recent trends in writing by women and minorities have emerged from the detective story tradition, and the detective story has also become an important component of a new global culture developing around the rapid international spread of telecommunications. Finally, the basic significance of the detective story to modern culture has been reflected in the frequent use of detective story patterns by major modernist and postmodernist writers such as William Faulkner, Vladimir Nabokov, Jorge Luis Borges, and Thomas Pynchon.

When the detective story first became widely popular through the great success of Sherlock Holmes, the social values and ideologies it expressed were generally conservative. Conan Doyle's attitudes were deeply Victorian and he strongly affirmed most of the values of traditional British culture in his stories by making his Holmes and Watson embody the combination of solidity, morality, and eccentricity so central to the ideal of the British gentry. His criminals often represented groups who threatened this traditional order. However, despite the conservatism of Doyle and most of the other successful writers of the "golden age" of the detective story, there has always been a subversive element in the genre as well. The combination of conservative and subversive elements in detective literature may even go back to the ambiguous mixture of rationality and decadence that Edgar Allan Poe built into his original creation. While most of the detectives of the 1910s and 1920s were gentlemen in the mold of Holmes and Watson—one thinks immediately of such eccentric paragons as Ellery Queen, Philo Vance, Lord Peter Wimsey, Sir Henry Merrivale, Albert Campion, and Hercule Poirot—the creation in the later 1920s of the hard-boiled detective, a plebian with distinctly subversive undertones, revolution-ized the genre.

The detective story has continued in that direction. Recently, the subversive element has manifested itself in the genre's increasing open-ness to women and minority groups. Indeed, one central aspect of the recent development of the detective story has been its growing domi-nance by women and by writers who, one way or another, seek to repre-sent minority groups.

Even in its early days, the detective story strongly attracted women writers, perhaps in large part because, as an area of literature considered mere entertainment, it was more open to women than "serious" litera-ture.[1] In addition, since the classical detective story depended to a con-siderable extent on the portrayal of what used to be called "manners," it may be that women, trained from childhood to be exceptionally alert to social cues, had a special gift for the skillful parading of clues and sus-pects. Whatever the reason, women's influence on the development of the detective story has been much greater than on any other literary genre except the romance. One of the first successful detective novelists was the late-nineteenth-century American author Anna Catherine Green while the bestselling detective-story writer of all time is Agatha Christie. Writers like Christie, Margery Allingham, Dorothy Sayers, Patricia Highsmith, Ngaio Marsh, and Josephine Tey were certainly as important in the so-called golden age of the detective story as their male counterparts.[2] The women writers of this early period generally expressed the same social values as their male counterparts, sometimes in so extreme a form as to be almost parodic. Never was there a more complete model of the casual but totally competent British gentleman than Lord Peter Wimsey or Albert Campion.[3] However the rise of the

1. Kathleen Maio lists twenty-five important mystery novels by women between 1861 and 1916 in *Murderess Ink* (47–49), while Michele Slung lists over one hundred women detectives from 1861–1974 in *Crime on Her Mind* (357–77).

2. Along with the continued appearance of new women writers and detectives, the literature on women mystery writers has grown considerably in the past three decades; among the important books are Dilys Winn, *Murderess Ink*, a compendium of information on women mystery writers and other aspects of women and crime, Michele Slung, *Crime on Her Mind*, an anthology of stories featuring women detectives, and Bobbie Ann Mason, *The Girl Sleuth*, a feminist study of mys-teries such as the once super-popular Nancy Drew books, featuring young girl detectives. See also Elaine Budd, *13 Mistresses of Murder*.

3. Significantly, however, both Wimsey and Campion fall in love with highly brilliant and in-dependent women and must work very hard to understand and accept their needs as feminists.

hard-boiled detective story changed all that. The hard-boiled story was initially dominated by male writers and had a distinctively antifeminist and even misogynistic animus, though, aside from this rampant sexism, it had a socially liberal and even, in some ways, radical ethos.[4]

The hard-boiled story's misogyny proved in the long run to be only a temporary aberration. At the present time, two of the best and most popular hard-boiled writers, Sara Paretsky and Sue Grafton, are women, and they have imported feminist values into the tough-guy genre in a way that would doubtless have put Mike Hammer into a tizzy. Paretsky's V. I. Warshawski is not only an arch-feminist, but has mixed Italian and Polish parentage, so that she represents ethnic minorities as well. Warshawski is the kind of character who was typically either villain or victim in the traditional hard-boiled story. It is as if Brigid O'Shaughnessy or Velma Valento had become the detective. In addition, Warshawski is tough; she runs, does judo, and is able to handle herself in a fight. She bitterly resents the attempts of various men to seduce her back into a more traditional woman's style and will only accept protection from another woman, Dr. Lotty Herschel, who runs a clinic serving Appalachian, Chicano, and other immigrant women.

In spite of her toughness and independence, Warshawski also represents many traditional "feminine" values like nurturing and devotion to family. Several of her cases develop out of her attempts to protect more vulnerable members of her family, such as her ne'er-do-well Aunt Elena, in *Killing Orders*. In addition, Warshawski is presented as quite brilliant in her own right—she is a trained lawyer who has also developed considerable expertise in the investigation of complex financial crimes, her particular specialty as a private investigator. Paretsky has

---

Though Wimsey defends Harriet Vane against a false charge of murder in *Strong Poison* she is still not willing to marry him until she is sure that he has become sufficiently nonsexist to be willing to support her full independence. It takes another mystery, one of Sayers' longest and most complex books, *Gaudy Night*, before the two lovers are able to negotiate an *entente cordiale*.

4. Dashiell Hammett, for example, was, at least in some sense a committed Marxist, though a highly individualistic and rebellious one. It is easy to read *Red Harvest* as a Marxist parable, though his best works, *The Maltese Falcon* and *The Glass Key*, largely resist that kind of interpretation. In the 1950s Hammett even went to jail for refusing to testify about other people's involvement in communist causes. Raymond Chandler was largely apolitical, though his stories express a similar critique of American society and the decadence of the rich. The only significant hard-boiled writer with a strongly conservative bent was Mickey Spillane, though he was more a member of what used to be called the radical right and his criticism of the decadence of the rich was even more strident than that of Hammett and Chandler.

imported a whole range of feminist concerns and ideals into the detective genre and she has, to a considerable extent, succeeded in synthesizing these with the hard-boiled world. Warshawski has all the toughness and independence traditionally associated with men, but has not abandoned the traditionally feminine concerns of family and nurturance. She is a trained professional, yet has rejected the lure of bureaucratic success to become a reluctant and lonely crusader in the best hard-boiled tradition. Much the same can be said of Sue Grafton's Kinsey Milhone. The considerable success of these writers illustrates that the detective story is flexible enough to allow the expression of new constellations of value and style in their relation to traditional social values.[5]

While feminism has been the most striking source of new developments in the detective story, other minorities have also reached out to claim their right to a corner of the action. One of the first areas in which black actors achieved a broad success with white as well as black audiences was in the detective genre in such films as *Shaft* and *In the Heat of the Night*, though these films were, ironically, based stories on written by white writers. However, Chester Himes, a black writer, made the detective story particularly his own and the genre continues to attract younger black writers such as the gifted Walter Mosley, who created a new kind of cool hard-boiled hero, Easy Rawlins, in his *Devil in a Blue Dress*. In addition, the detective story has provided a frame for the exploration of black and white partnerships within the important Hollywood tradition of the "buddy" movie. Significantly, the first black-white "buddy" movies revolved around convicts, as if only on the illegal margins of society could a close relationship between black and white men be imagined. In this context, *48 Hours* starring Nick Nolte as a white policeman and Eddie Murphy as an escaped black convict, represented a transition to the full-fledged black-white detective teams of the highly successful *Beverly Hills Cop* and *Lethal Weapon* series.

While many earlier detective writers were from a Jewish American background, they tended to suppress their Jewishness and to write

5. The hard-boiled story is not the only type of detective story on which feminist writers have made their mark. There are also many women practitioners of the more ratiocinative detective story who, like Amanda Cross (Carolyn Heilbrun) are very much concerned with expressing feminist ideas in their work. Even somewhat more traditional women writers like the English P. D. James and Ruth Rendell may still use male detectives like Inspectors Dalgleish and Wexford, but these male characters are very different in their relationship to women than the traditional male detective. Significantly, these writers are probably also the most successful of today's detective writers from the standpoint of sales.

about white protestant detectives. A younger generation has more fully exploited Jewish cultural traditions as in the Rabbi David Small stories of Harry Kemelman or in new detective types such as the schlemiel detective developed by Stuart Kaminsky, Roger Simon, and Andrew Bergmann. The Latino detective has emerged in the Luis Mendoza stories of Dell Shannon. Even Native Americans now have their detective representatives in the bestselling Navajo series of Tony Hillerman and many others. Though Hillerman is not himself a Native American, his knowledge of Southwestern Navajo and Pueblo cultures gained from his many years of living in New Mexico is extraordinary. Many American readers have probably gotten more insight into traditional Navajo culture from his detective stories than from any other recent books.

Sexual minorities, too, have increasingly turned to the detective story. In addition to the important feminist school of detective fiction already discussed, a thriving school of lesbian detective novels by authors such as Katherine Forrest, Lee Lynch, and Claire McNab developed in the 1980s.[6] The male homosexual detective is represented as well by the excellent Dave Brandstetter series by Joseph Hansen.[7]

The remarkable ethnic and gender diversity of recent detective stories suggests that the genre has become more than simply a popular literary entertainment. Increasingly the detective story is a genre in which writers explore new social values and definitions and push against the traditional boundaries of gender and race to play imaginatively with new kinds of social character and human relations. The creation of representative detective heroes has become an important social ritual for minority groups who would claim a meaningful place in the larger social context.

Another related recent trend in the detective genre is the remarkable flourishing of regional and local detectives. Once most American detective stories were set in the urban centers of New York and Los Angeles. However, in recent years an ever larger variety of locales supply the setting for detective series: there are now women detectives from Chicago, Cajun detectives from New Orleans, black detectives from Los Angeles,

6. I'm particularly grateful to Beth Heston, Ph.D. student at the University of Kentucky for introducing me to the Lesbian detective novel through her unpublished paper "'A Twice-Written Scroll': The Lesbian Detective Novel." A version of this paper was presented at the 1991 convention of the Popular Culture Association.

7. See Hansen, *Nightwork, Gravedigger, Skinflick, The Man Everybody Was Afraid Of, Troublemaker, Death Claims*, etc.

and Catholic detectives from Detroit in addition to "regional" detectives from Cincinnati, Denver, Minneapolis, and many other specific American locales. Many of these novels contain highly accurate representations of these locales—for example, Paretsky shows a keen awareness of particular neighborhoods in Chicago, and Hillerman portrays the differences between Navajo, Hopi, and Zuni cultures in the Southwest. It is as if, to establish a distinctive place in the national consciousness, particular places must also see themselves portrayed in the detective story. In this way, the detective story is becoming our most serious and complex form of popular literature.

Beginning as an expression of conservative, bourgeois ethnocentric Anglo-American values,[8] the detective story has expanded to accommodate a much greater diversity of social values and ideologies until, in the aftermath of the Cold War, it seems on the verge of becoming a truly global mythos. The stages through which this transformation occurred suggest that the genre has a sort of dynamic that enables it to push against the seemingly rigid boundaries of the formula.

The early history of the detective story clearly displays this interplay between Anglo-American ethnocentricity and an involvement in other cultures. On the one hand, there is a very strong emphasis on the values of Anglo-American bourgeois culture in the stories of Conan Doyle and other early masters of the genre. On the other, there is the fascination with the exotic and the strange, which even Doyle clearly represents in such stories as *A Study in Scarlet* and *The Sign of Four*. In this respect, the detective story mirrored the ambiguous mixture of fear of and attraction to cultures on the fringes of the empire that the English experienced and to the Native American cultures that Americans were simultaneously exterminating and romanticizing.

This same mixture of fear of and attraction toward non-Anglo-American cultures continued to dominate the detective story and its near relative the spy story well down into the 1920s. The doubling of Anglo-American hero and ethnic or third-world villain so characteristic of the period is clear in some of the most compelling duos in the literature, such as Doyle's Sherlock Holmes and Professor Moriarty (presumably Irish), Sax Rohmer's Nayland Smyth and Dr. Fu Manchu, John Buchan's Richard Hannay and his various German, Near Eastern, and mixed antagonists. Such duos continue to appear in the literature even in the post–World War II period as in the colorful racially mixed

8. Several studies such as Palmer and Knight interestingly discuss detective story ideologies.

figures of Dr. No, Goldfinger, and Blofeld who bedevil James Bond, but these are already showing the signs of self-parody clearly foreshadowed in the conflict between Sam Spade and the devious alliance of Joel Cairo, Caspar Gutman, and Brigid O'Shaugnessy.

Actually, in the 1930s and 1940s two important developments begin to undercut the detective story's Anglo-American ethnocentricity. Writers in other countries, such as Georges Simenon in Belgium and France, Edogawa Rampo in Japan, and Arthur W. Upfield in Australia, as well as the American hard-boiled writers, began to develop important new varieties of mystery fiction, a trend that became increasingly international in the 1960s, '70s, and '80s. Also in the 1930s and '40s the quest for new kinds of detectives led to the invention of a rich galaxy of non-English detectives created in large part by English and American writers. Among them were Earl Derr Biggers' Charlie Chan, John P. Marquand's Mr. Moto, Robert van Gulik's Judge Dee, Upfield's half-aborigine Napoleon Bonaparte, and Simenon's Inspector Maigret. Charlie Chan and Mr. Moto might almost have been benevolent transformations of Dr. Fu Manchu suggesting that the detective story, instead of remaining an expression of ethnocentrism, was on the way to becoming a means of exploring rather than condemning other cultures. This trend continues with a growing number of detective series dealing not only with a great variety of national cultures, but also with regional cultures within large countries like America.

In short, the internationalization of the detective story seems to be another major contemporary trend The extent to which the detective story has expanded from its Anglo-American roots into an ever more international genre is further indicated in an extensive guide that appeared in a Dutch publication, the *Vrij Nederland,* in 1991 to who were considered the best writers of detective novels and other kinds of thrillers.[9] This annual guide listed seventy American and thirty-five English authors, symbolizing not only the national origins of the genre, but also demonstrating the extent to which, through the thriller, certain English and American writers have become a significant part of other cultures. In Holland, most of these authors are distributed in both the original English and in Dutch translations. In addition the *Vrij Nederland* guide listed eight Belgian, thirty-one Dutch, one Canadian, one Dutch/ Swedish collaboration, one Norwegian, one Swiss, two Swedish, one

9. This periodical is published in Amsterdam. I'm grateful to my friends from Groningen, Birgit Lijmbach and Petro van der Veen, for sending it to me.

Flemish, three Russian, two French, and one Danish author of mystery novels. And this listing does not even include such international best-sellers as Umberto Eco's *The Name of the Rose* and *Foucault's Pendulum*, perhaps because they are considered more complex novels rather than thrillers, though like many modernist and postmodernist works, their basic structure is that of the detective story.

The detective story is thus a pervasive phenomenon of the contemporary world, not only in books but also in many other media. It's hard to imagine what our culture would be without it. And also to understand why this is so. I can't pretend in the rest of this paper to offer more than a couple of tentative speculations about why the detective story has become so canonical. One of them has to do with the special significance of the unique form of the detective story itself, while the second is a notion about why the theme of crime and detection has become increasingly important on a global level.

The unique formal pattern of the detective story genre lies in its double and duplicitous plot. The plot is double because the story is first narrated to us as it appears to the bewildered bystanders who observe the crime and are to some extent threatened by it, but who cannot arrive at its solution. Finally, through the detective's reconstruction of the crime, the true story of the events is given along with their explanation. This doubling is duplicitous because, in the first presentation of the story, the writer tries to tantalize and deceive the reader, while, at the same time, inconspicuously planting the clues that will eventually make the detective's solution plausible.[10] This double plot has fascinated many major modernist and postmodernist writers because it reflects their own highly self-conscious awareness of the artificiality of narration and the ambiguity of plots.

Among major modernist writers, Faulkner was perhaps most influenced by the detective story, for the structure of the double plot plays an important role not only in the actual detective stories Faulkner wrote— the novel *Intruder in the Dust* and the stories collected in *Knight's Gambit*—but is also a major element in *The Sound and the Fury*, *Absalom, Absalom!*, and *Light in August*. Adapting the detective story's play with clues and possible solutions, as well as its emphasis on the testimony of different witnesses, enables Faulkner to develop some of his

---

10. See the discussion of this aspect of the detective story in Cawelti, *Adventure*, 87–91. For a fuller discussion of the use of the detective story plot pattern by modernist and postmodernist writers see Cawelti, "Faulkner and the Detective Story's Double Plot."

most important themes. For instance, in *Absalom, Absalom!*, the detective story's double plot of murder and its solution is further complicated by the accounts of a number of storytellers, legend makers, and witnesses who have their own versions of the Henry Sutpen-Charles Bon murder case. To the problem of conflicting individual truths basic to the detective story, Faulkner adds the complexities of history, memory, and myth, through which the clues of the past are communicated to the "detectives" of a later generation, Quentin Compson and Shreve McCannon. While there is no firm evidence that the solution Shreve and Quentin arrive at is the truth — the investigation leads to some devastating truths about the culture. Faulkner's complex version of the double plot dramatizes imagination and the human capacity for empathy and identification as more vital to the pursuit of truth than ratiocinative brilliance and reveals that though truth is precarious and always elusive, its quest is the most important of human activities.

The double plot is even more pervasive in what we now usually refer to as the postmodernist writers. In addition to the explicitly antidetective novels of Alain Robbe-Grillet, Stanislas Lem, and others, the duplicitous parading of clues and false solutions is a pervasive element in the writing of Borges, Nabokov, and Pynchon.

Modern and postmodern twentieth-century authors express the pervasive philosophical and cultural skepticism of modern times by using or inverting the double plot of the detective story to create a structure in which their own sense of the problems of truth and meaning can be embodied. For Faulkner, the double plot serves as a means of dramatizing the complexity and difficulty as well as the human necessity of the quest for truth. For Borges, the inversion of the double plot exposes the delusion of rationality fostered by the traditional detective story. Finally, for Nabokov, it becomes the source of an incessant play of furtive meanings and ambivalences.[11]

Though the structure of the detective story has helped some of our most important writers to create fictions casting doubt on the very possibility of rational truths, others still produce straight detective stories in which the clues are correctly interpreted, the conflicting solutions transcended, and the mystery resolved. It is something of a puzzle that the genre can apparently accommodate both the pervasive skepticism of the postmodernists and a continued belief in successful interpretation

11. For a fuller analysis of the influence of the detective story on modernist and postmodernist writers see Michael Holquist, William Spanos, and Stefano Tani.

and solution but that is material for another investigation. Here we are limited to a brief exposition of what appears to be another source of the continued popularity of the detective story in its originating cultures of England and America as well as its increasing relevance on the international scene.

In essence the detective story constitutes a *mythos* or fable in which crime, as a distinctive problem of bourgeois, individualistic, and quasi-democratic societies, is handled without upsetting society's fundamental institutions or its world-view. When he/she solves the crime, the detective reaffirms the fundamental soundness of the social order by revealing how the crime has resulted from the specific and understandable motives of particular individuals; crime happens but is not fundamental or endemic to the society. In other words, the detective reveals to us by his actions that society, however corrupt or unjust it may seem, still contains the intelligence and the means to define and exorcize these evils. Even in the more pessimistic vision of some of the hard-boiled of detective stories, where the corrupt far outnumber the innocent, it is still possible for the detective to accomplish a significant act of justice or vengeance. Of course, it is precisely this optative and optimistic view of the world that many postmodernist writers are questioning. Since the detective story is so deeply pervaded by the bourgeois individualistic world-view, it is almost inevitable that postmodernist stories become inversions of the double structure of the detective story.

If these reflections are correct, the increasing internationalization of the detective story genre is related to the growing global influence of the ideologies of individualist, bourgeois democracy. As these ideologies spread throughout the world, more and more countries seem to be developing their own detective literature. Totalitarian societies have usually shown considerable hostility toward detective stories; they were virtually banned in Nazi Germany and in the more Stalinist periods of Russia and China. The genre is apparently just beginning to flourish in the latter two countries. Furthermore, the detective story did not even exist in earlier societies and, because of its relative modernity, is one of the few major popular literary genres that can be traced to a specific date and author. Of course, we frequently compare certain myths, legends, and folktales involving mysteries, like Oedipus the King, to detective stories. But there are some basic differences, as well as obvious similarities between the detective genre and these earlier mysteries. The tale of Oedipus does involve a kind of detecting and explaining, but the agency of the gods remains a mystery beyond investigation and solution. The true solution of the myth of Oedipus, if there is any at all, comes only much later when Oedipus is apotheosized at Colonnus, again through an inexplicable action of the gods. In the detective genre, however, the key point is that every mystery can be explained not only by human agency, but also by reference to the actions and motives of particular individuals. Even in *The Nine Tailors* when Dorothy Sayers metaphysically makes God out to be the murderer, it is clear that He is acting as an individual with the clearly understandable motive of punishing the guilty.

In short, the detective story is a key *mythos* of the ideology of individualistic bourgeois democracy embodied in a unique formal pattern that ritually involves the reader in the celebration of the myth. Therefore, the detective genre has become bound up with two major trends of modern democracy: the quest for greater equality among different regional, ethnic, and gender groups and the increasing international influence of the ideologies of individualism and bourgeois democracy.

21

Detecting the Detective:
Some Theories of Mystery

Previously unpublished in this form, this essay pulls together and expands on a number of reviews of important books on mystery fiction published since 1990. I realized that a common theme of these books was the attempt to understand how mystery relates to modernity so I tried in this essay to see how these different approaches related to each other and to suggest an agenda for the further development of mystery theory. The next essay after this attempts to reformulate parts of a theory of mystery. The original reviews appeared in ANQ *and* American Literature.

~

During the past quarter century, the number and variety of mystery-detective stories published annually has reached astronomical proportions. One important way in which the genre has increased its range is by developing a whole series of new subgenres that address some of the central cultural issues of the time. There's been an explosion of gender-oriented detection, for example. Three of the bestselling contemporary writers—Sue Grafton, Patricia Cornwell, and Sarah Paretsky—have created new detective personas that are both hard-boiled and feminine; alongside them, a new breed of sensitive, psychologically complex male detectives—what Fred Pfeil calls the "soft-boiled dicks"—also flourishes. Even the gay world now participates in detection with increasing numbers of homosexual and lesbian investigators.

Along with gender, ethnicity inspires another new corps of crime-solvers. Walter Mosley, Barbara Neely, Barbara Hambly, and others have considerably expanded the existing tradition of African American detection while writers like Les Roberts, Robert Campbell, and K. C. Constantine have explored variations on white ethnicity. In the wake of Tony Hillerman's bestselling Navajo policemen, Native American detectives swarm. Finally, the detective story has manifested a new regionalism, a new internationalism, and a new historicism, with mystery series set in every conceivable area of America and the world, from Viper, Kentucky, to Bombay, India, and from South Africa to Ancient Greece and Rome. I have yet to read a Neolithic detective story, but I am sure that, as I write, a Cro-Magnon investigator is hunting for clues in some aspiring mystery writer's prehistoric marshes.

Such a phenomenon has, not surprisingly, inspired a substantial critical literature. Some idea of the evolution of that literature can be found in Heta Pyrhönen's *Murder from an Academic Angle*. Pyrhönen painstakingly, if somewhat ploddingly, defines the three main areas of mystery story criticism—the formal, the thematic, and the cultural—and then carefully analyzes how they have grown since G. K. Chesterton's 1902 "A Defence of Detective Stories." Her well-chosen bibliography runs from 1900 to 1993. The largest number of works by far—those from 1970 to the present—testify to the recent expansion of mystery criticism and the impact on it of various kinds of critical theory: Lacanian psychoanalysis, semiotics, deconstruction, neo-Marxian ideology and Gramscian hegemony analysis, British-style cultural studies, and gender theory.

In this useful account, Pyrhönen shows how formal mystery criticism arose from early attempts to define and justify the peculiar limitations of the detective story genre. Later critics used formalist and structuralist methods to develop a more complex analysis of the narrative forms of the mystery, relating it to myth, folklore, and other traditional modes of narration. She then discusses more recent "postmodern" attempts to reveal a greater complexity, ambiguity, and self-reflexivity in the important texts of the genre. This has led to the recognition of a modernist and postmodernist subgenre of metaphysical or, as some would have it, just plain meta-detective stories.

Pyrhönen suggests that detective story criticism recurrently concerns itself with moral or ethical themes. She traces the many different critical discourses through which commentators have explored the fundamental idea that the "detective narrative [is] heavily coded by ethics, by the binary of good and evil," even though the classical and hard-boiled types of detective story "invest this moral structure differently" (63).

Detective story analysis has also centered around philosophical and psychological themes: many critics have offered epistemological interpretations of the genre showing how the mystery writer's preoccupation with problem solving exemplifies the quest for knowledge and the attempt to derive order out of chaos. Pyrhönen also treats the tradition of psychological interpretation that springs from the Freudian fascination with the detective genre as an archetypal narrative of the Oedipus complex. Among other things Pyrhönen makes some sense out of one of the most remarkable moments in the history of detective story criticism, Jacques Lacan's famous seminar on Poe's "The Purloined Letter," which has tantalized and baffled critical theorists and detective story specialists ever since it appeared. By approaching Lacan's analysis of the purloined letter with the help of the Lacanian Slavoj Žižek's discussion of the detective story, Pyrhönen offers one of the clearest accounts of the implications of Lacan's ruminations that I have seen.

In the last section of her book Pyrhönen discusses the evolution of ideas about the detective story's cultural significance. This aspect of the detective story was the area of greatest interest in the 1970s and 1980s, to judge from the number of books and articles it produced. In fact, since Pyrhönen's work appeared the methods of cultural studies have been widely applied to popular genres and several new books on the detective story take cultural analysis of the genre farther than it had gone before.

As Pyrhönen suggests, much cultural criticism of the mystery story up the 1990s tended to hover around antithetical cultural interpretations that were never been fully reconciled. One group of critics argued that the genre's origin in England and America in the nineteenth century associates it with the middle-class democratic values of law and order and equal justice for all. The other camp insisted that the mystery is escapist mass literature that seeks and finds easy solutions to social problems. In this way it expresses the ideology of a dominant group that wishes to preserve the status quo. Therefore, detective fictions reduce potentially revolutionary social issues to the moralistic simplifications of crime and punishment.

Pyrhönen's analysis traces the debate between "liberal" defenders and ideological critics of the detective story as it ran through the clash between mass culture critics and popular culture analysts in the 1950s and 1960s and into deconstruction, cultural studies, and gender analysis. While those familiar with these developments will not find much that is new in Pyrhönen's discussion, it is nonetheless useful as a summary of the major points at issue and as an analysis of the development of different approaches to the ideological and cultural analysis of the genre.

The concern with sexism and the construction of gender to which Pyrhönen refers has inspired a large and interesting body of new criticism of popular genres. In the case of the detective genre, perhaps the central question has been if, and if so to what extent, the detective story can be regendered as a nonsexist narrative or whether, like many popular genres, the form is inherently and inescapably patriarchal. In an important study concerned with this issue, *The Woman Detective*, Kathleen Gregory Klein argues that despite the important contributions of women to the detective story tradition, the sexist conventions of the genre drove earlier women writers to create mainly male detectives. She suggests that more recent feminist writers are, at best, only creating parodies of the form. Sally R. Munt in *Murder By the Book* takes issue with this and argues that several new mystery subgenres involving lesbianism, psychoanalysis, and African American woman detectives have created an authentic feminist detective story tradition. Moreover, she insists that even traditional mainstream women detective writers like Christie, Sayers, Patricia Highsmith, and Ruth Rendell bring feminist perspectives to the mystery. An interesting anthology edited by Glenwood Irons, entitled *Feminism in Women's Detective Fiction*, offers a variety of essays taking various positions on this debate. Finally, though the analysis of masculine images in the detective story lags behind feminist criticism, Fred Pfeil has shown the intriguing possibilities of such a critique in his essay on contemporary trends toward feminization in the hardboiled tradition (his chapter on "Soft-Boiled Dicks" in *White Guys*).

Discussion of the new ethnicizing of the detective story has not attracted the same kind of attention as gender criticism except in the case of the African American mystery story. Several books have dealt with this emergent tradition, and one of the most interesting is Stephen Soitos's *The Blues Detective*. Soitos's study develops the idea that African American detective fiction created distinctive versions of some of the basic conventions of detective fiction. He argues that a pattern of formulaic variations or "tropes" arose that was more or less distinctive to African American mystery writing because it reflected central themes of African American literature and culture. Soitos's tropes include a detective with a relationship to family and community outside the mainstream detective tradition. He also postulates a kind of detection making use of something like DuBois's "double consciousness" to reveal the deeper meanings of crimes as well as the significant use of black vernaculars and of hoodoo practices and hoodoo tradition. Soitos traces the use of these tropes in African American detective fiction from its origin in the early twentieth century through its initial flourishing in the work of Rudolph Fisher in the Harlem Renaissance to its culmination in the brilliant black mysteries of Chester Himes and the meta-detective fictions of Ishmael Reed and Clarence Major. This is a very useful and suggestive study. One only regrets that Soitos did not choose to deal more fully with contemporary popular African American detective writers like Walter Mosely and Barbara Neely whom he mentions briefly in an afterword only to suggest their relationship to the paradigmatic tradition he has defined.

William Marling's *The American Roman Noir* presents another kind of cultural criticism. Marling is interested in why the distinctively decadent, pessimistic, and dark type of novel and film that has come to be called "noir," and that included the ironic crime fiction of James M. Cain as well as the hard-boiled detective stories of Hammett and Chandler, arose and flourished. It is particularly puzzling that such a subgenre should originate in an America that seemed on the surface to be dedicated to optimism, success, and progress. Marling sees the "noir" type of mystery as a reaction to the accelerated pace of economic and technological change in America. He also thinks it reflects the cultural trauma resulting from the sudden loss of wealth and prosperity in the crash of 1929 and the depression of the 1930s: "How does [American] narrative represent having, and having had, too much? Never in the United States did wealth impinge on the national conscience as in the 1920s, and never was conscience so sharply rebuked as in the 1930s. What was the popular understanding of wealth after it vanished? What were the paradigms that explained accumulation and windfall, waste and failure?" (ix–x).

The answer to this question is the "roman noir" and Marling does a very interesting job in relating the work of Cain, Hammett, and Chandler to central cultural themes of the period. His argument that their works are all variations on the archetypal biblical story of the prodigal son is unconvincing. However, his analysis comes alive and is most insightful when he shows how contemporaneous technological and economic themes of the culture are reflected in the style and images of "noir" writing and film. In addition, his treatment of the specific historical circumstances mirrored in the work of these writers is quite fascinating. For example, he persuasively demonstrates that Dashiell Hammett's *Red Harvest,* even though set in a western mining town nicknamed "Poisonville" by the detective protagonist, actually draws on characters, events, and even places that are thinly disguised versions of Hammet's San Francisco. Above all, Marling's work shows the importance of the refraction of specific historical and cultural materials in the mirror of the mystery story.

One of the important issues that Pyrhönen takes up in the course of her discussion of the cultural analysis of the genre is what she calls "genealogical explanations of the detective narrative" (94). The origin of classical genres like tragedy and comedy is lost in the mists of time, but it is possible to relate the emergence of many of the most important popular genres to specific works and writers. The gothic sprang originally from Walpole's *The Castle of Otranto,* the popular romance from Richardson's *Pamela* and *Clarissa,* the western from James Fenimore Cooper, etc. There is nearly universal agreement that in spite of many different precursors, the detective genre originated with the C. Auguste Dupin stories of Edgar Allan Poe. For this reason Poe's work will always have a particular importance in discussions of the detective story, whether formal, thematic, or cultural, as two recent books in the field indicate.

Two different explanations have commonly been offered for what Pyrhönen calls the "genealogy" of the detective story. The first suggests that the genre is a modern version of a traditional mythical archetype while the second treats the genre primarily as a distinctive, new cultural phenomenon. The latter critics usually see the mystery as linked to some aspect or aspects of modernism, such as the rise of middle-class society; new ideologies of crime, justice, and law; or the development of modern scientific and rationalistic epistemologies. The first kind of explanation refers the problem of the detective story's popularity to its embodiment of a quasi-universal narrative archetype. The only question that remains to be answered is why this particular form of the archetype seems so pervasively present in the later nineteenth and twentieth centuries.

John Irwin's awesomely brilliant *The Mystery to a Solution: Poe, Borges, and the Analytic Detective Story* offers a complex analysis of the underlying archetype of the detective story. In fact, Irwin's book is an elaborately developed intellectual detective story in itself. It begins with a problem — the mysterious connection between the three Dupin stories of Edgar Allan Poe and the three major mystery stories of Jorge Luis

Borges that, as Irwin shows, were written as a kind of reflection of, or homage to, Poe. The tale then passes through a series of baffling clues represented by Irwin's discussions of such diverse matters as Sir Thomas Browne, Lewis Carroll, chess, Freudian and Jungian psychology, classical archeology and mythology, Platonism, astrology, the history of mathematics, and Frazerian anthropology, to say nothing of Lacan, Derrida, and other delicious red herrings. Finally, it arrives at a solution, or, since this is truly a meta-detective story, a sort of a solution. Poe created a brilliant allegory of the development of self-consciousness by creating the detective story, "whose central mystery is the self-conscious description of its own workings." It therefore dramatizes the paradox that "there will always be one more step needed, precisely because self-consciousness by its very nature can never really think its own ending, its own absence" (423). In other words, the detective story as art must seek a solution but at the same time it represents the impossibility of any real closure.

As a narrative of the development of consciousness, Poe's (and Borges's) detective stories thus become modern embodiments of archetypes found in classical myths like those of Oedipus and Theseus who, according to Irwin, were archetypal heroes of consciousness. Like these myths, Poe's and Borges's stories are richly embellished with riddles, reflections, doubles, and labyrinths. Much of Irwin's text and many of his ingenious and fascinating interpretations lead to the uncovering of such archetypes in Poe and Borges's stories. He then tracks them from their origins in classical mythology to Poe and through the mediating figure of Lewis Carroll into Borges.

Irwin points out at the beginning of his work that "in creating the detective story, Poe produced the dominant modern genre" (xvi). However, he does not offer much illumination about why the popular simplifications of Poe's creation constituting most of the detective story tradition have been so successful. It's revealing that, in the 464 dense pages of Irwin's text, there is only one brief reference to Arthur Conan Doyle and none at all to Agatha Christie, Dorothy Sayers, or most of the other popular practitioners of the analytic detective story. In fact, Irwin's analysis does not pretend to be a discussion of the detective story as popular genre. Instead, he is mainly interested in the possibilities of the detective story as "high art": "How does one write analytic detective fiction as high art when the genre's central narrative mechanism seems to discourage the unlimited rereading associated with serious writing? That is, if the point of an analytic detective story is the deductive solution of a mystery, how does the writer keep that solution from exhausting the reader's interest in the story? How does he write a work that can be re-read by people other than those with poor memories?" (1).

This may be a little hard on detective story fans, many of whom have gone to considerable effort to master the art of selective — or is it inadvertent? — forgetting. In spite of its limitations and its unregenerate elitism, Irwin's speculations about the genius of Poe and Borges are often fascinating on the subject of the modern obsession with analysis and a certain kind of knowing. They may thereby offer the basis for new insights into the unique role of detection in both literature and popular culture since that day in 1841 when Poe's C. Auguste Dupin first strode the fictional streets of Paris in "The Murders in the Rue Morgue."

Irwin's study, then, is not really about the detective story as a popular genre but is a commentary on Poe as a writer in a Borgesian library where every single text refracts the universe. In the course of his study, Irwin shows how Poe's original Dupin tales and Borges's three meta-detective stories assimilate many of the archetypal patterns of human consciousness into a brilliant set of fictional images. Whether these ruminations shed much light on the detective story is another matter.

The "cultural studies" approach to the emergence of the detective story is illustrated by Jonathan Elmer's *Reading at the Social Limit*. This is one of those exasperating books that is so densely written and so larded with the jargon of critical theory that it requires the skills of a master detective to figure out just what it is talking about. Elmer tries to situate Poe in relation to the development of what he sees as a new relationship between the individual and society characteristic of modern mass cultures. It was Poe's special genius, he feels, to become a major explorer of the "social limit," that ambiguous area of liminality between the individual and society that arises when "the figure of social power is no longer a monarch but the sovereign people." In this new cultural landscape

> society reflects into itself its own totality, which effectively renders that totality an internally unattainable limit. And the fissure this limit produces means that, since no one person can coincide with the representation of social power, society henceforth exists only in the form of an impossible or failed representation, one riven by an instability between statement and enunciation. This is the social limit, simultaneously exposing the self as social, unnervingly plural, and the social as self, uncannily singular. (20)

Like a lot of "theory," this is much more difficult to understand than the texts it supposedly illuminates. Apparently Elmer believes that Poe's explorations of the uncanny, his treatment of horror, doubling, and identification, his fascination with psychopathic confessions, and his interest in the mechanism of hoaxes and dupings are expressions as well as symptoms of profound instabilities in the relationship between self and society brought about by the "cultural logic of modernism."

Sorted out, this kind of analysis might lead to some useful insights into the significance of the mystery genre as archetypal mass cultural narrative, but Elmer is rather disappointing when it comes to analysis of Poe's Dupin stories. He is much more interesting when he discusses some of Poe's other works—"The Man Who Was Used Up," "William Wilson," and "The Raven." What he has to say about the Dupin stories draws mainly on the Lacanian controversy over "The Purloined Letter" and on Franco Moretti. Moretti analyzes the detective story as a transmutation of the possibility of deep social meaning into the surface meaning of individual motives and crimes, an ideological move that further reinforces mass culture as "the culture of unawareness" (150). Elmer's interpretation of Lacan's interpretation of Poe's interpretation of Dupin's interpretation of—well, you get the idea!—presents still another twist in the meaning of the famous relationship between letter, Queen, King, and Minister. As Elmer sees it, Poe (Lacan) makes the letter represent signifying itself; thus, the dialectic of perception and blindness that swirls around the letter becomes Poe's symbolic exploration of the role of ideology as the ambiguous basis of modern social and political power. (There, he's got me doing it!) While this approach may offer some insight into modernism, Elmer does not choose to clarify its significance for the meaning of the detective story. In the end, while *Reading at the Social Limit* suggests some interesting new approaches to Poe and his place in the history of modern culture, its does not relate these new approaches directly to the importance of Poe as the inventor of the detective story.

Though Pyrhönen is certainly right in pointing out that the vital center of mystery genre studies today lies in the area of culture, it's interesting that an occasional book will offer a new take on the most traditional sort of detective story commentary, the rules of the genre. However, the problems and ambiguities that emerge in Marty Roth's *Foul and Fair Play* make clear that, as Pyrhönen's account of the history of mystery criticism suggests, the detective story genre cannot be defined entirely in formalistic terms. Increasingly it seems evident that any analysis of a popular genre that fails to take into account its cultural location and its ideological or thematic components is incomplete. Actually, though Roth does his best to concentrate on the kind of formalistic analysis and generic definition that characterized much of the early commentary on the detective story, he frequently imports historical and cultural comments into his account. For example, he remarks that when "Holmes makes his first appearance in *A Study in Scarlet,* he is a version of the engineer-hero of Wells and Dreiser; when he appears in *The Sign of Four,* he has been recast as a Bohemian and aesthete" (43–44). Or he discusses the theme of the frontier or the colony as a paradigm for the world of mystery. His stated intent is to "read classical detective fiction as a genre, that is to read a range of separately authored stories . . . as variations on a tight set of conventions" (xii). However, Roth in fact spends most of his time on comparisons between the analytic detective story and such other forms of popular literature as the hard-boiled mystery, the gothic or horror story, and what he calls the "amateur thriller." It's never very clear how Roth sees the relationship among these narrative patterns—are they different genres altogether or simply different versions of the same conventions? This confusion results from Roth's failure to take into consideration the historical and cultural situation of the detective story.

However, despite this basic problem, *Foul and Fair Play* is an insightful discussion of such basic elements of the detective genre as the character of the detective, the crime and the criminal, the solution, and the manipulation of clues. One of the most interesting sections of his book is the discussion of clues. Roth suggests that the way in which certain crucial clues seem to be trifles or dirt is connected with new images of scientific discovery as in Lyell's and Darwin's investigations of evolution through the study of apparently trifling changes or the interest in dirt connected with the Freudian tradition. This discussion highlights again the importance of the relationship between formal patterns and cultural themes in the discussion of popular genres.

Unfortunately, much work on the formal aspects of the detective story is little more than the reinventing of the wheel. Because the genre had been considered a form of subliterature until recently, many intellectuals create their poetics of the detective story without paying much attention to the well-established body of criticism that already exists. This is especially true on the international level. English and American critics write about the genre without knowing of the excellent work that has been done by French writers like Caillois, Narcejac, Todorov, and Barthes, while French critics ignore the large body of critical work in English. The result is that the reader of mystery criticism is forced to wade through oceans of the obvious before reaching the happy isles of new insights. One is therefore very glad to see new attempts to close the great gaps in intercultural discourse on popular genres like the detective story. In this connection I'd particularly like to call attention to a new journal, *Paradoxa,* which in 1995 published a special issue on detective and mystery fiction featuring work by both French and American scholars. It includes the very useful intercultural studies of Paul Bleton, "French Espionage, Spy Fiction, and Readers in the 1930s" and Robert Conrath, "Pulp Fixation: The Hard-Boiled American Crime Novel and its French Public."

Another study giving an interestingly different spin to the formal definition of the detective story is George Dove's *The Reader in the Detective Story.* Dove sets out to apply reader response theory to the analysis of the detective story. Though his discussion sometimes repeats itself and is too digressive, it provides, on the whole, a fresh and interesting angle of vision of the formal aspects of the genre. Dove emphasizes the way in which the detective story reader is programmed to read new detective stories through knowledge of the conventions of the genre and shows persuasively how such conventions as false suspects, red herrings, and locked rooms shape the process of reading. Dove is particularly interesting in showing how detective story conventions work to turn the reader's involvement in the story from serious concern and anxiety about the fate of the characters toward play and the elimination of stressful feelings. I think that Dove is also right when he shows how the form of the detective story pretends to involve the reader in the effort of solving the crime along with the detective but actually discourages involvement in the detailed interpretation of clues.

Dove's approach seems to work best for the classical or ratiocinative type of detective story. Applied to the hard-boiled story, it seems less interesting, and he makes little attempt to deal extensively with more recent trends in mystery fiction. Nonetheless, *The Reader in the Detective Story* provides enough insight into the form of a variety of mystery texts to suggest that the reader response approach needs to be applied to a wider range of more recent detective fiction writing.

So, detective story criticism seems to be flourishing along with the genre that called it forth. The tradition of formalistic and genre criticism continues to thrive, while John Irwin's work shows how thematic, archetypal, and psychoanalytic criticism have reached new levels of complexity and richness. Gender analysis of the mystery is also proceeding at an accelerating pace. Historical, biographical, and critical work like that of Marling and Soitos is only a sample of much excellent work done recently on different periods of mystery writing and on individual writers like Hammett, Chandler, and Christie. The one area of great interest that has not yet generated much good criticism is that of the regionalization and internationalization of the detective story. I was hoping that Ralph Willett's *The Naked City* would partially fill this lack since it undertakes to study mystery fiction associated with different American cities. However, the book is more a catalogue with brief commentaries than a sustained analysis, and its discussion of "urban discourse" does not probe very deeply.

Much better and a pioneering attempt to analyze a particular regional version of the detective story is J. K. Van Dover and John F. Jebb's *Isn't Justice Always Unfair*. This book is a good catalogue of southern detectives, usefully treating both of detectives in "canonical" literature and books within the mystery genre situated in the South. Jebb and Van Dover begin, appropriately enough, with Poe who was both southern and the father of the detective story. However, they don't offer much insight into why a southern genius might have been the one to foresee the modern significance of the detective. Actually, Jon Thompson's *Fiction, Crime, and Empire*, does a more persuasive job with the Poe-as-originator problem. Jebb and Van Dover pass lightly over Poe's Dupin stories on the grounds that they are set in Paris, concentrating instead on "The Gold-Bug," which is set near Charleston, but not offering much wisdom into the relationship between the South and the detective story.

On the whole, Jebb and Van Dover concentrate more on describing southern writers who deal with detection than on analyzing the relationship between southern culture and the detective story. Though their introduction enumerates some of the standard cultural characteristics often ascribed to the South, the analysis of individual writers draws only sporadically on these southern cultural patterns. The book discusses the use of detective themes in canonic writers like Twain, Faulkner, Percy, and Capote. After that it deals with generic writers whose stories are set in the South: New Orleans with James Lee Burke, Julie Smith, etc; the Southern countryside with Sharyn McCrumb, Margaret Maron, Patricia Cornwell, etc; and Miami with John D. MacDonald, Elmore Leonard, Carl Hiassen, and others. Their listings and summaries will be extremely helpful to further researchers. However, the authors do not really discuss how cultural characteristics have been reflected in the type of detective literature written by southerners. Thus, *Isn't Justice Always*

Unfair does not deal very effectively with the regional or local aspects of southern crime literature. This is an area that still awaits its theorists.

This is a shame since whatever may be the reasons for the detective story's remarkable popularity since Poe created it over a hundred years ago, one of the genre's central features is the kind of light it sheds on particular cultures. The criminal act rips apart the social fabric and the detective must use his unique investigative skills to sew it back together again. In the process the skillful writer can reveal certain aspects of a culture that otherwise remain hidden, and this may be one reason the genre has increasingly proliferated into the representation of different national, regional, and ethnic cultures.

Not only is the mystery quite useful for uncovering the characteristics of different cultures, it also can deal effectively with distinctive subcultures like those of having to do with locality and occupation. For example, the academic subculture is a more and more influential part of most modern cultures and has often been the subject of mystery stories. This may reflect the fact that many mystery writers are themselves academics slumming in the genres for a change of pace and a little additional income. Among the many professorial mystery writers are Michael Innes, a.k.a. J. I. M. Stewart; Amanda Cross, a.k.a Carolyn Heilbrun; and Rex Burns. In D. J. H. Jones's recent mystery story *Murder at the MLA* we see an academic subculture strongly influenced by postmodern ideas even in the way it deals with murder. Jones's professor detective, Nancy Cook, explains:

> You see, if the whole set of killings is read as a contemporary text . . . then the underlying pressure would be irony, the text would be self-reflexive. It would deliberately disrupt its own patterning; it would subvert some parts of itself. It would have connections that are overdetermined. (179)

This insight enables scholar-detective Nancy to solve a series of puzzling murders seemingly connected only by the fact that they are all murders of professors and all take place at an MLA convention in Chicago.

Despite its seemingly nontraditional pattern of murders, *Murder at the MLA* is a conventional sort of mystery, drawing most of its elements from the academic branch of the "classical" tradition of Agatha Christie, Dorothy Sayers, Michael Innes, and Amanda Cross with a few nods in the direction of the contemporary police procedural novel. It follows the generic pattern of seemingly unsolvable crimes, bizarre clues, a distinctive and at least partially closed setting, and is finally solved by a brilliant amateur aided by the massive if uninspired investigations of the police. In fact, the use of seemingly unconnected murders to conceal the one crime actually intended by the perpetrator is a common pattern in the traditional detective story, perhaps most brilliantly developed in Agatha Christie's *The ABC Murders*. Compared with Christie's dazzling puzzler, *Murder at the MLA* is rather clumsy and protracted as a mystery. Because the crimes remain mysterious and the killer is not actually introduced to us until the crimes are almost solved, there is little play with red herrings or shifting interpretations of clues and suspects; nothing that remotely approaches "fair play" with the reader.

However, this hardly matters for *Murder at the MLA*, like many contemporary mysteries, is not primarily a witty game with the reader or a treatise on crime and punishment. Instead it uses the frame of the mystery genre to construct a mildly amusing satire of contemporary social institutions. In such works (they are legion) the crime disrupts the ordinarily seamless functioning of society and thereby sharply illuminates patterns of manners, ritual, and conflict. Jones is most reminiscent of two immediate predecessors who are also pseudonymous writers interested in the "inside dope" about the institutions they deal with: Emma Lathen who targets financial institutions and various businesses, and Amanda Cross whose mysteries relate to the university and the world of literature.

Jones doesn't try for Lathen's interplay between high finance and comic chaos, nor does she/he achieve Cross's acerbic cleverness and density of literary allusion. However, it offers a chuckle or two for anyone familiar with the vagaries of MLA conventions. For example, Jones does a delightful job in satirically describing that tic that every coventioneer descries as often as he/she practices it. Jones calls it the "MLA Swivel":

> At frequent intervals, your head swivels left and right, to see, first of all, whether anyone is paying attention to you, and second, whether anyone else nearby is more important than the person you're speaking to. In which case, you abruptly terminate your chat and move off in the higher-status direction. (110)

In more general terms, Jones diagnoses the current MLA as dominated by a fatuous and meaningless struggle between empty traditionalism (the "tweeds") and fashionable but vacuous critical theorizing (the "trendies"). Detective-professor Cook's animus is particularly directed at the latter, whom she describes at considerable length to her new police detective friend. Most of her targets are among the current sitting ducks of academic excess: deconstruction, political correctness, the new historicism, and feminist theory. The "trendies" are represented by catalogs of "typical" paper presentations, some of which the author obviously had a lot of fun coming up with:

> Tonight at the Hyatt, for instance, there would be "A Bard in the Hand; Masturbatory Arcs in *As You Like It*," and "Sex-texualities: The Erotics of Early Irish Manuscript Study." ("However, if you preferred to avoid all suggestion of a physical world, there was "Primatology, Immunology and Cyborg Praxis.") (73)

Murder at the MLA is pleasant enough as a lighthearted nose-thumbing at some of the current and past pieties of the profession of literary studies. It can be recommended to any scholar who wants to while away an hour or so, or to share temporarily a somewhat jaundiced view of the meaning and practice of "postmodernism."

So much for a "postmodern" murder mystery. What about a postmodern theory of crime and mystery fiction? For one thing, postmodernists have a tendency to theorize everything. Jon Thompson's *Fiction, Crime and Empire* is the work of a daring young man dizzily hung from an intellectual trapeze suspended between the poles of its comprehensive theoretical ambitions and the highly selective nature of the materials from which it is constructed. The title gives some idea of the scale of the work's theoretical purpose, and that isn't the half of it. The book argues for the general thesis that crime fictions are popular because they "offer myths of the experience of modernity, of what it is like to live in a world dominated by the contradictory forces of renewal and disintegration, progress and destruction, possibility and impossibility. The capacity of crime fiction to evaluate different historical moments in the experience of modernity is not an accidental feature; rather, it is a dominant convention of the genre" (2). Thus, in the course of its analysis the book touches on Victorianism, realism, modernism, imperialism, modernity, postmodernity, and lots more. The author attempts to corral this grand parade of -isms and -itys with the help of such redoubtable wranglers as Raymond Williams, Gramsci, and Bahktin, but often, despite his best efforts the theoretical stampede tramples over the reader with a thundering herd of generalizations.

Part of the problem results from the vagueness of the author's definition of what he is talking about and the limited and arbitrary selection of writers that he employs in his analysis. Though he insists at the beginning that his subject is "fictions of crime," his examples consist largely of fictions of detection and espionage—the detective story and the spy story. While the detective story is obviously a major category of crime fiction, there is a large range of crime literature both fictional and nonfictional that must surely be acknowledged if one is going to make a serious attempt to account for the modern fascination with crime. In addition, linking the fiction of detection and espionage in this way is at least problematic. There are certainly connections between these genres; many writers like Conan Doyle, Agatha Christie, and John le Carré have worked in both areas or combined the two. Nevertheless the traditions of the detective story and the spy story are separate enough that Thompson's treatment of their history as if they shared a single line of development seems an oversimplification. In order to maintain the rather tenuous connection between crime and empire, Thompson makes a number of generalizations that reveal the weakness of his grasp of the tradition of spy fiction. For example, Thompson asserts "unlike the modern espionage novel, the postmodern espionage novel is concerned not with the threat posed to a nation by a foreign power or conspiracy, whether internal or external, but with the threat posed to individual freedom and action by an increasingly determinative system of social relations and institutions" (152). However, this is almost exactly the distinction that prevailed between the romantic and heroic spy novel of the World War I era (Buchan, Oppenheim, Yates, Sapper, etc.) and the more skeptical and realistic espionage fiction of the thirties (Ambler, Greene, Maugham, Household, etc.). One must either postulate an emergence of postmodernism that is remarkably early or question the connection between these themes and the modernist-postmodernist distinction.

The biggest problem in writing about literary genres, particularly popular genres like the detective story, the spy story, the romance, the western, etc., lies in defining the dialectic between individual writers and the formulaic patterns of the genre. In many ways, a few highly successful individual practitioners whose versions of the generic formulas influence large numbers of other writers shape the history of a genre. Thus, in the history of the detective story such remarkable inventions as Poe's ratiocinative mystery, Doyle's Sherlockian detective and his bumbling narrator, Christie's country house comedies of manners, and Hammett's hard-boiled style have, in turn, influenced hundreds of other writers. Yet, important as these few individual masters of the genre are, the genre itself has an existence and an evolution that is more complex and extends beyond any individual writer. Studies of genres tend to be either too individualized, making a few writers serve as evidence for the entire genre, or too generalized, formulating a set of abstract principles or defining motifs or themes that can subsume all individual instances of the genre. This practice can all too easily lead to the amusing but highly dubious sets of rules for the detective story that were once a favorite exercise of devotees of the genre. My favorite was S. S. Van Dine's rule that "no Chinaman can figure in the story," which was paradoxically self-contradictory since one of the most successful detective sagas in the mold of Conan Doyle was Sax Rohmer's Fu Manchu series.

In his treatment of the fictions of "crime" and "empire" and their relationship to "modernism" and "postmodernism," Thompson overgeneralizes on the basis of an insufficient grasp of the diversity and richness of the popular literary traditions from which he draws his material. He is more interesting, if not always more persuasive, when he deals with the subject of detection and its relationship to modern and postmodern ideologies of knowledge. Here, Thompson rightly begins his analysis with Poe and the concept of "ratiocination" exemplified in C. Auguste Dupin.

Dupin's seeming omniscience, Thompson argues, represents Poe's projection of an aristocratic ideal of superior understanding antithetical to "the dominant mode of knowledge fueling the social transformations in the early decades of nineteenth-century America" (44). This dominant mode Thompson characterizes as embodying the empiricism driving industrial and technological progress (exemplified by the bumbling prefect of police in the Poe stories) and the progressivism of manifest destiny. Thompson suggests that in the detective story Poe gave expression to a "longing for a prebourgeois, settled aristocracy untainted by iniquity." Therefore he created a "definition of detective fiction as oppositional, as antagonistic to contemporary values, mores, ways of thinking and seeing" (57).

These important ideological inventions, Thompson argues, paved the way for the two major later developments of detective fiction. One was the "conservative modernism" of Agatha Christie and so many other English detective story writers with its nostalgia for traditional aristocratic institutions. The other was the hard-boiled fiction of Dashiell Hammett and others with its oppositional impetus.

The great significance of Conan Doyle's Sherlock Holmes, according to Thompson, was that he affirmed empiricism rather than ratiocination like Poe's Dupin. In Doyle, the detective's function "resides in affirming, not rejecting, the industrial society for which the labyrinthine complexity of London is the most obvious symbol" (135). Thompson also argues that by importing into the detective novel themes of imperial adventure and espionage, Doyle helped to create a new genre of fiction affirming the central values of modern bourgeois society, capitalism, and imperialism. "Through the figure of Sherlock Holmes, and through the empirical values he championed, Conan Doyle's fiction ratified the principles and ideologies of an imperial, patriarchal Britain" (75). Thus poor Holmes becomes the very model of a modern politically incorrect Englishman.

Detective fiction originates, Thompson thinks, in the literary embodiment of new ideologies of knowledge that seem to empower the detective hero either to assert his superiority over the mass of men à la Poe or, as with Sherlock Holmes, to valorize and redeem society and its imperial and class values. As detective and espionage fiction develop through the eras of modernism and postmodernism, the relationship between knowledge and power becomes more and more attenuated. In hard-boiled fiction, for example, the detective's knowledge, far from being liberating or redeeming, "reveals the corruption in civil society, and the effects and limitations this corruption places on the individual, including the detective figure" (172). Finally, by the time one reaches a writer like Pynchon, who Thompson somewhat arbitrarily selects as the archetypal postmodernist writer of "fictions of crime and empire," the value of knowledge is even more questionable. "Knowledge is always contingent, always incomplete. Power exists, but the machinations of power . . . are more difficult to identify and resist" (172). Thus with the emergence of a postmodern ideology of knowledge, the symbolic association between the detection of crime and the possibilities of social power becomes very attenuated. However, all is not lost, for in its characteristic reworking of many of the conventions of detective fiction, postmodern crime fiction moves outward "from a highly localized murder (or similar) mystery, until the movement of the novel encompasses the evaluation of a whole culture or society." Thus, these more recent novels transcend the ideological limitations of the earlier traditions of detective and espionage fiction and "exploit the critical possibilities of crime fiction . . . to critically examine the failures and corruption of political life" (176).

According to Thompson, then, crime fiction arose out of Poe's ambivalent relationship to modernism. Then, Doyle and Kipling found a way to fully embody the ideologies of empiricism, capitalism, and imperialism, in a fictional form that would appeal to the public. These ideologies continued to dominate the genre, though the "conservative modernism" of English writers like Christie still echoed some elements of Poe's aristocratic rejection of these ideologies. Finally, in the hard-boiled subgenre and in postmodern crime and espionage stories, the genre became increasingly critical of the ideologies it had once not only expressed, but also helped to produce.

It's interesting to note that this developmental thesis is itself an expression of a postmodernist ideology in which the modernist attempt at cultural synthesis becomes a kind of villain overcome by the deconstructing multicultural criticism of postmodernism. Thus Pynchon as a postmodernist redeems the tradition of crime fiction by turning it from the production of capitalist and imperialist parables into criticism of these as ideological.

There's a good deal else in Thompson's book such as a critique of the traditional distinction between high and popular culture and an account of how in the era of modernism the detective story preserved certain aspects of nineteenth-century fictional realism. Thompson also develops a related notion, based on Bahktin, of genres as composites of previously existing genres. Many of the observations based on these concepts are useful and suggestive and help to make Thompson's study the best and most complex of a number of recent analyses of the ideologies embedded in detective and spy stories. However, in spite of its many interesting insights into individual writers like Poe, Doyle, Kipling, et al., Thompson does not successfully overcome what seems a basic ambiguity in many of these "ideological" analyses of popular genres. The essential argument of such discussions is that genres like the detective story, the western, the spy story, etc. become popular primarily because they reflect or produce the dominant ideologies of their times, or antithetically, because they create, like Poe, effective critiques of these ideologies. But how can we understand popular genres as both affirmations and rejections of the prevailing hegemony?

Another scholar's more recent work parallels and to some extent improves upon Thompson's cultural speculations. Like Thompson, he also tackles the fundamental cultural question of why the detective story arose in the mid-nineteenth century and flourished in the twentieth. Ronald R. Thomas, in *Detective Fiction and the Rise of Forensic Science*, sees in the emergent detective story the reflections of a debate over new concepts of society and the individual.

> For all its investment in elaborate plotting, the typical detective novel of the nineteenth century came to focus most attentively . . . upon a fundamental transformation taking place in the representation of human character . . . the century-long process in which modern urban and industrial societies began defining persons in terms of their identities rather than their characters. (287)

This new concept of the individual, Thomas argues, was implicit in the rise of such forensic technologies as the lie detector, fingerprinting, and the use of photography for criminal identification. Developed concurrently with the detective story, these techniques, and the ideologies of crime, identity, and citizenship they implied, were an important part of the emergence of new means of social control and manipulation. Detective stories reflected the ambiguity people felt toward these new techniques and ideologies. At times, they affirm the new conceptions. In other cases, they criticize and attack them.

Thomas's study seems to me one of the best of the large number of books on mystery literature published in the past decade. Applying methods of literary and cultural analysis derived from cultural studies, Thomas relates the development of detective fiction to a substantial body of clearly relevant social and cultural material connected with the rise of forensic science. When he discusses how detective writers used such developments as fingerprinting, photography, the lie detector, and other technologies of criminal investigation and then interprets the significance of these developments in terms of emergent ideologies of identity, nationality, citizenship, and crime, Thomas is wonderfully interesting and highly useful. However, the further he gets from this specific relationship and the more he ventures into broader speculations about the social meanings of the works of the detective writers he has chosen to deal with, the less convincing he becomes. An instance is his interpretation of Hammett's *The Maltese Falcon* as a parable affirming post–World War I American capitalism and isolationism. It seems to me that one could also argue the opposite, that Sam Spade's ultimate failure to establish any meaningful human relationships is a criticism of isolationism while his dealings with the Maltese Falcon amount to a burlesque of capitalism. In fact, at the end of his discussion of Hammett's classic, Thomas suggests that though *The Maltese Falcon* might seem to be "a defense of the ethos of American isolationism" important elements of the narration such as the "Flitcraft story" in fact caution "that it is not merely that" (269). The ambiguities in this conclusion nicely illustrate the difficulty inherent in the ideological interpretation of literary works of any complexity, even popular ones.

In trying to make a cultural analysis of a popular genre based on a quite limited number of texts one does run into problems as is demonstrated in the case of one of Thomas's central theses. He uses *The Maltese Falcon* and *Murder on the Orient Express* to argue that in the twentieth century the fascination with forensic science gave way to a concern with the larger political issues that the new technologies and ideologies were implicated with. He does make a very good case that these two very different works both evince a lack of interest in the details of fingerprinting and other aspects of forensic science. However, there were many other works in the period and down to the present time in which forensic science remained a central theme and not just a matter of nostalgic historical interest as Thomas suggests (274–75). In fact the subgenre of detective fiction known as the police procedural has consistently kept forensic science at the center of its stories and currently writers like Patricia Cornwell, Kathy Reichs, and Jeffery Deaver have gained far greater popularity than Hammett and Chandler ever achieved by exploiting the fascination with new methods of forensic science.

As he constructs his framework Thomas offers insightful and sometimes brilliant interpretations of the major creators of the generic detective story, Poe, Doyle, Christie, Hammett and Chandler. He also treats some important novels that give the theme of detection a major role, Dickens' *Bleak House,* Collins's *The Woman in White,* Twain's *Pudd'nhead Wilson,* Hawthorne's *House of Seven Gables,* and Conrad's *The Secret Agent.* The selection is narrow in terms of the number of texts, but very wide in variety and significance and, on the whole, Thomas's argument is interesting and convincing.

A somewhat different perspective on the literary and cultural issues dealt with so interestingly by Thompson and Thomas suggests that specific political, social, moral, and cultural values do not inhere in narrative and dramatic elements like story, character, and theme. When Poe invented Dupin, for instance, he created a narrative model of the brilliant and eccentric investigator that could be used in connection with the expression of a wide range of values. Thompson, himself, points out how different aspects of Poe's creation could lead to very different developments within the detective story genre ranging from the conservative vision of Agatha Christie to the leftist criticism of Dashiell Hammett. However, he doesn't seem to recognize that the dialectic between form and ideology may cast some doubt on the very kind of ideological analysis he is attempting to carry out. Thomas is more complex on this point and recognizes the presence of multivalent meanings in most of the specific texts he discusses. There is still, however, considerable certain uncertainty in the way in which he deals with the problem of different ideological interpretations that can be derived from such writers as Poe, Doyle, and Hammett.

Other students of popular genres have tried to develop a more complex way of treating the relationship between generic constructions and ideologies. These analysts see the genres of popular culture as patterns of narrative and drama that offer the possibility of ideological conflict within them. Though a particular ideology may temporarily establish its hegemony over several different popular genres, it is more typical of complex and diverse societies that individual genres become arenas of ideological struggle. In addition, once well established, a successful popular genre can itself have some influence on the way in which certain historical and ideological situations are perceived. Thus, in *Gunfighter Nation,* the third volume of his history of the myth of the frontier in American culture, Richard Slotkin shows how the western film was shaped in many ways by ideologies of American imperialism of the progressive period. However, he also suggests that certain long established patterns of the western film shaped the way in which Americans tragically failed to understand the limits of their power and thus misconceived the appropriate American political and military role in Southeast Asia. The complex interplay between generic form and ideological implications is an area that very much needs further investigation.

R. Gordon Kelly in *Mystery Fiction and Modern Life* tackles the question of the pervasive presence of the mystery story in a very different way. Kelly has a simple thesis, but his analysis is methodologically sophisticated and surprisingly illuminating. Rejecting the ideological analyses that traditional Marxists and contemporary cultural theorists have supplied, Kelly argues that the mystery story's peculiar significance and its special link to the nineteenth and twentieth centuries results from the way in which it "models" key interpersonal and social processes of modernity. Most significantly, the mystery story shows how one gains knowledge of the intentions of others through the interpretation of surface clues. Such skills are what a person needs to act effectively in the increasing number of encounters with people one doesn't know, sometimes Kelly sees as a central social phenomenon of modernity.

Hence, "correctly assessing the intentions of strangers with whom one must interact in the normal course of events is both a feature of modern life and a staple of mystery fiction" (xii).

Kelly chooses his examples carefully to show how the various sub-genres of mystery—ratiocinative and hard-boiled detective tales, police procedurals, spy stories and other kinds of thrillers—all centrally narrate the typically modern patterns of interaction with others that he defines. He shows how such diverse detective and spy writers as Conan Doyle, Dashiell Hammett, Raymond Chandler, Ross Macdonald, John Buchan, John le Carré, Marcia Muller, and Tony Hillerman all tell stories in which central characters read the intentions of others while concealing their own. In addition, Kelly analyzes how these writers explore the moral and pragmatic implications of this way of relating to others in terms of what is gained and what is lost in humane values.

Careful with his methodology, Kelly is well aware that proving the presence in literary works of certain themes or "models" is not the same as saying that these are what most affect readers or are the cause of a genre's popularity. The most one can say is that the pattern meant something to the writers and publishers. But in the case of the mystery story, there are certainly enough producers to represent a significant segment of the population, which argues for the validity of Kelly's thesis.

Kelly himself tackles the problem of reader effect in a later chapter entitled "Some Readers Reading." After examining some of the established theories about the popularity of the mystery story, he takes the ingenious tack of analyzing the commentary on DorothyL, an internet forum for mystery readers, and comparing this with the standards of valuation used by a long-term mystery reviewer, Anthony Boucher. These approaches are obviously useful, but somewhat inconclusive in the case of Kelly's own theory, since the major value espoused by these readers is the ill-defined notion of "realism."

In my view, popular genres do not serve one overriding function nor can their success be explained by reference to a single cause; rather I think they succeed because they meet a large variety of needs and values. Kelly's discussion is a very persuasive account of one important factor in the mystery story's development. However, his concept of modeling interpersonal processes of modernity now needs to be analyzed in relation to some of the other explanations of the mystery of mystery, such as those I have examined in this essay.

What is one to make of all this? Are these various explanations—formal, archetypal, ideological, and historical—mutually exclusive or is some further synthesis possible? One of the problems with the development of mystery criticism and scholarship is that it has come from many different disciplines and has emerged out of many different perspectives that often are not aware of one another. I suggested earlier that it's a shame that English and American critics are largely unaware of the work done by the French and Germans in this area. To a certain extent the reverse is true, though European scholars are more likely to be multilingual than Americans and therefore are usually more aware of Anglo-American scholarship. In addition to the language barriers, there have also been differences of perspective like those between formalist critics and scholars of cultural studies that have hindered the task of synthesis. This is not unlike the current situation in literary and cultural studies in general where there has been such an explosion of new theories and methods in the last two decades that the task of understanding how these different approaches relate to each other has lagged far behind. In the case of detective fiction there is also a large gap between writers and fans on the one hand and scholars and academic critics on the other. Heta Pyrhönen's work with which I began this essay is a serious attempt to catalogue mystery criticism and analyze the way in which different approaches have developed, but it does not make much attempt to understand how these different approaches might be synthesized. This is clearly one of the major tasks awaiting a new generation of scholars and critics.

22

Take That, You Commie Rat! The Cold War's Imaginary Spies

In the spring of 1999, Indiana University organized a conference on Cold War culture and Peter Bondanella, the conference director, asked me to give a talk. I felt a bit intimidated by being asked to speak in the same forum as real heavyweights like David Halberstam, but the conference turned out to be one of the most interesting I've ever attended. The paper I presented goes over some of the same material I dealt with in *The Spy Story*, which I coauthored with Bruce Rosenberg, but examines more directly the relationship between spy fictions and the political events of the period that produce them. The essay has never been published before.

$$\approx$$

Almost by definition, the Cold War was a conflict of secrecy and spies. Of course there were open conflicts like the Korean "police action," the Russian suppression of anticommunist movements in Eastern Europe, and the Vietnam War. However, in America at least, the period was perhaps equally affected by the public exposure of episodes or alleged episodes from the secret war. The Hiss Case, the Rosenberg trials, the China Lobby's hysterical claim that China had been secretly betrayed to the Communists, Senator McCarthy's attacks on the State Department and other government organizations, the U-2 incident, the Cuban missile crisis, the conspiracy theories that proliferated around the assassination of John Fitzgerald Kennedy, and the Philby, Burgess, and McLean escapes to the Soviet Union all had a deep impact on the public. Though the Cold War era fostered a widespread obsession with secrecy,[1] it was also, paradoxically, a time when mass media coverage of government activities and scandals reached a new level of intensity. In this climate, those alphabetic runes concealing the clandestine espionage organizations of the major contestants under a facade of bureaucratic blandness—CIA, KGB, MI-6—became household words.

This ambiguous fascination with the secret war transformed the spy thriller, which had been a dominantly European preoccupation,[2] into a genre of international popularity, as the enormous output of spy fiction, films, and television series in America, England, France, and other European countries during the period suggests. Mickey Spillane's Mike Hammer, the bestselling detective character of the late 1940s and early 1950s, was part of this trend when, in 1951, the year after Senator McCarthy launched his crusade against communism in the state department, he started chasing American communists. Spillane's Manichean version of the Cold War was soon in fictional competition with a much more critical and less heroic portrayal of the secret war in English writers like John le Carré and the later Graham Greene. Le Carré's bleak fictional accounts of Cold War espionage became very popular after the great success of *The Spy Who Came in from the Cold* in 1962. However, by far the most popular member of this vast legion of imaginary spies was Ian Fleming's James Bond who at least temporarily replaced the great detective Sherlock Holmes as the best-known hero of thriller and suspense stories. Bondisms like "Bond, James Bond," "shaken, not stirred" and "license to kill" joined the hallowed company

---

1. Edward Shils's *The Torment of Secrecy* is one of the best contemporaneous discussions of this obsession.

2. From its beginnings in the late nineteenth century, the spy thriller was, until World War II, primarily a genre of European and especially English writers and filmmakers. Names like William LeQueux, Edgar Wallace, E. Phillips Oppenheim, John Buchan, Dornford Yates, Sax Rohmer, Somerset Maugham, H. C. Neile, Eric Ambler, Graham Greene, and the early Alfred Hitchcock, all English, dominated the genre. Between the first and second world wars, American thriller writers were mainly interested in crime and hard-boiled detection; see, e.g., Dashiell Hammett, Raymond Chandler, Rex Stout, Ellery Queen, James M. Cain, Jim Thompson, Erle Stanley Gardner. It was not until the aftermath of World War II and the emergence of the obsession with communist subversion that American writers turned to the spy thriller in great numbers.

of Sherlockisms like "elementary, my dear Watson," while the fiendish Blofeld, with his octopus-like criminal organization S.P.E.C.T.R.E., momentarily eclipsed the nefarious schemes of Holmes's great nemesis, Professor Moriarty.

At the height of the Cold War the espionage thriller became virtually a required literary indulgence for politicians and other government functionaries. John Kennedy was reportedly an enthusiastic fan of Ian Fleming, while a surprising number of the individuals who became notorious in the Watergate scandal were either already spy novelists—like Howard Hunt—or later gave birth to thrillers—like Erlichman and Liddy. Were it not for his aversion to literature, one would not be surprised to find, under suitable cover (or should we say cover-up), a spy novel by Richard Nixon. For a time the spy thriller seemed the form of popular narrative that most directly addressed the important issues of the day. Thus, one can find spy thrillers of every political complexion from leftist to reactionary. Many of these novels represented the Cold War like American politicians liked to portray it, as a great moral crusade against the treacherous tyranny of communism. In such stories the American agents mostly seem to be wearing haloes, while the Russians might as well be concealing horns and cloven hoofs.

The vast majority of these novels have faded into obscurity just as the spy story itself has been merged into the more general category of suspense thriller since the ending of the Cold War. However, a few spy novelists and filmmakers achieved amazing popularity at the time, and have become a permanent part of popular culture. Strangely enough, as one wanders through the bewildering landscape of the most popular espionage fictions, the real enemies usually turn out to be not Russians or Chinese, but treacherous fellow citizens, whose greed, folly, or incompetence led them to betray the "free world" to the communists. These narratives would seem to imply that the Cold War was not primarily about the conflict between Soviet Russia and the "free world," but a symbolic battleground on which an internal American political and cultural struggle was being fought out. Let us follow that symbolic conflict as it appears in the actions and characters of four of the most popular fictional espionage creations of the Cold War period: the hard-boiled spy novels of Mickey Spillane, the novels and films of John le Carré and Ian Fleming, and the suspense thrillers of Alfred Hitchcock.

It is something of a surprise to discover that Mickey Spillane is still alive and as recently as 1996 published a novel, for he is almost completely forgotten by most members of the public. Nevertheless, in the

1950s, Spillane was the bestselling popular novelist in America and the favorite writer of such diverse people as Cardinal Spellman and Ayn Rand. His success was so great that it revolutionized the publishing industry by making the production of original paperbacks a major concern and inspiring new kinds of publishers and publishing patterns. Yet, Spillane's ultimate fate was an ironic commentary on the rapid transformation of the public mood from the subversion-obsessed 1950s to the more ambiguous and conflicted 1960s. After producing six novels that brought the fictional portrayal of sex and violence to a new level of intensity and sold many millions of copies, Spillane, in 1952, announced his conversion to the faith of the Jehovah's Witnesses and his retirement from writing. He returned to writing nine years later but never recaptured his earlier mass popularity. By the 1970s, his readership had begun to fade. Despite the success of a very different Mike Hammer TV series in the mid-1980s (1984–1987), Spillane's own work continued its descent into obscurity.

Spillane's tremendous success in the 1950s and his rapid fall from popularity after the 1970s reflected a considerable shift in public attitudes toward the Cold War during that time. Spillane did not actually begin as a writer of espionage thrillers, but as a writer of hard-boiled detective stories. His first great success, *I, the Jury* featured a tough private eye, a seductive female villain, and a world of corrupt alliances between wealth and criminality that might have come off the pages of Dashiell Hammett and Raymond Chandler. However, where those earlier tough-guy writers were imbued with the left-liberal orientation that was widespread during the depression-ridden 1930s, Spillane was right wing and so gave a significantly different political and cultural spin to his version of these characters. Where Hammett and Chandler saw rampant individualism and greedy capitalists as the major sources of corruption,[3] Spillane blamed intellectuals, irresponsible professionals, women, homosexuals and discontented minority groups for the trouble. He praised what later became know as family values and moral purity. Unlike many moralists he apparently actually tried to practice what he preached by becoming a Jehovah's Witness.

The early 1950s was the time of the Hiss trial, the exposure of atomic espionage, and the beginning of the McCarthy hysteria. It didn't take

---

3. Dashiell Hammett refused to testify against former associates for the House Un-American Activities Committee and went to jail for a time. The corrupt alliance between businessmen, politicians, and criminals was one of Chandler's favorite themes.

much for Spillane to interpret what he, like J. Edgar Hoover and many other Americans, perceived as the pervasive internal subversion by communism as the major cause of moral decay and disillusion with American values. In *One Lonely Night* (1951), Mike Hammer announced his conversion to the Cold War and proposed an infallible solution to the problem of communist conspiracy:

> But some day, maybe, some day I'd stand on the steps of the Kremlin with a gun in my fist and I'd yell for them to come out and if they wouldn't I'd go in and get them and when I had them lined up against the wall I'd start shooting until all I had left was a row of corpses that bled on the cold floors and in whose thick red blood would be the promise of a peace that would stick for more generations than I'd live to see. (133–34)

The ironies in this passage are certainly unintentional and seem lost on Mike Hammer and, presumably, on Hammer's creator and many of his readers. 1951, which saw the publication of *One Lonely Night*, was rife with public fear and rage against alleged disloyalty. A paranoia like that of Mike Hammer blinded many Americans to the folly and hypocrisy of the House Un-American Activities Committee, the crusade of Senator McCarthy, and the manifold investigations into subversive activities carried out by the Federal Bureau of Investigation.

One Lonely Night deals with a remarkable communist plot. A pair of twins, Lee and Oscar Deamer, represents an America split between loyal and honest citizens and an increasing number of traitors who have become pawns of the communist menace. Lee is an ideal American and in the view of Pat Chambers, a New York police captain and Mike Hammer's best friend, is a political leader who could redeem a dangerously corrupted postwar America. Lee's twin, Oscar, is a madman who has long been institutionalized, but now has escaped and threatens his brother. Pat asks Mike to track down the maniacal Oscar in order to keep him from destroying Lee's blossoming political career. The problem is that, unknown to Pat and Mike, Oscar has not only taken his brother's place, but has become a devoted (and crazy) communist. He schemes to subvert the American political establishment in order to carry out some sort of atomic espionage for the communists. Mike finally figures all this out and murders the villainous Oscar, making sure that the public will think he is the noble Lee and has been murdered by communists. Then he brags to Oscar as he slowly chokes him to death, "You, the greatest Commie louse of them all, will be responsible for the destruction of your own party" (175).

Never noted for the clarity of his plots, Spillane outdid himself here in murkiness and confusion. The narrative is full of loose ends and unrecognized ironies such as the curious relationship between two scenes in which women are brutally abused. In one Mike forces a female communist convert to strip and whips her with his belt in order to make her see the error of her ways. Needless to say, he glories in administering this appropriate punishment. In the second such scene, however, Mike gibbers with rage when he sees his virginal but sexy secretary Velda similarly treated by the Commie rats. His response is to machine-gun the lot.

In spite of these confusions readers loved Spillane and read his books by the millions. Not all of them shared Spillane's primitive rightist politics but they were attracted by the sadistic and misogynistic indulgence in sex and violence that Spillane justified as being in the cause of righteousness. Others, however, certainly responded to Spillane's rage, paranoia, and furious sense of having been betrayed by intellectuals, artists, women, gay people, and ethnic minorities supposedly susceptible to the communist message. Spillane's anger, as well has his blindness to the hypocrisy and inconsistency of his attitudes toward violence and legality, was certainly widely shared in the first phase of the Cold War by the followers of McCarthy and other redbaiters including J. Edgar Hoover and many members of the House of Representatives.

While misogyny and gay bashing may not be explicitly political, they certainly have important political implications. Mike Hammer's kind of antifeminist and antigay agitation continues to be central themes of today's religious right and Spillane's fictional representation of the communist menace delineated some of the central themes of what some political analysts of the 1950s referred to as the radical right.

Spillane's view of the Cold War and the threat of communist subversion in America faded into the past along with Senator McCarthy's belief that communist agents pervade the government. Many of Spillane's bestselling novels of the early 1950s are out of print and can only be found in tattered copies in used bookstores. But his righteous view of the Cold War and his paranoia about American decadence continued to inform a sizeable number of otherwise quite different writers of spy fiction, such as William F. Buckley Jr. and Helen MacInnes.

However, as the 1950s went on, the redbaiting and blacklisting of the late 1940s and early 1950s began to seem excessive to many Americans. Senator McCarthy was ignominiously toppled from his position of power and the Korean War ended in an uneasy truce. Much of the American public tired of the hysteria, rage, and paranoia associated with the crusade against internal subversion and became more skeptical about unsubstantiated claims of large-scale communist infiltration of the government, the movie industry, and the universities. By the beginning of the 1960s, audiences were ready for a very different version of the secret war and the espionage thriller. Two Englishmen, the film director Alfred Hitchcock and the novelist John le Carré were instrumental in presenting this new paradigm of Cold War espionage in films and novels that achieved great popularity. Hitchcock introduced a more skeptical and critical version of the Cold War in his brilliant 1959 suspense thriller, *North by Northwest,* and le Carré gave it a definitive embodiment in the bestselling novel *The Spy Who Came in from the Cold* and the film of it.

The English public never shared the American obsession with the Cold War and with internal subversion. There were almost certainly far more communist sympathizers and actual double agents occupying important positions in the English government than there ever were in America. Even when Burgess and Maclean were exposed as double agents and fled to Russian in 1951, the British reaction was subdued enough that Kim Philby was able to continue his spying for another decade, rising to a high position in the Secret Service. And then when Philby fled in 1963, there was a scandal but nothing like the widespread American redbaiting connected with the Hiss and Rosenberg cases.

These attitudes toward internal subversion reflected different tensions within the two countries as well as the contrasting geopolitical situations of America and Britain after the war. World War II made America the most powerful country in the world. With what seemed its sole possession of the atomic bomb, America dominated the world. However, this dominance was quickly challenged by the discovery that the Soviet Union also had an advanced nuclear capacity, by the "loss" of China to the communists, and by the outbreak of the Korean War. The erosion of American confidence resulting from such events convinced many Americans that the country had been "sold out" by traitors. The quest for a scapegoat provided conservatives with a very powerful rhetorical weapon to use against liberalizing tendencies in the 1950s like feminism, the campaign against desegregation, incipient multiculturalism, and the further expansion of the welfare state. We have already seen how Mickey Spillane drew on this fear of internal subversion in creating his version of a Cold War espionage myth.

The British ended the war in a state of exhaustion, their manpower and resources depleted by six long years of fighting. The British empire, a dominant world political force for over a hundred years, was in the process of dissolution and the British were reluctantly becoming aware that they were doomed to play an increasingly smaller role in world politics. For many Englishmen, the real question was whether the traditional political establishment was competent to lead the country through the difficult times ahead. Diplomatic skill and economic knowledge were therefore more important considerations than loyalty and commitment to the defense of the "free world." Reflecting these circumstances, much British spy literature and many British spy films of the Cold War period center more on the competence of the Secret Service and the political establishment. Whether the earlier assumptions and traditions of the empire were relevant to the new global order were much more important than issues of loyalty and security. In le Carré's novels, the Secret Service seems as damaged by the incompetence and folly of its legitimate leaders as it is by the impact of double agents.

Hitchcock was an English director who, like many important European filmmakers, made the pilgrimage to Hollywood on the eve of World War II. In the 1930s he had made a brilliant series of spy films, most of them updated adaptations of World War I classic thrillers like John Buchan's *The 39 Steps* and Somerset Maugham's *Ashenden*. These films resembled the 1930s spy novels of Graham Greene and Eric Ambler in that their central character was usually a civilian who became accidentally trapped in a complex espionage plot. Often this protagonist was pursued not only by the enemy organization, but was mistaken by the police and his own secret service for a criminal or an enemy agent. In the end, the innocent narrowly escapes with his life, or, in some cases, becomes committed to the struggle against fascism.

Hitchcock adopted this pattern effectively into three World War II spy movies, *Foreign Correspondent* (1940), *Saboteur* (1942), and *Notorious* (1946). These films bore many similarities to American World War II espionage thrillers like *Casablanca* and *To Have and to Have Not*. However, with the end of the war, Hitchcock turned to other mystery themes (e.g. *Rope, Strangers on a Train, Dial M for Murder, Rear Window*, and *Spellbound*). While the American espionage film increasingly developed the theme of internal subversion during the early 1950s, Hitchcock evidently felt uncomfortable with this theme and did not return to the spy film for nearly a decade. His first attempt was with a 1955 remake of his 1934 classic *The Man Who Knew Too Much*. Only in the brilliant 1959 *North by Northwest* did the old master tackle a Cold War theme.

Though American in setting, this is a very British film beginning with the three leading male actors, Cary Grant, Leo G. Carroll, and James Mason who portray the innocent American, the CIA control, and the communist agent respectively. The movie begins with one of Hitchcock's most fascinating depictions of the innocent entrapped in a web of espionage. Cary Grant plays an advertising man who is mistaken by enemy agents for a CIA operative they are trying to capture. It turns out that this agent does not really exist, but has been created by the CIA in order to distract the enemy organization while they plant one of their own agents as Mason's mistress. This hall of mirrors is the plot that Grant mistakenly stumbles into. Captured by the enemy who thinks he is the nonexistent CIA spy he is forcibly made to drink himself into a state of total inebriation and then set loose in a car careening down a steep and winding road. When he narrowly escapes this trap, he is framed for the murder of a leading diplomat who is stabbed in front of a large crowd at the United Nations. And this is only the beginning. By the end of the film the hapless Grant has traveled across half the United States by train, has been machine-gunned by a crop-dusting plane in an Indiana cornfield, and nearly been pushed off the sculptured face of Abraham Lincoln at Mount Rushmore, all in Hitchcock's most brilliant cinematic style.

North by Northwest foreshadowed in richly comic fashion themes treated more seriously in many of the spy novels and films of the 1960s and 1970s. Above all, like le Carré, Hitchcock rejects the view that American agents are as honorable and good as the communists are treacherous and evil. In *North by Northwest* both sides are duplicitous and involved in constructing false versions of reality to the extent that nobody seems to know what is really happening. The choice of English actors to play the communist agent, the CIA control, and the innocent victim emphasizes the lack of distinction among them. In fact, if there is anything to choose between rival agents, James Mason as the ostensible enemy seems a good bit more attractive than the bumbling and totally unscrupulous Leo G. Carroll, who is prepared to sacrifice anyone to achieve ends he cannot even articulate. Even Cary Grant, though the sympathetic victim and the romantic lead of the film, becomes, to some extent, corrupted by his involvement in plots and counterplots. In the end he is just as willing to use deceit and violence to achieve what he wants as the film's professional agents. For Hitchcock and for the writers and filmmakers who followed the vision of Cold War espionage represented in *North by Northwest* the real enemies are not subversive fellow travelers but the espionage establishment itself and the distorted vision of the world it seeks to impose on reality.

The bleakest and most serious presentation of Cold War espionage as destructive of the basic political and moral values of the "free world" appeared in the novels of John le Carré. From *The Spy Who Came in from the* Cold and through his "Karla Trilogy" and other novels of the 1970s and 1980s, le Carré wrote bestselling novels in which decent and well-meaning individual British agents were betrayed, hampered, and compromised by incompetence, treachery, and bureaucratic rivalry at the top levels of the espionage establishment. Moreover, they discover that their very involvement in the political and ethical ambiguities of Cold War espionage increasingly forces them into moral compromises that erode the very ideals of patriotism and peace that they originally joined the Secret Service to pursue. Finally, these le Carré heroes realize that have lost their ability to differentiate between means and ends and have increasingly become a mirror image of the enemy agents they have long opposed. Le Carré's breakthrough with *The Spy Who Came in from the Cold* made him an international bestseller and inspired a school of English spy novelists like Len Deighton and Adam Hall who developed their own intricate versions of decadence, treachery, and incompetence within the secret establishment.

The Spy Who Came in from the Cold's Alec Leamas is a British agent who, at the beginning of the novel, discovers that the network of agents he has built up in Communist East Germany has been exposed and destroyed. The head of the Secret Service, Control, offers him a chance to avenge his agents' deaths by destroying the enemy masterspy, Dieter Mundt, believed by Leamas to be responsible for the disaster. Control's scheme is for Leamas to pretend that he wants to defect and sell British secrets to the East Germans. In this guise he is to reveal false evidence that will implicate Mundt and persuade the East Germans that their masterspy has become a double agent working for the British. Unknown to Leamas this is actually the case.

Leamas goes through with the scheme and successfully plays out the role of defector scripted by Control. Interrogated by Mundt's rival in the East German espionage apparatus, Leamas skillfully plants his misinformation and Mundt is arraigned as a traitor before a secret panel of judges. However, as the trial proceeds, Leamas discovers that he has been tricked by Control and that the real purpose of his mission has been to protect Mundt by destroying Leamas's interrogator, Fiedler, a decent and sympathetic human being who has long suspected Mundt's duplicity. The turning point of Control's plot involves Control's ruthless manipulation of an innocent and unsophisticated British communist, Liz Gold, who has fallen in love with Leamas. Liz is sent to East Germany unknowingly carrying evidence that will doom Fiedler and insure Mundt's future safety. When this happens, Leamas realizes the extent of the deceit he has been a party to and also understands that Mundt cannot possibly let Liz Gold escape from East Germany alive. In a powerful scene at the Berlin Wall, Leamas chooses to die with Liz at the Berlin Wall rather than to return to an organization that has betrayed him.

Le Carré's trilogy "The Quest for Karla," consists of a still more complex structure of three novels, *Tinker, Tailor, Soldier, Spy* (1974), *The Honourable Schoolboy* (1977), and *Smiley's People* (1979) based to some extent on the Kim Philby case. In the first novel, George Smiley, who has Leamas's basic human decency but operates at a higher level of the establishment, uncovers a double agent or "mole" at the very heart of the British Secret Service. This agent, Bill Haydon, appears to be the ideal gentleman spy in the best British tradition and is not only a leading candidate for the directorship of the Secret Service but the lover of Smiley's wife. After exposing Haydon, Smiley is called upon to redeem the Service. He decides to bring about the defection of the top Russian agent, Karla, who was responsible for training Haydon and setting him up as a "mole." In *The Honourable Schoolboy,* Smiley schemes with the CIA to capture a Chinese agent planted in Communist China by Karla only to have this prize snatched away from him at the last moment by the CIA who have conspired with one of Smiley's British rivals. In *Smiley's People,* the stakes escalate as Smiley returns to power and discovers a means of bringing about the defection of Karla himself. However, to trap Karla Smiley must ruthlessly exploit his enemy's one human vulnerability, Karla's great love for a schizophrenic daughter. When Smiley threatens to reveal the hidden existence of this daughter to Karla's superiors, he forces Karla to come over, though he understands that in doing this he has become as brutal and unprincipled as his adversary. In the final scene of *Smiley's People,* Smiley and Karla confront each other at the Berlin Wall, and Smiley realizes that he has become the mirror image of his enemy. For them both, the Cold War has ended in a total defeat of humanity.

Le Carré's bleak view of the Cold War was shared in many ways by Graham Greene who returned to the drama of espionage in several of his later novels, and by several other important espionage writers of the

1970s and 1980s most notably the prolific Len Deighton and Adam Hall—a.k.a. Trevor Elleston. In many ways this view of Cold War conflict replayed some of the left liberal criticism of the military industrial complex shared by many intellectuals and writers in the 1930s, including Greene and Eric Ambler. It also reflected the widespread belief in the existence of a rightist conspiracy within the establishment aimed at destroying leaders and programs that threatened the power of the military-industrial complex. The tragic political assassinations of the 1960s, particularly that of John Fitzgerald Kennedy, gave further credence to this vision as did the events surrounding the Watergate scandal and Nixon's resignation. In films like *The Parallax View* (1974), *The Conversation* (1974), *Three Days of the Condor* (1975), and *Blow Out* (1981) protagonists found themselves in jeopardy when they stumbled upon evidence of such conspiracies deep within the upper circles of the government and the corporate establishment.

On the surface, le Carré's critique of a decadent and incompetent espionage establishment seems antithetical to Mickey's Spillane's reactionary myth of a crusade to purge commie and pinko traitors who would betray the "free world" to what President Reagan called "the evil empire." Yet Spillane's righteous paranoia about the enemy within shared with these conspiracy fantasies a sense that the real enemy was not the Soviet Union or Maoist China, but an internal cabal that had subverted the government and become increasingly skillful at covering up its very existence. The main difference seemed to lie in whether the conspiracy was liberal or conservative and that, too, was increasingly ambiguous as the Cold War came to an end. The myth of an all-powerful conspiracy within a democratic America was less specifically political than it was a quasi-moral and spiritual vision of something going on in the world that was deeply threatening and out of control. In other words, the fear of an enemy within may have represented an inarticulate concern that fundamental changes in the American way of life had reached the point where they threatened it. In any case, the myth of an internal conspiracy continued to fascinate many Americans even after the Berlin Wall was torn down and the Soviet Union collapsed. Today it survives and flourishes in such popular films as Oliver Stone's *JFK* and the hit television series *The X-Files*, to say nothing of its significance in the postmodern novels of writers like Thomas Pynchon and Don de Lillo, who have transmuted the paranoiac vision of the Cold War espionage narrative into novels like *The Crying of Lot 49*, *Gravity's Rainbow*, *Libra*, and *Underworld*. Not surprisingly, the idea of conspiracy also surfaced in the debates about the impeachment of President Clinton.

Several thriller writers of a more conservative persuasion earnestly attempted to counter such attacks on the establishment by emphasizing the conflict between good American agents and the nefarious plots of Russians, Communist Chinese, Cubans, and, more recently, of international terrorists. The dean of this school was William F. Buckley Jr. whose Blackford Oakes series narrated the adventures of a sort of Americanized James Bond. Oakes heroically swashbuckled around the world attempting, not always successfully, to foil such communists plots as the East Germans' building of the Berlin Wall and a supposed Castro scheme to use a missile left over from the Cuban missile crisis against the United States. Others thriller writers ranging from Howard Hunt of Watergate fame to the contemporary bestseller Tom Clancy also glamorized the espionage establishment and its political, military, and corporate allies, though even Clancy could not resist exploiting the dangers of internal conspiracy in the third episode of his Jack Ryan series, *Clear and Present Danger*. Yet Buckley's romanticized espionage adventures were a far cry from the paranoiac hysteria of Spillane's earlier thrillers, while Clancy's conservative political message was less important a factor in his popularity than his remarkable ability to dramatize the technologies of war, both covert and overt.

The largely apolitical quality of these espionage narratives was also characteristic of the single most popular spy saga of the Cold War era. James Bond made his debut in Ian Fleming's 1953 thriller *Casino Royal* and was featured in further fictional adventures up until Fleming's death in 1964 and beyond (with further Bond adventures penned by Kingsley Amis, John Gardner, and others). The extraordinarily popular Bond films began in 1962 with *Dr. No*, Fleming's 1958 reinvention of Sax Rohmer's Dr. Fu Manchu. Sean Connery's brilliant incarnation of the superspy was featured in six further films. Connery's Bond was followed by fifteen further Bond films with George Lazenby, Roger Moore, Timothy Dalton, and Pierce Brosnan, successively. This great Bond success inspired a plethora of parodies and imitations, such as the amazing 1967 John Huston *Casino Royale* with David Niven and Peter Sellers playing duplicate versions of the great spy. By the later 1960s, the release of a new Bond film had become almost as important a part of Christmas ritual in America and England as the arrival of Santa Claus while television series imitating the Bond paradigm proliferated on the networks.

The Bond epic not only became (and remains) an international bo-
nanza, but was widely imitated by writers like the French popular novelist Jean Bruce and the American Donald Hamilton. Its television
clones included series like *The Man from U.N.C.L.E, The Avengers, The
Girl from U.N.C.L.E.*, the Dean Martin-Matt Helm series and the two
most successful of them all, *Mission: Impossible* and the farcical burlesque *Get Smart*. Most of these were short-lived and limited to the
1970s and none of them proved to have anything like the staying power
of the original. Bond's popularity even spread as far as the land of
SMERSH, the Soviet spy agency that furnished antagonists for Bond
in his early years. Anthony Masters reports that the KGB tried to get
into the act by commissioning a Bulgarian writer, A. Gulyashi, to write
a spy thriller, which was then serialized in *Komsomlskaya Pravda,* that
apparently portrayed Bond being defeated by a Communist hero (156).

The KGB was certainly being simple-minded if it viewed the Bond
stories primarily as anti-Russian propaganda, though Fleming's first
novels did show Bond in opposition to a mythical Russian secret organization. However, by the early 1960s when the hugely successful series
of Bond films got underway with Sean Connery as Bond in *Dr. No,* this
quickly changed. In this film, as in the novel it was based upon, the villain is vaguely identified as an agent of the Russians, but he is certainly
far more like Sax Rohmer's Dr Fu Manchu, a brilliant maniac with a
vast secret criminal organization bent on world domination. Though
the second Bond film was called *From Russia With Love* (1963) the putative Russian agent trying to assassinate Bond has actually defected from
the Russians to become part of a great outlaw corporation known as
S.P.E.C.T.R.E. From this point on, the Bond films typically start with
a situation in which Britain, the United States, and Russia are equally
threatened by the machinations of this multinational criminal syndi-
cate. In response to S.P.E.C.T.R.E's challenges to the existing super-
powers Bond must cooperate with assorted Russian agents. He does so
erotically in the case of the luscious Major Akhmatova of *Moonraker* or
as one professional to another with the amusing General Gogol who
appears in a number of films as the representative of Soviet espionage.

Aside from the skills of the remarkable creative teams put together
by Bond film producers Broccoli and Saltzman, the Bond saga's success
stemmed from its glamorized representation of a jet-setting lifestyle associated with the new world of multinational corporations. The increasing power of these organizations was rapidly transforming the
"free world" while the Cold War occupied the public's attention.

The myth of James Bond was quite different from that of his most successful and influential predecessors in thriller literature, Sherlock Holmes by the Englishman A. Conan Doyle and the American hard-boiled detectives Sam Spade and Philip Marlowe created by Dashiell Hammett and Raymond Chandler. Above all, Bond's characteristics reflect his membership in a large political-economic organization. Bond is "Bonded" as it were. By contrast Holmes, Spade, and Marlowe are all individualists who operate according to their own codes. Typically they are quite different from the official police organizations, which are portrayed either as incompetent (Holmes), or corrupt and venal as with Spade and Marlowe. Moreover, the most memorable aspect of Bond is his famous 007 number indicating that he has the "license to kill," that is, a permission from authority to act in a way for which ordinary people would be held criminally accountable.

Bond is also a gentleman and has luxurious tastes in food, drink, travel, clothing, cars and women that could once only be afforded by the aristocracy. His glamorous manner of living takes him to exotic places around the world where, when he is not fending off the enemy's thugs, he lives like royalty at the finest hotels and frequents the most elegant restaurants, clubs, and casinos where he clearly knows his way around. His manner of life presents a striking contrast to the cozy domesticity of Holmes and Watson or the dingy offices of Spade and Marlowe. Though his manner reflects that of the traditional British gentleman, Bond is not from the upper classes. A scion of the respectable middle classes, his professional skills have enabled him to become a corporate aristocrat supported in his lavish manner of life not by inherited money but by an expense account. His way of life and his scale of values are not primarily derived from social traditions, but from the conviction that his professional skills and accomplishments merit a life of pleasure, consumption, and sensuous fulfillment in his leisure moments. This unlimited expense account luxury represents his reward for the value of his professional services to the organization he so devotedly serves. Bond's ethos strikingly resembles that of another important contemporaneous cultural invention, the Playboy ethos of Hugh Hefner, designed, like the delights of Bond, not for the idle rich but for the young professional or executive. The emphasis on consumption, the centerfold-like representation of women, and the sophisticated graphic styles of the Bond films significantly resembled what could be found on the pages of Hefner's *Playboy* magazine.

Like *Playboy* and its numerous imitators, the Bond saga dramatized the life of a bureaucrat-executive in a large multinational corporation, portraying it as a heroic struggle against the nefarious machinations of rival corporations. Bond's life of skilled derring-do and hedonistic satisfaction glamorized this new kind of life and gave audiences a tantalizing glimpse of the way in which the new world of multinational corporations could offer undreamed of affluence and happiness to those belonging to it. It even assured us that the corporate world allowed some leeway for personal initiative and resistance as in those ritual episodes when Bond disobeys the orders of the bureaucratic M and destroys the technological wonders of the eponymous Q.

Seen like this in hindsight, the spy fictions of the Cold War used the widely accepted myth of the struggle between the free world and the evil empire of communism in several ways, the least of which was to portray the struggle between the United States and Soviet Russia. On the contrary the most successful and popular spy stories of the period were drawn to explore a kind of underside of the Cold War. One layer of this underside was the need to attach blame to someone for the great postwar changes in the political and economic structure of America and Britain that were perceived by many people as a betrayal of established patterns of life and traditions. Whether this betrayal resulted from the communist subversion of liberal intellectuals or from the rigidity, incompetence, and corruption of the political establishment or from the machinations of a rightist conspiracy seemed less important than that the cover-up should be uncovered and somebody exposed to censure and punishment. On the other hand, the most widely popular kind of spy story offered a more positive vision of these changes by glamorizing the possibilities of fulfillment and happiness within the new world of large international organizations. To a considerable extent, the interplay between these two attitudes toward the political and economic changes of the second half of the twentieth century continues down to the present day even though the myth of the Cold War is no longer available to distract our collective attention.

23

The Literature of Mystery: Some Reconsiderations

This essay attempts to get beyond the more formalistic approach to popular genres represented by most of *Adventure, Mystery, and Romance*. I've always been interested, as many people have, in the way in which popular genres reflect and influence the culture that produces them (see my essay on "Detecting the Detective"). However, this also seems to me an elusive and complex relationship very open to oversimplification. The many diverse cultural explanations of the detective story testify to that. Not too long ago it struck me that if we considered the literature of mystery as one "supergenre" with many branches like the gothic, the detective story, the spy story, the crime novel, etc. we might be able to construct a cultural history with more plausibility. This, then, was a preliminary attempt to "theorize" such a supergenre and to try out some of the cultural explanations it suggested. For some time I did not publish it, partly because its length exceeded by far the usual journal article. Part of it appeared in a new journal, *Storytelling*, edited by Bonnie Plummer from Eastern Kentucky University.

$$\rightleftharpoons$$

A large proportion of stories currently produced in the media of literature, film, and television involve three basic themes: mystery, transgression, and otherness. These stories represent actions that cross some fundamental moral, religious, legal, or natural boundary and enter a realm of otherness. Something about the transgressions or the transgressors seems inexplicable or beyond our ability to control or place within our ordinary sense of reality and order. Thus, an aspect of mystery is central to the narrative. Some of these stories represent investigations of the identity of a transgressor and his means. These we usually call detective or mystery stories with their manifold variants of classical, hard-boiled, police procedural, gendered, ethnic, and regional. Other narratives explore the mystery of transgression, itself, by focusing on the criminal in the crime thriller, or by representing still more monstrous and extreme forms of transgression in the gothic or horror tradition. Finally, there are spy stories and other kinds of thrillers that deal with the machinations and exposure of dangerous conspiracies. Some of these story types follow the quest for the transgressor's identity and the explanation of how the transgression was carried out, while others concern themselves more with the why of a transgression or focus on the relationship between victims and transgressors. Yet despite the diverse ways in which these elements can be deployed, these narratives all present different kinds of encounters with and resolutions of transgression and mystery, and perhaps in some ways explore what transgression and otherness mean.

These story types, once relegated to a sort of intellectual and cultural basement called subliterature or popular fiction, have received increasing critical and scholarly attention and, in addition, have become more obviously influential on the literary mainstream, especially in what is now often characterized as postmodern fiction. Many writers now considered part of the postmodern canon, Robbe-Grillet, Borges, Kafka, Pynchon, DeLillo, Gaddis, Oates, Morrison, Amis, Barnes, and Ackroyd to name a few, often use themes, situations, and plots derived from gothic, horror, mystery and spy stories.

However, most of the criticism of this kind of narrative has treated the traditions of the detective story, gothic horror, the crime thriller, and the spy story as separate genres. In many ways this makes sense for there are distinctive differences among such narrative types as the horror story, the espionage thriller, and the detective mystery. Nonetheless, these genres are also very similar, and have often influenced one another. This paper suggests that, despite important individual differences, these story types can be seen as subgenres of a single master genre, which I will call mystery literature. The emergence and development of this master genre is a major cultural and aesthetic phenomenon of the last 250 years.[1] The free interchange among these subgenres has been an important factor in the vitality of the literature of mystery. As Bakhtin suggests, the mixing of genres has been a significant force in the creative evolution of literature. It has certainly been a big factor in the history of mystery narratives.

A Brief History of Mystery Narratives

It's not surprising that critics and scholars have generally treated the gothic novel and the detective story as separate generic traditions, since, on the face of it, these narrative types are antithetical. One glories in darkness and irrationality while the other celebrates rationality and man's ability to solve the mysteries that threaten him. The central figure of the gothic novel can be a villain or criminal who seeks to seduce and murder innocent people, or it may be one of this villain's chosen victims, usually an attractive and virginal young woman. On the other hand, the detective story protagonist is a brilliant or at least dogged investigator who penetrates the mystery created by the criminal transgressor, saving the innocent from falling into the traps of the criminal or from being falsely accused of the villain's crimes.

The gothic plunges into extremes and mystifications of all sorts, while the detective story is one of the most controlled and orderly of all narrative forms, highly predictable in almost every respect except for the specific solutions revealed by the detective at the most appropriate moments. The detective story proceeds from a seemingly insoluble

---

1. Examples of the kind of criticism which treats these story types as separate genres include: Walter Albert, *Detective and Mystery Fiction;* Nina Auerbach, *Our Vampires, Ourselves;* Bernard Benstock, ed., *Art in Crime Writing;* T. J. Binyon, *"Murder Will Out";* John G. Cawelti, *Adventure, Mystery and Romance;* John G. Cawelti and Bruce Rosenberg, *The Spy Story;* Judith Halberstam, *Skin Shows;* Ralph Harper, *The World of the Thriller;* Jacqueline Howard, *Reading Gothic Fiction;* Maggie Kilgour, *The Rise of the Gothic Novel;* Bruce Merry, *Anatomy of the Spy Thriller;* Marie Mulvey-Roberts, *The Handbook to Gothic Literature;* David Punter, *The Literature of Terror;* Heta Pyrhönen, *Murder from an Academic Angel;* Marty Roth, *Foul and Fair Play* Julian Symons, *Bloody Murder* Anne Williams, *Art of Darkness* Robin W. Winks, ed., *Detective Fiction.*

One notable exception to the tendency to approach popular genres as separate traditions is Jerry Palmer's *Thrillers.* Palmer tries to treat detective, crime, and espionage novels as part of a larger genre of thrillers and he has many interesting insights to offer about the history and interrelations of these story types. However, he does not include horror and the gothic as part of his conception. The title of Stephen Knight's *Form and Ideology in Crime Fiction* would seem to suggest a consideration of the interplay between detective and crime narratives, but in fact is almost entirely concerned with detective fiction.

mystery—it may even appear to be supernatural—to a solution that explains everything in purely human terms. The gothic novel typically moves in the opposite direction from reluctance to acknowledge the unnatural nature of events to an acknowledgment of the presence of the unaccountable. There are, as always, exceptions. One is the ratiocinative gothic pioneered by Mrs. Radcliffe. In this subgenre, supernatural mysteries are ultimately revealed to be tricks or hallucinations. But this is clearly a move in the direction of the detective story.

The detective story's creator, Edgar Allan Poe, was a gothic writer and had already published some of the most radically terrifying, as well as eerily humorous, short narratives in the history of literature. Historical sequence indicates the close relationship between these major subgenres of the literature of mystery. Poe's 1839 gothic nightmare, "The Fall of the House of Usher," seems directly connected in several ways to his creation of the first detective story, the 1841 "Murders in the Rue Morgue." The great detective C. Auguste Dupin has much of the brilliant strangeness of Roderick Usher, dazzling the narrator, as Usher does, with his intuitions and theories. The "time-eaten and grotesque mansion" inhabited by Dupin and his narrator friend might be an urbanized version of the mysterious House of Usher itself. Multiple parallels make the connection unmistakably clear: "Usher" is full of doubling and reflections, while Dupin's strange double nature makes the narrator think of the "old philosophy of the Bi-Part soul." The theme of doubling appears again in "The Purloined Letter" in the oft-observed analogies between Dupin and the Minister D. Poe may have gotten his fascination with the double from his German predecessor in the literature of mystery, E. T. A. Hoffman, who also influenced Dostoyevsky, another important figure in the emergence of the detective story. The double became an even more compelling obsession in such Poe tales as "William Wilson" and reached a crescendo in "The Fall of the House of Usher" where everything is doubled and the boundary between the psychological and the physical boundary is broken down. It's almost as if the detective story appears as a double of the gothic fantasy, a sort of antidote to the chaotic mirroring and reflecting that destroys all order in the house of Usher.

Poe, Radcliffe, and others link the gothic tradition to the detective story. This tradition of modern mystery literature is generally thought to have begun with the eighteenth-century gothic revival and Horace Walpole's pioneering gothic novel, *The Castle of Otranto*. Walpole's example was widely influential and the gothic quickly became a genre.

Gaining increasing popularity through the work of Ann Radcliffe (1764-1823) and the "Monk," Matthew Gregory Lewis (1775-1818), the gothic continued to flourish in the nineteenth century. There was the invention of the android-monster (Mary Shelley's *Frankenstein*), and also the vampire (John Polidori's *The Vampyre*, Thomas Prest's *Varney the Vampire*, Sheridan Le Fanu's *Carmilla*, and the definitive realization of the myth in Bram Stoker's *Dracula*). In the twentieth century, such gothic themes and forms have pervaded the development of all the major media of print, film, and television.

There seems little doubt that Poe invented the detective story. Scholars have rightly suggested assorted precursors like Godwin's *Caleb Williams* and the *Memoirs* of Eugène Vidocq, and noted that Thomas de Quincey clearly foreshadowed the genre in his marvelously perverse 1827 essay aestheticizing the worst of transgressions, "On Murder Considered as One of the Fine Arts." However, no significant fictional detective appeared until 1841 when C. Auguste Dupin emerged from the amazing mind of Edgar Allan Poe to solve "The Murders in the Rue Morgue." Poe not only invented the detective as character but he created a narrative form for his adventures. Following Poe, many novelists in the mid-nineteenth century, including Collins, Hugo, Dickens, Dostoyevsky, and the American Anna Katherine Green, wrote novels that included detective characters. In 1887 and 1891 Arthur Conan Doyle established the definitive detective character and codified Poe's formal inventions in *A Study in Scarlet* and *The Adventures of Sherlock Holmes*.

The spy thriller is another form of mystery literature closely related to the gothic and the detective story, though with a slightly different line of development. Early nineteenth-century historical novels like those by Scott and Dumas often have situations of international intrigue as a background, while James Fenimore Cooper wrote the first novel to use *The Spy* as a title. *The Spy* was a historical novel about the American Revolution and one can see that Cooper had a little trouble treating a spy as the protagonist of a heroic adventure. After this experiment, Cooper turned instead to the figure of the Leatherstocking hero and began a long tradition in which spying and scouting are portrayed as related skills on the western frontier.

The theme of international intrigue also appeared in connection with mystery and detection in Poe's third Dupin story, "The Purloined Letter." Moreover, in the later nineteenth century, detective stories sometimes contained elements of espionage and counterespionage. A number of Sherlock Holmes stories, including "The Naval Treaty,"

"The Greek Interpreter," "The Bruce-Partington Plans," and "His Last Bow" certainly adumbrate the contemporary spy thriller.

Several candidates have been suggested as the first modern spy story. Some scholars consider Erskine Childers's 1903 *The Riddle of the Sands* to be the first true spy story, while others suggest that it came out of the literature of imaginary wars that first appeared in Chesney's 1871 *The Battle of Dorking* and that flourished in the wake of the Franco-Prussian war. Other candidates include Joseph Conrad's 1906 *The Secret Agent*, the novels of William LeQueux, the work of the prolific Edgar Wallace, the stories of E. Phillips Oppenheim, and the 1915 *Thirty-Nine Steps* of John Buchan. This last was the first great success of several spy fictions by Buchan and helped establish the basic shape of the modern spy narrative for some time to come. Whatever the actual genesis, the spy thriller apparently originated in the very late nineteenth or early twentieth century, about fifty to sixty years after the appearance of the detective story.

Thus, the gothic gave birth to the detective story. The detective story, in turn, mixed with other narrative traditions to produce the spy story. The fourth subgenre of mystery, the literature of crime, is also related to this sequence, but with different earlier roots. Seventeenth- and eighteenth-century broadsheet ballads and picaresque accounts of famous outlaws and criminal life like Fielding's *Jonathan Wild the Great* and the *Beggar's Opera* antedated both the gothic novel and the detective story. However, the treatment of the outlaw in these earlier types of crime narrative was quite different from the treatment of criminals in the literature of mystery. Later crime narratives reflected the gothic influence in emphasizing the mystery of criminal psychology and in presenting tales about the criminal underworld of modern cities. Mid-nineteenth century works like Eugene Sue's wildly popular *Les mystères de Paris* were criminal "mysteries" that showed many signs of gothic influence (by, for example, Radcliffe's *The Mysteries of Udolpho*, which may have suggested Sue's title).[2]

The literature of crime developed further in the nineteenth century through accounts of horrendous serial crimes like those that de Quincy analyzed in "On Murder Considered as One of the Fine Arts." This kind of literature evolved in a complex dialectic with the horror and detective story traditions. For example, one of Poe's three Dupin stories, "The Mystery of Marie Roget," reconstructed and offered a solution to

2. Sue's book appeared in 1842 and was followed rapidly by "Mysteries" of London and New York by other authors.

the notorious "real-life" New York murder of Mary Rogers. As chronicled by Richard Altick in *Victorian Studies in Scarlet,* proper Victorians delighted in the goriest and most gothic details of horrendous crimes. This tradition culminated in the incredible proliferation of narratives about Jack the Ripper, the archetypal serial killer, whose deeds (1888–89) were strikingly contemporaneous with the fictional cases of Sherlock Holmes and the horrific depredations of Count Dracula (1897).[3]

The next major stage in the evolution of crime stories came some thirty years later in America when the American hard-boiled detective tradition created by Dashiell Hammett, Raymond Chandler, and others and the cinematic influence of German expressionism brought to America by refugee film directors like Fritz Lang converged to create several important new crime subgenres. One was the psychological crime novel of writers like James M. Cain, Horace McCoy, and Jim Thompson. A second was the gangster novel and film. These evolved into film noir with its modern transmutations of such traditional gothic themes as the mysterious mansion, the world of darkness and shadow, the obsessional villain, and the entrapped victim.

Historically, then, the literature of mystery began around the middle of the eighteenth century and proliferated through the nineteenth, resulting in the development of such major subgenres as the detective mystery in 1841, and the espionage thriller toward the end of the century. The crime story developed in a complex dialectic with these other subgenres of mystery. These dates clearly suggest a connection between the development of the literature of mystery and the many contemporaneous cultural changes associated with the modernization of European and American civilizations.

The Historical Significance of Mystery: From Mythic Ritual to Generic Narrative

Interpretations of the significance of the literature of mystery and the sources of its appeal range widely. Some are theological (Auden, Sayers, Chesterton), or psychological (Freud, Pederson-Krag, Auerbach); others offer political and ideological interpretations (Tropp, Knight, Mandel, Thompson). Some have examined the structural and aesthetic aspects of mystery (Todorov, Cawelti), the role of gender (Williams, Irons,

---

3. Norbert Spehner's enormous bibliography of *Jacques L'éventreur* details the amazing proliferation of books and articles about Jack the Ripper in many different languages.

Pfeil, Munt), and the connection with modernity (Kelly, Klein, Thomas, Thompson). Such a variety of explanations appropriately reflect the diverse appeal of the literature of mystery. Different readers and viewers seem to take different pleasures in horror stories, detective novels, and spy thrillers in print, in the movies, and on television and to find various uses for their experience of them.

Such diverse audience responses to mystery make it very difficult to generalize persuasively about the cultural significance of the emergence and development of this vast area of storytelling. However, there may be some useful clues to the meaning of the genre in the historical evolution of the term "mystery" itself, which is, on the face of it, rather paradoxical. The term today has a variety of meanings that seem almost antithetical to each other. One meaning relates to things that lie beyond the boundaries of ordinary human experience and touch on the realm of religion and the supernatural. But another meaning of mystery has to do with certain kinds of stories in which human actions and the use of reason lead to nonsupernatural solutions, for example, mystery stories.

In earlier times, the term was especially associated with religion, as in the ancient Greek mystery religions, the mystery of the Trinity, or the medieval mystery plays, which were dramatic presentations of biblical stories. Originally "mystery" was a Greek word apparently derived from the root *mu*, thought by some to have had some connection with the sound made by muttering with closed lips. The same root can be found in mute, and also in myth and mythology (in Greek *muthos*, originally meaning something spoken in a special way; later a story and then a special kind of narrative). Mystery itself derives from the verb *mueo*, which means to initiate into secrets. Thus *mustes*, an initiate, and *musterion*, a secret rite or mystery applied by the Greeks to such secret cults as the Dionysian rites of Eleusis. Gradually the meaning of *musterion* widened to mean any mystery or secret thing and this carried over into the Latin *mysterium*, though there were still very strong religious or ritual implications adhering to the word.

Around the time of the Renaissance, the word *mystery* began to take on nonreligious meanings. For example, it denotes "the mysteries of nature" (1638), which may yield their secrets to human reason. Shakespeare, for example, has a character say in *All's Well That Ends Well* (1601): "Plutus himself . . . / Hath not in natures mysterie more science than / I have in this ring." This is a little ambiguous since it suggests that nature's mysteries are more complex than those of human craft, yet also that there is a "science," that is, some kind of comprehensible order in those mysteries. Mystery also came to be applied to the secrets of statecraft and in 1738 one author talked of the mysteries of Masonry, referring to secret rituals that were human in origin and anti-religious in intent. By the beginning of the nineteenth century, mystery was being applied to almost any unsolved riddle of human life or history. In 1835, Thirwal, a great classicist, noted, "the origin of the Homeric poetry is wrapt in mystery." Though it wasn't until 1908 that G. K. Chesterton, essayist, philosopher and writer of mystery stories, made the first reference to "mystery story" recorded in the OED, it's clear from such literary titles as the already mentioned *Mysteries of Udolpho* and *Mysteries of Paris* as well as Dickens's *The Mystery of Edwin Drood* (1870) that the association between mystery and a certain kind of story goes back at least to the end of the eighteenth century.

We may find one key to the literature of mystery in this strange ambiguity and tension between the idea of mystery as supernatural and religious and the use of mystery to denote secular secrets accessible to rational solution. In 1973, a reviewer in the *New York Times* observed that "good mystery writers have always known that a man himself is the greatest mystery of all," a sentence that nicely combines the two antithetical meanings subsumed in the word "mystery." There is a strong modern fascination with the intersection between larger mysteries and lesser mysteries, those that are beyond human understanding and those that can be solved or at least resolved through human reason and action. This interaction underlies and inspires the literature of mystery. Dorothy Sayers elegantly suggested something like this in the introduction to her *Omnibus of Crime:* "it may be that [in mystery stories, the reader] finds a sort of catharsis or purging of his fears and self-questionings. These mysteries made only to be solved, these horrors which he knows to be mere figments of the creative brain, comfort him by subtly persuading that life is a mystery which death will solve, and whose horrors will pass away as a tale that is told" (qtd. in Winks 53).

Tzetvan Todorov's theory of the fantastic is also useful in this context. Todorov argued that the emergence of a genre of fantastic literature, lying somewhere between fantasy and realism, was a key feature of the transition from romanticism to realism. This genre featured narratives characterized by unresolvable ambiguity as to whether the events of the story were supernatural or could be explained in naturalistic terms as the result of material causes or by insanity or delusion on the part of the characters. In other words, Todorov suggested that the genre of the fantastic reflected a sense that the dialectic between the supernatural and the natural could never be resolved. He saw this genre as flourishing particularly in stories from the late eighteenth and nineteenth centuries by writers like E. T. A Hoffman, Edgar Allan Poe, Nathaniel Hawthorne, Sheridan LeFanu, and others. Henry James's great novella *The Turn of the Screw* stands as a perfect example of Todorov's idea of the fantastic. To this day, critics and readers of that story continue to puzzle over the mysterious appearances of Peter Quint and Miss Jessel. Are they "actual" ghosts or delusions or hallucinations resulting from the emotional stress of the governess who is both protagonist and witness of the story? James surely never intended that this brilliant ambiguity should be clarified.

Todorov argues that the fantastic arose during a period in the evolution of Western culture when traditional religious faith in a transcendent supernatural reality had been eroded by the rise of science and naturalism but not entirely destroyed. Thus the fantastic particularly flourished in the nineteenth century because this was a period in which what Matthew Arnold called "the Sea of Faith" had reached a critical point in "its melancholy, long, withdrawing roar." Todorov sees the genre of the fantastic as symbolizing the tension between religious faith and doubt felt by so many people in the aftermath of the eighteenth century "Age of Reason."

In my view, the literature of mystery reflects this conflict between explanation and inexplicability, between reason and the incomprehensible. What Todorov calls the fantastic is actually, I think, a particularly rich and complex branch of the literature of mystery. Unlike Todorov's fantastic, however, most examples of the literature of mystery actually work out at least a temporary resolution of the conflict between explanation and the inexplicable that the fantastic resists. The detective story replaces the elusive lack of closure with a seemingly rational solution. Nonetheless, the best and most influential mystery stories usually retain an element of uncertainty no matter how clearly the mystery has been solved or the evil villain destroyed. The inherently serial character of the literature of mystery indicates this. The detective may solve one crime, but he can never overcome crime itself and therefore must face a new crime in the next story, just as Dracula always rises from the grave and Frankenstein's creature is continually reassembled and reanimated.

The literature of mystery and its relationship to the ambiguity or tension between religion and the secular has existed since the eighteenth century. This would suggest that the literature of mystery is a relatively modern cultural phenomenon that addresses in secular terms the concerns and themes that were once dealt with in religious myth and ritual.[4] An account of this development might go something like this. The Reformation, the rise of modern scientific cosmology, and other secularizing trends significantly transformed the role of religion in European cultures by displacing God from the center of the universe and placing him at the margins. The literature of mystery, then, developed out of the need for a narrative form capable of exploring the boundaries between the new secular world of man, society, and nature and the traditional world of the supernatural and mythical.

Ronald Thomas in *Detective Fiction and the Rise of Forensic Science* suggests that there was a close relationship between the emergent detective story and the development of "scientific" methods of criminal investigation like photographic "mug shots," fingerprinting, and the lie detector, which materialized at the same time. He interprets the connection between them as reflecting the need to explore, define, and justify new concepts of identity based on the physical body rather than the soul or psyche that were invented because the modern state needed a more tangible way of identifying and controlling its citizens. This interpretation spells out at least one aspect of the cultural transformation between a dominantly religious conception of reality and a more secular and political one. There are probably other factors, such as the rise of capitalism and the middle class, that were also involved in the transformation of mystery from a mythic and religious experience to one involving the concepts of crime, detection and punishment that underlie modern mystery genres.

In short, the new mystery genres arose when writers invented literary plots and symbols that reexamined the central religious issues of sin, death, and salvation in secular terms. This is the reason why some of the most influential stories in the history of the genre seem almost like parodies of traditional myths and rituals. Linda Bayer-Berenbaum in *The Gothic Imagination* is one of many readers who have observed the parodic or inverted treatment of central religious themes and stories in gothic novels. Sometimes this parody is clearly consciously intended by the writer, as, for example, in the case of Mary Shelley who purposely alludes to *Paradise Lost* and the biblical account of creation as well as to

---

4. Karen Halttunen's discussion in *Murder Most Foul* of the role of gothicism and the murder mystery in replacing the religious treatment of evil with various secular narratives shows convincingly how this process shaped the emergence of the literature of mystery and horror in eighteenth and early nineteenth century America.

the Prometheus myth in *Frankenstein*. In others, the religious allusions seem more ambiguous and latent. Bram Stoker's *Dracula* inverts the Christian gospels with Dracula's promise of immortality, the ritual of blood drinking, and the ultimate crucifixion of the vampire. It also suggests certain aspects of spiritualism and theosophy, such as the transmigration of souls. Bayer-Berenbaum further suggests that *Dracula* reflects even earlier religious rituals in the themes of cannibalism and human sacrifice. It's certainly suggestive that Bram Stoker (1847–1912) was a near contemporary of Sir James Frazer (1854–1941) and that *Dracula* (1897) embodied many of the themes that Frazer developed in *The Golden Bough* (1890–1912), though it seems unlikely that there was any direct influence either way. What these two very different works share is a very complex and ambiguous attitude toward traditional religious narratives and their validity.

It's almost a cliché that the relationship between criminal and detective in the mystery story is analogous to the relationship between sinner and priest. In this sense, the detective's solution of the crime is a secular inversion of the confessional. Torn between orthodox Christianity and modernity, Dostoyevsky created a great tragic novel out of the struggle between criminal and detective. He portrays his detective Porfiry Petrovich as a true son of Saint Peter, the gatekeeper, as he attempts to help the desperate Raskalnikov confess his crime and thereby gain the possibility of redemption. *Crime and Punishment* powerfully develops the conflict between the two worlds of traditional religious faith and modern secular society. On the other hand, the generic detective story seems to erase or conceal this conflict by placing its primary emphasis on the identity of the criminal and the means of the crime rather than on its moral meaning. The generic detective is thus comparable to another modern investigative specialist who has also often been compared to a priest. Like the psychoanalyst, the detective seeks to uncover not the ultimate mystery of sin, which is really the prerogative of God alone, but the psychological motives that drive someone to destructive and antisocial actions. The connection between detective and psychoanalyst has inspired more than one fictional meeting between Sherlock Holmes and Sigmund Freud. Indeed, Freud was well aware of the connection that could be drawn between what he was doing and the investigations of Sherlock Holmes (Shepherd 8–9).

Religious symbolism is even more overt in the horror story. From the beginning the gothic reveled in the ambiguously supernatural realm suggested by such phenomena as the gigantic helmet of *The Castle of*

Otranto. Even in the late twentieth century, horror calls upon demonic forces that rise out of the depths of small-town Maine in Stephen King's imagination or the satanic avatars that afflict the heroines of *Rosemary's Baby* and *The Exorcist.* The detective story would seem almost the antithesis of that vision since it places such importance on the rational explanation of mysterious events and the rejection of supernatural causes. Yet, many of the most powerful detective stories seem to reenact in many ways that brilliant move that led Poe to create the form in the first place by substituting a rampaging ape for the apocalyptic and mythic chaos enveloping the House of Usher. In this fashion he transformed poor, mad Roderick Usher into the eccentric and brilliant explainer of mysteries, C Auguste Dupin. But the detective story never moves too far toward order, for its fascination continues to depend on the possibility that the mysterious will really turn out to be inexplicable. One of the great mystery novels, Doyle's *The Hound of the Baskervilles,* begins with the legend of the Baskerville curse, a demonic hound that hunts down and destroys each Baskerville heir. In the end, the canine specter turns out to be a big dog with chemicals added to make it glow in the dark. However, we never quite lose the *frisson* of that great moment when Dr. Mortimer describes the fearsome sign he has observed near the dead body of Sir Charles Baskerville. "Mr. Holmes, they were the footprints of a gigantic hound."

The Aesthetics of Mystery

Patterns of action involving transgressions and complex doubling relationships between protagonists and antagonists help define the basic elements of all mystery narratives and also outline some of the central aesthetic effects that mysteries seek to achieve. The first and most important of these effects is the maximum possible tension between explicability and inexplicability. More than anything else, this tension defines the idea of mystery in narrative form. In the detective novel, the writer allows us to feel we can solve the crime, but must, at the same time, keep us from doing so. In a good detective story there is a point where the reader feels that all possible solutions have been disproved and that he cannot imagine the identity of the murderer. This is the ideal point for the detective to reveal that he or she knows the answer. Ellery Queen and John Dickson Carr sometimes used to interrupt their narratives at this point and issue a challenge to the reader. Of course, not all mysteries succeed in creating this effect. Readers solve many mysteries long before they reach this point. However, that they do so clearly indicates that the mystery has failed aesthetically. Skillful readers even develop the ability to suppress the correct solutions even if they have hit upon them, in order to enjoy the pleasure of the mystery.

The horror story involves different emotions and themes, but also depends on evoking the liminal state between explicability and inexplicability. In the gothic novel, the question of whether the horror is rational or irrational, natural or supernatural, often dominates the first section of the narrative. The reader is made to wonder whether the horror can be controlled or defeated. The possibility that the monster is beyond human power is the gothic tradition's version of inexplicability and is as much a source of suspense as the apparent insolubility of the crime in the detective story.

The espionage thriller often employs both of these variations of the dialectic of explicability vs. inexplicability. There is the question of discovering just what the conspiracy is about and which characters are involved with it and which are not. This is like the characteristic tension between inexplicability and solution characteristic of the detective story. But the conspiracy can also take the place of the monster in the horror story, raising the issue of whether or not it can be exposed and defeated. Something of this sort also works in the crime novel, though the latter often creates an additional tension concerning the moral responsibility of the criminal and whether or not he or she deserves to be punished. This tension generates the disturbing and labyrinthine moral ambiguity that seems to be a central characteristic of what we now call "noir" narratives and films.

Just as the literature of mystery takes place along the borderline between reality and fantasy, between what can be explained and what cannot, it also explores the dialectic between self and other. Some mysteries are based on a simple antithesis between the self, represented by characters with whom the reader identifies, and that which is antithetical to the self. In such narratives the other is a horrible monster, an evil demon, a ruthless or maniacal criminal and its near victory followed by a climactic defeat constitutes the central structure of the story. However, the most powerful and influential forms of mystery seem to develop a higher degree of ambiguity in the self-other dialectic by exploiting various kinds of doubling, particularly those in which the other can appear as some sort of projection of the self. Works of mystery that have come to seem canonic or archetypal in the genre often possess this kind of tension to a high degree.

The original reception and later history of two important mystery creations nicely illustrate this tendency toward doubling and increasing self-other ambiguity. When Bram Stoker's *Dracula* originally appeared, most readers apparently perceived him as a sinister figure of otherness. For them, Dracula's story represented the clash between Christian purity and its demonic antithesis or, in more ideological terms, the struggle between Western civilization as represented by Victorian England and the corrupting temptations of other racial or religious cultures. The original Dracula was a sinister shadow who remained offstage for most of the story. However, the figure of Dracula was reinterpreted in the proliferating series of films that began to appear in the early 1920s starting with *Nosfteratu*. In later novels and films and in such television manifestations as the vampiric soap opera *Dark Shadows,* the relationship between the vampire and "ourselves" became increasingly complex. In '*Salem's Lot,* Stephen King shows how the coming of vampirism is in fact a reflection of the actual lusts and desires of the citizens of a sort of "Our Town," or a Maine version of *Winesburg, Ohio.* Anne Rice's *Vampire Chronicles* invert the Dracula narrative by making the vampire's "quest for a deeper meaning to his macabre existence . . . a reflection of our own sometimes fruitless quest for life's meaning" as Gary Hoppenstand suggests (4). Francis Ford Coppola's misleadingly titled film, *Bram Stoker's Dracula* actually turns the clash between self and other into a very un-Stokeresque love story in which the Count becomes the doomed Romeo to Mina Harker's Juliet.

Recent feminist criticism has been remarkably sympathetic in its treatment of the sinister Count. Several feminist critics treat the self vs. other dialectic in the novel as a struggle of white male patriarchy, as represented by Jonathan Harker, Van Helsing and the other ostensible "heroes," against a more liberal and complex view of gender associated with the many affinities between Dracula and women. Anne Williams even argues that

> Van Helsing and his band of four and one-half men (the half being Mina's rational self) struggle against the most powerful "other" of all— mindless, soulless "nature red in tooth and claw," the archetypal "Terrible Mother." What they are fighting *for,* is, ironically, also what they are fighting *against,* because even the most "virtuous" of human women can betray the cause, either seduced, like Lucy or forced, like Mina. But this is the system's flaw: if the maiden is to be worth rescuing she must become a mother; but when she becomes a mother, she invites the enemy Death into the house of culture." (129)

If Dracula is thus both male and female and the ostensible heroes are both rescuers and enemies of women, the proliferation of doubling becomes mind-boggling.

That very near contemporary of Dracula, Sherlock Holmes, has a similarly complex relationship with the self-other dialectic. From the beginning Holmes was a double figure, first in himself as the mixture of scientist and poet and then even more significantly in the double figure of Sherlock Holmes-Dr. Watson. The doubling of Homes and Watson is also a complex self-other pattern. Dr. Watson both represents the reader and is a kind of double for Holmes; the two characters have such complementary traits in relation to late nineteenth century ideas of personality that they seem at times like the two parts of a single person. Finally, the doubling of Sherlock Holmes and Professor Moriarty, though a very minor part of the original Holmes saga, came to assume a major role in the legend of Holmes, indicating how important doubling is in eliciting reader interest.

The history of adaptations and interpretations of Sherlock Holmes shows how, as in the case of Dracula, mystery texts that remain important tend to be reinterpreted in such a way as to maximize the complexity of doubling and of self-other relationships. In the most successful recreations of Sherlock Holmes, such as the Holmes pastiches of Nicholas Meyer, the Holmes films starring Basil Rathbone and Nigel Bruce, and the television adaptation with Jeremy Brett as Holmes, the figure of Professor Moriarty typically assumes a much larger role. In Meyer's *Seven-per-Cent Solution* the whole idea of Moriarity as a master criminal and Holmes's opponent is presented as an obsessive projection on the part of Holmes while the actual Moriarty turns out to be an innocent mathematics professor. The need to deal with Holmes's obsession then requires the intervention of another figure often seen as a kind of counterpart or analogue for Sherlock Holmes—the real Sigmund Freud. In the film and television adaptations, Moriarty is implicated in a number of Holmes cases from which he is totally absent in the original Doyle stories.

Successful mystery texts become the subject of adaptations and imitations as well as of critical interpretations that sometimes significantly reshape the meaning of the original texts. This suggests another important aesthetic feature of the literature of mystery: the central role of reader involvement in the narrative. Most obviously, the literature of mystery depends on arousing elemental, visceral, and immediate emotions of fear and perplexity that other kinds of literature either avoid or do not pursue to the same extent. As Stephen King points out in *Danse Macabre*, "the gross-out can be done with varying degrees of artistic finesse, but it's always there" (4). Similarly, in the detective story the reader must be kept in an intense state of curiosity mixed with bewilderment. Thus, the literature of mystery requires a kind of reader participation that is more immediate and extreme. It does not usually evoke the complexity of feelings and interests that more sophisticated literature does.

In order to evoke powerful emotions and to manipulate and deceive the reader about what is going on, the mystery writer must be continually alert to the possible responses of his audience to specific actions and characters. Because of this, mystery writing may be more analogous to traditional oral taletelling than any other current literary form. In fact, the popularity of ghost stories as material for oral taletelling is a significant aspect of the residual oral folk culture characteristic of modernity. In Kentucky, there is even an annual festival devoted to the telling of such stories. The writer, unlike the storyteller, must imagine his or her audience's responses. Yet there are many ways in which the audience for the literature of mystery makes itself known to the interested writer. For example, writers must be especially responsive to sales since publishers are reluctant to publish mystery or horror writing that does not garner significant sales. In addition, mystery writers are quick to imitate success. Stephen King and Anne Rice have many imitators. Tony Hillerman's best-selling Navajo detective mysteries inspired a number of other Native American detective series, just as the success of Sue Grafton and Sara Paretsky prepared the way for a legion of female private eyes.

Still another way in which audience response plays a major role in the literature of mystery is through the complex history of adaptations of successful mystery figures to other media. Detectives and monsters like Dracula, Sherlock Holmes, Frankenstein, and Raymond Chandler's Philip Marlowe have been frequently adapted to films and recreated in new versions. Sometimes these reinterpretations become so successful in their own right they have a considerable influence on future interpretations of the figures in question. Humphrey Bogart's remarkable portrayals of the hard-boiled detective in *The Maltese Falcon* and *The Big Sleep* certainly had a strong influence not only on the interpretation of Hammett and Chandler, but also on the acceptance of the hard-boiled detective by a broader public. In the same way Bela Lugosi's Dracula and Boris Karloff's portrayal of Frankenstein's creature deeply influenced the next generation's concept of horror.

Sometimes adaptations of mystery texts involve a sort of updating as when the Basil Rathbone-Nigel Bruce recreation of Sherlock Holmes brought the great detective into action against Nazi spies in World War II, or like the way some current vampire films transport Dracula to contemporary California or Brooklyn. Such transformations can also lead to an interesting dialectic between these films and others that claim to be restorations of the original tradition. Kenneth Branagh and Francis Ford Coppola's recent horror films were entitled *Mary Shelley's Frankenstein* and *Bram Stoker's Dracula* because they claimed to be more authentic versions of the original sources of these important horror traditions. However, these films were certainly drastic reinterpretations of Stoker and Shelley's original conceptions. Coppola's film was quite successful, perhaps because its transformation of the Count into a tragic lover pursuing his lost love across the centuries was right in line with contemporary feminist interpretations of Dracula as an androgynous antipatriarchal figure. It will probably have some influence on future version of Dracula, while Branagh's version, even though closer to the original, did not succeed in the same way and will probably be soon forgotten.

Mystery's emphasis on immediate audience response is one reason that some people condemn most of the literature of mystery as escapist literature that can only be read once with any pleasure. Many people will stop reading a detective story if they recall that they have read it before (even if they have forgotten how it comes out.) Similarly, good horror films are rarely as powerful the second time around, which may be another reason why reinterpretations are so frequent in this area. Seen too often a horror film becomes funny rather than terrifying. The extreme situations that once aroused fear seem exaggerated and silly as they become more familiar. Some readers even feel that it is a waste of time to read works that cannot be enjoyed even more on a second reading. John Irwin suggests that the true mystery of the mystery story is "how . . . the writer keep[s] [the] solution from exhausting the reader's interest in the story[.] How does he write a work that can be reread by people other than those with poor memories?" (1). Yet Irwin has written a very large and quite fascinating critical work on the meaning of mystery as defined by two major figures, Poe and Borges.

Irwin's criticism applies in part to many mystery texts, suggesting the extent to which mysteries depend on the manipulation and deception of readers to create fear and suspense. A reader is likely to feel less suspense when he or she knows from a prior reading what is coming next. Most mystery texts are easily consumable and then dispensable.

This is one reason why so many of them are written and why they are widely read by for relaxation. Only the most powerful and influential works of mystery literature generate more complex relationships with their readers.

The special kind of reader involvement characteristic of the most successful mystery creations seems to require the story to contain a high degree of doubling and to encourage projection. This also leads to a paradoxical aspect of the mystery protagonist and/or antagonist. The successful mystery character usually embodies a set of highly contradictory characteristics. The master detective combines scientific method and poetic imagination while the hard-boiled detective embodies both an intense sense of honor and the kind of amorality that enables him to break the law when necessary. Dracula is a labyrinth of oppositions—he is immortal and doomed, asexual and highly erotic, aristocratic and animalistic, human and inhuman and, at least in recent criticism, male and female. One important result of these conflicting aspects of the figure is that he/she seems both very distinctive and strangely opaque and blank. Nina Auerbach points to the famous early scene in *Dracula* where Jonathan realizes that he cannot see the Count in his shaving mirror: "in Jonathan's mirror the vampire has no more face than does Dickens's Spirit of Christmas Future. In his blankness, his impersonality, his emphasis on sweeping new orders rather than insinuating intimacy, Dracula *is* the twentieth century he still haunts" (63). I believe Auerbach is wrong in thinking that this blankness of character is solely a reflection of the twentieth century. Actually most of the lasting figures of the literature of mystery generate this opacity and thus become blank screens for projections of all sorts of meanings. Mystery protagonists or antagonists that do not ultimately have this opacity do not last. Some figures, like the lascivious monk, or the predatory aristocrat, possess this quality for a certain cultural era, but then lose it in a later time with the result that the texts that feature them no longer continue to draw readers and recreations.

Thus, the archetypal mystery figure can evoke diverse and even antithetical interpretive projections on the part of readers. Later recreations of these figures reflect the way in which such characters tantalize and tease us into attempting to resolve the contradictions and fill in the blankness, to struggle without success to explain them . Until the recent development of popular culture criticism, most literary critics did not consider the literature of mystery worth much commentary. Instead, writers and filmmakers carried the tradition forward by adapting and recreating the primal detectives, monsters, and spies, thereby offering imaginative interpretations by creating new works in the tradition. In recent years there has been a great proliferation of highly creative and imaginative mystery criticism as well. However, though many of these reinterpretations or critical analyses offer fascinating explanations of or solutions to the meaning of such characters as Dracula, Sherlock Holmes, or James Bond, they are usually short-lived, for another important characteristic of the mystery text is its resistance to closure. While the detective mystery seems to reach an end with the detective's solution of the crime and the apparent restoration of order, the serial character of mystery texts assures us that in the next story or novel, the detective will encounter still another crime. When one encounters a title like Sue Grafton's *"L" is for Lawless,* it's pretty evident that we can look forward to *"M" is for Malice* and back to *"K" is for Killer.* In the horror novel, we usually arrive at a point where the monster seems to have been destroyed and his secrets exposed. However, even though the writer may not explicitly signal a possible return of the horror, we are well aware that Dracula always rises from the grave and that Frankenstein's creature waits only to be reanimated. In more contemporary horror novels, like Stephen King's *'Salem's Lot* or Anne Rice's *Interview with the Vampire,* even the pretense of closure is abandoned. The defeat of one avatar of the monster only makes way for the encounter with an even more complex and less resistible form of monstrosity. In Anne Rice's *Vampire Chronicles* and her Mayfair Witch saga, the transgressors who were once sources of terror have become the protagonists of a seemingly inexhaustible metaphysical soap opera. Even the "slasher" films of the last two decades, cruder offspring of Hitchcock's *Psycho,* trumpet the failure of closure in their serial titles. At last count we were up *Scream 2, Halloween 5, Nightmare on Elm Street 4,* and the ultimate anticlosure film text *Friday the 13th,* which will soon reach its own 13. Even the brilliant *Psycho* has suffered two sequels and has been slavishly remade in full color!

Mystery's structural characteristics—maximum tension between explicability and inexplicability, complex play between self and other and the tendency toward doubling, heightened intensity of immediate response, and continued audience involvement and resistance to closure—reflect a distinctive modern tension between religious ideas about man's place in the universe and the new worldview of scientific naturalism and rationalism. Naturalism ignores God and the supernatural, giving the divine no place in explanations of the universe, except perhaps as alleged experiences to be explained as psychological phenomena. Some scientists credit God with the origin of the cosmic design, but view his act of creation as anterior to the actual processes of nature. In either case, the kind of supernatural visions that dominated the human imagination up to the seventeenth and eighteenth centuries no longer do for the most part. Evil and sin have been replaced by social disorder and criminality. This, however, leaves a great hole in the human imagination, which both fears and yearns for the supernatural. The literature of mystery dramatizes this ambiguity and thus becomes the narrative embodiment of some of the key myths of modernity. With this in view certain aspects of the history of the literature of mystery, such as the strange interconnection between the seemingly antithetic narratives of gothic horror and detective ratiocination, can be explored more fully.

Toward a New History of Mystery

This preliminary essay is no place to attempt a more complex history of the interlinking of the various subgenres of mystery, horror, crime, detective, and conspiracy-espionage, or to fully define how such a history would transform our understanding of the cultural significance of these highly popular narrative forms. However, a few examples may suggest how the contemporaneous impact and mutual influence of certain major mystery creations have shaped the history of mystery. We have already commented on the interplay in the work of Edgar Allan Poe between the total gothic disorder of "The Fall of the House of Usher" and the seemingly rational order imposed on apparent chaos by the brilliant solutions of C. Auguste Dupin. We've also referred to the striking historical congruity of Conan Doyle's Sherlock Holmes and Bram Stoker's Dracula. Both authors were Anglo-Irish and thus subject to similar cultural tensions about self and other. Moreover, Doyle's great detective was at least partially mirrored in Stoker's dedicated vampire hunter, Van Helsing, while Dracula's ability to command the services of an international group of vampires, gypsies, and even bats, wolves, and insects is comparable to the criminal organization of Dr. Moriarty. The plot thickens when we observe that two important historical phenomena of the same period—the unsolved murders of Jack the Ripper and the psychological discoveries of Dr. Sigmund Freud—are so clearly connected to Holmes and to Dracula that these relationships have become central to commentary on these figures.[5] In addition, many reinterpretations of Sherlock Holmes and Dracula, like the novels of Nicholas Meyer and Francis Ford Coppola's film version of *Dracula*, explore the interplay between these archetypes of detection and horror and Freudian ideas of human sexuality and consciousness. Exploring the related cultural and ideological patterns that became manifest in the treatment of these real and fictional figures should give us rich insights into the deeper imaginative patterns pervasive in the England and America in the later nineteenth and early twentieth centuries. For example, one pattern manifest in these characters is that of frightening forces erupting from below and unleashing dangerously uncontrollable energies that threaten the very fabric of society. Dracula rises from his coffin to convert innocent young women into monsters while the criminals in Doyle's stories typically seek to improve their lot in society through fraud and murder. Freud struggled to understand and control the repressed secrets rising from the unconscious while Jack the Ripper's horrifying murders were perceived as an example of animalistic savagery breaking out in the very center of civilization. All of these instances of mystery can be understood as symbolizing some form of what Freud brilliantly defined as the return of the repressed in an essay that meditates, among other things, on the literature of mystery.

By the 1930s, the shape of the literature of mystery had changed considerably. The first highly successful film adaptation of Dracula shows us a very different Count from the shadowy figure in Bram Stoker's novel. This 1931 Tod Browning-Bela Lugosi reinterpretation frames the vampire more in terms of social inclusion and exclusion than as a force from the depths of the psyche. Though Lugosi's Dracula can still evoke that original fear of primeval forces, there are other aspects of his characterization that are quite different from Stoker's Dracula. As Nina Auerbach suggests, Lugosi's Dracula is a far more humanized figure than Stoker's archetypal original, who is so mysterious that, after the opening section in Transylvania, his actions are mainly reported to us and he hardly ever actually appears. It is certainly significant that

5. Christopher Bentley's "The Monster in the Bedroom: Sexual Symbolism in Bram Stoker's *Dracula*" and Burton Hatlen's "The Return of the Repressed/Oppressed in Bram Stoker's *Dracula*" are two of several essays included in *Dracula: The Vampire and the Critics*. Freud also makes a frequent appearance in Williams and Auerbach. Psychoanalytic criticism of the detective story is pervasive while Michael Shepherd in *Sherlock Homes and the Case of Dr. Freud* discusses the specific connections between Freud and Holmes.

such Draculaisms as "Velcome to Transylvania," or "The children of the night. They make such lovely music." Or "I never drink—Wein," though based on things said by Stoker's original, are inextricably connected in our minds with Bela Lugosi's memorable voice and accent. It's hard even to even imagine what Stoker's Count looks like, but Lugosi-Dracula in his swanky evening clothes and Transylvanian cape stands out in the streets of London like a tarantula on a slice of angel food cake, to quote another contemporaneous mystery writer.[6] It's certainly important that Stoker's Dracula is an Eastern European and thus invokes that deep English ambivalence about the East and all it represents. However, Lugosi looks and talks like a foreigner and this makes him more like an outsider than a force from the depths. There is even something comic and ridiculous, as well as disturbing, about Lugosi-Dracula that relates to the anti-Semitic and ethnic stereotypes of Eastern European immigrants so characteristic of isolationist 1930s America. Lugosi-Dracula, as well as other 1930s film monsters, like Boris Karloff's creature of Frankenstein, were often portrayed as social outsiders looking in through windows on a scene they long to be part of but are excluded from. Their attempts at entrance threaten the imminent destruction of that comfortable social order.

Shortly after *Dracula* Tod Browning made his most powerful and original film, *Freaks*. This film inverted the theme of the social outsider by portraying a society made up of people forced to the margins of ordinary society by their deformities. The freaks join ranks against a normal person, a scheming woman who invades and threatens their world. The harrowing conclusion transforms the normal woman into the most horrendous of freaks and proved to be too upsetting for audiences in the 1930s, thereby virtually ending Browning's career. In Browning's *Dracula*, Van Helsing, Harker and Seward unite to repel the outsider's invasion, just as society unites to destroy the other two of what Auerbach nicely describes as "the three captivating monsters of the 1930s—Bela Lugosi, Boris Karloff, and King Kong." We might add Lon Chaney Jr.'s werewolf, and Boris Karloff's Mummy to this unholy trio. These are all monster figures for which one feels a considerable degree of human sympathy. After all, they are not really responsible for what they are and what they seem to want is mainly to be accepted as human beings. Yet this is not possible, for their presence in society is dangerous and disruptive.

---

6. Raymond Chandler's Philip Marlowe describing the hoodlum Moose Malloy, another social outsider, in the opening scene of *Farewell, My Lovely*.

Therefore ordinary normal people must join together to repel and destroy them.

These highly successful monster figures of the early 1930s shared important thematic characteristics with another of the most popular developments in mystery narrative at that time, the gangster story, represented by such novels and films as *Little Caesar, Public Enemy, Scarface, High Sierra,* and *The Roaring 20s.* These texts are also about social outsiders whose monstrosity seems as much a result of accident and circumstances as of evil intentions. One can even sympathize with their attempts to gain acceptance or success in respectable society. But the desire to move from the margins to the center of society leads them to overreach themselves and to threaten society itself, thus necessitating their destruction. Needless to say, this portrayal of the gangster is very different from the Mafia and Godfather narratives more characteristic of the Cold War period of the 1960s and 1970s, just as Lugosi-Dracula represents something very different from the vampires of Stephen King's *'Salem's Lot* and Anne Rice's *Vampire Chronicles.*

In addition to the gangster, another version of the crime narrative appeared in the early 1930s in the work of writers like James M. Cain and Horace McCoy who have become known as the "noir"[7] school. These criminals, like some of the 1930s gangsters, are as much victims of accident and confused social values as they are agents of primal evil. Like Frankenstein's creature and the werewolf, they are forced to become social outsiders because their desire for a normal life is thwarted by society's inability to understand their true motives.

---

7. The "noir" writers like James M. Cain, Patricia Highsmith, Cornell Woolrich, Jim Thompson, David Goodis, Chester Himes, and others were thought of in their own day as sensational pulp novelists, popular enough with a certain class of reader but certainly not bound for literary immortality. Though not much respected by the critics of the period, many of these books were turned into sensationally successful movies like Billy Wilder's *Double Indemnity* and Tay Garnett's *The Postman Always Rings Twice* (both based on novels by James M. Cain). After the war, these writers were taken up by French intellectuals. The publisher Gallimard had many of them translated into French and issued in a series called (after its black covers) the "Série noire," thereby coining a name for this type of fiction (and film), which would stick not only in French but in English. After the Série noire's great success in France where it was praised by literary heavyweights like Jean-Paul Sartre and Albert Camus, these writers were resurrected in America with fresh credentials and admired by intellectuals as popular existentialists writing a black literature of the absurd. Today the "noir" writers are turning up all over the place. New movies based on their works have done well, while a younger generation of writers like Elmore Leonard, and of filmmakers like Quentin Tarrentino, have been inspired by their work. The noir tough guys are now classics, memorialized in such volumes as the Library of America's *Crime Novels: American Noir of the 1930s and 40s.*

Two other important mystery inventions of this period were the hard-boiled detective story and the narrative of international intrigue in which innocent persons become social outsiders because the authorities mistakenly identify them as spies, or because their accidental knowledge of secret conspiracies threatens to expose powerful members of the establishment. They are forced out "into the cold," as later spy stories would put it. Both of these narratives have protagonists who live outside the patterns and values of normal society. The hard-boiled detective is an outsider by choice and his cynicism about respectable society and his rejection of its values enables him to deal with criminal transgressions involving gangsterism and the wholesale corruption of normal society. Just as Poe's ratiocinative detective was a sort of antidote to the chaotic disorder of gothic horror, so the hard-boiled detective was a counter to the endemic corruption of a "world ruled by gangsters" (Chandler, "The Simple Art of Murder" 207).

Together these new forms of the literature of mystery evoke a world in which the protagonist is suddenly forced out of the comfortable daylight world of ordinary society into a night world of insecurity, doubt, accident, corruption, and amorality. One striking fable of this "noir" world was a story about a man named Flitcraft told by Sam Spade in Hammett's *The Maltese Falcon*. The "Flitcraft story" was about a man nearly killed by a safe that had fallen from a building as he was walking past. The respectable Flitcraft suddenly became aware of the real nature of the world and it led him to reject his ordinary life in order to unite himself with the chaos and chance of reality. In Flitcraft's case what he found was another orderly niche within ordinary society. But, for the typical protagonist of "noir" mysteries, there was no return once the line had been crossed. The other side of the line for most "noir" protagonists was death.

In the aftermath of World War II, major changes in the literature of mystery led to the emergence of another constellation of forms. In horror, for example, the two most influential figures of the 1960s were Alfred Hitchcock and Stephen King. Hitchcock began as a filmmaker in the 1930s and his most important prewar films were versions of spy narratives like *The Thirty-Nine Steps, The Lady Vanishes,* and *Sabotage* and gothic romances like *Rebecca* and *Suspicion*. These films typically developed the themes of the social outsider and the noir world so characteristic of that time. However in 1960 with the shocking impact of *Psycho*, Hitchcock launched a new kind of horror film that would become increasingly important in the 1970s and 1980s. The theme of *Psycho* might be defined in simple terms as the story of the next-door neighbor as serial killer. The presence of frightening evil in the most ordinary places became the central theme of Stephen King, whose tribute to *Dracula*, *'Salem's Lot*, could be subtitled "Our Town as Vampire Acres." *'Salem's Lot* laid out several of King's central narrative concerns. A representative of evil visits a small town in New England and quickly seduces most of the citizens. The now wholly corrupted town is about to self-destruct in a terrible apocalypse when a counterforce of innocents, often a group of children, discovers the spiritual strength necessary to withstand the subversion and temporarily avert the apocalypse.[8]

Two highly popular films (and novels) of the period, *Rosemary's Baby* (1968) and *The Exorcist* (1973), exemplified another way in which the idea of the monster next door could be developed. In these films and their many imitators, the subject was demonic or satanic possession of an ordinary person or, in the *Amityville* series, of a typical suburban house (*The Amityville Horror* [1979] and its eight sequels). These persons or objects become infested with a demonic force that intends to use its disguise as a typical person as a base from which to enter the world and to dominate it. As in Stephen King's novels, most people in these movies either quickly come under the demon's control or turn out to be already part of secret covens, like Rosemary's New York neighbors. Not surprisingly, this was a period in which public belief in the widespread existence of satanic cults and active covens of witches rapidly proliferated.

Just as the horror novel of the 1960s and '70s explored the evils lurking behind the mask of ordinary people and places, the detective story also moved from the criminal centers of major cities like New York, San Francisco, and Los Angeles to regional America. The outsider detective of the hard-boiled tradition developed into the detective as part of the community or as representative of some significant social group like women, African Americans, or ethnics. In addition, this detective, instead of being a lone individual like Sam Spade, Philip Marlowe or Mike Hammer, was typically part of a team like a police squad. Others were backed up by a group of recurrent characters, like many of the new women detectives or Walter Mosley's Easy Rawlins, who belong to a sort of loose family of friends and neighbors.[9] Just as Poe's Dupin was a

---

8. King has openly acknowledged the sense in which *'Salem's Lot* was an homage to *Dracula* in his own delightful book of horror criticism, *Danse Macabre*. Other King works that follow a pattern similar to *'Salem's Lot* include *It*, *The Stand*, *Needful Things*, and *The Tommyknockers*.

9. Easy Rawlins has his homicidal friend Mouse, his adopted children, his various lovers, and

counterforce against the gothic villain he so much resembled, the new detectives of the 1960s and 1970s seem to be positive counterparts of the new monstrosity disguised in the ordinary. He or she symbolizes the boy or girl next door helped by a symbolic family to defeat the neighborhood serial killer.

The most influential crime narratives of this period were Mario Puzo's *The Godfather* and three immensely successful movies made by Francis Ford Coppola based on Puzo's original: *The Godfather* (1972); *The Godfather: Part II* (1974); and *The Godfather: Part III* (1990). The central theme of these narratives was that of the criminal "family." In *The Godfather* the original family created by Don Vito Corleone is a positive source of warmth and support in a world hostile to recent immigrants. However, as the "family" seeks respectability under the leadership of Michael Corleone, it becomes gradually corrupted and turns into a heartless organization concerned only with its own power and aggrandizement. The treatment of the Mafia as ambiguous family and stories about serial killers pretending to be ordinary people were central themes of crime narratives during the 1960s and 1970s.

On the surface, the Cold War espionage novel remained an oasis of exoticism and unfamiliar glamour in this world of ordinary monstrosity. However, some of the most powerful spy thrillers of the time, in particular those of John le Carré and Graham Greene, portrayed the greatest threat as coming not from the foreign enemy but from the double agent or mole who had penetrated to the heart of our own bureaucracy. The moles of le Carré and Greene, based to some degree on the actual English double agent Kim Philby, were the espionage thriller's counterpart to the serial killer next door and indicated that some of the same mystery themes also influenced the espionage thriller of the 1960s and 1970s. Even James Bond, despite the traditional exoticism of his antagonists, the foreign strangeness of many of the settings of his adventures, and the pneumatic glamour of his female conquests, was still linked to the ordinary by Fleming's obsessive fascination with brand names and widely familiar manufactured products. No matter how strange Dr. No's underwater lair, its accommodations had the same basic lineaments and even better toiletries than a good Holiday Inn.

---

assorted neighborhood friends. Patricial Cornwell's Kay Scarpetta has her niece Lucy, her pseudo-father figure Captain Pete Marino, and her lover Benton Wesley while Grafton's Kinsey Milhone and Paretsky's V. I. Warshawski have important woman friends, elderly neighbors, and assorted other friends and allies.

Final Considerations

I have tried to suggest that by considering the popular narratives of horror, detection, crime, and espionage as a changing series of constellations we can see how different mystery narratives of the same times share essential themes and patterns. I have not attempted to elucidate the relationship between those patterns and the historical and cultural trends that shaped these periods. However, it seems clear that the eras I have briefly discussed, the turn of the century, the thirties, and the Cold War era, produced mystery constellations responsive to the historical events and trends that shaped these periods. Further clarification of the history of mystery will better enable us to define these connections.

The development of the literature of mystery can be analyzed, as suggested here, by looking at the contemporaneous similarities in theme, character, and situation to be found in the different areas of horror, detection, crime, and espionage. It can also be seen in somewhat larger terms through an analysis of how the structures of mystery have interacted since the origin of gothic in the mid-eighteenth century. From this perspective, it would appear at first glance that there are three major phases in this development. The first resulted from the original fascination with the gothic and from the coalescence of important mystery themes, characters, and situations from other literary forms like the novel and the romance into gothic forms. The second phase can be dated from Poe's great invention of the detective in the early 1840s. It lasted for more than a hundred years until the 1960s and was dominated by forms of specialization in which a variety of narrative types proliferated from the original mystery tradition and established semiautonomous traditions—different forms of horror, of detective mysteries, of crime stories, and of thrillers. Finally, beginning in the 1960s, while the specialized forms continued to exist, the distinctions between horror and investigation, crime and detection, espionage and other forms of conspiracy became increasingly blurred. The relationship between science fiction and mystery also became more complicated. The result was a combination and synthesis of mystery narratives with elements of science fiction that resulted in such highly successful texts as the futuristic thrillers of Arnold Schwarzenegger (the *Terminator* films, *Running Man*, *Total Recall*, etc) and the highly synthetic series *The X-Files*. By 1997 this new type of synthetic thriller had become so well established that it could generate the highly successful parody, *Men in Black*. These developments certainly reflect in some way the major cultural transformations of the last 300 years: the rise of individualism, democracy, and romanticism from 1750-1850; the development of modernism and the industrial and technological revolutions from 1850-1950, and the emergence of postmodernism from 1950 to the present. Further investigations of the literature of mystery along the lines I have suggested in this essay should lead to a richer and more complex understanding of the way in which human cultures have created popular imaginary narratives in response to these developments.

24

Stuart Kaminsky: Place and Irony in the Mystery Story

These last two essays are recent attempts to apply formula and genre analysis to specific contemporary mystery writers. Discussing the work of Stuart Kaminsky, I try to deal primarily with some aspects of his artistry as a mystery writer, while, in the paper on contemporary southern mystery writing, I am especially concerned with the way in which certain key cultural themes recur in several writers, and how these themes are related to the mystery's role in modernist cultures.

—

My discussion of Stuart Kaminsky's work will be unusual in at least one respect. Unless we're dealing with a modernist drama like Pirandello's *Six Characters in Search of an Author*, it's not at all usual for a character to have a chance to comment on the author who created him. However, that is at least in part what's going to happen here. Let me introduce myself. I am John Cawelti, a retired professor of English from the University of Kentucky. I'll let you draw your own conclusions about my personality and character. But I have an alter ego. This John Cawelti is a detective sergeant in the Los Angeles polices force in the 1930s and 1940s and he is not a nice man. He appeared for the first time in one of Kaminsky's early Toby Peters mysteries and he has turned up recurrently and nastily ever since. In his most recent appearance he is introduced in the police interrogation room, about to grill a suspect in the most brutal fashion:

> [The interrogation room] was probably John Cawelti's favorite place in the world: small, single bulb, no windows, wooden table with two chairs and a phone book on the table. The phone book was used in the heads of suspects. . . . Cawelti's sleeves were rolled up. He was having a good time. He hadn't changed much in the years I had known him. He was about my height and weight but that was the end of the resemblance. John Cawelti had bright red hair parted straight down the middle. His face was pockmarked and angry and he always wore suspenders. (*A Few Minutes Past Midnight* 149)

Now while the John Cawelti writing this was certainly once thinner than he is now, he has never been near Toby's height or weight. Moreover, there are not many people around any more who know that this John Cawelti did once have "bright red hair." Actually, I still had it when Stuart Kaminsky first met John Cawelti many years ago in Chicago. In addition, and I don't think Stuart knows this, John Cawelti started to wear suspenders a few years ago, mainly because they are more comfortable with my excessive avoirdupois. Perhaps this is an example of the mystical insight of writers.

However, in this presentation, I will try to be a little more generous to the mysteries of Stuart Kaminsky than might be expected, given the way my alter ego treats poor Toby Peters. In fact, I find Kaminsky one of the most delightful and interesting writers of detective stories working today and I have never read one of his mysteries, and I believe I've read all of them, without thoroughly enjoying it. His gift for creating interesting characters (present company excepted of course), his brisk and witty style, and his ability to keep a story moving have always given me great pleasure in reading his mysteries. However, I want to concentrate on what is perhaps Kaminsky's most remarkable accomplishment: his creation of four distinctive mystery series and his ability to sustain these different series over an increasing number of books.

When I first met Stuart Kaminsky and I still had red hair, it was in the late 1960s or early 1970s and I had no idea he was going to be a major mystery writer. But he was already an incipient film scholar and knew more about movies than I would ever know. I had the good fortune once during those years to teach a summer course on the gangster film with him and another film expert, and I certainly learned much more than I taught—the ideal situation for a teacher. Stuart had arranged weekend film showings and I'll never forget the Saturday I watched something like twelve straight gangster films from early dawn to late at night. Stuart, of course, seemed to have virtually memorized all of them.

That Kaminsky's first mystery series, debuting in 1977 with *Bullet for a Star*, involved the movies is not surprising, then, given his background in film scholarship. *Bullet*, appropriately enough, concerned the filming of *The Maltese Falcon* and *The Sea Hawk* in the early 1940s. Its detective was an incompetent, but delightful schlemiel named Toby Peters, né Tobias Pevsner, and his client was the dashing Errol Flynn who came flying to the detective's rescue on a rope from the adjoining set of *The Sea Hawk*. This was the first of those memorable Kaminsky climaxes where the mystery is solved and the beleaguered detective is rescued at the last minute by some symbolically characteristic action on the part of his stellar client.

This basic pattern—the incompetent hero, the star client, the historical Hollywood background, and the climactic rescue—was obviously a formula well conceived, since it has carried the Peters saga through twenty-two rollicking and mysterious adventures with another on the way.

Four years later, Kaminsky opened his second major series with the 1981 *Death of a Dissident*. This series was a startling departure from the first, though, as we will see later, there are certain recurrent and interesting patterns that link all the Kaminsky series. The new series was set in Communist Russia near the present time and as it developed through fourteen subsequent volumes, it had to adapt to the fall of communism and the rise of a new political society, which it did with remarkable persuasiveness. The detective in this series, Porfiry Petrovich Rostnikov, got his name from both the detective and the criminal of Kaminsky's all-time favorite novel, Dostoyevsky's *Crime and Punishment*. Rostnikov is a Soviet policeman, but a very generous and humane man who continually struggles to balance political reality with his own sense of justice and decency. He is a very interesting and compelling creation, as is the oddly assorted team of superiors and subordinates with whom he works. Rostnikov's team is a little like Ed McBain's 87th precinct, another of Kaminsky's favorites, set down in Moscow and confronted with political issues much more complicated than those faced by Kaminsky's model.

But what probably struck most readers with amazement was Kaminsky's apparent mastery of place. The Rostnikov books seemed steeped in detailed and precise knowledge of the Russian capital and of what it was like to live and work in it. When I discovered that Kaminsky had never been to Russia until after the appearance of the first several Rostnikov novels, I was astonished at his ability to imagine this setting through research at a distance. And I was not the only one. A group of French critics awarded Kaminsky the *Prix du Roman d'Aventure* for *A Cold, Red Sunrise,* fourth in the Rostnikov series, apparently under the impression that he was a Russian. When they discovered that he was actually an American, Stuart told me, they were apparently quite shocked that this citizen of Russia's Cold War antagonist could draw such a sympathetic and knowing picture of the Soviet world and tried to withdraw the award.

As a fellow Chicagoan, I suppose I was always waiting for the third Kaminsky series, which is set in the city that Kaminsky knows so well from his own growing up. In my opinion, the only other mystery writer who shows anywhere near Kaminsky's perceptiveness about Chicago is Sara Paretsky who acknowledges learning much about the mystery trade from Kaminsky. Among other things, she invokes the same very specific sense of place in her novels. This series features homicide detective Abraham Lieberman and his partner William Hanrahan, known to each other as "Rabbi" and "Father Murphy." These two police detectives investigate murders in Chicago's North and West sides, a territory known familiarly to Kaminsky since his childhood. The Lieberman series debuted in the early nineties and has developed a rich cast of recurrent characters who become increasingly important with each new episode. They include Lieberman's wife and family, the other police officers at the North Clark Street station where Lieberman is headquartered, fellow members of the synagogue where Lieberman's wife is president, his partner Hanrahan's estranged family and the Chinese American woman he falls in love with, the gang leader El Perro who becomes a strange ally of Lieberman and many others. There's almost a Dickensian flavor to the series, which, owing to both this and its setting, makes it my personal favorite of the Kaminsky opus.

Kaminsky moved to Sarasota, Florida in 1989 to become head of a new film division of Florida State University, but it wasn't long before his fertile imagination, responding to a new place, developed a fourth series featuring Lew Fonesca, an ex-Chicago policeman, who has left Chicago in despair at the death of his wife and now ekes out a marginal existence in Florida as a process server and tracer of lost persons, perhaps in homage to that great radio character, Mr. Keene. Fonesca has so far only appeared in three adventures, but the series has already developed a distinctive character, though it, too, shows some of the characteristic patterns of Kaminsky's mysteries.

Though each of Kaminsky's series has a character of its own, there are several patterns common to most of his different creations. One of them is the way his detectives invariably gather around them a group of associates, family, and friends, who not only play an important role in the investigation of mysteries, but whose individual concerns become increasingly significant as each series develops. This kind of group detection is a common feature of contemporary detective stories. Kaminsky has often acknowledged here the influence of Ed McBain whose 87th Precinct series he admires. Two other things stand out for me as important sources of Kaminsky's distinctiveness and importance as a mystery writer. The first is a singular treatment of the setting of his mysteries. Second, Kaminsky's use of allusions and irony is pervasive in his work and contributes significantly to the overall atmosphere of his stories.

Mystery writers as different as Raymond Chandler, James Lee Burke, and Sharyn McCrumb carefully construct the places where their mysteries occur by evoking a distinctive mood or atmosphere that seems to hover over the setting. These writers are, we might say, in the tradition of Edgar Allan Poe in their treatment of place. Conan Doyle brilliantly evoked the fogbound atmosphere of Victorian London, but, on the other hand, he was also very much concerned with the social aspects of setting. Other writers have shared this interest including such various mystery creators as Dorothy Sayers, Agatha Christie, Reginald Hill, Robert Parker, and Michael Malone. While Kaminsky certainly evokes both atmosphere and social setting when appropriate, two other aspects of place play a much more important role in his creation of the settings for his mysteries. First there are the exact particulars of place, or what critics used to call verisimilitude of setting. I suspect Stuart spends a lot of time poring over guidebooks and maps because, in Kaminsky's stories, one learns the precise names, addresses, and appearances of, as well as the distances between, the places visited by his characters:

> He was sitting in the Paris Café a few hundred yards from his apartment on Krasikov Street. The Paris Café bore no resemblance to anything Parisian, nor was it a café. . . . There were six plastic tables with four chairs at each. (*Trans-Siberian Express* 90)

This might be called Kaminsky's guidebook version of places and it is the product either of close personal knowledge, as in the case of Lieberman's Chicago or Fonesca's Sarasota, or extremely diligent research, as with Rostnikov's Moscow or Toby Peters' Los Angeles of the 1940s. As we read a Kaminsky mystery these precise details accumulate and eventually we come to understand just what sort of places the characters live in and how they move around them. This total clarity of place provides an effective contrast with the mysteriousness of the events that the detective is called on to deal with.

Kaminsky's construction of place is also strongly influenced by his interest in the historical dimension of his settings. This is obvious in the case of the Toby Peters series where every place is pervaded by references to the songs, radio programs, ads, and front-page news that were the historical particulars of the era. But Kaminsky's sense of history manifests itself in many other ways. Important characters and places are usually introduced with a brief background note and in some cases, a whole novel, like the recent *Retribution*, is framed by a historical dimension:

> In about fifty thousand years, give or take a few centuries, the state of Florida will be gone. The Gulf of Mexico and the Atlantic Ocean will cover the peninsula that rests just above sea level. Geologists tell us it has happened before and they know about when it will happen again. (11)

Kaminsky continually sets his places and characters in a historical context and this relates to another central characteristic of his writing, his frequent use of historical and literary allusions and his quirky and pervasive sense of irony. Kaminsky's sense of irony derives, I think, from the cultural style of black humor and absurdity and the philosophy of existentialism so widespread in American writing and humor in the period when Kaminsky began writing. The humorously absurd and allusive climaxes that so often lead to the denouement of Toby Peter's cases illustrate Kaminsky's particular sense of irony well. In *Bullet for a Star*, Toby Peter's first case, when the detective is nearly killed by the criminal on the set of *The Maltese Falcon*, Toby's client Errol Flynn comes swinging to the rescue on a rope, just like the star does in the movies. In another Peters climax from a book published twenty-five years later, Cary Grant rescues Toby from the face of a steep cliff in obvious allusion to the hero's rescue of the heroine from Mount Rushmore in Hitchcock's *North by Northwest*. These allusive collages of fiction, film, history, and reality are among the many marvelously witty examples of meaningful absurdity that are among the many delights of Kaminsky's books.

Another kind of irony, a sense of the ultimate futility of human efforts against the cycles of time and history reflected in the statement about the rise and fall of the state of Florida I just quoted, emerges in the later Kaminsky series. . This view of things reflects fairly closely the concept of vanity set forth by another well-known Jewish writer, Ecclesiastes. It is particularly strong in the Lieberman books, not inappropriately, since the detective in that series is an aging Chicago Jew known to his partner and friends as "Rabbi." In the most recent Lieberman book, *Not Quite Kosher,* one of the opening episodes details a man named Melvin Sokol being mugged on the shore of Lake Michigan by three young hoodlums. Having turned on the hoodlums and beaten them, Sokol thinks incorrectly that he has killed one of them. Being a Jew who has turned Catholic on the insistence of his wife, he goes to a temple to confess to a rabbi, but encounters Abe Lieberman instead. Thinking the policeman is a rabbi he confesses what he thinks to be his crime. Lieberman senses that Sokol is a deeply troubled man, and when he finds that the supposed victim is only slightly wounded and in a hospital, he persuades Sokol to go the hospital with him to ask forgiveness of his victim. In a tense confrontation in the hospital room, Sokol instead seizes Lieberman's gun and tries to finish off his attacker. The actual rabbi, who also happens to be present, prevents Sokol from doing this by throwing himself across the intended victim's body. This Dostoyevskian catharsis seems to bring about a kind of redemption in Sokol who leaves feeling more at peace with himself and with the world. Lieberman, of course, does not tell either Sokol or the Rabbi that the gun was not loaded. Later Lieberman discovers that, after this episode, someone murdered Sokol. Only at the end of the tale, do we find out that it was Sokol's wife who killed him.

This extraordinary tale, which Kaminsky narrates much more effectively than I have retold it here, is a striking existential-Ecclesiastes parable of the futility of human efforts, especially those of the detective, against the absurdity of life and the inertia of evil. Of course, this doesn't mean that effort isn't worth making or that there's anything else for a human being to do. In spite of their continual encounters with the meaninglessness and absurdity of life, Kaminsky's detective heroes persist in, and insist on, hoping that it will somehow all get worked out, acting as if their struggles to find truth and justice will at least temporarily grant some sort of significance to human life. Let's hope it is so.

25

Cornpone Detection? Notes on Southern Mystery Writing

The detective story is surely one of the most important popular myths of modernity. Simple as its basic outlines are, it is ubiquitous in fiction, film, and television, and seems to be of inexhaustible fascination to contemporary audiences. One significant thing marking the modernity of the detective story is that, unlike most traditional literary genres whose origins are lost in the past, we can actually name its creator and date the time of its first appearance. This remarkable act occurred in the middle of the nineteenth century (April 1841 to be exact) and was the work of Edgar Allan Poe, a southerner.

It seems strange that the American regional culture seemingly most oriented toward tradition and the past should have been involved in the birth of one of the most modern of genres. In fact, once Poe had created it, the impetus of the detective story passed for the rest of the nineteenth century and the opening decades of the twentieth to England, which was, at that time, the leading European industrial and imperialistic power and therefore at the cutting edge of modernization. The further development of the detective story was carried out by Wilkie Collins and Charles Dickens and then by that crucial figure, A. Conan Doyle, creator of the archetypal detective, Sherlock Holmes.

However, the South continued to play a crucial role in the mystery genre's development. The best American detective novel of the nineteenth century was, arguably, Mark Twain's *Puddn'head Wilson,* one of his many experiments with the genre, which included the much less successful *Tom Sawyer, Detective,* and others. Still later in the 1920s, a southerner from Baltimore, Dashiell Hammett, played a crucial role in the emergence of a new tradition within the detective genre, that of the hard-boiled story. And of course, William Faulkner, the major southern novelist of the twentieth century not only produced a collection of detective stories *(Knight's Gambit)* and a full-length detective novel *(Intruder in the Dust),* but he also drew on the generic patterns of the detective story to create his greatest novels. Both *The Sound and the Fury* and *Absalom, Absalom!* are mystery stories in many ways, with writer, reader, and sometimes the characters, playing the role of detectives.

The crucial role of the South in the development of the detective genre continues down to the present time. In the last decade or so, there have emerged significant regional schools of southern detective fiction — New Orleans with James Lee Burke, Julie Smith, Norman Donaldson, and James Sallis; the Piedmont with Margaret Maron, Patricia Cornwell, and Michael Malone; Florida with Elmore Leonard and James Hall, the Appalachian region with Sharyn McCrumb and even Texas with Kinky Friedman. Clearly southern detection constitutes one of the most important and vital areas of contemporary mystery fiction.

My own conception of southern mystery writing has been strongly influenced by the one excellent and comprehensive book on the subject, Van Dover and Jebb's *Isn't Justice Always Unfair?* Van Dover and Jebb list the central characteristics of southern detective fiction in terms that, not surprisingly, recall the features of southern literature and culture as initially set forth by the major writers and critics of the southern renaissance and then refined by the influential southern historian, C. Vann Woodward in *The Burden of Southern History.* These characteristics include:

1. regional self-consciousness
2. focus upon place as a central condition of action and behavior
3. obsession with history
4. experience of defeat
5. critical attitude toward regional customs and traditions
6. strong awareness of racial differences
7. concern over the condition of the landscape and environment
8. response to new problems arising from economic and social changes. (9)

This is an excellent list and a good thematic guide to a wide variety of southern mystery writing. Indeed, it seems to me that the crucial characteristic of southern detective fiction is the ambiguous but powerful interplay between two of these themes: the obsession with the past, with history and tradition, and the sense that a new society is emerging in which the patterns of the past are no longer an effective guide to action. And it is this tension that I believe accounts for southern detective fiction's central relationship to modernity. Since one of the central patterns of the detective story is the bringing to light of a past evil, one can see how the "burden of Southern history," as Woodward puts it, might be a particularly compelling setting for the investigation of crime. It may account for why it is that the South has made such an important contribution to the development of the detective story as a central myth of modernity.

In this presentation I want to explore how three of the most effective contemporary southern mystery writers, James Lee Burke, Sharyn McCrumb, and Michael Malone, deal with the complex of themes associated with the burden of the past. Let's begin with the detective protagonists created by these writers. Most of them are haunted by their own pasts and thereby reflect on a personal level the troubled relationship with the past that defines the cultures whose crimes they investigate. Burke's Dave Robicheaux is a recovering alcoholic whose addiction continues to tempt him despite years of victory over it. Though he is married several times and adopts and raises a child in the course of the series he is still tortured by horrifying mental flashbacks to episodes of combat in Vietnam and by the desire for a drink that he must always resist. He is also haunted by the southern past and, in one of the novels, appropriately entitled *In the Electric Mist with Confederate Dead,* these metaphorical phantoms take on a kind of ectoplasmic substance in Dave's mind as the ghost of Confederate general John Bell Hood.

Michael Malone and Sharyn McCrumb resemble many contemporary mystery writers in using a collective detective-protagonist. In Malone's case, this is a group of characters belonging to the police force of Malone's imaginary small southern city of Hillston, North Carolina. Two central characters are both narrators and protagonists of the three novels in Malone's series. Justin Savile and Cuddy Mangum are both deeply ambiguous about aspects of their past which continue to obsess them. Justin, a recovering alcoholic like Dave Robicheaux, is deeply troubled by his relation to the southern aristocracy from which he springs. Cuddy Mangum comes from the working classes and is dominated by the hopeless passion he has long cherished for a young woman from the Hillston upper classes he fell in love with as a teenager.

In Sharyn McCrumb's "Ballad Series" four "detectives" recurrently appear in central roles. The first is an old woman, Nora Bonesteel, who has second sight and is regularly visited by ghosts from the past at her cabin in the mountains near Hamelin, Tennessee, the setting of Mc-Crumb's series. Like Dave Robicheaux, Joe Le Donne, a member of the Hamelin police force, has recurrent Vietnam nightmares that continue to torture him and make it difficult for him to enter into long-term relationships. His colleague and lover, Martha Ayers, not only has to cope with Joe's frequent nightmares, but is herself haunted by the failure of two earlier marriages, one of them violent and abusive. Only Spencer Arrowood, Hamelin's chief of police, seems relatively free of the past, though he is obsessed with the death of his older brother in Vietnam.

These interesting and complex detective protagonists are archetypal citizens of the modernizing South after the Civil Rights era and the Vietnam War. In this new "New South," some African Americans have become members of the establishment and the old explicit racism and segregation is publicly rejected. However, racism continues to lurk in the culture's depths, emerging at times in ambiguous controversies like that over the Confederate flag. As I was sketching this paper, Senator Trent Lott made his notorious observation about Strom Thurmond's 1948 attempt to win the presidency on a segregationist platform and was greeted with obloquy from all sides, including from President Bush, never noted for his championship of equal rights. Yet the real significance of the episode is the way in which southern racism still returns from the repressed, even in the contemporary South.

The burden of southern racism became increasingly important as Burke's Dave Robicheaux series developed. The first books, like *Neon Rain* and *Black Cherry Blues*, reflected the immediate post-Vietnam era's concerns about government conspiracies and organized crime in the situations that the detective protagonist encounters. However, by the middle 1990s, Dave has resigned from his position in the New Orleans police force and, moving closer to his Cajun roots, has become a sheriff's deputy in Burke's archetypal New Iberia. In these surroundings the crimes Dave deals with reflect more strikingly the residual effects of racism and elitism in southern culture. In *Cadillac Jukebox*, Dave becomes involved with the case of an old Klansman who is being tried for the decades-old murder of a Civil Rights leader. He discovers that this trial is deeply intertwined with the long-kept secrets of some powerful members of the southern aristocracy in a way that symbolizes how the evils of slavery and segregation lay at the root of southern history. In *Purple Cane Road*, Robicheaux investigates the case of a mulatto woman about to be executed for the murder of an old Cajun who had long been the official executioner of the state of Louisiana. Dave discovers that the victim had been a child molester as well as a racist and that his murder was caused by his attempt to sexually exploit and abuse a young black girl in the same way he had earlier exploited and abused the woman and her sister. That women of mixed blood were especially vulnerable to such torment is one of the hidden truths of racist sexuality and the southern past that Burke's detective uncovers in his investigations.

Like Dave Robicheaux's protagonists, Michael Malone's Justin Savile and Cuddy Mangum repeatedly encounter situations in which criminal actions reflect a reemergence of traditional southern racism. In *Time's Witness*, Malone's representative North Carolina city of Hillston has tried to leave the racist past behind. An African American has recently been elected as mayor and several blacks have been added to the police force. Nonetheless the past continues to haunt Cuddy and Justin in the form of a wrongfully convicted African American awaiting execution on death row. While demonstrators seek to win a pardon from the governor, the convict's brother, a civil rights activist, is murdered. This sets off a complex chain of events that lead Cuddy and Justin right back into the heart of traditional southern racism as they uncover and expose a deep-seated connection between Hillston politics and racist violence.

Racism was less a part of Appalachian history than in other areas of the South, since there were relatively few plantations in the rugged mountains, and most of the mountain people were too poor to own slaves in any event. Nevertheless Sharyn McCrumb's ballad series of detective novels, set in the symbolic Appalachian town of Hamelin, Tennessee, shows that a ghost from the past still haunts the new Appalachian culture. This is the residue of the traditional mountain culture and it exists on many levels in what is arguably McCrumb's best work in the ballad series, *She Walks These Hills*.

The title character of *She Walks These Hills* is the ghost of Katie Wyler,[1] a legendary figure out of the past who was captured by the Indians and then heroically escaped and returned to her family only to die mysteriously shortly after her return. Nora Bonesteel, an old mountain woman and one of the few remaining living representatives of the old

---

1. This figure is obviously based on the legendary figure of Kentucky heroine Jenny Wiley.

culture, has long been aware of the restless ghost of Katie Wyler roaming the mountains, but Katie also becomes present to another character, a young historian who has embarked on a hike along the Appalachian trail hoping to find out something about the life of the real Katie Wyler.

McCrumb's symbolic town of Hamelin, Tennessee, where the story takes place, is a progressive community with a modern police force that still, nevertheless, must occasionally deal with the residue of the old mountain culture in the form of the redneck Harkryders, best known for their fecklessness, violence, and drunkenness. However, more typical of the modern Hamelin is a popular radio host known as Hank the Yank, a Northern migrant to the area. Hank represents the New Appalachia with its bemused curiosity about the past and he serves as a sort of chorus for a mystery involving the tragic return of another representative of the old mountain culture, the escaped prisoner, Harm Sorley. Harm, originally a subsistence farmer, has been in prison for many years after being convicted of the apparently senseless murder of a wealthier neighbor. This apparently harmless convict surprisingly escapes from prison and is pursued throughout the novel as he makes his way across the mountains to Hamelin. By the end of the novel, the police have discovered that Harm killed in self-defense in the course of a quarrel after discovering that his neighbor had poisoned his land to force Harm to sell out to him. This wealthy neighbor wanted to make the land part of a large development project.

Mc Crumb symbolizes many intersections of present, past, and future but the central theme of her mysteries, like those of Burke and Malone, is that the New South cannot ignore its past without bringing about the tragic destruction of relatively innocent victims caught in the struggle between present and past.

This basic southern cultural concern with the tension between past and present is a central reason why southern writers are particularly able to create the rich and complex social setting that good detective stories require. In fact, if we look at the periods of greatest creativity and invention in the history of the detective story, such as early twentieth-century Britain, from which emerged the classical detective story, or America in the 1930s and the hard-boiled detective tradition, they do tend to be periods in which accelerating social change generated great tensions between present and past. The goal of the narrative in almost all detective stories is to reveal the truth of specific past actions, to make clear the motives behind these actions. Thus, the detective is, in some ways, like a historian and in others like a psychiatrist in the way that he or she undertakes to heal a social disruption by uncovering its causes. In the best detective stories, such as those I have discussed in this paper, the uncovering of the truth of a specific past crime is also frequently connected to the revelation of past social evils or failures to resolve the problems caused by changing social patterns. This may be why in times of particularly disturbing social change the detective story is challenged to transcend its established formulas and seek out new patterns of character, theme, and action that will more powerfully reflect the disruption between present and past.

As a final observation, it seems significant that two areas with the greatest creative vitality in the contemporary detective story are the southern mystery that I have discussed, and the mystery story involving Native American characters and settings. Perhaps southern and Native American mystery stories share a similar concern with radical disruption between the present and the past and an awareness of the burden of the past. They sense that dangerous evils can arise from the unresolved tension between present and past requiring a new kind of investigator to bring them to light.

Afterword

Mystiquing the Western; or, How I Started Doing Popular Culture

This essay was first presented at a fascinating film and history conference organized by Peter and Susan Rollins in 2002. I'm very grateful to Peter and Susan for encouraging me to write it and being such wonderful hosts in Kansas City.

When I first arrived at the University of Chicago as an instructor in the humanities, I was fresh out of grad school. In fact, I was not quite finished with that since I had not yet completed my dissertation, or, in fact, even started it. I assumed that this appointment at Chicago would be only a temporary one and when I looked at the distinguished phalanx of scholars who made up the English department, my gloomy prognostications about any future prospects there were seemingly confirmed. I knew that I would never be accepted in their midst. Many of these scholars were internationally renowned for their work in particular areas, like Shakespeare, Goldsmith, Swift, and Medieval English. Some had been pivotal figures in the rise of what had become known as the Chicago school of neo-Aristotelianism, an important theoretical rival to the pervasive New Criticism with which I had been strongly imbued.

So I was under considerable pressure to get my dissertation finished and to get some publications accepted. I always imagined an axe swinging over my head and before it fell, I hoped to have enough published to save my neck. At this time, I don't believe I had ever heard of popular culture, though my dissertation, on ideas of success in America, certainly touched on things that later became part of pop culture studies. However, like many students of my generation, I took an approach to studying popular culture that consisted largely of looking at popular myths and themes in canonic works of literature since this was what most of the American studies scholars I tried to model myself on had done. As some indication of what this implied, I confess that the last chapter of my dissertation on success in America was, of all things, a long analysis of Henry James! When I revised the dissertation for publication this was the first thing to go.

Negative assumptions about mass culture dominated the intellectual scene of the 1950s; a common view of popular culture was that it was a "vast wasteland" with few redeeming qualities. Critics were interested in what we now call canonic works of literature and culture or in traditional folk cultures and their offshoots in only a few areas, most notably in popular music and theater. These genres were supposedly "authentic," to use a favorite buzzword of the times, while the rest of popular culture including most of popular literature, film, and television, were characterized as derivative, manipulative, purely commercial, and a very bad influence on the mass of the people.

There was no reason to get involved in the academic study and teaching of mass culture. Nonetheless, I drifted into it mainly because, as I searched for topics I could turn into publications in the hope of getting tenure somewhere, I came to an important realization. Though my knowledge of most canonic literature was pretty fragmentary, I had a large fund of knowledge about westerns and mystery stories, having misspent my youth watching movies and reading popular fiction. I also noticed that, though I might be teaching poetry and other high culture to my students, when I came home after a hard day in the classroom it was to mysteries and other popular genres that I turned for solace.

The Six-Gun Mystique was my first significant venture into popular culture studies. Its immediate catalyst was my reading, sometime in the early 1960s, an article on the western written by another young University of Chicago scholar, who later became a friend. In this article, Peter Homans had analyzed a few major westerns of the 1950s and argued that the popularity of westerns was tied to recurrent cycles of Puritanism in American culture. Since I discussed my response to this argument in the introduction to *The Six-Gun Mystique*, I won't go into that here. However, though I disagreed with many of Homans' conclusions, I was quite excited by his structural method of approach and I began to toy with it and to wonder what other attempts had been made to analyze the cultural significance of the western. Researching the literature, I found that there were a few interesting attempts beside Homans' essay to account for the popularity of the western, which at that time was a pervasive genre in movies and television. I don't think anyone would have predicted that within fifty years, new westerns would be extremely rare on television and only infrequently attempted in feature films.

I published an early version of my ruminations on the western and Homans' version of it in 1962 as "A Prolegomena to the Western." It appeared in the same journal, *Studies in Public Communication*, that had published Homans' "Puritanism Revisited: An Analysis of the Contemporary Screen-Image Western" a year earlier. If this journal is not immediately familiar to you I'm not surprised as it ceased publication the year it printed my essay. I hope its demise wasn't caused by the pompous title I had given my article, since I had drawn on my background in classics, adapting it from one of the most famous and important books in classical studies, Jane Harrison's *Prolegomena to the Study of Greek Religion*. In retrospect, I shudder at the presumption.

Both Homans and I were particularly influenced by those western films that had been so successful in the 1950s — *Shane, High Noon, The Gunfighter, Rio Bravo,* and others. We drew, too, on John Ford's remarkable series of westerns between *Stagecoach* and *Cheyenne Autumn,* especially *My Darling Clementine, The Man Who Shot Liberty Valance, The Searchers,* and the Cavalry trilogy.

I also depended a lot on my memories of the Lone Ranger radio program that began in 1936 when I was six years old, by the B westerns and serials that had been the staples of that movie matinee, and by the television westerns so popular in the later 1950s. At that time I was much less aware of the history of the western film than I later became and, of course, Sergio Leone's "spaghetti Westerns" and Sam Peckinpah's *The Wild Bunch* had not yet appeared. Thus my original definition of the western formula was biased toward the gunfighter theme. I later came to realize that the western genre was a much richer and more complex thing than I had originally thought. Many of my later revisions in the original *Six-Gun Mystique* resulted from my attempts to expand my definition of the western to include the range of different version of the genre that I was increasingly discovering.

I'd originally thought to edit an anthology of some of these early scholarly analyses of the western with an introduction commenting on different methods of approach. However, as I worked on it, that introduction grew and grew until it was far too long for the purpose originally intended. At this point, as he so often has done in the history of popular culture studies, Ray Browne stepped in. In the mid-1960s, Ray was creating the *Journal of Popular Culture,* the Popular Press, and the Popular Culture Association, among many other things. I met Ray for the first time at this point this and was involved with him in a panel on Popular Culture at the MLA that led directly to the first meeting of the PCA. I told Ray something about my work on the western and he greatly encouraged me. When my introduction spread beyond its proper boundaries, Ray came up with the solution of publishing it as a small book. Thus, *The Six-Gun Mystique.* It was published so casually that none of us remember whether it appeared in 1970 or 1971. The title, tempting fate again, I drew from Betty Friedan's recently published *The Feminine Mystique.* Somehow the connection seemed appropriate for the discussion of a popular genre that certainly had many sexist characteristics. I was greatly helped by my undergraduate students at the University of Chicago, many of whom, like Barbara Bernstein and Charles Flynn, knew more about the movies than I did. Another student, Dennis James, drew the cover, which alluded not only to the subject of the book, but also to the pop artist Roy Lichtenstein and to the final scene of the first film western, *The Great Train Robbery.* Some people thought it was the best part of the book.

By this time I had tenure at the University of Chicago, but I was still quite concerned about the reaction of my colleagues to a book on such a popular topic. I had already come to know the redoubtable Norman Maclean who would later so movingly recreate the image of the West in *A River Runs through It and Other Stories.* My first encounter with Norman did not augur well. He and many of my other colleagues had attended my first public lecture at the University of Chicago, which I gave a couple of years after arriving there in 1957. In it I tried to use some nineteenth- and twentieth-century popular fiction to trace changing ideas of social reform in America. The audience responded warmly and I thought the lecture had been quite successful so the next day I was floating on air when I encountered Norman walking across the campus.

I knew who he was, but had not actually met him. After he had introduced himself, he congratulated me on my first public performance and then launched into a stinging critique of my argument and method that thoroughly crushed me. The day after this I found I had a high fever and most of the symptoms of a good case of the flu and I have always attributed this to Norman's response to my lecture. In fact, I had to take to my bed for three days before I recovered.

However, after I got over the initial shock, I realized that Norman was not criticizing the kind of thing I was attempting to do, but the facile clumsiness and lack of real insight that had in fact characterized this early effort. I've always been grateful to Norman for his honesty. In the following years we became close friends and colleagues and even taught a course on the West and the western together. Before he began, in his later years, to write the stories about the West that made him famous and his book on the Mann Gulch fire, Norman had been fascinated by the figure of Custer and his legend. I'm sorry he never got around to writing up the ideas he had on that subject. I'll never forget his response to the Errol Flynn version of Custer in *They Died with Their Boots On*, which we showed to our western class. I thought Norman would hate the film, but he loved it, though of course it had little to do with the Custer whom he knew. Since Norman was himself a man of considerable flair and dash, I think he particularly appreciated the panache that Errol Flynn brought to his portrayal of Custer.

I soon discovered that many of my other colleagues at the University of Chicago were also quite supportive of my explorations in popular culture. The austere elder statesman of the English department, Ronald Crane, a leader of the Chicago critics and a well-known eighteenth-century scholar, was famous for his savage criticisms of conference papers and he terrified me at first. But when he found out what I was working on, he invited me to his summer cottage up in Wisconsin, where he had walls full of paperback westerns and mystery stories as well as a large collection of the works of Horatio Alger. He loved to spend the summer reading these books, as a break from his "serious" literary and philosophical investigations.

I realized from conversations with Crane and other Chicago scholars that most American academics had a background in popular culture, as I did, and that many of them were very interested in understanding this aspect of their culture more fully. On the other hand, most of them were not prepared to accept the idea that popular culture was an academic discipline comparable to literature or philosophy or history.

Through these experiences, I came to feel that the most effective way to study popular culture was by striking a balance between popular materials and established academic disciplines. That is, it seemed to me that the best way to study popular culture was by approaching it through the lenses of well-developed methods like literary history and criticism and some of the concepts of philosophical aesthetics.

In the early 1960s when I began trying to figure out how to deal with popular materials, two dominant ideas about the study of literature prevailed and, in spite of certain tensions between them, they had arrived at a more or less harmonious alliance. The first was what used to be called "philology" (the love of words), an approach that had dominated literary studies since the middle of the nineteenth century. Philology involved the scholar in investigating the linguistic, historical, bibliographical, and biographical background of the great works of literature and bringing this knowledge to public attention through scholarly editions, literary history, and biographies of important writers so that others might better understand how these works came into being. The bias in philological studies toward works that were clearly great, or at least old enough to have become part of a cultural tradition, was, of course, one of the reasons that literary scholars avoided, for the most part, the study of popular culture.

The second method of literary study was both new and old. It was old in that it harked back in many ways to what is generally viewed as the first significant work of literary criticism, Aristotle's *Poetics*. It was new because it had been reinterpreted by some of the most influential twentieth-century literary minds, most notably Ezra Pound and T. S. Eliot, and it was generally referred to as the New Criticism. New Critics tried to put the literary text itself, rather than its historical background or the biography of its creator, at the center of literary study. And they tried to read that text in a complex fashion using the old Aristotelian concepts of plot, character, setting, and form, along with modernist ideas like irony and ambiguity. This approach, too, had some problems with popular works, most of which were not particularly long on irony and ambiguity, at least on the surface.

However, the myth and symbol concepts developed especially in American Studies suggested a way in which popular works like the western could be seen as embodying complex meanings. Actually, Henry Nash Smith had already used this approach to the western in his seminal study *Virgin Land* and I drew heavily on Smith's work in relating the western to American culture. However, Smith had only carried

his analysis up to the end of the nineteenth century and seemed to regard the modern western as having degenerated from the richness of
Cooper's *Leatherstocking Tales*. I, on the other hand, was particularly
interested in the films, television programs, and novels of the twentieth
century on which I had spent so much time in my youth. The opening
bars of Rossini's *William Tell Overture*, used to introduce the Lone
Ranger on radio and then on television, still sent shivers up and down
my spine. I wanted to know whether there was anything more to my
interest than nostalgia for those movie theaters of my young years where
I had spent so many hours peering into a cinematic West.

I was quite surprised at the success of *The Six-Gun Mystique*. Published as casually as it was by what was then a newly founded and rather
obscure press, it sold surprisingly well. Ray once told me that it was the
Popular Press's bestselling book though I'm not sure that is still the case,
as the Press went on to publish many important theoretical and historical works in popular culture. I don't even know how many copies the
book has sold in its various revisions, but it has remained in print in one
form or another for over thirty years. I found myself growing fond
enough of this flawed literary orphan that I have tried to remedy its de-
fects in the two revised editions, the last of which involved a complete
rewriting and expansion until it gradually accreted to the length of a
regular scholarly book. I'm not sure that was such a good idea since one
of the principal virtues of the original edition was its brevity. That,
along with the various bibliographies and filmographies, evidently
made the book useful in teaching popular culture and much of its sales
were as course texts or supplementary readings.

Aside from its brevity, I think there were two aspects of *The Six-Gun
Mystique* that were quite different from the prevailing mass culture critiques of the 1950s. First of all, I emphasized the idea that popular works
like the western were forms of art, not simply cultural products, and I
tried in what now seems a somewhat oversimplified fashion to define,
through the concept of formula, what sort of artfulness was involved in
popular works. I think that was an important and influential shift in
emphasis and it related to much other contemporaneous work in the
field. It was a time when many people like Reuel Denney, Irving and
Harriet Deer, Paddy Whalen, and Russell Nye were also developing the
idea of popular culture as an art form. This was an important idea needed
as an alternative to the negative and critical animus of many earlier
scholarly dissections of popular culture.

Related to the concept of popular culture as art was the idea of the genre itself, or what I was then calling the formula, as the major work of popular culture. Though individual instances of the western might seem to present an oversimplified view of life, one could see the genre as a highly complex embodiment of artistic form and cultural meaning that was worth considering among the creative masterpieces of modern culture. I later developed this idea more fully and tried to apply it to genres other than the western in *Adventure, Mystery, and Romance*. A few years later Richard Slotkin published the first of his great trilogy on the myth of the frontier and thereby gave us an even richer sense of the manifold meanings of the western genre.

Since the first appearance of *The Six-Gun Mystique*, many new critical theories have arrived on the scene with important implications for popular culture studies. Such approaches as structuralism, Bakhtinism, deconstruction, auteur theory, media theory, feminist criticism, race and gender analysis have dazzled us all and challenged us to understand what their implications are for our own work. I first became aware of this new challenge to our traditional way of doing things in a conversation with another Chicago colleague, Wayne Booth. Wayne was an extraordinarily widely read literary scholar and critic whose book on *The Rhetoric of Fiction* had already established itself as an important extension of the New Criticism into the rhetoric of narrative. I knew that Wayne was on the cutting edge of critical developments so I asked him one day about a particular novel that puzzled me (I've forgotten now what it was). Wayne replied that he thought the understanding of that novel required a little application of Bactine, at least that's what I thought he said. Since the only Bactine I had ever heard of at that time was an over-the-counter antiseptic it struck me that this was a very strange comment, indeed. Wondering whether Wayne had lost his grip, I quickly ended the conversation.

However, in the next couple of days, I learned that the Bakhtin Wayne had in mind was Mikhail Bakhtin, a recently rediscovered Russian literary critic of the 1930s now recognized as a major contributor to what we have come to call literary theory. So I went back to Wayne and ate a little crow about my mistaken understanding of his remark and asked him what he could tell me about this literary theory. He suggested I go hear a lecture by the Yale scholar Paul de Man who, it happened, was due to speak at Chicago that week. I dutifully trotted to de Man's lecture, which was, I think, about irony, a complex subject in any case but when approached through what I came to understand was called the "deconstructive method" a real mind-boggler. I have to confess that this remains the only lecture I can remember attending at which I understood not a single word.

I've spent much of my time since *The Six-Gun Mystique* and *Adventure, Mystery, and Romance* in trying to figure out whether these new theories and methods can be synthesized with the basic approach of my work. To some extent, I think I have effected such a synthesis, in *The Six-Gun Mystique Sequel* and some of my more recent essays. However, we must remember that if Art is eternal, Scholarship is ephemeral and quickly superseded by new ideas and new information. Still, I am grateful to the little book I so accidentally wrote some thirty odd years ago, for, among other things it has given me the pleasure of being at this very interesting conference and to be talking with you now.

Works Cited

Adler, Mortimer J. *Art and Prudence: A Study in Practical Philosophy*. New York: Longmans, Green, 1937.

Adler, Richard, and Douglass Cater, eds. *Television as a Cultural Force*. New York: Praeger, 1976.

Albert, Walter. *Detective and Mystery Fiction: An International Bibliography of Secondary Sources*. Madison, IN: Brownstone Books, 1985.

Altick, Richard D. *Victorian Studies in Scarlet*. New York: Norton, 1970.

Appel, Alfred, Jr. *Nabokov's Dark Cinema*. New York: Oxford UP, 1974.

Arlen, Michael J. *The Camera Age: Essays on Television*. New York: Farrar, Straus, Giroux, 1981.

Arnheim, Rudolf. *Visual Thinking*. Berkeley: U of California P, 1969.

Auden, W. H. "The Guilty Vicarage." *The Dyer's Hand and Other Essays*. New York: Vintage, 1989.

Auerbach, Nina. *Our Vampires, Ourselves*. Chicago: U of Chicago P, 1995.

Bakhtin, Mikhail. *Rabelais and His World*. Cambridge, MA: MIT P, 1968.

Baldwin, James. *Go Tell It on the Mountain*. New York: Grosset and Dunlap, 1953.

Bandura, Albert. *Aggression: A Social Learning Analysis*. Englewood Cliffs, NJ: Prentice-Hall, 1973.

Barth, John. "The Literature of Exhaustion." *Atlantic Monthly* 220. 2 (Aug. 1967): 29–34.

Bayer-Berenbaum, Linda. *The Gothic Imagination: Expansion in Gothic Literature and Art*. Rutherford, NJ: Fairleigh Dickinson UP, 1982.

Bazin, André. *What Is Cinema?* Berkeley: U of California P, 1967.

Bell, Daniel. "Crime as an American Way of Life." *The End of Ideology: On the Exhaustion of Political Ideas in the Fifties*. Glencoe, IL: Free P, 1960. 115–36.

Bellah, Robert N. et. al. *Habits of the Heart: Individualism and Commitment in American Life*. Berkeley: U of California P, 1985.

Bellow, Saul. *Adventures of Augie March*. New York: Viking, 1953.

——. *Dangling Man*. New York: Vanguard, 1944.

————. *Herzog*. New York: Viking, 1964.

————. *Mr. Sammler's Planet*. New York: Viking, 1970.

————. *Ravelstein*. New York: Viking, 2000.

Benstock, Bernard, ed. *Art in Crime Writing: Essays on Detective Fiction*. New York: St. Martin's P, 1985.

Berkowitz, Leonard. *Aggression: A Social Psychological Analysis*. New York: McGraw-Hill, 1962.

Berryman, John. *The Dream Songs*. New York: Farrar, Straus, and Giroux, 1969.

Bettinotti, Julia, ed. *La Corrida de l'amour: Le roman Harlequin*. Montréal, Québec: Université du Québec à Montréal, 1986.

————. "Race, Gender, and Genre: News from the Indian Romances." *Roman contemporain et identité culturelle en Amérique du Nord*. Ed. Jaap Lintvelt et al. Montréal, Québec: Nota Bene, 1998.

Bettinotti, Julia, et al. *Femmes de rêve au travai: Les femmes et le travail dans les productions écrits de grande consommation, au Québec, de 1945 à aujourd'hui*. Montréal, Québec: Nota Bene, 1998.

————. *Les 50 romans d'amour qu'il faul lire*. Montréal, Québec: Nuits blanche, 1996.

Binyon, T. J. *"Murder Will Out": The Detective in Fiction*. New York Oxford UP, 1989.

Blair, Walter. *Native American Humor*. San Francisco: Chandler, 1960.

Blair, Walter, and Hamlin Hill. *America's Humor: From Poor Richard to Doonesbury*. New York: Oxford UP, 1978.

Bleton, Paul. "French Espionage, Spy Fiction, and Readers in the 1930s." *Paradoxa: Studies in World Literary Genres*, 1.2 (1995): 187-209.

————. *Western, France: La place de l'Ouest dans l'imaginaire français*. Paris: Encrage, 2002.

Blotner, Joseph. *Faulkner: A Biography*. 2 vols. New York: Random, 1974.

————. *William Faulkner's Library: A Catalogue*. Charlottesville: UP of Virginia, 1964.

Bode, Carl. *Anatomy of American Popular Culture 1840–1861* Berkeley, CA: University of California, 1959.

Bold, Christine. *Selling the Wild West: Popular Western Fiction, 1860–1960*. Bloomington: Indiana UP, 1987.

Borges, Jorge Luis. *A Personal Anthology*. Ed. Anthony Kerrigan. New York: Grove P, 1967.

————. *Ficciones*. Ed. Anthony Kerigan. New York: Grove P, 1962.

Brackett, Virginia. *Classic Love and Romance Literature: An Encyclopedia of Works, Characters, Authors, and Themes*. Santa Barbara, CA: ABC-CLIO, 1999.

Brackman, Jacob. "Onward and Upward with the Arts: The Put-on." *New Yorker* (24 June 1967): 19–23+.

Bridgman, Richard. *The Colloquial Style in America*. New York: Oxford UP, 1966.

Brooks, Cleanth. *William Faulkner: Toward Yoknapatawpha and Beyond*. New Haven: Yale UP, 1978.

Brooks, Van Wyck. *America's Coming-of-Age*. New York: E. P. Dutton, 1915.

Brown, Norman O. *Life against Death*. New York: Vintage, 1959.

Browne, Ray. *Against Academia: The History of the Popular Culture Association and the Popular Culture Movement, 1967–1988*. Bowling Green, OH: Bowling Green State U Popular P, 1989.

Buchan, John. *The Thirty-Nine Steps*. London: William Blackwood and Sons, 1915.

Buckley, William F., Jr. *The Blackford Oakes Reader*. Kansas City, MO: Andrews and McNeel, 1995.

―――. *Mongoose R. I. P.* New York: Random, 1987.

―――. *The Story of Henri Tod: Blackford Oakes in Berlin*. Garden City, NY: Doubleday, 1984.

Budd, Elaine. *13 Mistresses of Murder*. New York: Ungar, 1986.

Burch, Barbara. "Nabokov and the Detective." Unpublished paper. University of Kentucky, 1987.

Burke, James Lee. *Black Cherry Blues*. Boston: Little, Brown, 1989.

―――. *Cadillac Jukebox*. New York: Hyperion, 1996.

―――. *In the Electric Mist with Confederate Dead*. New York: Hyperion, 1993.

―――. *The Neon Rain*. New York: Holt, 1987.

―――. *Purple Cane Road*. New York: Doubleday, 2000.

Buruma, Ian. *Behind the Mask: On Sexual Demons, Sacred Mothers, Transvestites, Gangsters, Drifters, and Other Japanese Cultural Heroes*. New York: Pantheon, 1984.

Butler, Christopher. *Interpretation, Deconstruction, and Ideology: An Introduction to Some Current Issues in Literary Theory*. Oxford, UK: Clarendon P, 1984.

Cage, John. *Silence: Lectures and Writings*. Middletown, CT: Wesleyan UP, 1961.

Cahan, Abraham. *The Rise of David Levinsky*. New York: Harper and Brothers, 1917.

Camus, Albert. *The Stranger*. Trans. Stuart Gilbert. New York: Knopf, 1946. (Original French work published 1942.)

Carter, Margaret L., ed. *Dracula: The Vampire and the Critics*. Ann Arbor: UMI Research P, 1988.

Cawelti, John G. *Adventure, Mystery, and Romance*. Chicago: U of Chicago P, 1976.

―――. "America on Display: The World's Fairs of 1876, 1893, 1933." *The Age of Industrialism in America*. Ed. Frederic Jaher. New York: Free P, 1968. 250–70.

―――. "Faulkner and the Detective Story's Double Plot" *Clues* 12.2 (Fall/Winter 1991): 1–15.

―――. *The Six-Gun Mystique*. 2nd ed. Bowling Green, OH: Bowling Green State U Popular P, 1984.

―――. *The Six-Gun Mystique Sequel*. Bowling Green, OH: Bowling Green State U Popular P, 1999.

Cawelti, John G., and Bruce A. Rosenberg. *The Spy Story*. Chicago: U of Chicago P, 1987.

Chandler, Raymond. *Farewell, My Lovely*. New York: Knopf, 1940.

―――. *Later Novels and Other Writings*. New York: Library of America, 1995.

―――. "The Simple Art of Murder." *Later Novels and Other Writings*.

Chesterton, G. K. "A Defense of Detective Studies." *The Defendant*. New York: Dodd Mead and Co., 1902.

Cohn, Jan. *Romance and the Erotics of Property: Mass-Market Fiction for Women*. Durham: Duke UP, 1988.

Conrath, Robert. "Pulp Fixation: The Hard-Boiled American Crime Novel and Its French Public." *Paradoxa: Studies in World Literary Genres*, 1.2 (1995): 161–75.

Cooper, James Fenimore. *The Deerslayer; or, The First War-Path*. Philadelphia: Lea & Blanchard, 1841.

―――. *The Last of the Mohicans: A Narrative of 1757*. Philadelphia: H. C. Carey and Lea, 1826.

————. *The Spy: A Tale of the Neutral Ground.* New York: Wiley and Halsted, 1821.

Cripps, Thomas. *Slow Fade to Black: The Negro in American Film, 1900–1942.* New York: Oxford UP, 1977.

Critchley, T. A. *The Conquest of Violence: Order and Liberty in Britain.* London: Constable, 1970.

Crouch, Stanley. *The All-American Skin Game; or, The Decoy of Race: The Long and the Short of It, 1990–1994.* New York: Pantheon, 1995.

Davidson, Cathy N. *Revolution and the Word: The Rise of the Novel in America.* New York: Oxford UP, 1986.

Davis, David Brion. *Homicide in American Fiction, 1798–1860: A Study in Social Values.* Ithaca, NY: Cornell UP, 1957.

Davis, Kenneth C. *Two-Bit Culture: The Paperbacking of America.* Boston: Houghton Mifflin, 1984.

Deer, Irving, and Harriet Deer, eds. *The Popular Arts: A Critical Reader.* New York: Scribner, 1967.

Delamater, Jerome H. , and Ruth Prigozy, eds. *Theory and Practice of Classic Detective Fiction.* Westport, CT: Greenwood, 1997.

Denney, Reuel. *The Astonished Muse.* Chicago: U of Chicago P, 1957.

Denning, Michael. *Mechanic Accents: Dime Novels and Working-Class Culture in America.* London: Verso, 1987.

Dostoyevsky, Fyodor. *Crime and Punishment.* Trans. Constance Garnett. London: Heinemann, 1960. (Translation first published 1914.)

Douglas, Ann. *The Feminization of American Culture.* New York: Knopf, 1977.

Dove, George N. *The Reader and the Detective Story.* Bowling Green, OH: Bowling Green State U Popular P, 1997.

Doyle, Arthur Conan. *The Adventures of Sherlock Holmes.* London: George Newnes, 1892.

————. *A Study in Scarlet.* London: Ward, Lock, 1887.

Durgnat, Raymond. *Films and Feeling.* Cambridge, MA: MIT P, 1967.

Durham, Philip. *Down These Mean Streets a Man Must Go: Raymond Chandler's Knight.* Chapel Hill: U of North Carolina P, 1963.

During, Simon. "Popular Culture on a Global Scale: A Challenge for Cultural Studies?" *Critical Inquiry* 23.44 (Summer 1997): 808–33.

Eliot, T. S. *Selected Essays, 1917–1932.* New York: Harcourt, Brace, 1932.

Ellis, John. *Visible Fictions: Cinema, Television, Video.* London: Routledge and Kegan Paul, 1982.

Ellison, Ralph. *Invisible Man.* 1952. New York: Viking, 1989.

Elmer, Jonathan. *Reading at the Social Limit: Affect, Mass Culture, and Edgar Allan Poe.* Stanford, CA: Stanford UP, 1995.

Emery, F. E. "Psychological Effects of the Western Film: A Study in Television Viewing." *Human Relations* 12 (1959): 201–5.

Emrys, Barbara. "Does Formula Matter? Notes Toward a Narratology of Popular Fiction." Unpublished paper. University of Nebraska, Kearney, 2002.

Erikson, Erik. *Childhood and Society.* 2nd ed. New York: Norton, 1963.

Fariña, Richard. *Been Down So Long It Looks Up to Me.* New York: Random, 1966.

Faulkner, William. *Absalom, Absalom!* New York: Random, 1936.

————. *Intruder in the Dust.* New York: Random, 1948.

————. *Knight's Gambit*. New York: Random, 1949.

————. *Light in August*. New York: Vintage International, 1990.

————. *The Sound and the Fury*. New York: Cape and Smith, 1929.

"Fatal Television." *Louisville Courier-Journal Sunday Magazine* (25 Feb. 1985): 14–17.

Feiffer, Jules. *The Great Comic Book Heroes*. New York: Dial, 1965.

Fiedler, Leslie. *Love and Death in the American Novel*. New York: Criterion, 1960.

————. *What Was Literature? Class Culture and Mass Society*. New York: Simon and Schuster, 1982.

Fish, Stanley. *Is There a Text in This Class? The Authority of Interpretive Communities*. Cambridge, MA: Harvard UP, 1980.

Fiske, John, and John Hartley. *Reading Television*. London: Methuen, 1978.

————. "Television and Popular Culture: Reflections on British and Australian Critical Practice." Iowa Symposium and Conference on Television Criticism, University of Iowa, Iowa City, May 1985.

Fitzgerald, F. Scott. *The Great Gatsby*. New York: Scribners, n.d.

Forman, Henry James. *Our Movie Made Children*. New York: Macmillan, 1933.

Forrest, Leon. *The Bloodworth Orphans*. Chicago: Another Chicago P, 1987.

————. "FAULKNER/Reforestation." *Faulkner and Popular Culture: Faulkner and Yoknapatawpha, 1988*. Ed. Doreen Fowler and Ann J. Abadie. Jackson: UP of Mississippi, 1990.

————. "In the Light of Likeness—Transformed." *Contemporary Authors Autobiography Series*. Farmington Hills, MI: Gale Group, 1987. 7:21–35.

Fredriksson, Kristine. "*Gunsmoke:* Twenty-Year Videography: Part 2." *Journal of Popular Film and Television 12.2* (Fall 1984): 127–43.

French, Philip. *Westerns: Aspects of a Movie Genre*. New York, Viking, 1974.

Frohock, W. M. *The Novel of Violence in America*. Dallas: Southern Methodist UP, 1957.

Frye, Northrop. *Anatomy of Criticism: Four Essays*. Princeton, NJ: Princeton UP, 1957.

Fussell, Edwin. *Frontier: American Literature and the American West*. Princeton, NJ: Princeton UP, 1965.

Gates, Henry Louis, Jr. *Loose Canons: Notes on the Culture Wars*. New York: Oxford UP, 1992.

————. *The Signifying Monkey: A Theory of Afro-American Literary Criticism*. New York: Oxford UP, 1988.

Gayle, Addison. *The Black Aesthetic*. Garden City, NY: Doubleday, 1971.

Ginsberg, Allen. *Howl*. 1956. San Francisco: Grabhorn-Hoyen, 1971.

Gitlin, Todd. *Inside Prime Time*. New York: Pantheon, 1983.

Gluckmann, André. *Violence on the Screen: A Report on the Research into the Effects on Young People of Scenes of Violence in Films and Television*. Trans. Susan Bennett. London: British Film Institute, 1971.

Goddu, Teresa A. *Gothic America: Narrative, History, and Nation*. New York: Columbia UP, 1997.

Gombrich, E. H. *Art and Illusion: A Study in the Psychology of Pictorial Representation*. New York: Pantheon, 1960.

Graff, Gerald. *Professing Literature: An Institutional History*. Chicago, U of Chicago P, 1990.

Grella, George. "Murder and the Mean Streets: The Hard-Boiled Detective Novel." *Contempora* 1.1 (Mar. 1970): 6–15.

Halberstam, Judith. *Skin Shows: Gothic Horror and the Technology of Monsters*. Durham, NC: Duke UP, 1995.

Hall, Stuart, and Paddy Whannel. *The Popular Arts*. New York: Pantheon, 1964.

Halttunen, Karen. *Murder Most Foul: The Killer and the American Gothic Imagination*. Cambridge, MA: Harvard UP, 1998.

Hammett, Dashiell. *The Dain Curse*. New York: Grosset and Dunlap, 1929.

————. *The Glass Key*. New York: Knopf, 1931.

————. *The Maltese Falcon*. New York: Knopf, 1930.

————. *Red Harvest*. New York: Grosset and Dunlap, 1927.

————. *The Thin Man*. New York: Knopf, 1934

Hardison, O. B. "The Rhetoric of Hitchcock's Thrillers." *Man and the Movies*. Ed. W. R. Robinson . Baltimore, MD: Penguin, 1969. 137-52.

Harper, Michael. *Images of Kin: New and Selected Poems*. Urbana: U of Illinois P, 1977.

Harper, Ralph. *The World of the Thriller*. Cleveland: P of Case Western Reserve U, 1969.

Harris, Neil. *Humbug: The Art of P. T. Barnum*. Boston: Little, Brown, 1973.

Hart, James D. *The Popular Book: A History of America's Literary Taste*. Berkeley: U of California P, 1967.

Haycraft, Howard, ed. *The Art of the Mystery Story: A Collection of Critical Essays*. New York: Simon and Schuster, 1946.

Heller, Joseph. *Catch-22*. New York: Simon and Schuster, 1961.

Henderson, Brian. *A Critique of Film Theory*. New York: E. P. Dutton, 1980.

Hernadi, Paul. *Beyond Genre: New Directions in Literary Classification*. Ithaca: Cornell UP, 1972.

Heston, Beth. "'A Twice-Written Scroll': The Lesbian Detective Novel." Unpublished paper. University of Kentucky, 1991.

Himmelweit, Hilde T., et al. *Television and the Child: An Empirical Study of the Effect of Television on the Young*. London: Oxford UP, 1958.

Holland, Norman. *The Dynamics of Literary Response*. New York: Oxford UP, 1968.

————. *5 Readers Reading*. New Haven: Yale UP, 1975.

Holquist, Michael. "Whodunit and Other Questions: Metaphysical Detective Stories in Post-war Fiction." *New Literary History* 3.1 (1971): 135-56.

Hoppenstand, Gary, and Ray B. Browne, eds. *The Gothic World of Ann Rice*. Bowling Green, OH: Bowling Green State U Popular P, 1996.

Howe, Irving. *World of Our Fathers*. New York: Harcourt Brace Jovanovich, 1976.

Howard, Jacqueline. *Reading Gothic Fiction: A Bakhtinian Approach*. New York: Oxford UP, 1994.

Hunt, E. Howard. *The Hargrave Deception*. New York: Stein and Day, 1980.

————. *The Kremlin Conspiracy*. New York: Stein and Day, 1985.

Irons, Glenwood, ed. *Feminism in Women's Detective Fiction*. Toronto: U of Toronto P, 1995.

Irwin, John. *Doubling and Incest/Repetition and Revenge: A Speculative Reading of Faulkner*. Baltimore: John Hopkins UP, 1975.

————. *The Mystery to a Solution: Poe, Borges, and the Analytic Detective Story*. Baltimore; Johns Hopkins UP, 1994.

Jacobs, Lewis. *The Rise of the American Film: A Critical History*. New York: Harcourt, Brace, 1939.

Jameson, Fredric. *Marxism and Form: Twentieth Century Dialectical Theory of Literature.* Princeton, NJ: Princeton UP, 1971.

Joyce, James. *Ulysses.* New York: Modern Library, 1934.

Kallen, Horace M. *Culture and Democracy in the United States.* New York: Boni and Liveright, 1924.

Kaminsky, Stuart M. *A Few Minutes Past Midnight.* New York: Carroll and Graf, 2001.

—————. *American Film Genres: Approaches to a Critical Theory of Popular Film.* Dayton, OH: Pflaum, 1974.

—————. *Bullet for a Star.* New York: St. Martin's P, 1977.

—————. *Death of a Dissident.* New York: Ivy, 1981.

—————. *Murder on the Trans-Siberian Express.* New York: Mysterious Press, 2001.

—————. *Not Quite Kosher.* New York: Forge, 2002.

—————. *Retribution.* New York: Forge, 2001.

Kaplan, E. Ann, ed. *Regarding Television: Critical Approaches—An Anthology.* Frederick, MD: University Publications of America, 1983.

Kasson, John F. *Amusing the Millions: Coney Island at the Turn of the Century.* New York: Hill and Wang, 1978.

Kawin, Bruce F. *Faulkner and Film.* New York: Ungar, 1977.

Kazin, Alfred. *Writing Was Everything.* Cambridge: Harvard UP, 1995.

Kelly, R. Gordon. *Mystery Fiction and Modern Life.* Jackson, MS: UP of Mississippi, 1998.

Kilgour, Maggie. *The Rise of the Gothic Novel.* London: Routledge, 1995.

King, Stephen. *Stephen King's Danse Macabre.* New York: Berkley, 1983.

Kitses, Jim. *Horizons West: Anthony Mann, Budd Boetticher, Sam Peckinpah: Studies of Authorship within the Western.* Bloomington: Indiana UP, 1970.

Klapper, Joseph T. *The Effects of Mass Communication.* Glencoe, IL: Free P, 1960.

Klein, Kathleen Gregory. *The Woman Detective: Gender and Genre.* Urbana: U of Illinois P, 1988.

Klein, Marcus. *Easterns, Westerns, and Private Eyes: American Matters, 1870–1900.* Madison: U of Wisconsin P, 1994.

Knight, Stephen. *Form and Ideology in Crime Fiction.* Bloomington: Indiana UP, 1980.

Kouwenhoven, John A. *Made in America: The Arts in Modern Civilization.* Garden City, NY: Doubleday, 1949.

Krentz, Jayne Ann. *Dangerous Men and Adventurous Women: Romance Writers on the Appeal of the Romance.* Philadelphia: U of Pennsylvania P, 1992.

Larsen, Otto N. *Violence and the Mass Media.* New York: Harper and Row, 1968.

Lawrence, D. H. *Studies in Classic American Literature.* New York: Viking, 1964.

Lee, A. Robert. "Towards America's Ethnic Postmodern: The Novels of Ishmael Reed, Maxine Hong Kingston, Ana Castillo, and Gerald Vizenor." *Roman contemporain et identité culturelle en Amérique du Nord.* Ed. Jaap Lindvelt et al. Montréal, Québec: Nota Bene, 1998.

Levine, Edward. "The Twist: A Symptom of Identity Problems as Social Pathology." *Israel Annals of Psychiatry and Related Disciplines* 4.2 (Autumn 1966).

Levine, Lawrence. *Highbrow/Lowbrow: The Emergence of Cultural Hierarchy in America.* Cambridge, MA: Harvard UP, 1986.

Levi-Strauss, Claude. *Structural Anthropology.* New York: Basic Books, 1963.

Lintvelt, Jaap, Richard Saint-Gelais, Wil Verhoeven, and Catherine Raffi-Béroud, eds. *Roman contemporain et identité culturelle en Amérique du Nord.* Montréal, Québec: Nota Bene, 1998.

Lipsitz, George. "Listening to Learn and Learning to Listen: Popular Culture, Cultural Theory, and American Studies." *American Quarterly* 42.4 (Dec. 1990): 615-36.

MacDonald, Dwight. *Against the American Grain.* New York: Vintage, 1963.

Madden, David, ed. *Tough-Guy Writers of the Thirties.* Carbondale: Southern Illinois UP, 1968.

Malone, Michael. *Time's Witness.* Boston: Little, Brown, 1989.

McCrumb, Sharyn. *She Walks These Hills.* New York: Scribner's, 1994.

McLean, Albert F., Jr. *American Vaudeville as Ritual.* Lexington: U of Kentucky P, 1965.

McLuhan, Marshall. *The Gutenberg Galaxy: The Making of Typographic Man.* Toronto: U of Toronto P, 1962.

————. *Understanding Media: The Extensions of an.* New York: McGraw-Hill, 1964.

————. *War and Peace in the Global Village.* New York: McGraw-Hill, 1968.

McWatters, George S. *Knots Untied: Or Ways and By-ways in the Hidden Life of an American Detective.* Hartford: Burr and Hyde, 1871.

Mailer, Norman. *The White Negro.* San Francisco: City Lights, 1957.

Malamud, Bernard. *The Assistant.* New York: Straus and Cudahy, 1957.

Mandel, Ernest. *Delightful Murder: A Social History of the Crime Story.* London, Pluto, 1984.

Marc, David. *Demographic Vistas.* Philadelphia: U of Pennsylvania P, 1984.

Marling, William. *The American Roman Noir: Hammett, Cain, and Chandler.* Athens: U of Georgia P, 1995.

Mason, Bobbie Ann. *The Girl Sleuth: A Feminist Guide.* Old Westbury, NY: Feminist Press, 1975.

Masters, Anthony. *Literary Agents: The Novelist as Spy.* London: Basic Blackwell, 1987.

Mayer, Milton, "Faust in the Hashberry." *Progressive* (Oct. 1967): 9.

Merry, Bruce. *Anatomy of the Spy Thriller.* Montreal, Quebec: McGill-Queen's UP, 1977.

Metz, Christian. *Film Language: A Semiotics of the Cinema.* Trans. Michael Taylor. New York: Oxford UP, 1974.

Meyer, Leonard B. "The End of the Renaissance." *Hudson Review* 16.2 (Summer 1963): 174-75.

————. *Music, the Arts, and Ideas: Patterns and Predictions in Twentieth-Century Culture.* Chicago: U of Chicago P, 1967.

Meyer, Nicholas. *The Seven-per-Cent Solution: Being a Reprint from the Reminiscences of John H. Watson, M.D.* New York: Dutton, 1974.

Mitry, Jean. *John Ford.* Paris: Éditions Universitaires, 1954.

Moretti, Franco. *Signs Taken For Wonders.* London: Verso, 1988.

Morrison, Toni. *Playing in the Dark: Whiteness and the Literary Imagination.* Cambridge, MA: Harvard UP, 1992.

Mosely, Walter. *Devil in a Blue Dress.* New York: Norton, 1990.

Mott, Frank Luther *Golden Multitudes: The Story of Best Sellers in the United States.* New York: Macmillan, 1947.

Motz, Marilyn F., and Jack Nachbar, Michael T. Marsden, and Ronald J. Ambrosetti, eds. *Eye on the Future: Popular Culture Scholarship into the Twenty-First Century in Honor of Ray B. Browne.* Bowling Green, OH: Bowling Green State U Popular P, 1994.

Mulvey-Roberts, Marie, ed. *The Handbook to Gothic Literature*. New York: New York UP, 1998.

Munt, Sally R. *Murder by the Book: Feminism and the Crime Novel*. London: Routledge, 1994.

Murray, Albert. *The Omni-Americans: New Perspectives on Black Experience and American Culture*. New York: Outerbridge and Dienstfrey, 1970.

Mussell, Kay. *Fantasy and Reconciliation: Contemporary Formulas of Women's Romance Fiction*. Westport, CT: Greenwood, 1984.

————. *Women's Gothic and Romantic Fiction: A Reference Guide*. Westport, CT: Greenwood, 1981.

Nachbar, Jack, ed. *Focus on the Western*. Englewood Cliffs, NJ: Prenctice-Hall, 1974.

National Commission on the Causes and Prevention of Violence. *To Establish Justice, to Insure Domestic Tranquility: The Final Report*. New York: Praeger, 1970.

Nabokov, Vladmir. *Pale Fire*. New York: Putnam's Sons, 1962.

————. *The Real Life of Sebastian Knight*. Norfolk, CT: New Directions, 1941.

Newcomb, Horace. *Television: The Critical View*. New York: Oxford UP, 1976.

————. *TV: The Most Popular Art*. Garden City, NY: Doubleday, 1974.

Newcomb, Horace, and Robert S. Alley. *The Producer's Medium: Conversations with Creators of American TV*. New York: Oxford UP, 1983.

Nolan, William F. *Dashiell Hammett: A Casebook*. Santa Barbara, CA: McNally and Loftin, 1969.

Novak, Michael. *The Rise of the Unmeltable Ethnics: Politics and Culture in the Seventies*. New York: Macmillan, 1972.

Nye, Russell B. *The Unembarrassed Muse*. New York: Dial, 1970.

Ong, Walter J. *Interfaces of the Word*. Ithaca, NY: Cornell UP, 1977.

————. *The Presence of the Word*. Minneapolis: U of Minnesota P, 1981.

Palmer, Jerry. *Thrillers: Genesis and Structure of a Popular Genre*. New York: St. Martin's P, 1979.

Paradoxa: Studies in World Literary Genres, 1.2, 1995. Vashon Island, WA.

Paterson, John. "A Cosmic View of the Private Eye." *Saturday Review of Literature* 36 (22 Aug. 1953): 7–8.

Paretsky, Sara. *Killing Orders*. New York: Morrow, 1985.

Pederson-Krag, Geraldine. "Detective Stories and teh Primal Scene," *Psychoanalytic Quarterly* 18 (1949): 207–14.

Pfeil, Fred. *White Guys: Studies in Postmodern Domination and Difference*. London: Verso, 1995.

Piaget, Jean, and Bärbel Inhelder. *The Child's Conception of Space*. Trans. F. J. Langdon and J. L. Lunzer. London: Routledge, 1956.

Poe, Edgar Allen. "The Fall of the House of Usher." *Burton's* (Sept. 1839).

————. "The Murders in the Rue Morge." *Graham's Magazine* 18.4 (Apr. 1841): 166–79.

————."The Mystery of Marie Roget." *Ladies Companion* 18 (Nov. 1842–Feb. 1843).

————. "The Purloined Letter." *The Gift* (1845): 41–61.

Polito, Robert, ed. *Crime Novels: American Noir of the 1930s and 40s*. New York: Library of America, 1997.

Punter, David. *The Literature of Terror: A History of Gothic Fictions from 1765 to the Present Day*. New York: Longman, 1980.

Puzo, Mario. *The Godfather*. New York: Putnam, 1969.

Pynchon, Thomas. *The Crying of Lot 49*. Philadelphia: Lippincott, 1966.

—————. *Gravity's Rainbow*. New York: Viking, 1973.

—————. *Slow Learner: Early Stories*. 1984. New York: Bantam, 1985.

—————. *V.* 1963. New York: Bantam, 1964.

Pyrhönen Heta. *Murder from an Academic Angle: An Introduction to the Study of the Detective Narrative*. Columbia, SC: Camden House, 1994.

Radford, Jean, ed. *The Progress of Romance: The Politics of Popular Fiction*. London: Routledge and Kegan Paul, 1986.

Radway, Janice. *Reading the Romance: Reading, Patriarchy, and Popular Literature*. Chapel Hill: U of North Carolina P, 1984.

Reilly, John M."Beneficent Roguery: The Detective in the Capitalist City." Unpublished paper. The State University of New York at Albany, 1979.

Rein, David M. "The Impact of Television Violence." *Journal of Popular Culture* 3.4 (Spring 1974): 934–45.

Riesman, David, et al. *The Lonely Crowd: A Study of the Changing American Character*. New Haven: Yale UP, 1950.

Rosenberg, Bernard, and David Manning White, eds. *Mass Culture: The Popular Arts in America*. Glencoe, IL: Free P, 1957.

Rosenberg, Harold. *The Tradition of the New*. New York: Horizon, 1959.

Roth, Marty. *Foul and Fair Play: Reading Genre in Classic Detective Fiction*. Athens: U of Georgia P, 1995.

Roth, Philip. *Goodbye, Columbus and Five Short Stories*. Boston: Houghton Mifflin, 1959.

—————. *Portnoy's Complaint*. New York: Random, 1969.

Rourke, Constance. *American Humor: A Study of the National Character*. 1931. Tallahassee: Florida State UP, 1986.

Ruehlmann, William. *Saint with a Gun: The Unlawful American Private Eye*. New York: New York UP, 1974.

Russell, Don. *The Lives and Legends of Buffalo Bill*. Norman: U of Oklahoma P, 1960.

Sarris, Andrew. *The American Cinema: Directors and Directions, 1929-1968*. New York: Dutton, 1968.

Sayers, Dorothy L. "Introduction," *The Omnibus of Crime*. New York: Payson and Clark, 1929.

Schaefer, Jack. *Shane*. Cambridge, MA: Houghton Mifflin, 1954.

Schatz, Thomas. *Hollywood Genres: Formulas, Filmmaking, and the Studio System*. Philadelphia: Temple UP, 1981.

Scott, Robert Lee. *The Rhetoric of Black Power*. New York: Harper and Row, 1969.

Seldes, Gilbert. *The Seven Lively Arts*. New York: Harper, 1924.

Sennett, Richard. *The Uses of Disorder: Personal Identity and City Life*. New York: Knopf, 1970.

Seydor, Paul. *Peckinpah: The Western Films*. Urbana: U of Illinois P, 1980.

Shils, Edward A. *The Torment of Secrecy: The Background and Consequences of American Security Policies*. Glencoe, IL: Free P, 1956.

Shepherd, Michael. *Sherlock Holmes and the Case of Dr. Freud*. London: Tavistock P, 1985.

Sitkoff, Harvard. *The Struggle for Black Equality, 1954-1980*. New York: Hill and Wang, 1981.

Slotkin, Richard. *The Fatal Environment: The Myth of the Frontier in the Age of Industrialization, 1800–1890*. New York: Atheneum, 1985.

―――――. *Gunfighter Nation: The Myth of the Frontier in Twentieth-Century America*. New York: Atheneum, 1992.

―――――. *Regeneration through Violence: The Mythology of the American Frontier, 1600–1860*. Middletown, CT: Wesleyan UP, 1973.

Slung, Michelle B., ed. *Crime on Her Mind: Fifteen Stories of Female Sleuths from the Victorian Era to the Forties*. New York: Pantheon, 1975.

Smith, Henry Nash. *Virgin Land: The American West as Symbol and Myth*. New York: Vintage, 1950.

Soitos, Stephen F. *The Blues Detective: A Study of African American Detective Fiction*. Amherst: U of Massachusetts P, 1996.

Sollors, Werner. *Beyond Ethnicity: Consent and Descent in American Culture* New York: Oxford UP, 1986.

Sontag, Susan. *Against Interpretation*. New York: Noonday P, 1966.

Southern,Terry, and Mason Hoffenberg. *Candy*. New York: Putnam, 1964.

Spanos, William V. "The Detective and the Boundary: Some Notes on the Postmodern Literary Imagination." *Boundary 2 1.1* (1972): 147–68.

Spehner, Norbert. *Les Fils de Jack l'éventreur: Guide de lecture des romans de tueurs en série*. Québec, Montréal: Nuits Blanche, 1995.

Spillane, Mickey. *I, the Jury*. New York: E.P. Dutton, 1947.

―――――. *One Lonely Night*. 1951. New York: New American Library, 1980.

Stevens, Wallace. "The Snow Man." *Harmonium*. New York: Knopf, 1923. 24.

Stocking, George W. *Race, Culture, and Evolution; Essays in the History of Anthropology*. New York: Free P, 1968.

Stoker, Bram. *Dracula*. Westminster: Archibald Constable, 1897.

Symons, Julian. *Bloody Murder: From the Detective Story to the Crime Novel, A History*. New York: Viking P, 1985.

Tani, Stefano. *The Doomed Detective: The Contribution of the Detective Novel to Postmodern American and Italian Fiction*. Carbondale: Southern Illinois UP, 1984.

Thomas, Ronald. *Detective Fiction and the Rise of Forensic Science*. Cambridge, UK: Cambridge UP, 1999.

Thompson, Jon. *Fiction, Crime, and Empire: Clues to Modernity and Postmodernity*. Urbana: U of Illinois P, 1993.

Thorburn, David. "Television Melodrama." *Television as a Cultural Force*. Ed. Richard Adler and Douglass Cater. New York: Praeger, 1976. 77–94.

Thurston, Carol. *The Romance Revolution: Erotic Novels for Women and the Quest for a New Sexual Identity*. Urbana: U of Illinois P, 1987.

Tocqueville, Alexis de. *Democracy in America*. New York: Vintage, 1954.

Todorov, Tzvetan. *The Fantastic: A Structural Approach to a Literary Genre*. Trans. Richard Howard. Cleveland: P of Case Western Reserve U, 1973.

Tompkins, Jane P. *Sensational Designs: The Cultural Work of American Fiction, 1790–1860*. New York: Oxford UP, 1985.

―――――. *West of Everything: The Inner Life of Westerns*. New York: Oxford UP, 1992.

Toll, Robert C. *On with the Show! The First Century of Show Business in America*. New York: Oxford UP, 1976.

Tropp, Martin. *Images of Fear: How Horror Stories Helped Shape Modern Culture (1818–1918)*. Jefferson, NC: McFarland, 1990.

Turner, Victor. *Dramas, Fields, and Metaphors: Symbolic Action in Human Society*. Ithaca, NY: Cornell UP, 1974.

————. *The Forest of Symbols: Aspects of Ndembu Ritual*. Ithaca, NY: Cornell UP, 1967.

Twain, Mark. *The Tragedy of Pudd'nhead Wilson; and, The Comedy, Those Extraordinary Twins*. Hartford, CT: American Publishing, 1894.

Van Dover, J. Kenneth. *Murder in the Millions: Erle Stanley Gardner, Mickey Spillane, Ian Fleming*. New York: Ungar, 1984.

Van Dover, J. Kenneth, and John F. Jebb. *Isn't Justice Always Unfair?: The Detective in Southern Literature*. Bowling Green, OH: Bowling Green State U Popular P, 1996.

Veeder, Willam R. *Henry James: The Lessons of the Master: Popular Fiction and Personal Style in the Nineteenth Century*. Chicago: U of Chicago P, 1975.

————. *Mary Shelley and Frankenstein: The Fate of Androgyny*. Chicago: U of Chicago P, 1986.

Verhoeven, Wil. "How Hyphenated Can You Get? A Critique of Pure Ethnicity." Unpublished manuscript, 1990.

Vidocq, Eugène. *Mémoires de Vidocq: Chef de la police de sûreté, jusq'en 1827, aujourd'hii propriétaire et fabricant de papiers à Sainte-Mandé*. Paris: Tenon, 1828–1829.

Walpole, Horace. *The Castle of Otranto*. London: Bathoe, and Lownds, 1764.

Warshow, Robert. *The Immediate Experience: Movies, Comics, Theatre, and Other Aspects of Popular Culture*. Garden City, NY: Doubleday Anchor, 1964.

Wertham, Fredric. *Seduction of the Innocent*. New York: Rhinehart, 1954.

Wilbur, Richard. "The Poe Mystery Case." *New York Review of Books* 13 (1967): 16, 25–28.

Willett, Ralph. *The Naked City: Urban Crime Fiction in the USA*. Manchester, UK: Manchester UP, 1996.

Williams, Anne. *Art of Darkness: A Poetics of Gothic*. Chicago: U of Chicago P, 1995.

Williams, Raymond. *Culture and Society, 1780–1950*. New York: Columbia UP, 1958.

Wilson, Edmund. *The American Earthquake: A Documentary of the Twenties and Thirties*. Garden City, NY: Doubleday, 1958.

————. *The Shores of Light: A Literary Chronicle of the Twenties and Thirties*. New York: Farrar, Straus, and Young, 1952.

Winks, Robin W., ed. *Detective Fiction: A Collection of Critical Essays*. Rev. and exp. ed. Woodstock, VT: Countryman P, 1988.

Winn, Dilys, ed. *Murderess Ink: The Better Half of the Mystery*. New York: Workman, 1979.

Wister, Owen. *The Virginian*. 1902. Ed. Hohn Seelye. New York: Viking Penguin, 1988.

Wright, Louis. *Culture on the Moving Frontier*. Bloomington: Indiana University Press, 1955.

Wright, Will. *Six Guns and Society: A Structural Study of the Western*. Berkeley: U of California P, 1975.

Wolfe, Tom. *Radical Chic and Mau-Mauing the Flak Catchers*. New York: Farrar, Straus, and Giroux, 1970.

Wollen, Peter. *Signs and Meaning in the Cinema*. Bloomington: Indiana UP, 1969.

Wood, Robin. *Arthur Penn*. New York: Praeger, 1970.

————. *Hitchcock's Films.* 2nd ed. New York: Castle, 1969.

————. *Howard Hawks.* Garden City, NY: Doubleday, 1968.

Wright, Richard. *Native Son.* New York: Harper and Row, 1940.

Wynn, Dilys. *Murderess Ink: The Better Half of the Mystery.* New York: Workman, 1979.

Index

Absalom, Absalom! (Faulkner), 273, 274, 285, 365
aesthetics: Black Aesthetic movement, 232; interpretations of mystery litera-ture and, 334; modern, 35-36; of mys-tery, 340-48; pluralistic, 71; popular, 68-69; visual, 67
African Americans: Black Aesthetic movement, 232; formula or tropes of mystery and, 291-92; improvisation and re-creation in black culture, 242; popular culture and desegregation, 256-57. *See also* race; racism
Aliens (film), 93-94
Altman, Robert, 208
ambiguity, 102
American Culture Association, 120
American Dream, 247-49
American Studies, 79
Amityville series (films), 353
amusement parks, 223-24, 227, 255
anarchy as context, 185-86, 199
Anglo-American cultural hegemony, 235, 253, 255, 258, 261, 282
antagonists: ethnicity of, 282-83; execu-tion *vs.* exposure or self-destruction of the criminal, 196; gangsters as, 163, 186; parallels between detectives and

master criminals, 267; relationships with protagonists, 16, 267, 339, 340, 343; in westerns, 176; women as, 189-90, 197, 283
antidetective novels, 285
anti-Semitism, 237, 242, 250, 257
archetypes, 66; in American culture, 160-61; detective story archetype, analysis of, 293-95; gender and, 92; genre and, 8-9, 136; hunter archetype, 169-70, 188-91, 213-14; mystery figures, 346; stereotypes and, 76; western hero, 142, 177-78
Aristotle, 95-96
Arlen, Michael J., 66-67
Arnold, Matthew, 75
assimilation in American culture, 255-57, 258; education of ethnic groups and, 224; separatism and, 232, 240, 259-60
audience: accessibility as aesthetic princi-ple, 69; audience communities in re-sponse to gender and multicultural-ism, 106-7; audience research, 104-5; authors' responsiveness to readers, 344; canon and, 128; celebrity and, 50-51; characters as representative of the reader, 343; commercialization of popular culture, 221-22; engagement

A RAY AND PAT BROWNE BOOK